SPECIALIST COMMUNICATION SKILLS FOR SOCIAL WORKERS

SPECIALIST COMMUNICATION SKILLS FOR SOCIAL WORKERS

DEVELOPING PROFESSIONAL CAPABILITY

2ND EDITION

JOHANNA WOODCOCK ROSS

First edition published 2011 by
PALGRAVE MACMILLAN

Second edition published 2016 by
PALGRAVE

Palgrave in the UK is an imprint of Macmillan Publishers Limited, registered in England, company number 785998, of 4 Crinan Street, London, N1 9XW.

Palgrave Macmillan in the US is a division of St Martin's Press LLC, 175 Fifth Avenue, New York, NY 10010.

Palgrave is a global imprint of the above companies and is represented throughout the world.

Palgrave® and Macmillan® are registered trademarks in the United States, the United Kingdom, Europe and other countries.

ISBN 978–1–137–54532–9 paperback

This book is printed on paper suitable for recycling and made from fully managed and sustained forest sources. Logging, pulping and manufacturing processes are expected to conform to the environmental regulations of the country of origin.

A catalogue record for this book is available from the British Library.

A catalog record for this book is available from the Library of Congress.

CONTENTS

Acknowledgements   vii

1 Introduction   **1**
The increased policy impetus   2
The 'professional turn'   4
Outline of the underpinning research   5
A practice-led focus   7
Organisation of the book   8

2 Introducing Communication Skills   **11**
Developing communication capacity from basic social work
   communication skills to 'specialist social work communication'   11
A 'relationship-based practice' approach   14
Reflexivity   19
Communication obstacles and the wider communication environment   21
The 'social work' in social work communication skills   23
Social work communication skills do not 'come naturally'   24

3 Assessing Communication Skills   **28**
From 'assessing competence' to 'assessing capability'   29
What am I measuring when I assess communication capacity?   31
How can I measure communication capacity?   34
Different assessment methods for producing different types of
   evidence for developmentally progressive, holistic assessment   38
   Supervision and Supervision Records   39
   Direct Observation   44
   Service User Feedback   48

4 Basic Universal Communication Skills   **54**
'"Beginning Skills" to establish purposeful work'   55
'Tuning-in' (Shulman, 2009)   55
'Achieving a shared purpose'   60
'Empathy skills'   68
   'Reflective Listening'   68
   'Skills to encourage the discussion of unarticulated feelings'   70
Skills for 'gathering facts'   73
Skills for 'ending work'   73

5 Working with Children **77**
Policy and background literature 77
Practice application 83

6 Working with Young People with Offending Behaviour **105**
Policy and background literature 105
Practice application 108

7 Working with Parents **130**
Policy and background literature 130
Practice application 136

8 Working with People with Problematic Substance Use **159**
Policy and background literature 159
Practice application 164

9 Working with Adults with Disabilities **187**
Policy and background literature 187
Practice application 191

10 Working with People with Mental Health Problems **211**
Policy and background literature 211
Practice application 215

11 Working with Older People **230**
Policy and background literature 230
Practice application 234

12 Working with Refugees and Asylum Seekers **253**
Policy and background literature 253
Practice application 255

Conclusion **273**

Research Appendix 282
Bibliography 286
Index 306

ACKNOWLEDGEMENTS

In addition to the research for the first edition, this second edition publishes preliminary research findings and conceptual ideas from my doctoral study at the Institute of Education, University College London (IOE UCL), concerning specialist social work communication with parents of practising religious faith. This venture has given me the opportunity to question and develop the tenets of the first edition for exploring the potential for theoretical linkages to the real life challenges of practice actions in particular settings. I would like to thank the service users and carers, the qualifying social work students and practising social workers who participated in the study. Particular thanks go to my PhD supervisor, Professor Andrew Wright, for his encouragement and wisdom thus far in my explorative journey. It is no mean feat to be conducting doctoral study while working full-time, and living in transitional arrangements while the family home has been, literally, resurrected. I could not have achieved this second edition without the encouragement of my husband (Mark) and daughter (Lauren) or the support from my parents (Jackie and Stuart, Ken and Estelle, Frank and Diane) and siblings (Sharon and Martin, Denise). This book is dedicated to all of them, and, in accordance with my faith, to God – You never let go.

1

Introduction

The main driver for this new edition is the implementation of the Professional Capabilities Framework (PCF) in England (TCSW/BASW, 2012); an overarching professional standards framework which presents a new way of viewing the skills, values and knowledge that social workers bring to their practice at the different stages of their career. In pragmatic terms, this new framework reduced the relevance of the references to the National Occupational Standards at the end of each of the first edition chapters to Northern Ireland only. The Health and Care Professions Council in England (HCPC), the Northern Ireland Social Care Council, the Scottish Social Services Council (SSSC) and the Care Council for Wales operate the regulatory function for UK social work. These bodies set out threshold standards for what a social worker should know and have capability to do at the point of qualification. For example, the HCPC has produced a set of Standards of Proficiency for Social Work (HCPC, 2012) and also Standards of Conduct, Performance and Ethics (HCPC, 2016). The standards for social work are akin to those detailed in the Professional Capabilities Framework, and have been mapped to the PCF capability level for the end of final assessed placement (Qualifying Capability Level). This gives an educator confidence that a qualifying or qualified social worker who meets this capability level or above will equally meet the HCPC Standards of Proficiency (Williams and Rutter, 2013).

In wider terms, the PCF contains a significant philosophical change to practice learning and professional development, setting out developmental pathways of expected capability – framed as 'capability statements' – for all stages of a social worker's career, from the beginning entry to qualifying training to the most advanced social work practitioner. The emphasis is upon progressing a person's developmental capacity to engage in increasingly complex professional activity. Qualifying and qualified social workers aspire to each new stage of expected capability, the success of which is determined through a practice educator's professional judgement drawing upon different sources and types of evidence reflecting nine interdependent domains of professional capacity: Professionalism; Values and Ethics; Diversity; Rights, Justice and Economic Wellbeing; Knowledge; Critical Reflection and Analysis; Intervention and Skills; Contexts and Organisations; and Professional Leadership. At any one time, social work practice is an interwoven nexus of several, if not all the, PCF domains. In rejecting the exclusiveness of each domain and emphasising their inter-dependence, both professional capability and the professional judgement of it have to be 'holistic'. This is a significant step away from the previous checklist approach of assessing demonstrable behavioural competence against occupational standards.

What does this movement away from 'occupational competence' to 'professional capability' mean for the study of social work communication skills? Is skilled communication now to be conceptualised as 'communication capacity', and if so, how can this embrace the interdependence of several domains of professional capability (such as 'Contexts and Organisations' and 'Rights, Justice and Economic Wellbeing') rather than just the behavioural manifestation of just one ('Intervention and Skills')? What knowledge do we have of how these linkages can be drawn? This is the focus for this second edition. Extending the distinctive place of the first edition in taking beginning steps to bridge the knowledge gap of relevant 'specialist social work communication skills' by discerning and applying theoretical linkages to the real-life challenges of practice actions for social workers in different practice settings, this second edition seeks to enable social workers to map those emerging linkages to the different professional capabilities of the PCF. It is a task that warrants attention. There have been persistent criticisms of the lack of theoretical underpinning to the learning and teaching of social work communication skills for the demands of the reality of frontline practice in differing practice contexts (Dixon, 2013). Theoretical content is regarded as often implicit, and when explicit, lacking critical analysis and attention to structural forces arising from the context and influencing the interpersonal communication capacity of both social worker and service user (Trevithick et al., 2004; Dinham, 2006; Luckock et al., 2006; Dixon 2013).

The increased policy impetus

The continued limited research attention occurs despite the fact that in the past five years (since the first edition) the fundamental human right to be communicated with and consulted about decisions affecting one's life not only remains central, but has received increased attention to that within recent and existing policy and practice frameworks (The Children Acts 1989 & 2004; Department of Health, 2001b; Department for Education and Skills, 2003). New legislation has cemented the person-centred approach within 'personalisation' as a policy and practice agenda (The Care Act 2014 in England, Wales and Northern Ireland; The Social Care (Self-directed support) (Scotland) Act 2013; The Social Services and Well-being (Wales) Act 2014). No longer just a matter of 'good practice', now social workers are required to elicit the personal views and wishes of each service user of how to address their health and wellbeing to meet outcomes and goals deemed most important to them. Signalling a reformed system away from the process-driven, tick-box practice of considering what service to fit a service user into, social workers must adopt a flexible, individualised approach to have a 'genuine conversation'. Wherever possible, they must create a co-produced assessment of the care and support needs that matter most to the person concerned. Effective communication figures significantly within this active involvement and/or 'co-productive' approach. Social workers must identify service users' communication needs, particularly where service users might have substantial difficulty in engaging with the assessment and planning processes. These include difficulties in understanding and retaining information, as well as difficulties in weighing up information to consider and express preferences, alongside difficulties in communicating their views, wishes and feelings. Social workers must also consider the emotional and physical impact of the assessment when planning interventions upon service user wellbeing, taking steps to mitigate this within their communication approach.

New approaches to adult safeguarding within the Care Act 2014 echo these same principles of empowering people to speak out and express informed choices in managing the risk encountered in their lives. Respecting the concepts of both dignity and quality of life, the emphasis is not upon risk avoidance but risk appraisal of the circumstances, history, personal preferences and lifestyle of the person concerned. The aim is not for over-protection but a proportionate response that can tolerate acceptable risks. Within this, social workers must ensure that they use the least restrictive options for freedom of action, complying with the Human Rights Act (1998) and the Mental Capacity Act (2005). Skilled communication is needed to attain this level of shared information-gathering and shared judgement in order to achieve proportionate solutions for safety and support.

The increased emphasis upon individual wellbeing through self-expressed outcomes and person-centred practice does not only pertain to adult social care. Rather, policy highlights an alignment with principles and provisions within new legislation for children's services that places children, young people and their parents and carers as central actors in assessment and planning through similar person-centred processes of co-production, involvement and decision-making (The Children and

Families Act 2014 (England, Wales and Northern Ireland)). Government guidance accompanying the Care Act specifies a more joined-up 'whole family approach' by drawing simultaneously upon the provisions of The Children and Families Act to assess and support families (Department of Health, 2015). A picture must be gained of the whole family context, and how preferred outcomes for one individual's wellbeing might impact positively or deleteriously upon another's. The matter, again, is one of shared service user and professional judgement concerning 'proportionate intervention', a decision-making process which arguably requires considerable communication expertise. Indeed, social work communication has to be sufficiently skilled so as to ensure that children, young people and their parents and carers are not just passive players but have communication agency to explore such dynamics of individual and familial wellbeing. Moreover, the new children's legislation itself reinforces principles of 'involvement' and 'participation', with social workers not only required to ascertain views, wishes and feelings, but to provide information and support to enable a child and his or her parents, or a young person to fully participate in decisions. The increased prominence given to service user rights to be communicated with in a way that facilitates involvement in decisions (as fully as possible) is, therefore, an important second driver for this new edition, particularly as service users frequently say that their communication method is often undervalued or unrecognised in such contexts (Diggins, 2004; Cree and Davis, 2007; Lishman, 2009).

The 'professional turn'

The de-emphasis upon process-driven, bureaucratic approaches, and preference for professional interpersonal expertise and judgement, reflects wider discussion and developments arising over the past five years concerning the 'professional turn' and 'professional reform' of social work (Higgins et al., 2015). Social work educators and practitioners have voiced alarm at the impact of 'managerialism' upon the professional task, seeking a reclaiming of professional autonomy and expertise within a relationship-based and person-centred practice (Barlow and Scott, 2010; Ruch et al., 2010). Managerialism has been manifest through administration systems designed to increase individual and organisational accountability through target-driven, procedural processes, but with a consequential side-effect of significant reduction in social work time spent face-to-face with service users (Halliday, 2009; Ash, 2013). Studies indicate that the majority of time has been occupied with electronic case-recording systems designed to 'manage' the uncertainty of high-risk service user situations and lessen potential error arising through professional discretion (TCSW/

BASW, 2012; All Party Parliamentary Group on Social Work 2013). The prescription over the type and nature of information recorded, alongside the sheer cumbersome nature of the electronic systems, has negative consequences for the creative quality of social workers' enactment of personalised responses and professional autonomy (Broadhurst et al., 2010, Wastell et al., 2010; McGregor, 2013; Gillingham, 2014a; Gillingham, 2014b). Moreover, the severe financial constraints upon public spending have affected the level and choice of service available to ameliorate the circumstances of social work service users. Such uncertainty about performance and inability to enact aspirational professional social work values and creativity creates 'role conflict' and job dissatisfaction. In the face of such low control in professional autonomy, studies have identified high levels of social worker stress and burnout (Moriarty et al., 2015).

To address the difficult position of social work, and increase public and professional social workers' confidence in the profession, government has engaged in intense scrutiny of frontline social work practice, and the adequacy of education to prepare social workers for it. Previous governmental reviews from Labour (Social Work Task Force, 2009) and the Conservative-Liberal Democrat Coalition (Social Work Reform Board, 2010; Munro, 2011a; Munro, 2011b; Social Work Reform Board, 2012) proposed a chain of reforms aimed at equipping social workers with the knowledge and practical interpersonal and communication skills for the unrelenting demand and complexity of frontline practice. It is exactly these reforms that have produced the aforementioned overarching professional standards framework – the Professional Capabilities Framework (PCF) (The TCSW/BASW, 2012). Thus, this second edition echoes the professional reclaiming of social work by propounding the relational dynamics inherent within social work communication – those arising both from within and between the individual service user and social worker and from the wider practice context. At the same time, it recognises that such professional reclaiming takes place within a backdraught of recent and continued public scrutiny, alongside political uncertainty concerning the parameters of social work's role and tasks.

Outline of the underpinning research

The content draws partly upon empirical findings from an innovative research methodology and teaching method that I used to elicit the practice learning of qualifying social workers of 'specialist communication skills' for the first edition, and which I have since repeated and updated for the purposes of my current doctoral research concerning communication with parents. These findings continue my progress towards a provisional early mapping of theoretical linkages to communication skills employed by social workers. As such, the findings do not stand alone within the book, but within each of the chapters I have situated and considered them within the context of policy and existing knowledge of communication issues and skills as they relate to different practice settings. The research methodology explicitly used Schön's (1983) approach to experiential learning to enable groups of qualifying social workers at the very point of graduate qualification (the original study), and combined groups of qualifying and qualified social workers (my doctoral study) to bridge the aforementioned knowledge gap themselves by using a 'bottom-up' method to learning with the participants actively discerning theoretical linkages to the real-life challenges and actions of their practice learning settings. This meant observing and analysing their communication while they were 'in action', as well as collating their critical reflections 'on action' immediately after it occurred. 'Reflection-on-action' denotes learning taking place after the individual actions, such as considering why the participants acted as they did and unpicking what exactly took place. However, 'reflection-in-action' is described as thinking independently on the spot, engaging with feelings that are raised on a personal level and addressing the theories being used. Indeed, the second, crucial, dimension to the study was that the knowledge sought through the 'reflection-in-action' was embodied (felt) and not solely derived through abstract thought. A flexible application of Schön's concepts to practice is considered by other authors as useful, particularly in encouraging a holistic understanding of the social, personal and political contexts of service user situations (Darragh and Taylor, 2009).

The 'reflection-in-action' was achieved through the use of the drama technique of the Forum Theatre method within designated classroom workshops. The Forum Theatre method facilitates conscious and embodied (felt) recognition of collective problems (in this case, identifying specialist communication) and develops realistic and dialogical strategies for action (Boal, 1979; Houston et al., 2001). In the original study, a group of qualifying (stage 3) undergraduate social work students (n=55) were divided and assigned to one or more Specialist Social Work Communication Skills workshops corresponding to eight different practice settings in which they were undertaking their practice learning: children; parents; older people; adults with disabilities and their carers; people with mental health difficulties; asylum seekers and refugees; young offenders; and people who misuse substances. In my recent doctoral study, a combined group of qualified social workers alongside qualifying undergraduate (Stage 3) and graduate (MA) social work students (n=31) engaged in one Specialist Social Work Communication Skills workshop focusing upon the practice setting of parenting assessment. Each workshop involved two paid experienced actors performing a scripted role play to the audience of students within each workshop. A third person acting as 'facilitator' encouraged students to interact with the actors, ensuring that: a) interaction and discussion occurred with the role play and b) that the discussion focused on communication issues, and the type and nature of communication skills relevant for particular settings. The scripts were written in consultation with volunteers recruited from service user and carer consultative groups in order to reflect the 'typical' 'everyday' issues of communication between a service user and a social worker within different practice settings. These performances and on-the-spot role-play discussions were video recorded, transcribed and analysed. The practice examples that I use within the book to illustrate the specialist social work communication skills are drawn from these research transcripts.

The 'reflection-on-action' was acquired through the participants' responses to a semi-structured questionnaire at pre and post stages of the method (i.e. immediately before and immediately after each of the workshops). The semi-structured questionnaire contained a combination of closed and open-ended questions to facilitate participant reflection of issues of communication and the type and nature of communication skills required by their practice setting. Participants received and responded to it before the workshop, and then revisited their answers at the end of it. More details of the research methodology are supplied as an appendix at the end of the book.

A practice-led focus

Thus this second edition continues my intention to ground findings and discussions in the reality of practice actions and practice learning. The presentation of the content is 'practice-led' and meaningful for social work students and practitioners to use in their practice learning. Drawing on feedback from the first edition, I have kept the material accessible and concrete with vivid illustrations of practice. I have retained the separation of the denser detail of my theoretical justifications for why particular communication skills are 'specialist' and 'social work' orientated in nature within a separate chapter of its own (Chapter 2). It is in this chapter that I address the core issue of whether it is possible to distinguish 'specialist social work communication skills', encompassing differing communication capabilities linked to specific knowledge and policy implications of different social work practice settings, from fundamental social work communication skills that might be relevant to all service user situations across all social work practice settings in varying degrees. The way in which I have addressed this possibility is to differentiate between what I have termed as 'basic, universal social work communication skills' for all settings which are integrated with and extended by 'specialist social work communication skills' for the different practice settings in which they occur.

I want to emphasise that this second edition continues what is essentially an exploratory mapping of theoretical linkages to the communication skills employed by social workers in different practice settings. I recognise that the position is not without its problems, and before the book proceeds I should reiterate the following rider. First, the complexity of some service user situations means that there will be occasions when social workers will need to refer to the specialist knowledge covered within other settings in order to complete an analysis of their practice. Human beings are complex, with their characteristics not being so easily assigned to a particular 'practice setting' that constitutes an administrative category used by agencies to structure service delivery (Sapey, 2009). Rather, self-definitions of identity should be encouraged within an individualised, person-centred philosophy. For the purposes of this book, this means that readers must recognise that different communication skills may be needed for different people.

Second, it should be noted that the focus of the book is upon face-to-face interaction (verbal and non-verbal) rather than written or more interactive media methods. There are pragmatic reasons for this. The contextual knowledge is almost entirely based upon face-to-face interaction, and the research methods used face-to-face dialogue and body language to examine the communication issues and skills.

Organisation of the book

The next two chapters focus upon the theoretical ideas from current social work that I have taken to examine skilled communication, including the influence of 'professional capacity' in both the conceptualisation of those communication skills and the assessment of communication skills. In Chapter 2 ('Introducing Communication Skills') I contextualise the theoretical conceptualisation of communication skills taken by the book by outlining recent trends in social work practice that have led to the emphasis upon 'professional capacity', and, in particular, a resurgence in relationship-based practice. The discussion goes on to emphasise how skilled communication is inherently 'embodied' and 'deep', comprising multiple layers that include the contextual environment and its interface with the individuals concerned, as well as their own reflexive responses. Chapter 3 ('Assessing Communication Skills') considers further the issues underlying the PCF, such as the influence of the new model of professional capacity upon professional assessment, and explores what holistic assessment means in relation to communication capacity. It considers what exactly is being measured when assessing communication capacity and how it can be measured.

In Chapter 4, I describe a range of those basic 'universal' social work communication skills that are relevant to all social work practice settings in varying degrees. As such, they constitute a foundational base for effective communication. These basic 'universal' social work communication skills are drawn from the wider communication skills literature and chosen on their basis of relevance to communication issues arising from current and dominant themes in social work practice more generally. The skills are applied to vivid social work practice examples. At the end of the chapter, the capacity for skilled communication at this basic, 'universal' level is mapped to the Readiness for Direct Practice PCF statements of capability.

In Chapters 5 to 12 of the book, I describe and discuss the specialist social work communication issues and skills relevant to the eight different social work practice settings considered in the research study. These are: Chapter 5, 'Working with Children'; Chapter 6, 'Working with Young People with Offending Behaviour'; Chapter 7, 'Working with Parents'; Chapter 8, 'Working with People who Use Substances'; Chapter 9, 'Working with Adults with Disabilities'; Chapter 10, 'Working with People with Mental Health Problems'; Chapter 11, 'Working with Older People'; and Chapter 12, 'Working with Refugee and Asylum Seekers'. The structure and style of these chapters follow a more or less standard pattern, beginning with a practice example of dialogue (drawn from the research study) to illustrate some of the communication issues and skills that social workers need to be aware of and utilise in working in each relevant practice. This is followed by a section that sets out a broad summary of the 'contextual' knowledge, which includes: a) service user perspectives on intervention; b) policy directives on communication issues in the specific practice setting (where it exists); and c) what we know from existing literature about communication issues and skills relevant to that practice setting. The final part of each chapter contains an illustration and analytic commentary of the application of specific social work communication skills to the practice example, which draws on the research findings with further reference to the contextual knowledge. Thus, each of these individual social work practice setting chapters stands alone in presenting specialist social work communication skills pertinent to that setting. However, before turning to an individual chapter, the reader is advised to read Chapter 2 ('Introducing Communication Skills') to understand the conceptualisation of communication and Chapter 4 ('Basic Universal Social Work Communication Skills') in order to achieve the full benefit of the teaching and learning.

At the end of each of the specialist communication chapters, readers will find that I have mapped the capacity for specialist communication skills to the Qualifying Level PCF statements of capability. At the time of writing, definitions of the key knowledge and skills required by newly qualified social workers in statutory children's settings and in adult social care settings have been issued by the Chief Social Worker for Children (Isabelle Trowler) and Chief Social Worker for Adults (Lyn Romero). Framed as the Knowledge and Skills Statements (KSS), with one set for children and one set for adults, the KSS 'strengthens and enhances' the PCF by defining the expectation of 'specialist knowledge and skills' for all newly qualified social workers. Thus, I have included the KSS that seem most appropriate to communication capacity to my mapping of the PCF.

2

Introducing Communication Skills

Summary of Specialist Communication Skills in this Chapter

This chapter presents the theoretical framework that I used to analyse communication issues within the book:

➢ that it is possible to conceive of developing communication capacity from basic 'universal' social work communication skills to 'specialist social work communication'

➢ that the teaching and learning of communication skills takes place within a 'relationship-based approach' which is informed by the social model of disability to locate barriers in communication

➢ that effective communication requires an engagement in reflexive processes about the influence of 'self' upon communication

➢ that the legislative authority role of the social worker inevitably influences communication and must be attended to

➢ that social work communication is not instinctive but must be learnt, evaluated and rehearsed.

Developing communication capacity from basic social work communication skills to 'specialist social work communication'

The current emphasis within the professional development of social workers is to develop the qualities and capacity required to work with service user situations of increasing complexity, risk and uncertainty. This indicates that social workers must develop the capacity to communicate in a way so as to engage fully with the dynamics arising within those risk-ridden situations. Authors of core textbooks on social work communication (Koprowska, 2005; Seden, 2005; Trevithick, 2005; Lishman, 2009;

Shulman, 2009) have long proposed that the communication between a social worker and a service user is influenced by the context in which it occurs. The context changes the assumptions and meanings underpinning the words being used – a significant concern, given that good communication is largely understood as the conveying of information to achieve shared understanding which promotes the participation and wellbeing of the service user (Seden, 2005). To this end, these authors have sought to make particular skills transferable across different contexts and service user groups. The skills are drawn from a number of counselling approaches and methods for interviewing, such as those described by Mehrabian (1972), Egan (1990 and 2007), Agazarian (1997), Kadushin and Kadushin (1997), Hargie (1997), McLeod (1998), Hargie and Dickson (2004), Nelson-Jones (2005), Ivey and Ivey (2008) and De Jong and Berg (2008), and can be summarised as:

> 'active' or 'reflective' listening, attending; acceptance, often demonstrated through summarising, paraphrasing, reflecting back or 'mirroring';

> 'questioning', such as through open or closed questions, probing or prompting;

> 'demonstrating empathy', identifying feelings, using silences;

> 'challenging', recognising psychological defences and ambivalence;

> 'identifying and using non-verbal communication', such as body language;

> 'focusing', such as creating and working on a shared purpose, and keeping the communication focused, setting goals, encouraging self-efficacy and identifying service user strengths;

> 'avoiding assumptions' and self-checking for unhelpful judgemental attitudes;

> 'managing aggression and hostility', looking for the feeling behind the words and actions.

However, I would argue that there is justification for separating out these basic 'universal' social work communication skills that are relevant to all social work practice settings in varying degrees, from 'specialist social work communication skills' encompassing the more integrative work of linking particular knowledge, policy, values and skills pertinent to different social work practice settings. The import of the new PCF is in emphasising such integrative, holistic practice. The nine domains of professional capacity are not considered to be mutually exclusive, but employed interdependently and in varying degrees according to the demands of the practice context. The danger of privileging one domain is to diminish the influence of the others. Thus, a 'transferability of skills' argument does not deal adequately with the requirement for more theoretical linkages specific to different social work contexts. If different contexts create different meanings and assumptions that affect communication practice, then those differences should be identified, and the communication strategies ('skills') for dealing with those differences labelled. I would argue that it does not seem sufficient to hone or adapt existing skills.

The potential for communication differences to be identified through such integrative work was borne out by my earlier research. This research study sought a beginning identification, and overcoming, of barriers to inclusion that related to social work communication with a particular marginalised group (Woodcock and Tregaskis, 2008). The study took a combined social work and social model of disability perspective to analysing communication with parents of disabled children. Particular issues impacting on communication processes, as well as different social work strategies for communication, were identified. Given these differences, I thought it important to ask the same questions in relation to other marginalised groups. Were there particular communication issues pertinent to these groups? What barriers to communication were specific to these groups, and what communication strategies could be utilised to overcome those barriers? Certainly, I expected differences, as the policy literature identifies discrete factors relevant to different groups that can create or reinforce such barriers to communication, or encourage liberation from them. There are signs of this position, or the need for such a position, within findings of other studies. For example, the similar idea of there being 'inhibitory factors' to communication arising within a particular social work setting, for which a social worker develops capacity to identify and overcome, has been recently articulated by Lefevre and colleagues (Luckock et al., 2006; Lefevre, 2012) in relation to social work communication with children.

The distinction between basic universal communication skills and specialist communication skills is also made on pragmatic grounds. The PCF is presented as a developmentally progressive pathway of staged levels of increasing capability, with each stage mapped to the corresponding nine domains of professional capacity. The first four capability levels (or stages) are contained within the period of a qualifying degree programme. They commence with selection and entry to the programme and move on to a level of Readiness for Direct Practice. It is during this early Readiness for Direct Practice stage of their qualifying degree programme that social work students are required to learn and be assessed upon more basic universal communication skills. Indeed, currently such assessment requires the demonstration and reflection upon 'live communication skills' within a simulated practice environment. In later stages of the qualifying programmes, when students aspire to the capability levels of End of First Practice Placement and End of Final Practice Placement/Qualifying Social Worker level, they have to experience practice learning in different social work settings, engaging in increasingly complex work. For this they require learning and application of 'specialist communication skills'. Thus, the differentiation and inclusion of both types of communication skills across a range of settings meets students' learning needs as they accelerate through the PCF levels of capability. Moreover, the identification of specialist knowledge that corresponds to specific practice settings responds to the learning needs of social workers undertaking post-qualifying academic study at specialist and advanced levels. The distinction of specialist communication skills that correspond to their own practice setting, as opposed to particular types of skill, is therefore more pragmatic in facilitating the 'integrative' work of linking knowledge, policy requirements and skills.

However, as stated in the introductory chapter, I recognise that my position is not without its problems. It could be argued that the idea of identifying people as belonging to 'marginalised groups' or particular 'practice settings' is juxtaposed to an individualised person-centred philosophy. Certainly, human beings are more complex than having their characteristics assigned to the administrative categories used by agencies to structure service delivery (Sapey, 2009). Service users could be offended by my categorising and labelling different groups of people in ways that potentially disrespect their own self-definitions of identity. However, I would refer readers back to the rationale of this book of helping social workers in the reality of their practice learning, and so I took a practice-led perspective to its organisation.

A 'relationship-based practice' approach

The theoretical principles underpinning the teaching and learning of communication skills within the book are situated within the contemporary framework termed 'relationship-based practice' (Bower, 2005; Ruch, 2005a, 2009; Wilson et al., 2011) and are informed by the social model of disability (Finkelstein, 1980; Oliver, 1990; Oliver, 1996; Thomas, 1999; Oliver and Sapey, 2006; Sapey, 2009). The past five years has seen the ascendancy of relationship-based and person-centred practice (Barlow and Scott, 2010; Ruch et al., 2010). This has been partly in reaction to the impact of organisationally driven 'managerialism' upon the professional task, with a reclaiming of the professional relationship as the medium through which the social worker can engage with the complex, uncertain and high-risk dynamics inherent within service user situations (Higgins et al., 2015). The techno-bureaucratic administrative systems designed to 'manage' the uncertainty of high-risk service user situations which are so espoused by organisations and expected of their social workers bear little resemblance to the actual experiences of social workers in encountering erratic, irrational, emotionally charged behaviour and uncertain outcomes (Broadhurst et al., 2010; Ruch, 2012). More than this, it sidelines the traditional nuanced relational work of social workers in engaging with such difficult feelings, and processing affective responses to shed light on potentially harmful situations (Munro, 2005; Munro, 2010). Writers are keen to point out that while administrative systems and procedures which promote rational sourced knowledge to achieve safeguarding outcomes are important, one should recognise that they reflect a positivistic view of the world as being certain with regularities in causation, and human behaviour regarded as mainly rational, straightforward and predictable (Wilson et al., 2011; Ruch, 2012). Such a worldview has privileged the formal 'evidence-based' approach to knowledge-for-practice than the more relationally gained informal sources of intuition, emotion and prac-tical wisdom, which are not so open to scientifically measureable criteria. There is a call for a more balanced approach, which includes both formal and informal knowledge sources as legitimate knowledge-for-practice, one that values the relational processes that service users consider so critical (Wilson et al., 2011).

This is not to say that the relationship-based approach is solely predicated upon informal knowledge; it is equally derived from formal knowledge sources. Over the past decade there has been the dominance of a developmental perspective to understanding and intervening within service user lives, with the identification of 'wellbeing' constituting a central concern. Physical and mental wellbeing, growth and develop-ment are predominately understood as being determined by the quality of relationships with other people within the immediate social network, but also mutually influenced by factors within the wider social environment. This dynamic interrelationship model is also referred to as the ecological approach, with interactions understood as occurring across a number of sub-systems at micro-level, meso-level, exo-level and macro-level (see Bronfenbrenner, 1979; Jack, 2001; Jack and Gill, 2003). An example of the application of the approach within social work practice is its incorporation within the government policy guidance 'Working Together to Safeguard Children' (HM Government, 2015). Termed 'The Assessment Framework', it provides a way of assessing children's welfare needs by investigating how wider social factors, such as structural inequality, influence children's welfare directly, or more indirectly through affecting parents' needs and parenting capacity. However, the interrelationship model is not just for use in children's services. Developmental trajectories, at any point in the life cycle, can be adversely affected by difficulties experienced by any one or more of these interrelationships and create instances of developmental risk. At the same time, relationships could act as 'protective influences' to mitigate some of the developmental harm and put people on more successful developmental pathways. As an example, social support has been seen to act as a buffer against stress for individuals, particularly in the case of maternal depression where the provision of a confidante can reduce symptoms (Brown and Harris, 1978).

The 'relationship-based practice approach' essentially encompasses a re-conceptualisation of concepts from the psychodynamic approach, including those that relate to the 'use of self' within the professional helping relationship, alongside theoretical ideas that are social constructionist in orientation. Both orientations relate to the 'use of self' (psychodynamic processes) and the 'influence of self' (culturally derived constructions of service user situations, strengths and difficulties). As Ruch (2009: 350) states, 'relationship-based practice' is not an entirely new concept but rather a contemporary reworking of the psycho-social model (Hollis, 1964). A fundamental tenet of the relationship-based approach is its focus on the individual in context and on the psychological and the social, as 'neither the individual nor the context make sense without the other.' She cites the following as being the central features of the approach (Ruch, 2009: 350–351):

> ➤ it recognises that each inter-personal encounter is unique;
> ➤ it understands that human behaviour is complex and multi-faceted, i.e. people are not simply rational beings but have affective – conscious and unconscious – dimensions that enrich, but simultaneously complicate, human relationships;
> ➤ it focuses on the inseparable nature of the internal and external worlds of individuals and the importance of integrated – psycho-social – as opposed to polarised – individual or structural – responses to social problems; and
> ➤ it places particular emphasis on the 'use of self' and the relationship as the means through which interventions are channelled.

Thus, significant emphasis is made of the working relationship being the interaction between two actors (the service user and the social worker) who are themselves socially situated with the potential to influence the dynamics of an encounter by virtue of their own characteristics, perceived status, cultural vision and understandings, and the way they relate to other people. The psychodynamic elements of the approach emphasise the emotional dimensions of a person's developmental growth, particularly how the interactional quality of early relationship experiences affect psychological health and social functioning with others (Bower, 2005). Herein, modern attachment theorists, in particular, have explored the importance of the parent-child attachment relationship in the way the mind processes interpersonal information to use as a psychosocial template for future relationships (Howe, 2005). People bring these relationship templates to the working relationship between a service user and social worker (Howe, 2005). Powerful feelings about these relationship experiences can be 'repressed' but then 'aroused', 'revived' and 'transferred' to the present (Salzberger-Wittenberg, 1970). Indeed, when operating the relationship-based approach, social workers need to be aware of how the process of 'transference' of feelings influences their relationship with the service user. According to the classic work of Salzberger-Wittenberg (1970), 'transference' affects the way people perceive and interpret new situations with others, and then, how they themselves influence those situations, because our behaviour tends to elicit responses in others which fit in with our own expectations. Countertransference has been used to describe the reaction set off in the worker as a result of being receptive to a service user's transferred feelings. Bowlby (1962: x) neatly summarises the importance of recognising these processes of transference and counter-transference in relationships with service users:

> Transference reactions and counter-transference reactions are the stuff of which the caseworker's daily life is made. Her job is not to avoid them but to learn how best to deal with them, recognizing always that the way the [service user] and she treat each other is neither wholly a matter-of-fact coping with the present, but the result by each of an unconscious appraisal of the present in terms of more or less similar situations that each has experienced in the past.

Thus transference is inevitable and can be incredibly useful in identifying service user feelings (Mattinson and Sinclair, 1979; Howe, 1998; Agass, 2002; Ruch, 2005b). However, there are dangers if an uncritical approach is taken. For the social worker, there is a need to consider whether particular service user situations or problems tend to trigger off unresolved problems and feelings for the social worker which then distort perception and interfere with the interaction with the service user. Acknowledging another's pain can be unbearable, as extremely intense and frightening feelings can be aroused. For example, in Rustin's (2005) analysis of how it was that professionals would not see what was happening to privately fostered Victoria Climbie, she states that they erected various psychological defences to prevent personally witnessing and experiencing acute mental pain. Taylor (2008) similarly describes how social workers' feelings of vulnerability and anxiety about complex, emotionally challenging situations can create psychological defensive behaviours. She uses the classic study by Menzies (1960) of health organisations to identify how psychological defences of splitting and projection seem culturally required to manage professional anxiety. Taylor found that social workers operated less hierarchically than nurses and projected their feelings across the organisation, criticising colleagues for carelessness and non-acceptance of responsibility, but fearing the level of their own expertise. The psychologically defensive response by some workers to this professional anxiety and responsibility was a routinised adherence to structures and procedures, to split the anxiety-provoking situation of the relationship with the service user, and to promote ritualistic task performance (Buckley, 2000; Taylor, 2008). Equally, it points to the defensive response of social work organisations rather than just individual practitioners (Wilson et al., 2011). The increasingly procedural-driven practice documented as occurring within social work organisations is proposed to similarly operate to separate social workers from the anxiety-filled dynamics of emotionally charged interpersonal encounters. The aim, as Ruch (2012: 73) puts it, 'is to polarise and sanitise practice'. Such over-defensive organisational practice attends to neither the service user nor the social worker, producing recurrent patterns of detrimental states of mind, poor physical health and destructive relationship patterns within the family and workplace (Ruch, 2007; Munro, 2010).

The discussion signifies the need for social workers to engage in thoughtful, reflexive processes about their 'use of self'. They must ask themselves whether the feelings that they have about what a service user is trying to communicate to them is valid, or whether it is the social worker reacting to what they are bringing to the situation (Salzberger-Wittenberg, 1970). Thus, the need to become attuned to the ways in which feelings might be expressed is a vital component of relationship-based practice (Wilson et al., 2008). As complex beings, we find that our rational thoughts are shaped by our emotions, and we often express our thoughts through our feelings (Ruch, 2009). It is critical, therefore, that social workers expect feelings to be a medium of communication, and be prepared for it. Operating ritualised task performance within a problem-solving approach is not going to be sufficient to attend to service user concerns for social workers to spend time listening to their perspectives. The theoretical position that I have adopted here posits that until both thoughts and feelings are identified within the communication encounter (and in some cases actually 'felt' in an affective sense through transference), those perspectives will not be 'heard' or understood. Psychodynamic processes of 'containment' are considered crucial for achieving this attention to thoughts and feelings (Bower, 2005; Ruch, 2009). Containment involves enduring, considering and understanding anxiety-provoking feelings (Bion, 1962). It is when these feelings are not sufficiently contained that defensive responses occur (Bower, 2005). Thus, it would seem that the professional capacity to be able to engage on a thoughts-and-feelings level with emotional content is crucial for communication. This requires a level of self-awareness and self-examination about the influence of personal and professional experiences upon practice (Ward, 2010). The PCF locates this capability within the 'Values and Attitudes' domain rather than 'Intervention and Skills', reflecting again how skilled communication is a more integrated and thoughtful personal-professional activity than solely learned behaviour. It points to a picture emerging of communication skills being less about proven behavioural competence and more about the *capacity to communicate*.

Reflexivity

The emphasis upon engaging in reflexive processes about the 'use of self' corresponds to a central emphasis within contemporary social work literature upon the social worker as an 'active critical thinker' self-examining the knowledge and assumptions underpinning their practice (Sheppard, 2000; Taylor and White, 2000; Sheppard and Ryan, 2003). The process of reflexivity explicitly specifies that social workers recognise that they are social actors who actively influence the process and outcomes of a socially situated context (the social work interview) with service users who are in a social context themselves (Sheppard, 1998; Sheppard, 2000). Indeed, social constructionist ideas that inform the relationship-based approach encourage the social worker to actively consider how their personal and professional experiences 'get brought into' practice, such as through their culturally derived constructions of service user situations, strengths and difficulties (Ruch, 2009; Ward, 2010). These constructions are often reflected within the language or other communication methods with service users and social work colleagues. Equally, they are also evident by the methods that are not utilised, or not validated as being communication. Indeed, in some of my earlier publications, I identified that social workers may bring obstacles to the communication within the relationship with a service user that stem not only from a privileging of formal knowledge but also from preconceived notions and cultural stereotyping of service user situations and concerns (Sheppard, 2000; Woodcock, 2003; Woodcock and Tregaskis, 2008, Woodcock Ross and Crow, 2010). For example, literature has documented the way in which social workers have been found to apply social prescriptions of parenting which reinforce gender categories and normative expectations of motherhood and fatherhood (Nicolson, 1993; Richardson, 1993; Smart, 1996; Sheppard, 2000).

Such ideals concern providing warm, sensitive care which is responsive to a child's developmental needs regardless of the social circumstances in which it occurs (Woodcock, 2003). When parenting does not appear to fit with this construction of normative behaviour, it is frequently considered 'unreasonable' or 'deviant' (Urek, 2005).

Clearly the operation of such cultural stereotyping as common-sense reasoning is oppressive and should be identified and avoided. Indeed, the dangers have been well-versed in relation to issues of cultural relativism. As long as it is consistent with their authority role and function, social workers must respect the values and beliefs of the service users with whom they work. An awareness of cultural norms and values enables social workers to be sensitive to cultural differences and variations in patterns and styles of communication. Yet, it is important not to assume homogeneity in the values and practices of any family, faith, community or ethnic group. There are dangers in assuming all values are culture specific, that they should only be appraised within the context of a particular culture and that the values of another culture cannot be applied to another (Compton et al., 2005; Laird, 2008). Such extreme presentations of cultural relativism have been argued to be evident in normative assumptions or stereotypes or generalisations being applied by professionals when seeking to disentangle 'abuse' from 'cultural practice' (Chand, 2000; Williams and Soydan, 2005; Barn, 2007). For example, as early as the Maria Colwill Inquiry Report in the 1970s, cultural differences in relation to class and gender between the social worker and Maria's stepfather were cited as contributing to different understandings of Maria's emotional responses (Parton, 2004).

The example and discussion illustrates the importance for communication of the professional capacity to critically reflect upon wider social and cultural influences that are often taken for granted but are nevertheless invisible and powerful within communication processes. By this I mean there is an importance in revealing the social situatedness of social work communication and the social worker within it. It requires social workers to engage in what Archer (2003) refers to as an 'internal conversation', the reflexive activity of questioning preconceived assumptions and interpretations acquired and arising from the sociocultural context with resultant deliberation for subsequent action. Again, this conceptualisation of communication reinforces the idea of communication capacity as being more than behavioural skill and integrates several aspects of professional capability from the PCF. The PCF domains most relevant to this reflexive aspect of social work communication capacity are 'Critical Reflection' and 'Diversity'. Moreover, as it necessarily involves drawing upon both formal and informal knowledge sources, the capacity to communicate includes the PCF's domain of 'Knowledge' too.

Communication obstacles and the wider communication environment

The above example highlights how communication capacity is not an enactment of agency which is simple or straightforward. Rather, communication obstacles relating to normative expectations indicate that structural forces affect communication processes and the capacity to communicate. In my opinion, a practical application of the social model of disability approach provides greater appreciation of the impact upon communication of obstacles relating to normative expectations and required social work communication strategies than achieved by the relationship-based approach alone. The social model of disability approach validates insider accounts as representations of everyday reality, but also focuses on identifying structural, systemic and attitudinal barriers to disabled people's access to society, suggesting ways in which these can be overcome (Finkelstein, 1980; Oliver, 1990; Oliver, 1996; Thomas, 1999). An example is evident in my earlier work (Woodcock and Tregaskis, 2008). When I applied a social model of disability analysis in addition to a social work analysis to my study of social work with parents of disabled children, I found an alternative explanation to finding that parents tended to communicate in strong terms which prioritised their child's development over other aspects of parenting. The alternative explanation was that the strong communication reflected parental attempts to overcome systemic barriers to their child receiving effective help, such as preparation for significant life stages (like going to school). The combined analysis highlighted how social workers need to find a communication mechanism whereby they identify and discuss systemic barriers with parents, expecting such communication in direct and indirect ways. The analysis also found that communication strategies were needed to address attitudinal barriers within the social worker themselves. Some social workers within the study were either unwilling or unable to validate and recognise service user 'private' knowledge of the individual characteristics of an impairment, and the individual way it affected family life.

As a response to these findings, I have sought within this book to propose specific communication strategies to tackle the issue of identification and addressing of attitudinal and systemic obstacles that occur in the different practice settings. The conceptualisation of skilled communication as the *capacity or capability* of the social worker in identifying and addressing communication obstacles is supported by the work of Lefevre and colleagues (Luckock et al., 2006; Lefevre, 2012). For them, all such obstacles constitute 'inhibitory factors' which act like 'noise' in distorting the potential for "participative 'noise-free' dialogue and unconstrained, authentic and mutual exchange" (Outhwaite, 1994 in Lefevre, 2012: 33). In their 'Knowledge Review' for SCIE (Luckock et al., 2006), Lefevre and colleagues applied this conceptualisation of skilled communication to communication with children, creating an interpretive framework of 'inhibiting factors' arising from the service user, social worker and context which 'impeded' the communication process. A framework of 'Core Conditions' was created to enable mediation of inhibiting factors and create a more facilitative environment for communication with children (Luckock et al., 2006). Lefevre's most recent work grouped these capabilities into 'Capability Domains', conceived as interactive and interdependent such that capacity for enacting effective communication ('Doing') cannot be achieved without drawing on knowledge ('Knowing') and personal attributes ('Being'). The task for the social worker is in integrating the capabilities in a way that meets the communication demands for each individual situation with a child.

While not focusing on communication skills specifically, wider literature regarding learning for higher education has similarly identified the overlapping domains of 'Knowing', 'Doing' and 'Being' as being a useful model for considering the different learning development demands of subject specialisms (Barnett and Coate, 2005). 'Being' refers to the attributes of the person, the integration of personal and professional knowledge, and the preparedness to be self-aware and self-evaluative. 'Doing' refers to the actions taken, including the appraisal of relevant actions for the situation and skilled way of using them. 'Knowing' refers to the understanding of legislation and procedural knowledge as well as theories and research. It also refers to understanding how to appraise and apply knowledge. For Williams and Rutter (2013), it is this last element – 'knowing when to do things and why' – which is the most important element for developing the kind of critical approach that is consonant with 'capability'. Certainly it is a framework for understanding the integrative, holistic, progressively developmental nature of the PCF for social work (Field et al., 2014). When taken with the consideration of professional social work development, it is possible to see how the PCF, as a framework of developing capability, demands social workers (qualified and qualifying) to engage with their formal and informal knowledge ('Knowing' as evident in PCF Domain 3, 'Diversity' and Domain 5, 'Knowledge'), to inform their strategies ('Doing' as found in PCF Domain 6, 'Critical Reflection and Analysis' and Domain 7, 'Intervention and Skills') while critically reflecting upon their 'use of self' ('Being' as shown in PCF Domain 1, 'Professionalism'; Domain 2, 'Values and Ethics'; Domain 3, 'Diversity'; Domain 4, 'Rights, Justice and Economic Wellbeing' and Domain 8, 'Contexts and Organisations') to affect their professional role (Field et al., 2014). The 'Knowing', 'Doing',

'Being' model exemplifies the integrative, holistic nature of the PCF. Moreover, it enables the particular demands for 'Knowing', 'Doing' and 'Being' to be drawn out for particular service user settings, and particular capacities for successful communication to be identified.

What the discussion thus far is proposing is that the communication between a social worker and service user is an interpersonal process in which social workers embody or incorporate an integration of elements from within and across the PCF domains (encompassing 'Knowing', 'Doing' and 'Being') during the interaction (as 'capacity'). Payne (2007) refers to this idea of embodiment and enactment of different kinds of knowledge in interpersonal practice as 'practical wisdom'. For him, the knowledge that is enacted in what seems a practical manner is in fact rooted in theoretical and structural understanding which is potentially identifiable. It is knowledge that 'goes with the social worker' about how to understand the issues and emotions arising within the situation, about how to go about increasing the service user's involvement in deliberating risk to personal and familial safety, about how to address the rights and expectations of the service user and carer(s), and about how to present in a humane and personable way that encourages the discussion of thoughts and feelings while also working within organisational procedures and legislative conventions. There has been renewed interest in the exercise of practical wisdom as professional action (Bondi et al., 2011; Clark and Volz, 2012). Based upon the Aristotelian concept of 'phronesis', the revival of practical wisdom is considered a response to the rise of technical rationality and its associated flawed attempts to reduce risk and uncertainty. Practical wisdom is not about technical competence, but through the exposure to a variety of personal and professional experiences and knowledge sources, involves the ongoing development of human qualities to make increasing sense of the world and act within it in a way for the public good. As summarised by Clark and Volz (2012: 63–64):

> Practical wisdom can be thought of as the mature human capacity for dealing with multi-layered, complex, under-determined problems, both concrete and abstract, both practical and moral, under conditions of uncertainty and under pressures of time, physical, mental and social constraints – all of which may be only poorly understood.

The 'social work' in social work communication skills

Both the social model of disability and the relationship-based approach espouse practice that respects the uniqueness of the individual person within their situation. While personalisation requires attention to the personal 'voice' of the service user and encouragement of service user decision-making and choice in service delivery, people who use social work services do not always do so by choice. They may be compelled to receive services through legal measures or due to material or social disadvantage. Social workers operate communication skills within these legal and procedural frameworks concerning safeguarding, care and control (Seden, 2005). The authority that the social worker brings through their legislative role presents a power differential which can dramatically influence communication with a service user. In my view, this context presents a critical distinction between the use of communication skills within social work and within counselling. Social work communication has to 'start where the service user is' but cannot always be 'service user-led'. Reflexive thinking requires the social worker to be mindful of the social situation that the service user and social worker are in, including the immediate social situation of the social work encounter/interview. Attention must be paid to the 'immediacy' of the communication within an encounter, where the social worker will be dealing with the service user's recurrent ambivalent, and frequently defensive and aggressive, feelings about the work based upon their fear and mistrust of social work authority (Seden, 2005). Thus, it is my contention that communication strategies for addressing this fear should be central, and include that of being clear on the purpose of intervention. If it is not attended to, it will become an ever-increasing obstacle affecting the capacity to communicate.

Social work communication skills do not 'come naturally'

My experience of teaching communication skills to social work students has found that many students share a common anxiety about the quality and extent of the communication skills that they bring to the learning. They place an expectation upon themselves that they should be able to communicate well by virtue of being 'a social work student'. The anxiety becomes compounded when they start a process of comparing their abilities to the other social work students within their peer group. Questioning and self-doubt occurs, raising such comments as 'She has tons of work experience with vulnerable people, so surely she has excellent communication skills?' or 'He has more life experience than me so he is used to communicating with people.'

Other students seem to start the learning process from a completely different angle. The perspective being presented by these students is that they are already effective communicators within service user settings. It is often the case that they had worked for health or social care organisations for some time and, when within that role, they received positive feedback about their communication ability being appropriate to the task. Subsequent questioning and ambivalence about the relevance of the teaching occurs, with comments such as 'I know how to do this already – I've been told I communicate satisfactorily' or 'This teaching is telling me different things than I operate in practice, so it cannot be relevant.' However, on examination, the comments often mask a deeper feeling that corresponds to the same anxiety concerning the expectation of being able to communicate well by virtue of being 'a social work student'. There is fear in being found in deficit of communication skills, particularly when they believe that they should have them already.

In both instances, the anxiety seems to rest on a belief that communication skills 'come naturally' to people, particularly the types of people who become social work students. Certainly, as Koprowska (2005) indicates, humans have a biological drive to communicate with other humans in order to have their physical needs addressed. From babies, we experience and engage in verbal and non-verbal behaviour patterns in order to survive. Koprowska describes these acquired behaviours as 'communication skills'. She encourages social workers to identify, deconstruct and build on these established communication behaviours in order to communicate more effectively within the context of social work situations. In so doing, she identifies that social work communication skills are related but different or extended from those acquired through life experience and development. Lishman (2009) similarly identifies that there are ways of communicating effectively with social work service users which can and should be learnt, particularly as service users repeatedly highlight the poor communication of social workers. My point is that we cannot rely on the fact that skills will be learnt in the same 'naturally acquired' manner within social work situations. Rather, an active thinking process is required.

In concluding this chapter it is important to state that the communication skills presented within this book emanate from such reflexive consideration. As an 'active critical thinker', I have sought to examine and make transparent the knowledge and assumptions underpinning my own interpretation of the responses of qualifying social workers within the research study and wider literature to service user perspectives and policy across the different practice settings. Thus in this chapter I have laid bare the theoretical premises upon which I have made sense of the way in which these communication skills reflect developing communication capacity, from 'basic' to 'specialist', and are 'social work' orientated in nature. In summary, these premises are:

> that it is possible to conceive of developing communication capacity from basic 'universal' social work communication skills to 'specialist social work communication';

> that the teaching and learning of communication skills takes place within a 'relationship-based approach' which is informed by the social model of disability to locate barriers in communication;

> that effective communication requires an engagement in reflexive processes about the influence of 'self' upon communication;

> that the legislative authority role of the social worker inevitably influences communication and must be attended to;

> that social work communication is not instinctive but must be learnt, evaluated and rehearsed.

Moreover, within each of the individual practice setting chapters that follow, the reader will find that I have situated my findings within the context of existing knowledge of communication issues and skills relating to those different practice settings.

Mapping of Communication Capacity Domains to the Professional Capability Framework

Please remember that these should be viewed as domains which overlap in an integrative manner rather than as a linear checklist.

Communication Capacity Domain – 'Knowing' (engaging with formal and informal knowledge in communication)	**PCF 3 Diversity: Recognise diversity and apply anti-discriminatory and anti-oppressive principles in practice**
	PCF 5 Knowledge: Apply knowledge of social sciences, law and social work practice theory
Communication Capacity Domain – 'Doing' (the enactment of communication strategies in interaction)	**PCF 6 Critical Reflection and Analysis: Apply critical reflection and analysis to inform and provide a rationale for professional decision-making**
	PCF 7 Intervention and Skills: Use judgement and authority to intervene with individuals, families and communities to promote independence, provide support and prevent harm, neglect and abuse

Communication Capacity Domain – 'Being' (the use of 'self')	PCF 1 Professionalism: Identify and behave as a professional social worker, committed to professional development
	PCF 2 Values and Ethics: Apply social work ethical principles and values to guide professional practice
	PCF 3 Diversity: Recognise diversity and apply anti-discriminatory and anti-oppressive principles in practice (appropriately placed in both 'Knowing' and 'Being')
	PCF 4 Rights, Justice and Economic Wellbeing: Advance human rights and promote social justice and economic wellbeing
	PCF 8 Contexts and Organisations: Engage with, inform, and adapt to changing contexts that shape practice. Operate effectively within own organisational frameworks and contribute to the development of services and organisations. Operate effectively within multi-agency and inter-professional partnerships and settings

3

Assessing Communication Skills

Summary of Specialist Communication Skills in this Chapter

➤ a relationship-based approach to the assessment of communication capacity

➤ holistic assessment of developmental progression

➤ an assessment process using methods which are valid, fair and transparent

➤ clarity about the conceptualisation of what we are assessing ('communication capacity') and associated learning objectives

➤ using the 'Knowing', 'Being', 'Doing' model for identifying learning objectives of progressive communication capacity

➤ tailoring different assessment methods to produce different evidence of developmentally progressive communication capacity

➤ appraising the preparedness to engage in reflexive processes of self-examination and willingness to discuss emotional content

➤ critical questioning.

The context for practice learning and assessment has changed dramatically with the introduction of principles of developing professional capacity. This chapter considers the implication of this underpinning philosophy for holistic and developmental assessment with reference to what holistic assessment means in relation to communication skills. A key point is that as communication capacity is understood using a 'relationship-based approach', so the *assessment* of communication should be undertaken from the perspective of a 'relationship-based approach'. This bears on matters concerning 'what to measure' when assessing communication capacity and 'how to measure it'.

From 'assessing competence' to 'assessing capability'

Previously a competency-based approach was taken to the assessment of the key roles or occupational standards of qualifying social workers. The competency model had been criticised for a narrow focus upon the demonstrated task-based behaviour of a professional, rather like a checklist approach, than the view of a professional continually developing their expertise throughout their career (Preston-Shoot, 2004; Higgins and Goodyer, 2014). The PCF brings a new developmental approach to assessment, with social workers' increasing *capacity* or *potential* to learn and adapt to increasingly complex situations and demands being a distinguishing feature (Higgins and Goodyer, 2014). All social workers, whether qualifying or qualified and registered as practitioners or managers, are assessed at designated levels of capability for the integration of their developmental learning of all the PCF domains with the provision of a sufficiency of evidence of this integration. The assessment itself must be 'holistic' by integrating the domains of the PCF and evidential sources. The assessment must also show how that learning has progressed developmentally over the assessment period. It is a 'professional judgement' involving critical thinking and not the completion of a checklist of behavioural competence. Guidance accompanying the introduction of the PCF (TCSW/BASW, 2012) characterised 'holistic assessment' by these central features:

➤ assessment that is progressive over time;

➤ evidence should demonstrate sufficiency and depth across all nine domains;

➤ PCF capability statements can be used diagnostically to identify learning and development needs;

➤ the assessment process must be trustworthy, reliable and transparent;

➤ evidence includes the ability to reflect critically, including reference to different sources of knowledge and research;

➤ evidence will come from a variety of sources over time.

The emphasis upon holistic and progressive assessment places the educator in the driving seat of assessing and evidencing the student's practice learning. No longer is assessment limited to the evidence that students produce. Instead educators must present their overarching professional judgement of the student's integrated practice, a judgement which must be defendable, drawing on all the evidence available to support their assessment that a student has capability in all nine domains, and in the integration of domains. It is in this way that holistic assessment has a 'parts and whole' function, as summarised by Biggs (2007) and quoted in the TCSW (2012) *Assessing Practice Using the PCF Guidance*:

> 'the judgment of the assessor is considered central in making a holistic decision about the quality of performance ... we arrive at [such judgments] by understanding the whole in the light of the parts', and that 'the assessment is of the integrated action, not of the performance of each part'.

As stated above, there is an emphasis upon the assessment process for being 'trustworthy, reliable and transparent'. The onus given to transparency recognises that the gathering of evidence must be a developmental process, which involves both the educator and student making the connections between what a student is learning and doing (Field et al., 2014). The obligation to trustworthiness and reliability recognises that the educator's professional judgement is inevitably subjective, but must be justifiable and 'fair'. There are two key matters in this regard. First, students must be assessed by educators deemed capable of making the professional judgements for the level of capability. For example, in England, when students are assessed upon their practice, educators should have undertaken learning and assessment to gain or maintain Stage 1 or 2 status under the Practice Educator Professional Standards for Social Work (TCSW/BASW, 2013). This bears on the second matter concerning fairness of assessment, for it is within those Practice Educator Professional Standards (Domain C: 4, TCSW/BASW, 2013) that principles are cited for an evaluation of the fairness of evidence. The principles are considered below:

Relevance – has an appropriate method of assessment been used to measure the capability being assessed?

Validity – this requires the assessor to be clear about what it is that they are measuring (such as the learning objective) and to question whether the evidence is really measuring or capturing it.

Reliability – this raises questions about the degree to which we can rely on the source of the data, which then reflects upon the data itself. Does the student consistently show their learning across different settings and is it shown in different sources?

Sufficiency – consideration must be given to whether there is enough evidence to support the assessment decision. Have enough opportunities been provided to the student to show their capability?

Authenticity – this concerns questioning whether what is being presented is actually the work of the student. When joint working is undertaken for very complex scenarios, how much of the evidence presented is due to the co-worker, and how much is that of the student? Is the peer or service user feedback truly from the originator, or could it be a fabrication?

A final point in this section concerns the relationship between the assessment processes for professional development (as provided by the PCF) and the requirements set by the regulatory body – The Health and Care Professions Council (HCPC) – for social work students to meet its Standards of Proficiency (SoPs) on qualification. The SoPs are threshold standards, and their delivery and assessment takes place across social work education programmes. The qualifying level of the PCF incorporates and extends the SoPs of the regulator (the HCPC). The PCF has been mapped to the SoPs, and, similarly, the SoPs have been mapped against the qualifying level of the PCF (TCSW/BASW, 2012). Thus, if a student has been deemed to have reached the qualifying capability level for the PCF, then they will automatically have met the required SoPs.

What am I measuring when I assess communication capacity?

For an assessment method, and the evidence drawn from it, to be deemed 'valid', it must assess what it purports to assess. In other words, first, we must be clear about the conceptualisation of what we are assessing, and the learning objectives associated with it. Only then is it possible to match an assessment method appropriate to it. Such 'constructive alignment' of assessment with learning objectives is considered important for encouraging student motivation. The transparency of the process encourages a perception that it is 'fair' (Biggs, 2003). In terms of clarity of conceptualisation for the concept under consideration here ('skilled communication capacity'), in the last chapter I proffered the conceptual idea of skilled communication being the embodied enactment of practical wisdom, grounded in a relationship-based approach. The social worker has the capacity to employ his or her 'holistic self' constituting personal and professional experiences and expertise encompassing knowledge which is both formal and informal in nature (Wilson et al., 2011). The embodied action is not only intrapersonal (internal world of thoughts and feelings) but also reflects an interplay with structural forces in which socio-cultural symbols, conventions, assumptions and stereotypes can serve to give meaning to, but also possibly obstruct shared understandings.

Communicating well means learning practical wisdom, and to practise in a way which maximises relational and interpersonal dimensions, but which equally has regard to structural obstacles and opportunities arising from differing practice contexts. To achieve such integration, and respond to constantly changing and increasingly complex contexts, involves critical, active thinking ('capacity'). In the last chapter, I drew upon Lefevre (2012) and Barnett and Coate (2005) to consider a model or tool for conceptualising such integration and progressive professional development: the 'Knowing', 'Being', 'Doing' model. This consists of three domains constituting the 'Doing' of communication action, alongside the 'Knowing' of what knowledge to draw upon to rationalise the approach and the personal attributes brought ('Being') to enact it in a particular manner.

The 'Knowing', 'Being', 'Doing' model has potential for identifying learning objectives upon which the assessment of progressive communication capacity can be formulated. Writing about professional social work capacity more widely, Field et al. (2014) propose the use of the model as an assessment tool to identify and review student and practitioner strengths and development needs. Put simply, if student learning is now understood as the continuous, progressive development of increasing capacity, then assessment can be considered as a continuous process of seeking whether and how a student makes links between their 'Knowing' of what to do, and the personal attributes they bring ('Being') to enact it using particular skills and interactions ('Doing'). The framework has potential for understanding and operating the integrative, holistic, progressively developmental nature of the PCF for social work (Williams and Rutter, 2013; Field et al., 2014). When taken to the consideration of professional social work development, it is possible to see how the PCF, as a framework of developing capability, demands social workers (qualified and qualifying) to engage with their formal and informal knowledge ('Knowing' as evident in PCF Domains 3 and 5), to inform their strategies ('Doing' as found in PCF Domains 6 and 7) while critically reflecting upon their 'use of self' ('Being' as shown in PCF Domains 1–4, and 8) to effect their professional role (Field et al., 2014). Accordingly, when setting learning objectives concerning communication capacity, the educator can use the 'Knowing', 'Being', 'Doing' model to:

I. identify (and continually review) their learner's strengths and areas of development within each area of 'Knowing', 'Being', 'Doing', by referring to the capability statements of the relevant PCF domains;

II. identify (and continually review) how well their learner makes links between the areas of 'Knowing', 'Being', 'Doing' to develop and assess integrative learning;

III. identify (and review) specific, more manageable-sized learning objectives than operating a larger, overarching conceptualisation.

Thus, when setting learning objectives with the student, it is important to remember that the progressive developmental learning of communication capacity is a very different task than the technical memorisation and behavioural output of specialised content. Rather, it rests upon a process of encouraging honest self-evaluation and reflection upon personal and professional experiences. This is relational work between the educator and the student, requiring the establishment of trust, transparency and purpose. Consequently, the discussion points to a pedagogic underpinning to the assessment of communication skills – the application of a relationship-based approach. The following practice example of Sallie's developing practice learning and assessment is used within the next section to illustrate how such an approach underpins the way that we measure communication capacity.

Practice Example 3.1

Sallie has worked within an inner city youth offending team for several years and has a qualification in criminal justice studies. Previously she worked as a teaching assistant in a large comprehensive school in a socially deprived coastal town. Now approaching her fiftieth birthday, she feels that it is time, finally, to pursue her dream of gaining a social work qualification to enable her to take on more complex work, and perhaps move into more general safeguarding children and families social work than solely youth offending.

Sallie has been selected for a university social work programme, and is coming to the end of her first term of study. She has been engaged in learning activities that are designed to enable her professional development to meet the Readiness for Direct Practice capability level. Social work students have to show the capacity to meet this PCF level in order to be able to then proceed and make use of the learning opportunities provided by a first assessed practice placement. In addition to lectures and seminars delivering theoretical and thought-provoking content, Sallie has engaged in designated practical skills development activities and workshops designed to promote understanding of the concrete aspects of the professional task and how to put the knowledge in use. When taken together, the learning opportunities span all aspects of the 9 PCF domains for this PCF capability level, with each learning opportunity involving an integration of several PCF domains at one time. Different assessment tasks are designed to capture the integrated learning, with the criteria mapped to the most relevant PCF domains. Positioning the tasks at regular but different points over the Readiness for Direct Practice period captures the progressive nature of the developmental learning.

▶

◄

As an example, an early skills-development activity was for Sallie to work with her tutor in setting out her aims and objectives for her learning within a Personal and Professional Development Plan. This included specifying, in measureable terms, what activities she will complete to meet those individual (but still PCF-domain related) objectives and how she will know when they are completed. This is a live document, which Sallie has updated throughout the term as she has engaged in the different learning tasks.

As she nears the end of the first term, Sallie is preparing for another skills development activity where she will be observed by a practitioner and social work service user upon her 'live' communication skills in conversation with another service user. The assessment of the capability for communication will be Sallie's subsequent written critical reflection of what went well and what did not go well in the conversation, drawing upon the observers' feedback and her learning from the taught sessions.

Sallie has prepared for the service user conversation by engaging in some seminar-based activities to consider service user perspectives of social work communication and her own assumptions about it. In addition, she has received several days of teaching about basic communication skills and been given some reflective tasks and directed reading. While she has been given the opportunity to rehearse those skills in simulated role plays with her student colleagues in small triad groups, Sallie has stated that she is 'too nervous' and avoids participation by being late to class or continually talking about other distracting matters. She openly expresses dissatisfaction at the impending observation of her communication.

How can I measure communication capacity?

For some people, Sallie's agitated and critical response to the impending observation of her communication with a service user might seem unsurprising. Observation by others of oneself in practice, whether in role play or in real life, is daunting especially when an assessment is being made of it. There is a power differential between the observer (the educator as assessor) and the observed (the student being assessed) that can create feelings of vulnerability and fear of 'getting it wrong'. Arguably such a fear may be particularly heightened for Sallie. Having been an experienced worker in education and social care organisations for some time, she may feel the strain of heightened expectation to be an effective communicator. She may believe that this expectation to 'know how to do it' and 'perform correctly' is placed upon her externally, or she may even place it upon herself. Her feelings appear to be influencing her thoughts and beliefs. The relationship-based framework to my conceptualisation of communication skills (Chapter 2) highlights the importance of recognising our complexity as human beings, and particularly how our rational thoughts are shaped by our emotions, and that we often express our thoughts through our feelings (Ruch, 2009). As such, as educators we should expect feelings to be a medium of communication within the practice education and assessment of our student social workers. Herein, we should not lose sight of the fact that our education and assessment work takes place within a professional relationship with our students. This means that relational dynamics need to be considered as potentially operating. Moreover, as discussed in the last chapter, it is not just service users who bring relationship templates to the work, but professional workers too. These templates are based upon the quality of early relationship experiences. The experience of early relationships which provide a secure base from which to explore and thrive (through consistent, emotionally warm care) create a healthy sense of 'self' as loved, as being able to relate well to others and of self-efficacy to act upon the world (Howe, 2005). When the individual is faced with anxiety-provoking situations, he or she might rightly feel anxious, but having had the aforementioned protective experience, have capability to operate relational and intrapersonal strategies to bring the feelings under control. However, feelings of vulnerability and anxiety about complex, emotionally challenging situations can create psychological defensive behaviours, especially for people who have experienced less protective relational environments (Buckley, 2000; Rustin, 2005). Professional social workers are not excluded from this, whether students or experienced educators. Rather, research has shown that when faced with the emotionally charged situations of risk, complexity and uncertainty, some social workers have been found to operate psychological defences to project their feelings across the organisation, criticising colleagues for carelessness and non-acceptance of responsibility, but fearing the level of their own expertise (Taylor, 2008).

The relationship-based analysis is helpful for questioning and understanding the response of Sallie to the impending observation of her communication with the service user. What deeper feelings underlie her expression of agitation and criticism at the prospect of the observation and demonstration of communication action? What thoughts underlie the verbal and non-verbal behaviour of avoidance? Drawing on the relationship-based concepts, we might consider how psychological defences might be operating whereby she has found her level of expertise to be challenged. As an example, she could be projecting fear about 'being found out' or 'getting the communication wrong' to the educator who is requiring her to complete the activity. Her avoidance in participating displays a non-acceptance of personal responsibility for those feelings, seeking to criticise others for 'being wrong' than herself.

Equally, the analysis is helpful for considering the potential response of the educator, who in engaging in the interpersonal process perceives and interprets those transferred feelings. This aforementioned process of 'transference' (Salzberger-Wittenberg, 1970) is important for the learning and assessment of communication skills, for it gives the educator some insight into the feelings and thoughts of the student about their capability and comfortableness with the communication or subject matter. However, by the same token, the educator must take care to critically reflect upon the accuracy of those perceived feelings because we tend to elicit responses in others which fit in with our own expectations. Herein, countertransference has been used to describe the reaction set off in the worker as a result of being receptive to a service user's transferred feelings (Agass, 2002). For example, Sallie's expression of agitation and reluctance to engage with the learning and assessment could trigger off unresolved problems and feelings for the educator. As an example, he or she may feel under scrutiny and that his or her expertise is being unfairly challenged. Potentially, such feelings could then distort perception and interfere with the interaction with the student. In the end, it could influence the assessor's professional judgement of capability, unless attention is given to such perception.

Thus, a relationship-based perspective to assessing communication skills requires recognition for such invisible but powerful dynamics between the educator-assessor and the student. These can be summarised as the 'influence of self'. In this regard, as set out in Chapter 2, there is the added dimension of a social constructionist component to the 'relationship-based approach'. The social constructionist component highlights how the social context 'gets brought into' practice through social workers' culturally derived constructions of service user situations, strengths and difficulties, and the wider invisible but powerful influences of the socioeconomic context (Ruch, 2009; Ward, 2010). In view of this, there needs to be acknowledgement by both the student and the educator of the context of the assessment action, in terms of the social situatedness of them as actors playing out their socially ascribed roles as assessor (educator) and assessed (student). Indeed, as we have seen, the examination of social situatedness extends beyond that of internal dynamics of 'fear of failure', but relates to the influence of wider structural social forces interacting with the communication action. For example, Sallie's feelings of heightened expectation to be an effective communicator – to be knowledgeable and capable to perform this role – is socially ascribed by virtue of being an experienced worker in education and social care organisations. Service users and other professionals expect her to be 'wise' in this respect (Payne, 2007). Other related personal or social assumptions that the social work student may bring to their relationship with the educator surround the students' exposure to the nature and tasks of a social worker based on earlier personal or professional experiences, or media images and policy prescriptions. In Sallie's case, with her experience of the realities of front-line practice, she may see a dissonance between the techno-rational strategies operated by her previous employer and the approach taken by the PCF for a reclaiming of the professional relationship. It may cause her to question her previous approach to service users (creating some painful memories), and/or she may question the veracity of the alternative approach being proposed by the educator (creating further defences).

Equally, the educator may bring personal and cultural assumptions to the relationship concerning the nature and tasks for teaching and assessment in social work, and/or the status and appropriate behaviour of a learner vis-à-vis the authority of the educator. In illustrating this to our practice example, the educator may feel that Sallie's avoidant response is a display of poor professional practice demonstrating an unwillingness to learn as opposed to a communication of fear of failure and uncertainty about the security and validity of the assessment. Other structurally derived power differences based upon structural relationships of inequality in society could potentially permeate the communication context. These include age, gender, physical ability, sexuality, mental health, religion and belief, and economic resources, among many others. Such inequality can create further communication barriers, with both parties bringing their prior personal and cultural experiences of overcoming such systemic obstacles.

For an assessment of communication skills, the discussion points to the need for the educator to establish the sort of professional relationship with the student which has a climate for honest discussion and constructive questioning and discussion (Field et al., 2014). It is within this climate that both the student and educator can engage in reflexive processes about the influence of 'self' within social work communication and within the assessment of it. This includes critical reflection about personal and social values and assumptions, such as considered in the paragraphs above. Put simply, it involves honest reflection with emotional content. In Chapters 2 and 4, writing about 'containment' in communication processes, I make the point that it is only when feelings are attended to and contained through explicit recognition and empathy that they feel shared and understood. In the context of an assessment relationship, this means that the educator and student must be prepared to openly question his or her perception of the feelings engendered within communication processes, whether they be between each other or as observed when communicating with a colleague or service user. This requires an element of self-disclosure, a preparedness to discuss feelings and it requires the tentative consideration of potential communication obstacles arising from power differentials and structural relationships.

Therefore, in summary, I would argue that any assessment of communication skills must include an appraisal of the learner's preparedness to engage in such reflexive processes of self-examination and willingness to discuss emotional content. This work is not, therefore, solely about 'Doing' but connects domains of 'Being' and 'Knowing' which can be mapped to the PCF domain areas of 'Value and Attitudes', 'Diversity', 'Knowledge' and 'Critical Reflection'. Indeed, an important note on this point is that the work for this self-evaluation begins from the start. Drawing upon the illustration in our practice example, it should have actually begun with the earlier Personal and Professional Plan, when Sallie's attitudes and motivations for learning, and strengths and areas of development arising in both personal and professional spheres were first identified. In other words, Sallie's communication capacity began prior to the learning tasks and assessment of the communication action (the 'Doing' of the 'observed conversation'), and should be considered as part of that assessment. Those learning objectives should be continually reviewed in different contexts and using different assessment methods to assess the progressing capacity.

Different assessment methods for producing different types of evidence for developmentally progressive, holistic assessment

With communication capacity being measured as an integration of the overlapping domains of 'Knowing', 'Being' and 'Doing' (drawing on the capability statements of the PCF domains), the methods for assessment need to be able to capture this integration, and provide evidence of it. The 'holistic' nature of assessment of the PCF refers to the need for a 'suffi-ciency' of evidence in this regard, both in terms of depth, but also breadth across the PCF domains. Indeed, it is in the use of different sources of assessment and different types of evidence that an educator can feel more confident that they are building a 'reliable' assessment of a student's pro-fessional capacity.

Students bring different motivations to their learning, prefer different learning styles and have individual learning needs. Students' learning objectives will differ in the degree of balance between the three overlap-ping domains of 'Knowing', 'Being' and 'Doing' (and corresponding capability statements of the PCF domains). Arguably, assessment methods should be creatively tailored to those individual differences, demonstrat-ing a commitment to diversity and the complexity of human experi-ence. Certainly, some assessment methods have the capacity to elicit the integration of 'Knowing', 'Being' and 'Doing' in varying degrees. Those methods contain the integrative vision still, but the balance for learning and assessment is weighted more to one domain of 'Knowing', 'Being' and 'Doing'. Some of these different assessment methods are presented below and illustrated with reference to some practice examples.

Supervision and Supervision Records

The reflective supervision meeting between a student and their educator is considered to be a forum for dialogue and assessment; a reflective space to gather and assess the student's 'workings out' (Field et al., 2014). According to my conceptualisation of communication capacity, the student needs to be assessed upon his or her capacity to analyse and explain the thinking behind their communication action, including potential communication obstacles and opportunities that may arise from the communication context and their socially-situated 'self' within it. This critically reflective thought activity refers primarily to the 'Knowing' and 'Being' domains of the 'Knowing', 'Being' and 'Doing' model. The student draws on formal and informal knowledge to explore their rationale for the communication and how well it went. They also express their thoughts and feelings about it, making links to the 'influence of self'. Thus, the process and record of the supervision discussion could constitute critical evidence upon which the educator can draw in his or her assessment of communication capacity.

Texts concerning the professional development of social workers have long identified the potential of professional supervision as constituting the kind of professional relationship suitable for critical reflection upon internal and external dynamics operating within the complexity of social work communication (Kadushin, 2002, cited in Beddoe, 2010; Social Care Institute for Excellence, 2013a). The supervisory relationship received increased attention in the recent reforms of social work practice in recognition that social workers needed to better engage with affective responses, and (emotionally and cognitively) process the complex, uncertain and high risk dynamics inherent within their work (Munro, 2011a; Munro, 2011b; Higgins et al., 2015). In particular, the reviews of child protection practice following the Peter Connolly tragedy had criticised the organisational systems designed to protect vulnerable individuals and families for being excessively techno-bureaucratic and creating less time for social workers to spend with families to experience and make sense of dynamics (Laming, 2009; Broadhurst et al., 2010; Munro, 2011a; Munro, 2011b). Research evidence from qualitative studies of supervisee and/or supervisor perceptions of supervision (across children's and integrated adult services in the UK, Canada and Australia) concur that there can be an overemphasis on performance review, recording and outputs of productivity (Lambley and Marrable, 2012; Bogo et al., 2011a; Bogo et al., 2011b; Bourn and Hafford-Letchfield, 2011; Gibbs, 2001). The reforms have since placed standards upon employer organisations to ensure that effective supervision is provided regularly to social workers. Social workers, in turn, have to show their capacity to be able to use professional supervision effectively. It is now an aspect of developing capability within the PCF for assessment and development.

The following practice example shows Sallie at a later stage of her practice learning development – her first assessed practice placement. The example is the record of a supervision meeting between Sallie and her Practice Educator, Angela. Sallie has been in her practice placement for a month. She has identified the development of her communication capacity as a learning objective. When constructing the Placement Learning Agreement with Sallie at the beginning of the placement, Angela used the 'Knowing', 'Being' and 'Doing' model to identify which specific aspects of Sallie's communication capacity needed to be developed and assessed. Sallie had expressed confidence at how she interacted with service users ('Doing'), citing some examples from her years of experience and professional standing in her workplace. She had less awareness of why this worked, such as knowing whether it was an enactment of her personal attributes ('Being') and whether it could be related to informal or formal knowledge sources ('Knowing'). Angela recognised that the supervision process would be crucial for developing Sallie's ability to 'work out' the links between 'Knowing', 'Doing' and 'Being'. However, beyond solely providing a relational context for learning, in meeting together to critically discuss Sallie's casework, the supervision process provided an *assessment method* by which Angela could hear and question Sallie's 'workings out' of these linkages. This is because the assessment method is based upon critical reflection of experience but uses dialogue and questioning to facilitate learning and check progression of it (Williams and Rutter, 2013).

It could be argued that the use of recording in supervision for the assessment of developing capacity could restrict the 'space' and candid discussion required for critical reflection (Bourn and Hafford-Letchfield, 2011). It is a criticism raised of structured proformas which are used to guide the supervision process and ensure coverage of the tripartite functions to the supervisory role: educative function; supportive function; and managerial/administrative function (Kadushin and Harkness, 2002). The structured approach potentially reinforces the process-driven, performance management culture that supervision is seeking to move away from. Some supervisors may fall prey to an overemphasis upon the managerial/ administrative function in this regard. Yet, there is a difference between a supervisory approach which asks systematic questions and takes notes of answers during the process of supervision, and an approach which encourages inductive exploration, adapting and holding the questions 'in mind' if needed, and then recording the notes after the session (Lambley and Marrable, 2012). It is this latter approach that Angela adopts within the practice example. Indeed, Angela deliberately makes use of a structured proforma for recording the process and outcomes of the supervision as it makes for an excellent tool to enable her student, Sallie, to make the links required of her 'Knowing', 'Being' and 'Doing'. Moreover, Angela co-created the form in collaboration with Sallie in order to accentuate 'shared ownership' of the process and thereby promote emotional safety for exploring thoughts and feelings. It was during this collaborative activity that Angela achieved some transparency with Sallie about the assessment method being 'fair'.

The practice example, at point 1, shows Angela using 'critical questioning' to enable Sallie's deeper learning of her communication capacity (Brookfield, 1987). Williams and Rutter (2013: 90) explain that 'critical questioning' is more than the asking of exploratory questions of 'what, when, where, who, and how' but involves 'taking the dialogue process one step further in drawing out not only assumptions and underlying thoughts but also personal givens and accepted public truths'. For example, Angela asked Sallie to consider why her communication seemed to be achieving more with one service user (Ashley) than another (Ravi) and possible reasons for this. In so doing, Angela encourages Sallie to engage in self-examination, helping Sallie to recognise that her communication response is not automatic but is culturally and socially embedded. Sallie ponders whether her different communication response relates to her feelings of 'hopefulness'; feelings engendered by her empathy with this service user based upon a previous experience with a family member. This critical reflection enables Sallie to make the links between how her 'Doing' relates to her 'Being'. It is sensitive work, with the educator alert to using their insight to empathise and encourage student self-inquiry. Indeed, Williams and Rutter (2013: 91) draw upon Brookfield to suggest guidelines for such critical questioning:

> ➢ Be specific – relate questions to particular events, situations, people and actions;

> ➢ Work from the particular to the general – exploring a general theme within the context of a specific event helps people feel that they are in familiar territory;

> ➢ Be conversational – informal, non-threatening tones help people feel comfortable.

I would add that communication strategies for facilitating the discussion of feelings, such as considered in Chapter 4 ('reflective listening', 'reach for feeling' and 'putting feelings into words'), along with the 'use of immediacy' and 'use of silences') will be crucial for the educator in achieving and displaying such attunement.

Angela deepens the learning of the links between 'Being' (personal attributes and values) and 'Doing' (communication action) by drawing on concepts from ethical theory at point 2. She draws Sallie into a discussion about 'virtue ethics' and how a communication approach might embody these attributes. Sallie identified her own 'virtue ethics' and gave examples of what they looked like in her interaction within professional and familial relationships. The example shows how knowledge can be brought into the supervision discussion to deepen the analysis of 'Being' upon communication capacity. In so doing, it is possible to demonstrate the linkage between 'Being' and 'Knowing', and how communication capacity is so much more than just 'Doing'. However, holistic assessment has to be 'reliable' with learning assessed using different methods and across different types of evidence. Sallie will need to show evidence of her learning of the interrelationship between 'Knowing', 'Being' and 'Doing' for communication capacity in more than one assessment context. Angela uses the supervision meeting to transparently discuss a second assessment method – 'the direct observation' (point 3). A discussion of 'direct observation' as an assessment method for communication capacity follows the practice example.

Record of Supervision between: Sallie Jones (Student Social Worker) and Angela Richards (PE) **Date of supervision:** 20 February 2015	
How are you feeling? How are things going generally? Any wellbeing issues that you would like to talk about? Sallie says she feels relaxed and enthusiastic. She feels she has the right amount of casework not to feel overwhelmed at this early stage and enjoys working with the young people and staff. She is impressed by the communication approaches used by some of the experienced staff and is worried about her ability to replicate it ('I wish I knew what they were doing exactly').	
How have the action items from the last supervision been met? 1. Complete preparatory sections of the Direct Observation form and email to PE by end of the week – Action completed by Sallie 2. Identify Robbie Gilligan's work on 'Resilience' and use some of the key concepts and research findings to identify 'protective' and 'vulnerability' factors in the situation of one of Sallie's service users with whom she is completing a Pathway Plan. Record as a mind-map in Reflective Journal and bring to supervision – Action completed by Sallie	

What learning opportunities have occurred since the last supervision? (e.g. case work, training, shadowing, feedback) 1. Continued with her casework with the two service users with whom she is completing Pathway Plans (Ashley and Ravi). Sallie said that her progress with Ravi had been hampered by Ravi's cancellations in meeting with her, and non-return of her phone calls and messages. She contacted the manager of his temporary sheltered lodging to inquire about his safety. Ravi had been given strong constructive criticism about hygiene, resulting in him withdrawing. We discussed the need to look for differing reasons for his absence – to raise 'multiple hypotheses' – and drew on Sallie's reading of Gilligan's research to consider protective influences and vulnerability factors. Sallie was able to identify how his development needs match expected milestones and stages. We discussed how Ecological-Systems Theory can unpack the way a social care organisation is influenced by the political context which in turn can influence the communication of both workers and service users. She has achieved more progress with Ashley's Pathway Plan. Sallie has met with him twice and also with his mother to look at development needs and choices for college education. He is complying with rules in his sheltered accommodation and expressing a strong desire to leave for independent living. Angela asked Sallie to consider why her communication seemed to be achieving more with Ashley than Ravi, and possible reasons for this. Sallie said that Ashley reminded her a little of a relative who had gone through a turbulent youth with similar difficulties. He had gone on to achieve a successful career in a more practical vocation. She wondered if the experience was giving her more 'hopeful' feelings for Ashley. She was a little more unsure of how to 'help' Ravi. 2. Sallie participated in a team meeting and took simultaneous minutes. Her minutes were checked by the team manager as being an accurate record and in a generally appropriate format. Feedback was provided to Sallie. It identified that the length could be reduced with key points identified. Sallie said that it was hard to determine what was most relevant. We looked at a section of the minutes and identified the key concepts. Sallie agreed to offer to record the minutes again to show her progressive learning.	Point 1
What have you covered in your Reflective Journal since the last supervision? (key points) Sallie had read two academic journal papers by Gilligan on developing resilience in young people and said she had thought that Gilligan's perspective for working on joint tasks and hobbies was relevant to understanding the working approach of the staff from the sheltered accommodation. Sallie identified the availability of a secure attachment relationship as being a protective influence and how to include this in the Pathway Planning approach. We talked about 'virtue ethics' and how a communication approach might embody these in conjunction with Standards of Conduct and Ethics. Sallie identified her own 'virtue ethics' and what they looked like in her professional and familial relationships.	Point 2

What aspects of the formal practice learning portfolio need to be planned and evaluated? Direct Observation: A date and time has been agreed, and the service user (Ashley) has given permission. We discussed Sallie's preparatory sections. She has identified the rights for services and different resources available. Angela identified that Sallie needs to add more information about the elements of the theoretical approach she is taking, and how she will ensure involvement in the communication. She will also consider her 'use of self' in light of this knowledge, such as preconceptions and communication approach. She will apply her learning from today's discussion about resilience.	Point 3
What is agreed to be provided as formal assessment evidence for this period since the last supervision? 1. Sallie's mind-map of protective and vulnerability factors influencing resilience for Ravi from her Reflective Journal. 2. Feedback from Team Manager on the minutes of the team meeting as evidence of producing documents for practice. 3. This supervision record in evidencing Sallie's capacity to discuss personal and professional values, and to reflect upon the processes of reasoning in casework (raising multiple hypotheses and querying information) and resource panels (evidence-based argument).	
How are you progressing towards your identified learning needs? Sallie wants to feel more confident about how to integrate the PCF domains in her work. We agreed that Angela will make the integration specific and visual within her assessment report of the Direct Observation to enable Sallie's understanding.	
What is the plan for work for the next period? Sallie will continue with her casework and not take another piece of assessment work until she has finalised the current assessments. She will continue to attend reviews, with the aim of presenting at a review in a couple of weeks.	
What are the action items for the next supervision? Complete the first direct observation, with final version of preparatory sections by end of the week – Action by Sallie and Angela	
Signed agreement of record of supervision	*Sallie Jones (Student Social Worker) 22 February 2015* Angela Richards (PE) 22 February 2015

Direct Observation

Traditionally, 'direct observation' has been considered a reliable assessment method for assessing the safety and effectiveness of a student's communication action (Field et al., 2014). It is a method whereby the educator watches and observes what their student is actually 'doing' in communication with a service user when undertaking an intervention. Having gained the permission of the service user, the educator takes on the role of 'observer' by sitting in the background watching the interaction, and taking no part in the actual dialogue process itself.

It would be an error, however, to regard the assessment method as the educator solely appraising the student's communication action in the light of whether the student has utilised certain behavioural techniques to increase communication effectiveness. Communication is not all 'Doing'. Rather, from a relationship-based approach, the two other domains of 'Knowing' and 'Being' are always present. Wilson et al. (2011) highlight how the 'Knowing' dimension relates to the student having a theoretically informed rationale for formulating his or her communication approach and responses. Drawing on theory and research evidence, the communication context may raise certain communication issues and potential obstacles, which the student will seek to address. This requires some preparatory thinking of potential communication obstacles before the communication action, but also during action. The reflection upon the interpersonal process is also a component of 'Knowing' (Wilson et al., 2011). It involves a 'step back' to consider 'what is going on' in the process of communication. In the next chapter I refer to this action as 'objective distancing', with the adoption of 'the third ear' to simultaneously listen to the content at the same time as wondering why it is being said and what might more deeply be going on (Lishman, 2009). In this regard, Seden (2005) refers social workers to 'listen to the baseline' communication; the deeper concerns that underlie the presenting information.

Many educators make use of the York model of 'direct observation' (University of York, 1999) which comprises three stages of: i) preparation and planning, specifying objectives for the observer to look out for (before); ii) the observed activity (during); and iii) feedback, reflection and evaluation (after). Students are encouraged to view the assessment method as a circular reflective learning process. If students can 'buy into' the use of the assessment as a developmental tool, and be involved at each stage of the method, it lessens the fear of 'being observed' (Field et al., 2014). I would go further and propose that the York model of 'direct observation' offers potential for enabling assessment of the linking between 'Knowing' and 'Doing' within communication capacity. The three-stage approach captures formal and informal 'Knowing' by asking students to make clear their rationale for their professional intervention before the observation, and then after the intervention they are asked to reflect upon how well they thought they were able to realise their communication strategy (and meet their aims). In other words, the student uses their 'Knowing' (their aims derived from the rationale) to reflect upon their 'Doing' (the communication action). The educator then provides feedback to the student of their observation of the communication action (in the light of the aims) and offers advice of the ways that he or she could alter their communication strategy accordingly. An illustration is found in the following practice example, which constitutes Angela's written assessment of Sallie's communication capacity following the Direct Observation of Sallie's Pathway Planning meeting with her service user (Ashley). Following the methodology of Direct Observation, in preparation for the meeting, Sallie had produced material setting out her aims to: i) show her use of communication skills to engage Ashley in discussion of realistic and achievable objectives for independent living; and ii) encourage his 'self-efficacy' within that communication strategy (drawing on her recently derived knowledge of resilience theory). The presentation of these aims provided a clear rationale for the communication strategy, demonstrating an awareness of how 'Knowing' impacts her capacity for 'Doing'. Angela's subsequent assessment describes her observation of how Sallie achieved her stated aims (between points 1 and 3). In this descriptive section, she draws on different domains of the PCF to show how Sallie's communication action encompasses several aspects of capability. Her descriptive evidence is holistic in this sense. It is not until points 3 to 4 that Angela presents her reasoning and judgement arising from the descriptive evidence. Again, it is 'holistic', with linkages to different domains of capability from the PCF.

Equally, the practice example illustrates how it is not just 'Doing' and 'Knowing' that are assessed through Direct Observation but also 'Being'. The relationship-based approach highlights that a student brings their 'self' to the communication; there cannot be a way of being neutrally involved (Wilson et al., 2011). As Wilson et al. (2011: 343) summarise:

> The being component of social work interventions is about reflecting on these processes, and coming to know about them through thinking about them.

One particular section of the practice example, between points 2 to 3, illustrates this point well. Sallie's service user (Ashley) becomes restless, and Sallie has to make a decision within the communication action as to how to respond. She thinks that Ashley is possibly experiencing painful feelings and he is seeking to be distracting to avert discussion of them. In her feedback, Sallie explores how her thinking related to the feelings raised within her self at the time. Going with this intuitive perception, she expressed empathy to Ashley at the possible pain caused by their discussion of difficult family relationships. Angela validated Sallie's use of 'self' (her 'Being') in her assessment (point 3), linking it to the way that the communication action then progressed (the 'Doing'). Interestingly, it was not just Sallie but also Angela as the observer that 'felt' the expressed feelings. It points to the importance for educator-assessors as well as students critically reflecting upon the veracity of transferred feelings. Indeed, the challenge of 'observer-effects' of differing kinds is frequently deliberated as offering both strengths (such as enabling the consideration of unspoken feelings) and weaknesses (Wilson et al., 2011). In the case of the latter, bias can be created through subjective perception or normal/natural behaviour can be altered by virtue of the presence of the observer (Silverman, 2004). The importance, of course, is to consider such possibilities than to ignore them. Every assessment method has its weaknesses – hence the need for multiple types of assessment method (and the evidence derived from it) to increase rigour and reliability of the overall judgement of capacity.

Practice Example 3.2

Holistic assessment of the student's capability demonstrated in the direct observation of practice

Sallie had ensured that Ashley had given permission for my observation of her meeting with him, and it was clear that he knew that I was observing her and not him. At the start, I observed Sallie making refreshments, using the time to re-establish rapport with Ashley by engaging a little in his banter, displaying amusement, and showing care by checking for his comfort **(PCF 2: Values & Ethics; PCF 7: Intervention & Skills)**.

Sallie showed communication skills to create a good beginning for purposeful work: 'clear on purpose' and 'reached for feedback' as to whether Ashley was prepared to work with her on a 'shared agenda' about the steps for securing independent housing and finances involved. | Point 1
Her non-verbal communication skills were congruent with expecting a focused, purposeful discussion, and were at an appropriate developmental level for engaging a young person **(PCF 7: Intervention & Skills).** For example, she used a pen and paper to mind-map the different options as they discussed the independent living options and issues raised, and she drew little images to illustrate consequences that might occur for the different options. The pictures were amusing (creating a lot of laughter) and provided a non-threatening medium for Ashley to increasingly identify for himself the different steps and issues as they went through the process.

▶

Sallie helped Ashley explore the challenges and possibilities of the issues he raised by referring to the particular personal characteristics and difficult family relationships **(PCF 3: Diversity)**. She did not shy away from having to relay this difficult information. On one occasion Ashley started to turn and look away, fiddling with a drink bottle. He made a couple of jokes. I wondered why he had not stuck with the discussion. Had he sought to divert the discussion because it was too painful or because he had lost focus? (In our reflection of the meeting afterwards, Sallie said that she had wondered about this at the time too.) Sallie showed respect by acknowledging the jokes, and gently brought him back to the agenda. She expressed empathy for the potentially difficult issues and feelings being raised, and praised Ashley for sticking with it **(PCF 2: Values & Ethics; PCF 7: Intervention & Skills)**.	Point 2
The communication medium and Sallie's exploration of Ashley's thoughts and feelings showed understanding of human growth and development **(PCF 5: Knowledge)**. Sallie's preparation for the meeting was thorough. She had looked into the different financial possibilities and the process required, thereby seeking to promote Ashley's economic status and access to housing **(PCF 4: Rights, Justice & Economic Wellbeing)**. The result was that her service user engaged purposefully in the work. Certainly the feedback from Ashley after the observation was that he had confidence in her ability to help him **(PCF 5: Knowledge)**. She had communicated a belief in Ashley's potential that had a motivating effect, yet at the same time had drawn attention to the realistic challenges.	Point 3
Sallie was able to keep a balance of showing friendliness, care and interest, but with sufficient authority to ensure that 'work' was achieved **(PCF 2: Values & Ethics; PCF 7: Intervention & Skills)**. Although friendly, it was not a 'chat' but a 'conversation with a purpose', which achieved outcomes. Thus I saw good evidence of her ability to demonstrate honesty, respectfulness and maintain professional boundaries **(PCF 1: Professionalism)**. In summary, I observed that she can establish an effective working relationship with capacity to communicate within even more complex and challenging situations.	Point 4

Service User Feedback

Incorporating feedback from people who use services and those who care for them should be considered an essential element in the holistic assessment of social work communication capacity. If the outcome for communication is largely understood as the conveying of information to achieve shared understanding which promotes the participation and wellbeing of the service user (Seden, 2005), then we should be asking our service users about whether those outcomes have been achieved for them, including processes of what worked and what did not, and how changes can be made. Moreover, given the emphasis upon professional capacity, students should not just describe how feedback from service users has been obtained, but how this has contributed to their learning and continual development.

There is still very little written about the involvement of service users in assessment. A key point, however, is a recognition of the complicated power differential between a social worker or student and service user. Service users should not feel obliged to provide feedback, and there is a danger that a service user may believe that the delivery of a service is contingent upon their feedback. The provision of feedback must be 'fair' and 'optional' in this regard. By the same token, social workers and students work with their service users in complex situations involving the balancing of risk and independence. Importantly in such situations, service users should be involved in making decisions about their safety, but there are occasions when a course of action is suggested that a service user does not welcome. Wilson et al. (2011) draw on Beresford et al. (2007) to illustrate this dilemma:

> In such circumstances, the challenge will be to reach a solution that respects the desires of each individual even if it does not equate with that person's wishes. We do not underestimate the skill that this will require!

Indeed, social workers and students may feel that the feedback provided by their service user does not reflect the complexity of the situation, and could be unduly negative of their intervention. It is again a matter of 'fairness'. Parker (2004: 100) draws on Thomas's research of the involvement of service users in social work practice learning to cite three issues for consideration when using service user feedback:

> ➤ Competence – the ability to give reasoned arguments that matched practice to set and agreed outcomes;

> ➤ Fairness – which concerned the rights of service users to make comments based on observed evidence without fear or favour, and the range of comments to be extensive enough not to unjustly affect the student's overall assessment;

> ➤ Training and methods – procedures and processes should be established to prepare people about the role and remit of feedback and/or assessment.

Importantly, for service user feedback to be useful for a student's developmental progress, the student needs to be clear about what the feedback should focus upon. A proforma or set of semi-structured questions can be useful in achieving such specificity, although it must be suitable for the cognitive ability of the service user. More creative methods, such as through pictures or communication cards, will be more appropriate for some service users. The following practice example is of a semi-structured feedback form developed and used by service users involved in the assessment of 'live' communication skills of social work students for their Readiness for Direct Practice at a university in the South of England. The service user and carer consultative group agreed the dimensions of communication capacity that they expected to be shown by the student and agreed the formulation of questions that attended to those dimensions. The educators checked those dimensions against the PCF capability statements to ensure that the desired practice outcomes matched those expected for the student level. The service users then rehearsed the use of the feedback form in fictional role plays, and then revised the questions. A critical issue was for the educators to emphasise to the service users the developmental learning nature of the assessment, that it is a process from which the student will further develop. The feedback form contains a section for brief narrative feedback, which encourages service users to raise issues that they feel that the structured questions do not cover, or to re-emphasise and expand on answers already given. Students then used the feedback to reflect upon whether their communication strategy (their 'Doing') did meet their aims for the communication (their 'Knowing') and whether they were aware of this during the communication or only afterwards (their 'Being'). The actual marked assessment was upon the student reflection with the service user feedback sheets attached to evidence their reflective evaluations.

Practice Example 3.3

Service User Conversation Feedback Form to Student: Readiness for Direct Practice

Name of Student **Observer Identifier:**	
Circle your score between 1–5, where 1 is not very well, 2 is fair, 3 is OK, 4 is quite well and 5 is excellent	
Did you feel that the student introduced themselves properly to you and explained why they were there?	1 2 3 4 5
Did they explain what they hoped to achieve in the meeting and ask you what you hoped to achieve?	1 2 3 4 5
Was the student on time for your meeting?	1 2 3 4 5
How well do you think the student listened to what you said?	1 2 3 4 5
Did you have enough time to put across your views?	1 2 3 4 5

▶

Did you think that the student understood your views accurately?	1 2 3 4 5
Did the student look out for your comfort? (e.g. any tiredness, asked how you were, took account of your commitments, checked any particular needs such as visual aids, access)	1 2 3 4 5
Did the student treat you with respect?	1 2 3 4 5
Did the student show care for any feelings that you expressed?	1 2 3 4 5
Did the student ask useful and pertinent questions?	1 2 3 4 5
Did the student convey honesty and trustworthiness to you?	1 2 3 4 5
Did the student answer your questions with clarity and without jargon?	1 2 3 4 5
Did the student seem prepared for the meeting?	1 2 3 4 5
Did the student end the conversation well?	1 2 3 4 5
How confident was the student in dealing with the conversation?	1 2 3 4 5

What did the student do that you really liked?
(Please write or explain verbally your honest views about what you think. Areas that you could also consider are: whether the student communicated a genuine desire to learn, showed humility, asked for your views, engaged with the process and identified confidentiality or privacy)

....
....
....
....
....
....
....
....
....

What things do you think that the student needs to work on?
(Please write or explain verbally your honest views about what you think. If a student shows any of the following then this must be written down here: student loses temper, student shows a lack of empathy or continuous lack of interest, or uses discriminatory language or is rude, or is not punctual)

....
....
....
....
....
....
....
....

Thank you for participating and for all your comments.

This chapter has provided an overview of the underpinning philosophy for holistic and developmental assessment with reference to what holistic assessment means in relation to communication skills. With communication capacity understood using a 'relationship-based approach', the chapter considered ways in which the *assessment* of communication could be undertaken from the perspective of a 'relationship-based approach'. Matters concerning 'what to measure' and 'how to measure' communication capacity were reconciled through the use of the 'Knowing', 'Doing', 'Being' model.

Mapping of Communication Capacity Domains to the Professional Capability Framework

Please remember that these should be viewed as domains which overlap in an integrative manner rather than as a linear checklist.

Communication Capacity Domain – 'Knowing' (engaging with formal and informal knowledge in communication)	**PCF 3 Diversity: Recognise diversity and apply anti-discriminatory and anti-oppressive principles in practice**
	PCF 5 Knowledge: Apply knowledge of social sciences, law and social work practice theory
Communication Capacity Domain – 'Doing' (the enactment of communication strategies in interaction)	**PCF 6 Critical Reflection and Analysis: Apply critical reflection and analysis to inform and provide a rationale for professional decision-making**
	PCF 7 Intervention and Skills: Use judgement and authority to intervene with individuals, families and communities to promote independence, provide support and prevent harm, neglect and abuse
Communication Capacity Domain – 'Being' (the use of 'self')	**PCF 1 Professionalism: Identify and behave as a professional social worker, committed to professional development**
	PCF 2 Values and Ethics: Apply social work ethical principles and values to guide professional practice
	PCF 3 Diversity: Recognise diversity and apply anti-discriminatory and anti-oppressive principles in practice (appropriately placed in both 'Knowing' and 'Being')

	PCF 4 Rights, Justice and Economic Wellbeing: Advance human rights and promote social justice and economic wellbeing
	PCF 8 Contexts and Organisations: Engage with, inform, and adapt to changing contexts that shape practice. Operate effectively within own organisational frameworks and contribute to the development of services and organisations. Operate effectively within multi-agency and inter-professional partnerships and settings

4

Basic Universal Communication Skills

Summary of Specialist Communication Skills in this Chapter

➢ beginning skills to establish purposeful work
    ➢ tuning-in
    ➢ achieving a Shared Purpose
        ➢ being clear on role
        ➢ being clear on purpose
        ➢ reaching for feedback
        ➢ communicating empathy
        ➢ using immediacy

➢ empathy skills
    ➢ reflective listening
        ➢ observing
        ➢ positioning
        ➢ paraphrasing
        ➢ summarising

➢ skills to encourage the discussion of unarticulated feelings
        ➢ reaching for feeling
        ➢ putting feelings into words
        ➢ using silences.

This chapter describes a basic level of communication capacity, which can be understood as 'basic "universal" social work communication skills' as found both within the research studies informing this publication, and also the existing literature concerning communication skills as they relate to social work. These skills are relevant, to a greater or lesser extent, to each practice setting, and it seemed redundant to keep repeating their definition and discussion within each ensuing specialist practice setting chapter. Illustrative examples of the various aspects of these 'universal' skills are provided throughout this chapter as it proceeds.

'"Beginning Skills" to establish purposeful work'

The importance of working with a clear purpose, as opposed to a conversation without any aim or direction, has been emphasised by service user feedback, research and official enquiries into social work practice and current governmental practice guidance (HM Government, 2015; Lishman, 2009). Research has also identified that first meetings have a lasting emotional impact upon service users and therefore are a significant stage for engaging service users in processes of help and change towards achieving that elusive state of 'partnership working' (Aldgate and Bradley, 1999; Bell, 1999; Brandon et al., 1999; Brandon et al., 2006). Put simply, beginnings are important. Given that the first meeting is such a 'critical moment' within the social work process, it is essential for the social worker to develop skills to a) prepare for meeting the service user and b) achieve a shared understanding of the purpose, nature and process of the social work that will occur.

'Tuning-in' (Shulman, 2009)

The skill of preparing oneself for communication with a service user in order to attend to his or her concerns is described by Lawrence Shulman (2009) as *'tuning-in'*. In much the same way as one might block out all other noise and listen intently to different sounds in order to tune into a radio station, so the social worker needs to spend quiet time focusing on the concerns that the service user might bring to the communication and the ways that he or she might communicate those concerns. Shulman's alternative form of words for the skill is 'preparatory empathy'. It is a helpful term, neatly summarising the two actions required to fulfil the skill. First, the social worker needs to do the activity before the meeting with the service user, i.e. *in preparation* for the meeting. Second, the aim of the activity is to achieve empathy with the concerns of the service user. Empathy is widely regarded to refer to the act of recognising what another person is feeling (Koprowska, 2005). Trevithick's (2005: 81) definition of empathy is that it:

> involves attempting to put ourselves in another person's place, in the hope that we can feel and understand another person's emotions, thoughts, actions and motives. Empathy involves trying to understand, as carefully and sensitively as possible, the nature of another person's experience, their unique point of view, and what meaning this conveys for the individual.

'Preparatory empathy' or *'tuning-in'*, therefore, involves the social worker seeking to become attuned to the ways in which the service user might express

their emotions. The need to become attuned to the ways in which feelings might be expressed was considered in Chapter 2 to be a vital component of relationship-based practice. As complex beings, we find that our rational thoughts are shaped by our emotions, and we often express our thoughts through our feelings (Ruch, 2009). It is critical, therefore, that social workers expect feelings to be a medium of communication, and be prepared for it.

Shulman provides a three-stage framework for employing the skill of *'tuning-in'*. This involves considering how the concerns that the service user is bringing to the communication are influenced by:

1. the way that society's norms, expectations and institutional structures (such as laws, organisational policies) have been experienced by the service user;

2. the issues or difficulties that this particular service user is experiencing in his or her immediate environment;

3. the immediate situation being faced by the service user in meeting with a social worker to discuss these difficulties.

It is useful to illustrate the operation of this tripartite framework through the use of a practice example (4.1). The chosen example is that of Gary, a 16-year-old A-level school student who is living with his 18-year-old brother Steve. Their father is an officer in the navy, and at the time of this referral he is working on his ship away at sea. In operating the first stage of *'tuning-in'*, the social worker must ponder the way that Gary experiences society's norms, expectations and institutional structures. In this instance a simple question to ask oneself is 'How does society treat teenagers?' The answer, in general terms in relation to the UK, is that the teenage years are viewed as a time of 'stress', a transitional period between being a child and becoming an adult. Teenagers are often viewed as being disruptive, moody and seeking to assert independence to the care and control of adults. They are expected to demonstrate greater autonomy, increasing rational thought and more social integration and concern for collective wellbeing, yet at the same time are considered incapable of rational decision-making by virtue of not yet being an adult (Department of Health, 1996). This occurs despite the fact that the cultural expectation of some families is for young people to take on caring roles for their relatives, or to take on leadership roles within faith communities.

While the teenage years are a time of stress and strain for some young people, it is not the case for all young people, with many experiencing good relationships with adults and their peers. However, these largely negative societal and cultural assumptions are what Gary expects the social worker to bring to the communication.

Practice Example 4.1

Gary

Preparatory Stage

Gary, aged 16 and of white British background, lives with his brother Steve in a well appointed home, in a well-resourced suburban area of a medium-sized city in south-west England. Steve is 18 years old. He left school the previous summer and has just started a job as a sales person for a large company. Their father is a senior officer in the Navy and is frequently away at sea. Their mother died of cancer when Steve and Gary were in primary school. They received counselling to help with their bereavement. Gary is currently undertaking A-levels at a local secondary school. He has a few friends whom he sees regularly. All the family would describe their ethnic origin as white British. Two weeks ago, Gary went missing. It was very unusual for him to do this, and his brother Steve was very concerned. He did not arrive at school or return home. Two days later he was found by the police being drunk and disorderly with a couple of friends and returned home. Last night, Gary ran away again. This time friends took him to the local hospital as he said he was desperately unhappy and would live on the streets. The nurse that saw Gary made a referral to the Children and Families Team of the local Social Services Department. She was very worried about his emotional wellbeing and physical health (should he keep running away and live on the streets). She was concerned that he did not have a parent at home to care for him. This seemed to be a particular concern as the Christmas holidays were due to start and support networks (such as school) might not be available. The social worker's role was to assess Gary's health and wellbeing, and to ensure that the care of him was adequate. Where it was consistent with this, the social worker would also offer support in the care of Gary.

The social worker is a 30-year-old white Scottish woman called Caroline Simpson. She telephoned Steve earlier in the day to explain about the referral and to request to meet with Gary that afternoon after school. Steve said that he would inform Gary of the visit.

The important consideration for the social worker is 'how might Gary demonstrate these feelings?'. Gary could communicate feelings of frustration and exasperation at being viewed as unable to make his own decisions by becoming defensive through aggression, or of withdrawal. He might communicate mistrust of adult authority through hostility, or choose to reveal true feelings in a piecemeal fashion over time. However, he might have positive experiences of caring communication from adults and so he might be more open with his feelings, expecting to receive emotional warmth and constructive help from the social worker. It is crucial that the social worker considers as many alternatives as possible. In doing so, he or she will be more able to identify the feeling when it is demonstrated within the communication. This is not about being assumptive and deterministic about the service user's feelings. It may well be the case that other anticipated feelings are demonstrated during the communication. Yet, incongruously, the preparation helps the worker to spot those differences and so attend to that unanticipated feeling, showing that he or she has understood the significance of the communication.

The second stage of 'tuning-in' requires the social worker to ponder the issues or difficulties that Gary is experiencing, as a young person, in his immediate environment. One aspect is that Gary has experienced considerable loss, both in his childhood with the death of his mother, and repeated departures of his father during his adolescence. We know that loss and other adversity affects children and young people differently, depending on age, sex, temperament, intelligence (in terms of IQ) and, most importantly, the quality of relationships with caregivers (particularly whether there is a secure attachment relationship – for a further discussion please see Howe, 2005). Children and young people go through stages of grief, but do so in a different way to adults and, depending on individual factors, may become 'stuck' at a stage (Jewett, 1984). Loss may remain unresolved and grief may continue to be misunderstood or unidentified by adults. Gary, for instance, could be 'stuck' in feelings of guilt about the loss of his mother. It was too early in his development for him to be able to rationalise why she was suddenly unavailable to him. This causes some children in their middle years to blame themselves for the death of a loved one, believing that if they acted differently a different outcome would have occurred. Boys, in particular, find it difficult to demonstrate and discuss painful feelings in the face of cultural stereotypes that 'boys don't cry'. Now, within adolescence, Gary is experiencing multiple losses when his father departs for periods of service. Subsequent losses are not considered to be experienced as easier but as doubly hard, with painful feelings brought to the surface.

Drawing on this analysis, Gary's expectation of adults could be that they are unable to identify his pain and help him resolve it. As before, the important consideration for the social worker is 'how might Gary demonstrate these feelings?' Gary might communicate feelings of sadness and helplessness, withdrawing from the conversation. He might seek to mask his feelings and keep the conversation at a superficial level. He may be so surprised to find an adult openly discussing feelings that he becomes defensive and aggressive to ward off further exploration because he does not know how to deal with the situation. Alternatively, Gary may be relieved that someone is willing to hear and understand his feelings. He may demonstrate tearful distress and let go of pent-up emotion.

The third stage of 'tuning-in' requires the social worker to consider how Gary might feel in meeting with a social worker to discuss the difficulties within his situation. The negative media portrayal of social workers is either that of 'busybodies poking their noses into private affairs', removing children or vulnerable adults from their homes without good evidence, or 'inadequate' by failing to protect children from harsh caregiving. These dominant negative media images concerning authority will influence Gary's expectations of how helpful the social worker will be to him. He might hide his feelings and concerns in an effort to convince the social worker that all is well so that the social worker leaves his home. He may become fearful and angry as the social worker explores the situation and his feelings. Another particular concern for Gary is that the communication with the social worker might result in his father being summoned home from his ship. Often, service personnel find this action embarrassing because their private life becomes public within their workplace. Frequently they fear repercussions upon their service career. Gary would be aware of this issue and may communicate feelings of embarrassment and guilt at the situation, and demonstrate anxiety about his father's return.

Crucial to *'tuning-in'* at all three stages is for the social worker to ponder on how her 'self' will influence and impact on the communication with the service user. Thus, at the first stage of *'tuning-in'*, when considering how Gary experiences society's norms, expectations and institutional structures, it is important for the social worker to ensure that they have an up-to-date knowledge base about teenagers in society. Where this is lacking, there is a moral and professional imperative to take steps to improve this knowledge base prior to the communication. Indeed, research tells us that in the face of knowledge deficits, social workers' own constructions of caregiving and parenting have been found to dominate their assessment work and affect their practice strategies (Howitt, 1992; Parton et al., 1997; Daniel, 2000; Woodcock, 2003). Such constructions could add to oppression already experienced by a service user through reinforcing negative cultural stereotypes.

Similarly, at the second stage of *'tuning-in'*, the social worker needs to reflect on 'self' in terms of whether they have sufficient knowledge of the kinds of issues or difficulties that Gary could be experiencing, as a young person, in his immediate environment. In this example, knowledge of theories of loss was required. By *'tuning-in'* to 'self' at this stage, it is important that the social worker recognises that the service user's feelings of loss, grief and bereavement have an emotional impact on the social worker themselves. The social worker may have experienced significant loss and so be able to identify the depths of the grief being communicated by Gary. By the same token, the social worker may find it difficult to acknowledge the pain being communicated by Gary because it resonates too acutely with his or her own pain. Alternatively, the social worker may not have experienced significant loss and so may find it harder to demonstrate understanding of Gary's pain in an authentic way. What is important is that the social worker takes time to reflect on these issues about themselves before the communication takes place, so that they have more chance to recognise the way in which their own feelings might be communicated and take steps to deal with this.

Finally, in thinking about the influence and impact of 'self' at the third stage of *'tuning-in'*, the social worker needs to consider how Gary might demonstrate his feelings, not just in meeting with any social worker, but themselves as a particular social worker. This requires Caroline to engage in an active consideration of the similarities and differences relating to personal characteristics between her and Gary across a range of variables, including age, sex, ethnic origin and other facets of cultural background. For example, the age difference between Gary and Caroline presents a power differential. In being an adult, Caroline is considered by society to be able to make rational choices and is accustomed to having her views heard and believed. Gary, however, is not. The fact that legislation states that children's wishes and feelings should be sought and their views established as central to any decision-making (Children Act 1989; Children Act 2004; The Children and Families Act 2014 (England, Wales and Northern Ireland)) does not mean that partnership occurs as much in practice as it should. Rather, young people frequently report that their social workers do not listen adequately to them. Children are among the most oppressed members of society with frequent experience of being overpowered – whether through being told to 'shut up' or having their views devalued, or as too often reported, being physically constrained or beaten (Kroll, 1995). Caroline needs to *'tune-in'* to how she might inadvertently devalue Gary's thoughts and feelings and prepare herself to find ways to communicate the opposite. Caroline might be able to empathise with Gary's feelings of being 'unheard' or 'disempowered'. She may have experienced these feelings in her own life and so draw on this similarity in order to better understand Gary's position. This is not to say that she should claim that she understands Gary's situation completely. Only he is the expert on that. Rather, the similarity gives her greater insight, which she can then look to have confirmed or disconfirmed during their meeting when the communication is played out.

'Achieving a shared purpose'

'Tuning-in' prepares the way to achieve the other aim for the beginning stage of communication within social work intervention, which is to achieve a shared understanding with the service user of the purpose, nature and process of the social work that will occur. The beginning stage of work is often replete with instances of the service user communicating

ambivalence, resistance and sometimes aggression. Often this occurs because there is no shared understanding of the purpose of the work and, crucially, how that work is beneficial to the service user within their situation. Yet, the policy requirements to 'think person-centred' in terms of finding out from the person's perspective what is important to them and how to live their life, places a demand for greater clarity in generating the aims and purposes of social work assessment and ongoing intervention. Co-production of those aims and purposes should be sought wherever possible (The Care Act 2014 in England, Wales and Northern Ireland; The Social Care (Self-directed support) (Scotland) Act 2013; The Social Services and Well-being (Wales) Act 2014).

Shulman's work on 'agendas' is helpful in understanding the interpersonal dimensions of this aspect of the communication process. Key to this understanding is an appreciation of how the authority that the social worker brings through their role and law dominates the proceedings. Some service users seek and/or receive social work services on a voluntary basis. They bring an *'agenda'* to the communication which is about having their needs and difficulties understood, identifying their strengths and seeking to change the difficulties within their situation. Frequently, however, there is a degree of compulsion or social control underpinning the reason for the social worker meeting with the service user. This is due to the social worker having legislative duties to safeguard and promote the wellbeing of individuals. The social worker brings their *'agenda'* of ensuring that the communication process enables him or her to fulfil that authority role. In the case of our practice example, the social worker's *'agenda'* was to communicate effectively with Gary in order to assess Gary's health and wellbeing, and to ensure that the care of him was adequate. Where it was consistent with this, the social worker would also offer support in the care of Gary. On meeting with Gary, the social worker, Caroline, might find that the two agendas coincide. Gary may be keen, if not relieved, about having his needs and difficulties understood, and looking to work with the social worker to change the difficulties within his situation. In this instance, the social worker and Gary could be said to be working to the same agenda.

However, Gary may be very ambivalent about meeting with the social worker, rejecting her agenda. Indeed, we have just *'tuned-in'* to the possibility of this occurring. His agenda might be to hide his feelings and concerns in an effort to convince the social worker that all is well so that the social worker leaves his home. Indeed, the authority role that a social worker brings to the communication with a service user inevitability carries with it the aforementioned negative media stereotype of social workers creating fear and suspicion. Beyond this, there were other potential reasons that might mean that Gary might not want to share the same agenda as the social worker, such as being reluctant to share painful feelings about loss. In all these instances, we would describe the situation as having two conflicting agendas operating. The consequence is that 'no work' can be said to be occurring as there is no shared agenda (Shulman, 2009).

Clearly, at the outset of meeting, the social worker needs to utilise communication skills that create the conditions for achieving a shared agenda. The interpersonal processes just described indicate that this should be understood as an interactive process of introduction and negotiation. The agendas of both the social worker and the service user need to be brought out into the open. There needs to be discussion about those agendas and agreement on how the agendas can be brought together in order to specify the purpose and processes for the ongoing work. This will involve the social worker identifying the service user's thoughts and feelings as they emerge through this discussion, for which the social worker's previous engagement in 'tuning-in' will have helped to prepare him or her to have the communication capacity do this work. Shulman (2009) suggests a three-part communication strategy called 'contracting' for the process. The three parts consist of: *'being clear on role'; 'being clear on purpose';* and *'reach for feedback'.* I have chosen to extend this strategy to include a fourth part: *'communicating empathy'.* In view of this change and the practice context of emphasising more clarity of purpose in social work intervention, I have chosen to rename this communication action as *'achieving a shared purpose'.*

The first part of *'achieving a shared purpose'* concerns paying attention to the aforementioned dominating influence of the authority role. The requirement is for the social worker to be *'clear on role'.* This means that, at a minimum, the social worker must tell the service user in an honest and direct way that they are a 'social worker'. Taking into account people's capacity for understanding, they should go on within the discussion to explain the parameters of the role, such as the duties to ensure that someone is safe from harm and the limitations to ensuring confidentiality. Smale et al. (1993: 48), in their discussion of the skills needed to empower service users within assessment processes in care management, regard such authenticity to be central and define it as:

> 'The care manager's ability to relate to others with integrity; to be aware of their own feelings and values, as well as the significance of their agency role and the other roles they occupy dependent upon gender, race and cultural background ... there are several levels to this from the straightforward demand that workers are honest with people about themselves, their agencies and resources, to the more sophisticated demands on the worker's self-awareness and use of self in facilitating complex processes of change'.

By way of illustration, let us go back to our practice example.

Practice Example 4.2

Gary

Beginnings

Social worker knocks several times at the door before Gary answers it

Gary: Hello …

[1] Worker: Hello, are you Gary? My name's Caroline Simpson and I'm the social worker that telephoned your brother earlier to say that I wanted to visit you this afternoon. I need to see how you are doing, to check if you are all right. Is that OK? Can I come in?

Gary: My brother said you would be coming. How long is this going to take?

[2] Worker: Oh, not long. I won't take up much of your time. I expect that you are very busy. I do need to talk things over with you though.

Gary: Well, all right then, but I haven't got long. It's not like there's anything wrong or anything. It's all sorted now.

Worker: Well, we'll see. Can I come in to talk to you about things then?

(Gary led the way into the living room, which was untidy but comfortable and clean.)

Worker: The house looks really comfortable and cosy.

Gary: Yeah. We manage fine. My dad's friend, Roy, comes round regularly to see if we need anything. He's a copper. He makes sure we've got enough money. Sometimes gets us a take-away.

[3] Worker: That sounds good that you have someone who is keeping an eye on you. I guess that you might be wondering whether I am here to keep an eye on you too. I do have a responsibility to check that young people are safe and well, but if I am satisfied that all is in order then I won't need to bother you and your brother any further. Is that what you expected a social worker to do?

Gary: Yeah. My brother said that social workers poke their noses in when they're not wanted. You're not going to contact my dad are you? He's not supposed to come home before his leave. I get on fine with Steve usually. I'm going to be OK now.

[4] Worker: That's what I need to check out with you – whether you are really feeling OK or whether you will feel like running away again.

(There was a period of silence lasting about a minute, when Gary was slumped in the chair and had his head down.)

[5] Worker: What happened to make you want to run away? It's quite a serious thing to do.

▶

◀

(There was another period of silence.)

[6] Gary: I don't know why I did it. I just wanted to get my head cleared. Me and Steve keep arguing a lot lately. He keeps getting at me about my schoolwork. It's not my fault that I find the work hard. They don't teach me properly. Dad's always saying that. He says there is nothing wrong with my brain. I'm going to get on with my work now.

[7] Worker: Have you got a lot of course work to do over the Christmas holidays?

Gary: Loads. If they didn't give me so much to do at once then I wouldn't get so fed up. Mrs Smith is the worst one. She doesn't like me and keeps giving me more than everyone else. Can you talk to my form teacher about it?

Worker: It doesn't sound right that you have more than anyone else does. I could talk to your teacher. Does the school know that you are living at home with your brother and that your dad is away at sea?

Gary: Probably. But I don't think they care. We get on with things all right at home.

[8] Worker: It sounds like you don't think that anybody cares about how you are feeling and that maybe you feel that you have to get on with life because you are expected to manage. If that's right, then it must be hard for you.

Gary: It is quite hard sometimes. I don't like being bossed about by Steve. He's not my dad, but he acts like he thinks he is. I don't want my dad being told about all this though. He'll be cross if he has to come back. It affects his job.

Worker: Your dad needs to know how you are doing. At the end of the day, he is your dad and he has a responsibility towards you, by making sure that you are well and happy. What's stopping you from contacting him and telling him how you feel?

(Another period of silence occurred lasting about a minute.)

Gary: I can't tell him. That's all. He'll be cross. I'll get him in trouble. I told you.

Worker: Sounds like you're feeling that you have let your dad down and you are disappointed with yourself. Is that right?

Gary: I feel like I've messed everything up.

[9] Worker: When you say that you have 'messed *everything* up' what do you mean? Perhaps I can help you with it?

[10] Gary: What can you do to help? Haven't you got loads of other people to see?

We find Caroline, the social worker, stating that she is a social worker (point 1) but it is not until point 3 that she seeks to explain and discuss what the social work role involves. She states:

> I guess that you might be wondering whether I am here to keep an eye on you too. I do have a responsibility to check that young people are safe and well, but if I am satisfied that all is in order then I won't need to bother you and your brother any further. Is that what you expected a social worker to do?

Caroline's reluctance to discuss the social work role up to this point (point 3) could be understood as fear of upsetting Gary at an early stage of their relationship. She might be assuming that he would not be able to understand the parameters of her role. Unfortunately, the lack of clarity about the role only caused him to become more wary of her presence as an authority figure, causing an obstacle within their communication. Caroline might think she is being friendly and trying to gain rapport, such as when she says 'the house looks really comfortable and cosy', but essentially she is going around the obstacle by seeking compliance. Rather, she needs to attend to the obstacle in a direct manner and seek to remove it. Her statement at point 3 begins to do this work: 'I guess that you might be wondering whether I am here to keep an eye on you too.'

The second part of 'achieving a shared purpose' requires the social worker to be *clear on purpose*. The social worker needs to state the nature of their agenda, and to do so using straightforward, non-jargon language that is developmentally appropriate to the service user. The social worker will achieve greater success with this, if they have prepared a statement in advance. Within our practice example (4.2), we find Caroline, the social worker, using simple terms to explain her agenda. For example, at point 3 she says 'I do have a responsibility to check that young people are safe and well', and extends the discussion at point 4 by saying 'That's what I need to check out with you – whether you are really feeling OK or whether you will feel like running away again.' Clearly, though, Caroline should not just assume that by saying these statements, Gary heard and understood them. She needs to check with Gary what was understood and whether he agrees with the information. This constitutes the third part of the skill – *'reaching for feedback'*. It should take the form of a question that communicates a genuine desire for the service user's viewpoint. A quick statement like 'is that alright by you?' will not suffice. Indeed, Shulman (2009) states that this part of the skill should actively seek for the service user's stake in the work, such as saying 'Do you think that this something that we could work on together in order to make the changes you need? Tell me your view on this.'

Practice experience has shown me that these three parts of 'achieving a shared purpose' cannot occur unless the social worker conveys to the service user with warmth that they are meeting with someone who is prepared to listen to their difficulties with care and sympathy. They might then be able to unfold their concerns without the fear of blame or misunderstanding. It involves communicating acceptance of the uniqueness of each new situation with warmth, interest and concern. This is about demonstrating respect. Smale et al. (1993: 51) identify respect as a core skill for 'joining with people' and define it as:

> The care manager's ability to communicate their acceptance and valuation of people irrespective of their personal qualities and social or professional position.

An intuitive understanding of another person and the difficulties within their situation is not sufficient, but rather involves 'the hard work of hearing, comprehending and communicating understanding of what other people say, the thoughts and feelings that they express and the way they make sense of the world' (Smale et al., 1993). This describes empathic processes that are involved in being attuned to the ways in which thoughts and feelings might be expressed. As described earlier, social workers must engage with feelings as a principal form of communication if service users are to feel that their views have been heard and understood. It is especially critical to do so at this beginning stage of work when seeking to uncover the service user's agenda and discuss how the agendas of both the service user and social worker can be brought together. Indeed, there are feelings that the immediate relationship will be arousing, such as anxiety, anger or fear at either the authority role of the social worker or the creation of a new relationship. The social worker must identify and attend to these feelings or it will be impossible to achieve a shared agenda.

Seden (2005: 48) refers to this skill of commenting directly on the process which is happening between the social worker and service user as *'using immediacy'*. It involves the worker identifying exactly what they observe or feel is happening to the service user in a direct manner. We can find the skill beginning to be employed within our practice example (4.2). In the dialogue between points 2 and 3, Gary shows his anxiety about the social worker's authority role by stating 'I haven't got long. It's not like there's anything wrong or anything. It's all sorted now' and 'we manage fine. My dad's friend, Roy, comes round regularly to see if we need anything. He's a copper. He makes sure we've got enough money. Sometimes gets us a take-away.' The social worker recognises that the narrative is revealing Gary's anxious feelings about her role and responds *'using immediacy'*: 'I guess that you might be wondering whether I am here to keep an eye on you too?' She could have taken this comment further and identified the unexpressed feelings more directly, such as 'I understand that you might be nervous about trusting me because you may be worried about me being a social worker, and there are negative things said in the news about social workers, like taking children away from their families when they don't need to.' Seden (2005: 48) considers *'using immediacy'* to be a skill that requires practice, and involves 'basic listening and responding skills and a willingness to be open and genuine, framing the words honestly in a calm way. It involves the practitioner in monitoring carefully their own feelings and being prepared to practice a level of self-disclosure'. These are all aspects of what I have placed under an umbrella term of 'empathy skills'. While these skills are a crucial fourth part of *'achieving a shared purpose'* within the beginning stage of work, they should be employed throughout the whole of social work intervention. As they are not limited to the beginning stage, they are discussed more fully in the following section.

Before leaving this 'Beginning Skills' section, it is imperative to draw attention to one last point. This involves the situation whereby the meeting continues but no shared agenda has been achieved. The skill of *'achieving a shared purpose'* may not have been successfully executed. In such instances, it is likely that the social worker is either completely on the service user's agenda, or is fixated on their own agenda, with the service user demonstrating superficial compliance and passive involvement. The social worker may think that work is occurring but in actual fact it is just, as Shulman (2009) puts it, 'the illusion of work'. To avoid this, the social worker must take steps to prevent becoming so immersed in the content of the narrative that they fail to see the feelings that are being unconsciously revealed by attitude, gesture or tone of voice as the service user pursues their line of thought. The social worker needs to simultaneously adopt some objective distance as well as achieving emotional attunement to the thoughts and feelings being expressed. The literature refers to this objective distancing as operating a 'third ear' (Lishman, 2009), or a 'second head', with the social worker having in mind questions like 'What is it that is really going on in the communication here?', 'Is the problem that she or he is describing the most immediate problem or is there something more worrying?', 'What is the nature of the obstacle in our communication?' and 'What skill should I use next?' When these questions are utilised, it is easier to recognise the illusion of work and seek to operate the skill of *'achieving a shared purpose'* once again. It would seem useful to *'use immediacy'* to achieve this as it allows the social worker to comment honestly and directly on what has occurred. An example of this is: 'You know, Gary, I feel like I haven't been as clear as I should have been about my job as a social worker. I think that you are feeling worried about me being a social worker and whether you can trust me, and this means you are reluctant to share your concerns with me. What do you think, can we start again?'

'Empathy skills'

Social workers need to be able to place themselves emotionally and psychologically in the situation of the service user if they are to be able to work out that person's thoughts and feelings. The communication skills required to achieve and communicate this level of emotional attunement include *'reflective listening'* (a term used by Cameron, 2008) as well as other skills, such as *'reach for feeling'* (Shulman, 2009) and *'putting feelings into words'* (Shulman, 2009) which I have placed under the umbrella heading 'skills to encourage the discussion of unarticulated feelings'.

'Reflective Listening'

Feelings may be evident by the narrative but also revealed through tone of voice and attitude, and non-verbally through gesture and body position. However communicated, the social worker needs to receive these feelings in an open, warm and receptive manner. The skill of *'reflective listening'* enables this to occur (Cameron, 2008). However, because, as Cameron (2008) highlights, listening is a psychological, cognitive or mind function that only focuses upon verbal expression, it needs to be carried out in tandem with *'observing'* non-verbal behaviour to fully attend to the service user's total communication of feeling. Indeed, it is cited that up to 70 per cent of the emotional content of our communication is manifested non-verbally (Stack et al., 1991: 41, cited by Cameron, 2008: 24). It is essential to state that the way a person behaves non-verbally is not culturally neutral but influenced by their social and cultural background. For example there are cultural and ethnic expectations about courteous and acceptable non-verbal behaviour, such as the amount of space and eye contact between the worker and service user. Social workers need to recognise that a wide variation of expectations exists, and as such they need to have a good awareness of their own non-verbal presentation (Cameron, 2008).

The physical positioning of the social worker to encourage the discussion of feelings through their non-verbal behaviour constitutes a first stage in demonstrating the skill *'reflective listening'*. The acronym SOLER is usefully provided by Egan (2007) to describe the key elements of such positioning. 'S' refers to the position of the worker as sitting 'square on' at 90 degrees to the service user, and 'O' refers to the 'open' stance taken within that position as having legs and arms unfolded and hands resting, relaxed, on the thighs or in the lap. Through 'leaning forward' – the 'L' of SOLER – the worker can lessen any height difference and demonstrate interest and attention through 'eye contact', as denoted by 'E'. Indeed, a position that enables good observation for both the service user and social worker of each others' facial expressions is critical in enabling the discussion of feelings. The 'R' refers to achieving all this in a relaxed way.

Clearly the social worker should not expect the service user to adopt the SOLER position. However, the social worker needs to try and make sense of the non-verbal behaviour that is presented by the service user. The practice example (4.2) describes Gary's body language immediately following a direct statement from the social worker about his well being at point 4: 'There was a period of silence lasting about a minute, when Gary was slumped in the chair and had his head down.' We could interpret this body language as being 'closed', with Gary withdrawing his eye contact and folding his body away from the service user. Essentially he is indicating that he is finding it difficult to communicate on the subject. In an 'open' position, he would be relaxed and sitting with his arms and legs unfolded and towards the social worker. He would be making some eye contact and other gestures to show he is participating in the conversation, such as rubbing his head when thinking. As stated earlier, there are cultural differences to these expectations. For example, some faith communities do not allow eye contact between an unmarried female and male. In such situations it would be wrong to label the lack of eye contact as demonstrating 'closed' body language.

The second part of *'reflective listening'* is for the social worker to be focused on hearing the experience of the other person. This means waiting until the other person has finished speaking, reflecting upon it and then responding to check back that the communication was heard and understood accurately. As Seden (2005) highlights, it does not mean selecting and labelling parts of the communication that the social worker thinks are significant. Neither does it mean that it is acceptable to rush in and offer advice or offer to make a referral to a service without obtaining the full picture. The other person needs time to express their feelings. This requires having the patience and tolerance of pauses and silences that seem longer in duration than usual conversations. Cameron (2008: 39) summarises the point well:

> Good listeners put the focus on the other person and on what they are offering, rather than asking for additional information, or talking about other things.

There are two communication skills that can be usefully employed to check back with the service user that you have heard and understood what they were saying. The first is *'paraphrasing'*. Cameron (2008: 51) views a paraphrase as 'an attempt to combine in a coherent and meaningful sentence, reflections about the client's feelings, the situations and/or their behavioral responses to it'. It encourages further exploration. This is distinct to *'summarising'* which involves integrating broader themes at the end of the discussion of a particular point.

'Skills to encourage the discussion of unarticulated feelings'

Seden (2005: 26) emphasises the importance of 'listening to the base line (what is not openly said but possibly is being felt)'. As described earlier, the social worker will often perceive that some parts of the service user's descriptions are charged with feelings, which though unarticulated are unconsciously revealed through tone of voice and attitude, and non-verbally through gesture and body position. Shulman's (2009) skills of *'reach for feeling'* and *'putting feelings into words'* are useful for drawing out these feelings which may not be immediately at the surface or are difficult to express.

'Reach for feeling' involves the social worker directly asking the service user about how they feel about a particular issue. It needs to be formed as an 'open question', that is a question for which a simple 'yes' or 'no' response is not sufficient. Although it should be said sensitively and in a gentle tone, it nevertheless makes a demand on the service user to work on the feeling. Examples of the skill are 'How does that make you feel?' and 'What are you feeling right now?' The communication skill of *'putting feelings into words'* makes the same demand, but is not framed as an open question. In operating this skill, the social worker describes, tentatively but as accurately as possible, the feelings that he or she perceives to be communicated and asks the social worker to confirm or disconfirm the accuracy.

The social worker must reflect on the interpersonal communication which has taken place in order to decide which of the skills to use in order to encourage the discussion of unarticulated feelings. I described earlier how the social worker needs to have in mind questions like 'What is it that is really going on in the communication here?', 'Is the problem that she or he is describing the most immediate problem or is there something more worrying?', 'What is the nature of the obstacle in our communication?' and 'What skill should I use next?' If the social worker reflects that there is an obstacle to the communication concerning anxiety or ambivalence relating to his or her authority role, then it makes little sense for the social worker to 'reach for feeling' and ask how the service is feeling. The service user is unlikely to reveal feelings of ambivalence or anxiety in response. However, if the social worker uses the skill of *'putting feelings into words'*, then by identifying the feeling and bringing it into the discussion, the service user may be more willing to discuss the accuracy and relevance of it. Alternatively, the social worker may reflect that the service user may be finding it difficult to express a feeling, perhaps through fear that upon expression of that feeling they may be unable to control their reactions, or perhaps they are not yet developmentally mature enough to name and explain the feeling. The practice example (4.2) provides an example of this between points 8 and 9. The social worker uses *'putting feelings into words'* by stating 'Sounds like you're feeling that you have let your dad down and you are disappointed with yourself. Is that right?' This enables Gary to respond with 'I feel like I've messed everything up'.

Clearly the social worker needs to use their emotional attunement to make these tentative observations, and he or she needs to engage in reflexive processes about how they may be wrong. This involves the social worker identifying how their own preconceived notions and cultural stereotypes (based on their own experiences and biography) might cloud their judgement or indeed their behaviour in tolerating painful feelings to be shared and the service user's personality to come forward. In Chapter 2, I highlighted that social workers need to be aware of how the 'transference' and 'countertransference' of feelings influences their relationship with the service user. Countertransference has been used to describe the reaction set off in the worker as a result of being receptive to a service user's transferred feelings. These emotions are considered to be a helpful guide to understanding transferred feelings which are unexpressed. As such, it is pertinent to ask oneself 'what does this person make me feel like?' and 'what does this tell me about the nature of their relationships, or the effect of themselves on others?' Social workers should check whether this intuition is valid according to what the service user is communicating, or whether the countertransference is the social worker reacting to what they are bringing to the situation. Particular service user situations or problems can trigger off unresolved problems within the social worker which then distort perception and interfere with the interaction with the service user.

The issue of 'sharing worker's feelings' to facilitate the working relationship has been the subject of debate. Yet, according to the theoretical relationship-based framework discussed here, the development of empathy, or identification with service user feeling, is crucial for gaining awareness of unexpressed thoughts and feelings that are conscious or are below the surface (Ferard and Hunnybun, 1962). Shulman considers the sharing of worker's feelings to be an essential skill related to the worker's ability to present himself or herself to service users as a real human being, rather than a clinical, detached, objective professional. When there is a dichotomy between the 'personal' and 'professional', Shulman considers there to be a loss of spontaneity, with the worker appearing as a guarded professional, unwilling to allow service users access to themselves and their feelings. They will have difficulty in relating to the worker as a person who is connected to feelings.

Concerns about sharing feelings are often raised in relation to the boundaries within which personal feelings can be shared. We might ask whether the sharing of such feelings is appropriate to the professional function and task. Shulman provides an answer: that if a social worker is clear about the purpose of work with the service user (through a verbal or written contract) and the particular professional function, then this offers direction and, indeed, protection. As he states, 'the worker's feelings about personal relationships can be shared only in ways that relate them directly to the service user's immediate concerns. For example, take a situation in which a worker feels the client is misinterpreting someone's response because of the client's feelings. The worker who has experienced that kind of miscommunication might share briefly the experience as a way of providing the client with a new way of understanding an important interaction.' He provides a contrasting example which elucidates the point well: 'If a client begins an interview by describing a problem with his mother-in-law, the worker would not respond by saying "You think you have problems with your mother-in-law? Let me tell you about mine!" The client and worker have not come together to discuss the worker's problems, and an attempt by the worker to introduce personal concerns, even those related to the contract area, is an outright subversion of the contract' (Shulman, 1998: 134).

A good skill for encouraging emotional attunement and the discussion of thoughts and feelings is to *'use silences'*. Sitting still and in silence while maintaining an open posture, and leaning forward demonstrates interest (Cameron, 2008). The silence provides thinking space. As such, the social worker should avoid speaking into it unless it has gone on for some time or the service user is communicating a feeling non-verbally and the social worker needs to verbalise empathy for this work. The silence can be used as a signal to the service user that it is the service user's turn to speak and express their thoughts and feelings. As some people can find silences in communication quite difficult to tolerate, this type of signal can be very powerful if used appropriately.

Skills for 'gathering facts'

'Questioning to obtain factual information' is a critical communication skill in social work. Lishman (2009) and Koprowska (2005) emphasise the importance of suitable questioning to obtain factual information, not just the communication of feelings. If significant information is lost, then the result will be an inappropriate and less holistic assessment of the service user's situation and needs. Lishman warns social workers against subsiding into an interrogative question-and-answer stance with a lot of questions being asked at a fast rate. Service users feel disempowered by the underlying assumption of this approach that the social worker is the expert, who, in focusing on the problems, has the expertise to solve them.

Lishman suggests that the social worker reflect on the following four issues in order to select the right kind of question. First, the social worker should be aware that they are asking a question. Second, he or she should consider the purpose of that question and whether it is essential to clarify information or encourage further exploration. Third is questioning the right skill to be used, or is an alternative, such as *'putting feelings into words'* better as it encourages the service user to work on their feelings? Finally, having decided that questioning for facts is appropriate, what type of question should be asked?

There are two main types of questions. First, 'closed' (Lishman, 2009), also called 'narrow' questions (Koprowska, 2005) elicit a 'yes or no' or other limited factual response. This is illustrated within the practice example (4.2) at point 7 when the social worker asks: 'Have you got a lot of course work to do over the Christmas holiday?' and Gary responds 'Loads.' Koprowska (2005) notes that too many of these questions can feel like an interrogation, and they should be avoided when discussing personal issues which require exploration. Second, 'open' (Lishman, 2009) or 'broad' questions (Koprowska, 2005) invite more extensive answers which encourage further exploration or explanation of issues. An illustration of an open question that is asked for the purpose of clarification is at point 9 when the social worker asks: 'When you say that you have "messed *everything* up" what do you mean? Perhaps I can help you with it?'

Skills for 'ending work'

Endings can be difficult for service users, as they not only bring to mind past losses but also trepidation for the future without the assistance that has been provided (Koprowska, 2005). It is important that, wherever possible, endings are planned with service users being reminded of the meeting schedule and end time or date. The skill of *'summarising'* is usefully employed to agree the main points that have been covered and the tasks that have been set to manage the next steps. If possible, it is better for the social worker to encourage the service user to do this summarising work. This enables the service user to recognise for themselves how their psychosocial situation has altered, how they will manage this period of change, and the mechanisms they have in place to achieve their psychosocial functioning in the future. Examples are: 'Tell me the main issues that we have covered today' or 'Tell me your understanding of what you have achieved over these past weeks.'

This chapter has provided an overview of the basic communication capacity required for effective communication with an individual within social work situations. Communication strategies or 'skills' involve more than a response ('Doing'), but flow from the integrated analysis of working out 'what is going on' in the communication and how this relates to formal and informal knowledge concerning societal assumptions and preconditions which inhibit the communication ('Knowing'). The analysis involves examination of the 'use of self' to elicit and respond to communication at the level of feelings ('Being'). The following chapters present more specific social work communication strategies that build upon this foundation base and relate to the more specific needs of individuals.

Mapping to the Professional Capability Framework

Readiness for Direct Practice Level Capabilities

Please remember that these should be viewed as domains which overlap in an integrative manner rather than as a linear checklist

'By the point of assessment of readiness for direct practice (prior to first placement), students should demonstrate basic communication skills, ability to engage with users, capacity to work as a member of an organisation, willingness to learn from feedback and supervision, and demonstrate basic SW values, knowledge and skills in order to be able to make effective use of first practice placement.'	
Communication Capacity Domain – 'Knowing' (engaging with formal and informal knowledge in communication)	**PCF 3 Diversity: Recognise diversity and apply anti-discriminatory and anti-oppressive principles in practice** ➤ Recognise the importance of diversity in human identity and experience, and the application of anti-discriminatory and anti-oppressive principles in social work practice

	PCF 5 Knowledge: Apply knowledge of social sciences, law and social work practice theory ➢ Demonstrate an initial understanding of the application of research, theory and knowledge from sociology, social policy, psychology, health and human growth and development to social work ➢ Demonstrate an initial understanding of the legal and policy frameworks and guidance that inform and mandate social work practice ➢ Demonstrate an initial understanding of the range of theories and models for social work intervention
Communication Capacity Domain – 'Doing' (the enactment of communication strategies in interaction)	**PCF 6 Critical Reflection and Analysis: Apply critical reflection and analysis to inform and provide a rationale for professional decision-making** ➢ Understand the role of reflective practice and demonstrate basic skills of reflection ➢ Understand the need to construct hypotheses in social work practice
	PCF 7 Intervention and Skills: Use judgement and authority to intervene with individuals, families and communities to promote independence, provide support and prevent harm, neglect and abuse ➢ Demonstrate core communication skills and the capacity to develop them ➢ Demonstrate the ability to engage with people in order to build compassionate and effective relationships ➢ Demonstrate initial awareness of risk and safeguarding
Communication Capacity Domain – 'Being' (the use of 'self')	**PCF 1 Professionalism: Identify and behave as a professional social worker, committed to professional development** ➢ Describe the role of the social worker ➢ Describe the importance of professional behaviour ➢ Describe the importance of personal and professional boundaries ➢ Demonstrate ability to learn, using a range of approaches ➢ Describe the importance of emotional resilience in social work
	PCF 2 Values and Ethics: Apply social work ethical principles and values to guide professional practice ➢ Understand the profession's ethical principles and their relevance to practice ➢ Demonstrate awareness of own personal values and how these can impact on practice

	PCF 3 Diversity: Recognise diversity and apply anti-discriminatory and anti-oppressive principles in practice (Appropriately placed in both 'Knowing' and 'Being') ➤ Recognise the importance of diversity in human identity and experience, and the application of anti-discriminatory and anti-oppressive principles in social work practice
	PCF 4 Rights, Justice and Economic Wellbeing: Advance human rights and promote social justice and economic wellbeing ➤ Understand the principles of rights, justice and economic wellbeing, and their significance for social work practice
	PCF 8 Contexts and Organisations: Engage with, inform, and adapt to changing contexts that shape practice. Operate effectively within own organisational frameworks and contribute to the development of services and organisations. Operate effectively within multi-agency and inter-professional partnerships and settings ➤ Demonstrate awareness of the impact of organisational context on social work practice

5

Working with Children

Summary of Specialist Communication Skills in this Chapter

➤ the avoidance of the 'why' and 'how' questions

➤ giving choice

➤ child-centred contract

➤ containing a child's feelings by providing and being a 'safe place' in which feelings can be explored

➤ tuning-in to experience the child's world

➤ identify, validate and use the child's medium of communication

➤ using a storyline

➤ observing

➤ showing respect (using sub skills of: 'Giving choice'; 'Taking time')

➤ establishing a vocabulary of feelings

➤ challenging in a comfortable/non-threatening manner

➤ using silences

➤ the use of the third object.

Policy and background literature

There are clear policy requirements relevant to social workers' communication with children and young people. Social workers should give due consideration to 'the wishes and feelings' of children and ensure their perspectives are central to service planning and delivery (The Children Act 2004; The Children and Families Act 2014). Policy and practice guidance requires social workers to safeguard and promote the welfare of children, by identifying how their development is influenced by the environment in which they are parented, including an assessment of their immediate safety (Department of Health, 2000a; HM Government, 2015). Moreover they have to identify how they can promote this development to meet government-specified outcomes for children in the UK as drawn out in the research for the Green Paper 'Every Child Matters' (Department for Education and Skills, 2003), and given effect in The Children Act (2004). An 'outcomes focus' to assessment is retained within the most recent policy (HM Government, 2015). Thus, policy exhorts social workers to communicate effectively with children and young people, in order to promote human rights to participation but also to ensure services are more effective by being responsive to the expressed developmental needs, including the immediate safety, of the service user. Social workers should look for 'developmental competence' in determining whether a child can make decisions about their welfare (Doyle and Kennedy, 2009). Case law set a precedent with the case of Gillick v. West Norfolk and Wisbech Area Health Authority and Department of Health and Social security [1985] 3 All ER 402. The House of Lords determined that a child under 16 years old could give consent to treatment as long as they had sufficient understanding. Arguably, though, while a child might not be deemed developmentally competent enough to have their wishes taken into account, any child should be encouraged to express their feelings on a matter to a social worker. Recent legislation has augmented the involvement of children, young people and their parents and carers as central actors in assessment and planning, emphasising person-centred processes of co-production, involvement and decision-making (The Children and Families Act 2014 (England, Wales and Northern Ireland)). Operating in conjunction with the new provisions for adult safeguarding in the Care Act (2014), a 'whole family approach' is proposed whereby a social worker must gain a picture of the whole family context, and how preferred outcomes for one individual's wellbeing might impact positively or deleteriously upon another's (Department of Health, 2015). The matter is one of shared service user and professional judgement concerning 'proportionate intervention'. One such approach gaining popularity is the solution-focused 'Signs of Safety' practice model which pursues rigorous, sustainable everyday safety solutions in the child's actual home (Turnell and Edwards, 1999; Turnell et al., 2007; Turnell, 2012). It begins with a process of mapping the concrete everyday living circumstances surrounding a vulnerable child, seeking both strength and exploration of danger and risk. The approach seeks not to assert a definitive picture of the processes of risk but to ask probing, rigorous questions attentive to the four domains of worries, strengths, goals and judgement. Key questions to hold in mind when thinking about the situation facing a family are: *What are we worried about? What's working well? What needs to happen?* The communication challenge for the social worker is to find an age-appropriate way to ask these questions of children and young people and gain answers to them in a way which entails full involvement.

However, social workers have been repeatedly criticised for the level and quality of their communication with children and young people. Child death inquiry reports, particularly the Jasmine Beckford, Cleveland, Victoria Climbie and Peter Connolly tragedies, continually condemn social workers for their failure to communicate and observe the development of children at risk of abuse (Blom-Cooper, 1985; Butler-Sloss, 1988; Laming, 2003; Laming, 2009). Recent inquiry reviews of organised and widespread sexual abuse of young people, such as occurring in Rotherham and Oxford, similarly highlight a lack of professional communication, with young people's reporting being disbelieved or regarded as being exaggerated (Jay, 2014; Oxfordshire Safeguarding Children Board, 2015). Young people frequently report that their social workers need to listen more adequately to them (Department of Health, 2000a; Luckock et al., 2006). Arguably, these communication obstacles reflect normative assumptions concerning the relationship between children and adults in Western society. In Chapter 3 I discussed how a power differential between children and adults exists in society with children having frequent experience of being overpowered – whether through being told to be silent or having their views devalued, or as too often reported, being physically constrained or beaten by parents or carers (Kroll, 1995). Societal notions exist of children being viewed as innocent and defenceless, but also condemned and blamed for their behaviour (Wilson et al., 2011).

The literature cites further reasons for the communication barriers, such as social workers' feeling a lack of confidence and expertise, or a less conscious fear that the work might evoke strong feelings from the social worker's own childhood experiences that they wish to avoid (Daniel, 2007). Rustin (2005), for example, analysed how professionals would not see what was happening to privately fostered Victoria Climbie because they erected various psychological defences to prevent personally witnessing and experiencing acute mental pain. This may have contributed to a lack of child protection focus and a family support approach with the family. The professionals in this situation questioned whether an explanation for Victoria's deferential behaviour and marks on her skin had a cultural base by virtue of Victoria being an African child (for a critical analysis, see Garrett, 2006). However, this apart, literature highlights how social workers working with people from different ethnic groups can become anxious to 'get it right' (Laird, 2008). A lack of cultural knowledge can cause normative assumptions and dominant stereotypes about the cultural practices of people from different ethnic groups to be applied. Specialist social work communication in this practice setting must demonstrate sensitivity to cultural differences and variations in patterns and styles of communication. Care must be taken not to assume homogeneity in the values and practices of any family, faith, community or ethnic group, and extreme versions of cultural relativism must be avoided.

Ironically, while the modernising policy agenda has sought to improve standards of social work practice, the impact upon practice of the regulatory processes contained within it provides one possible explanation for these perceived failures in effective communication. Researchers highlight how social work practice with children and families has become so overtaken by the processes and procedures involved in demonstrating achievement of prescribed quantified outcomes in an attempt to manage the uncertainties of complex families that the dominant objective of intervention is 'monitoring' and 'policing' (Stepney, 2006; Munro, 2011a; Munro 2011b; Featherstone et al., 2014; Higgins et al., 2015). Indeed, Doyle and Kennedy (2009: 50) describe social workers as 'having to navigate their way through a labyrinth of new rules and procedures whilst meeting deadlines and targets in new regulatory landscapes to achieve organizational performance indicators'. The context is of ever increasing scrutiny of individual safeguarding practice, with social workers fearing their practice being reframed as 'inadequate' both by the bureaucratic performance indicators, but also by the media at having individually 'failed' a child. As an example of the impact of such 'fear' of scrutiny, in the wake of Peter Connolly case not only did the number of child protection referrals increase but also the number of social workers' applications for care orders resulting in complex court work. This places additional strain on workers within teams that are frequently understaffed and reliant on agency workers (Pile, 2009; Unison, 2009). It is with perhaps little surprise that social workers describe frustration at spending too much time in front of the computer and spending too little time with service users. Indeed, child protection systems have been criticised for inordinate bureaucracy, such as the amount of time required to work through the restrictive eligibility criteria that gate-keep the limited resources available to help children and families (Doyle and Kennedy, 2009; Munro, 2011a; Munro, 2011b). These systemic barriers are influencing the effectiveness of the communication strategies of social workers.

Another possible explanation for the perceived failures in effective communication lies in the existing knowledge base about social work communication skills with children and young people being complex and limited. Indeed, Luckock et al.'s (2006) knowledge review of empirical studies relating to communication skills with children and young people within social work found that the concept of 'communication with children' was contested across studies with no coherent body of research. Certainly, a tension seems to exist within the literature over the purposes of social work communication with children in terms of whether it has a solely participative function or an additional therapeutic function. The latter is considered to emanate from notions of 'childhood' and the history of a dominance of psychoanalytic and psychodynamic approaches to working directly with children. Key concepts arising from this dominant literature include:

➢ recognise and reflect upon the worker's own 'inner child' (the 'child within') to promote emotional attunement;

➢ experience the child's world on an emotional level;

➢ hold the child 'in mind' and do not allow parental concerns to overwhelm;

➢ seek to contain a child's feelings by providing and being a 'safe place' in which feelings can be explored;

➢ help a child understand their feelings and link these to past and present experiences;

➢ identify and validate the child's medium of communication and use that medium to communicate with them (e.g. using symbols or play);

➢ recognise the psychological effects of adversity upon the child's communication strategy.

Other concepts to inform a specialist communication strategy with children and young people are apparent in the approaches already used by social work educators and social workers themselves within their practice. However, again, there is complexity and disagreement among the different approaches (Luckock et al., 2006). Social work educators and practitioners make distinctions between the need for students and practitioners to:

➢ develop their personal capacity to communicate effectively in a more general sense;

➢ to do so in a way that demonstrates ethical commitment to rights of participation and 'child-centredness';

➢ perform more micro-skills, underpinned by knowledge of child development theories which echo the psychodynamic approach:

  ➢ keeping the child informed

  ➢ child-centred communication (play, symbolic, creative, expressive techniques, going at the child's pace)

  ➢ listening to direct and indirect communication

- interviewing

- using tools like 'ecomaps', rating scales, assessment schedules and life-story books.

Communicating with children as a response to receiving communication concerning the safety or distress of that child presents further communication issues. These relate to the need for the social worker to capture the information that a child is providing, provide support for any distress, but not to do so in a way that might frustrate a joint social work-police enquiry through affecting the accuracy or completeness of that evidence (Jones, 2003; Crown Prosecution Service, 2007; HM Government, 2015). Even the most initial discussions with children must uphold these principles for 'accuracy' and 'completeness' while 'minimising distress'. Within the communication the social worker must avoid the use of leading or suggestive questions (HM Government, 2015). As Jones (2003: 1–2) states:

> Accuracy is key, for without it effective decisions cannot be made and, equally, inaccurate accounts can lead to children remaining unsafe, or to the possibility of wrongful actions being taken that affect children and adults.

The issue of whether a child has been made safe in their caregiving environment has an influence on whether that child feels able or safe enough to communicate the distress and/or fear that they are feeling. Drawing again on the example of Victoria Climbie (Laming, 2003), it could be argued that a reason for why she did not communicate her distressing home situation to the social worker and police officers in hospital was because she had not been made safe. The chapter on 'Tracey' in Madge Bray's 'Poppies in the Rubbish Heap' presents a wonderful example of responding to the child's need to be safe prior to communication about abuse.

Service user groups have identified particular communication skills needed for work with children and young people with disabilities. The need for social workers to be proactive in developing 'communication enhancing environments' for children who have or need augmentative and alternative communication has been promoted by literature and organisations such as Scope (Potter and Whittaker, 2001; Scope, 2007). Triangle's 'Howitis' website describes some useful tools and images for communicating about feelings, rights and safety, personal care and sexuality (www.howitis.org.uk). Disabled children are particularly vulnerable in being more susceptible to abuse than their non-disabled peers, and historically many of the communication systems that disabled people use do not have a wide range of words, signs or symbols to describe feelings, parts of the body (such as genitalia) or acts of maltreatment (Wilson et al., 2008; Wilson et al., 2011).

Practice application

In operating these concepts from the background literature, and adding further concepts and discussion from the research study, it becomes evident that the preparatory stage for communicating with a child is absolutely critical if a social worker is to 'experience the child's world on an emotional level' and achieve a 'communication enhancing environment'. Within this area of specialist practice, when operating the basic communication skill of *'tuning-in'* (discussed in Chapter 3), the social worker needs to engage with concepts from child development theory, as well as the psychoanalytic and psychodynamic literature. Kroll (1995) would agree, stating that such theoretical perspectives provide windows from which to glimpse the experiential world of a child and as such constitute the first stage of a meaningful 'child-centred' communication with them. I have called this early specialist communication capacity as *'tuning-in to experience the child's world'*.

Child development theory helps social workers understand the impact of physical and psychological adversity upon a child in terms of socio-emotional and cognitive development. The specification of developmental milestones at different ages and stages of development provide important indicators from which to compare children's progress across a number of developmental domains. Social work literature and practice has given particular attention to research about how the interactional quality of early relationship experiences affect psychological health and social functioning as well as biologically impacting on the rapidly developing brain (Zeanah et al., 1997; Armstrong et al., 2000; Schore, 2001). Modern attachment theorists have explored the importance of the parent–child attachment relationship in the way the mind processes interpersonal information to use as a psychosocial template for future relationships (Howe, 2005). Researchers have linked difficult early attachment relationships to children showing aggressive and disruptive behaviour, and adolescents who have anxiety disorders and/or impaired operational skills and self-regulation (Sroufe, 1983; Speltz et al., 1990; Lyons-Ruth et al., 1993; Jacobsen et al., 1994; Shaw et al., 1996; Warren et al., 1997). Neglected children show social and emotional difficulties as well as differences in brain size and structure (Hildyard and Wolfe, 2002; Perry, 2002).

Children bring these often insecure relationship templates to their relationships, and indeed communication, with social workers (Howe, 2005). Children with an insecure-ambivalent attachment relationship model will feel only conditionally worthwhile, uncertain of whether they will be understood and valued, and therefore constantly seek to test out the emotional and physical availability of the social worker. Alternatively, they might provide responses that 'seek to please' as opposed to risking any indication of their true feelings. Children with an insecure-avoidant relationship model, however, bring to the communication their experience of having their developmental needs consistently ignored by their carers. They are mistrustful of the potential of the social worker to be helpful, preferring to rely on their own coping strategies which generally involves keeping emotionally detached to avoid inevitable rejection. Their self-esteem is often very low – feeling unlovable and without worth. A smaller proportion of children that social workers meet have internal relationship models that are disorganised. These children are in a heightened state of fear and anxiety at all times, having repeatedly experienced pain and violence from their carers instead of protection and care. As their attachment system is set on 'red alert', they are unlikely to have been able to progress on other development pathways, exhibiting severe delay both cognitively and socially.

Our practice example (5.1) shows Danni, a 12-year-old white British girl, being visited for the first time by her social worker since the social worker moved her from her family home to a foster placement. In *'tuning-in to experience the child's world'*, the social worker could hypothesise from her family history that Danni is likely to have developed an insecure-avoidant attachment relationship pattern and anticipate Danni communicating reluctance to exploring her difficulties due to her mistrust of adults who are supposed to care for her. Insecure attachment relationship patterns present a developmental risk to children. Frequently they find themselves in uncertain, risky situations which cause them anxiety, such as experienced by Danni in her move to a new family, but yet they are unable to relate to people in a way that will reduce their anxiety. Indeed, we might hypothesise that Danni's recent behaviour in using alcohol and engaging in criminal behaviour indicates her catastrophic attempts to find a way to dissolve her anxious emotions.

Practice Example 5.1

Danni

Preparatory Stage

Danni, a 12-year-old white British girl, is being visited for the first time by her social worker since the social worker moved her from her family home to a foster placement. Earlier that day, when the social worker telephoned Danni to confirm the appointment, Danni said she did not want to stay in the foster placement.

▶

◀ Danni's mother has been using drugs for most of Danni's life, with Danni frequently left to care for herself. A year ago, Danni's mother resumed her relationship with Danni's father, who brought an initial stabilising influence to the family but latterly lapsed into illicit drug use. Both parents have health problems, exacerbated by the drug use, which affects their ability to work. Since starting at secondary school Danni's school attendance has declined, and recently there have been reports from neighbours and the police that she has been drunk and wandering the streets. Danni has never experienced a trusting, emotionally warm relationship. She has few friends among her peer group. Danni's foster placement is with Fred and Jan, a Korean couple who are both in their mid 30s, and their two younger children.

Yesterday, the police returned Danni back to the foster carer saying that she and some friends had thrown a brick through the window of the home of an elderly woman. No charges had been made. The social worker is unaware of this latest incident.

In drawing on the basic communication skills described in Chapter 4, the social worker will need to achieve and communicate empathy for this anxiety in order to enable Danni to feel understood, and in control of her emotional and social self (Howe, 1998; Agass, 2002; Ruch, 2005b). Bion's (1962) concept of 'containment' is frequently used to describe this process, which Agass (2002: 127) summarises as, 'not simply putting up with or absorbing whatever unpleasant or uncomfortable feelings the client stirs up in us. It is a much more active process of struggling to "contain", understand and work through our own emotional responses in the hope that this will enable our clients to do the same for themselves.' It is an important communicative medium for work with children because the effect of physical and psychological adversity upon their socio-emotional and cognitive development may mean that they are unable to communicate their feelings meaningfully in any other way. It is crucial for the social worker to communicate to Danni that he or she can do this containing work. To this end, I have labelled the capacity for this specialist communication as *'containing a child's feelings by providing and being a "safe place" in which feelings can be explored'.*

However, the social worker will only be successful in its execution if he or she prepares themselves for this emotionally charged situation. As discussed in Chapter 3, an important stage of *'tuning-in'* is to examine 'self'. This requires the social worker to reflect back upon their own childhood experiences; recognising the potential influence of the 'child within themselves' (Wilson et al., 2011) Questions should be brought to mind like 'who, where or what did they experience as a "safe place" in which to explore their most troubled, anxious experiences?' Identifying and recalling that feeling will help the social worker absorb some of the difficult feelings that Danni is likely to transfer. Similarly, they will be more able to transfer the message to the child that they are 'a safe place' and able to contain difficult feelings. Clearly, some people will find that reflection upon loss and childhood a very painful process. However, it is better that this occurs during the preparation period and not during the meeting when such feelings may emerge as counter-transference and as such be inappropriate and unhelpful to the child (see Chapter 3 for more discussion about transference and counter-transference). As Wilson et al. (2008: 317) state:

> draw honestly on your own personal experiences of loss and be scrupulous in reflecting on your own feelings and responses – for example, offering quick reassurance or breaking a silence may be because your own experiences/feelings make you uncomfortable, helpless, uncertain, or fearful of hearing painful emotions expressed.

Another crucial specialist communication skill to be carried out in preparation for meeting with the service user is to *'identify, validate and use the child's medium of communication'*. It is important that social workers do not view speech and language to be the only or preferred mode of communication. Such an attitude would undervalue and fail to recognise the variety of ways children make their wishes and feelings known, particularly disabled children (Morris, 2002; Marchant and Page, 2003). Child development theory indicates that children of different ages and stages of development use different mediums as their dominant form of communication (Piaget, 1983). Generally, children under eight years old communicate through play or having a story read to them. Children between 8 and 12 years old will respond well to symbolic, creative, expressive techniques which are delivered at the child's pace. Young people in their teenage years experience adults communicating with them verbally or through text-based mediums such email or letters.

Some young people will be sensitive to any communication that seems overly childish or patronising. However, frequently, children and young people in contact with social workers have experienced development delay across many dimensions of their development, including their cognitive and intellectual abilities. Talking alone is unlikely to be sufficient in ensuring meaningful communication with many of these children and young people. Rather, use needs to be made of tools that use visual, symbolic and culturally relevant mediums of communication alongside the dialogue, such as drawing or craft-based activities, writing poetry, using computer-based games and questionnaires or dramatic techniques such as role play. The medium of clay, for example, has been found to be useful by adolescents unveiling harrowing experiences of sexual abuse (Wilson and

Ryan, 2001). Structured visual tools such as the 'Three Houses' technique from the 'Signs of Safety' practice model have gained popularity (Bunn, 2013). As stated earlier, this model has a solution-focused emphasis, seeking rigorous, sustainable everyday safety solutions in the child's actual home (Turnell and Edwards, 1999; Turnell et al., 2007; Turnell, 2012). This 'Three Houses' technique involves the social worker encouraging the child or young person to draw three houses representing: a house of vulnerabilities (house of worries or fears); a house of strengths (positivity and happy feelings); and a house of hopes and dreams (a place for the miracle question – 'what would life be like if you woke up in a perfect place?'). In each house, the child or young person should be encouraged to write down anything internal that relates to each house, such as their thoughts, feelings, beliefs or experiences. External experiences, relationships, and events should be placed around the outside of the houses. After the picture is completed, the social worker can discuss how the fears might be addressed, and how the strengths and dreams can be encouraged. It is a vehicle for person-centred planning, with the child or young person being directly involved in the planning and the things that most matter to them being identified.

The social worker must prepare suitable materials in engaging these communication methods according to what they know about the child and young person's cognitive ability, talents and interests, while ensuring that the methods are age-appropriate. However, I should note that some older children and young people may not always see communication aimed at younger children necessarily as patronising or inappropriate. If they are disclosing abuse as a younger child, they may need to communicate at the age they were when they were abused. They may need to regress and so a variety and/or range of methods are needed. An example related by a social worker of their own practice is that they ensure that soft toys are available in the room during ABE interviews and older young people often pick them up and cuddle them as they are speaking about abuse.

Returning to our discussion, the social worker might be aware of particular issues from the child's situation for which the child or young person does not have the cognitive ability to completely comprehend, but which need explaining to their level of understanding. For example, events could have happened to a child at a younger age, of which they had little understanding, but which at an older age could be more fully explained and understood. Indeed, the modern attachment literature places importance on developing the 'reflective function' of young people as a significant protective factor for their development (Howe et al, 1999; Howe, 2005). This refers to the way a person can alter their insecure internal relationship model of relationships if they are able to reflect on and understand how past relationships affect their expectations of current relationships and view of 'self'. Such progression towards a secure internal model of relationships, in which a child feels loved and valued through consistent responses to developmental need, is a major protective factor for their ongoing development. The issue for the social worker, at this preparatory stage, is to plan how they might communicate the issues from the children's past in a way that is appropriate to their age and stage of cognitive and social development and uses a medium of communication that is familiar to the child. A specialist communication skill, identified by the British Agencies for Adoption and Fostering (BAAF) (1984; 1986) to achieve this purpose is that of *'using a storyline'*. In the same way that a scriptwriter for a soap opera uses a storyline to explore how a particular issue manifests itself and impacts on an individual, their friends and family, so the social worker uses a form of words, or even an analogy, to explain the impact of past issues to the child or young person.

By way of illustration, our practice example (5.1) indicates that the social worker could usefully prepare to explore how Danni's alcohol use is dangerous to her health and safety, and how it might be related to her feelings about present and past issues. Both of Danni's parents have health problems, exacerbated by the drug use, which affects their ability to work and care for her. She may be confused and rejected by their physical and psychological unavailability to her. Her self-esteem may be very low, feeling unloved and without worth. The social worker could prepare to *'use a storyline'* with a suitable form of words or analogy about how Danni might be using the alcohol to dull these feelings.

When first meeting with a child or young person, the social worker must employ the four parts of the basic communication skill from Chapter 3 of *'achieving a shared purpose'*, i.e. *'being clear on role'*; *'being clear on purpose'*; *'reach for feedback'* and *'showing empathy'*. The background literature highlighted how the authority that the social worker brings both through their legislative role, and their status of being an adult, presents a power differential which can dramatically influence communication with a child and young person. Consequently, the social worker must ensure that they *'show empathy'* to the child's feelings of ambivalence and frustration about being 'unheard' or 'disempowered' by adults generally, and apprehension at speaking to a social worker because of their legal role. Indeed, it is unfortunate but many children are warned by parents to 'behave or you'll go into care'. Moreover, some children who have been emotionally, physically or sexually maltreated have often been threatened to keep the maltreatment a secret. This means that the social worker must use specialist communication skills to communicate clarity about their role.

First, the social worker must take into account the child's capacity for understanding and *'use the child's medium of communication'* to tell the child in an honest and direct way that they are a 'social worker'. They should go on to explain the parameters of the role, such as the duties to ensure that someone is safe from harm and the limitations to ensuring confidentiality. By way of an illustration, Wilson et al. (2008: 102) describe a social worker, Sheila, who introduces her work with a new child by sharing her handmade booklet 'All About Me'. The booklet contains hand-drawn pictures about her self and her role, which she uses to talk about how she will work with the child.

The skill of *'achieving a shared purpose'* also involves *'being clear on purpose'* and *'reaching for feedback'* about whether the social worker and service user can work together on a shared agenda. In Chapter 3, we discussed how this involves the social worker stating the nature of their agenda using straightforward, non-jargon language that is developmentally appropriate to the service user. Greater success is achieved if a statement is prepared in advance. The aforementioned specialist communication skill of *'using a storyline',* as illustrated by Sheila's use of her book 'All About Me' to explain how she will work with a child, is helpful for achieving this with children and young people. Another illustration is the use of the 'loving and caring liquid' visual analogy to show children how, having once been filled with loving and caring feelings (a cup filled with water), these can be lost ('water is spilt') or 'stirred up' and confused ('cup is shaken'), or guarded ('cup is sealed') until a time when the child will safe and be able to give and receive more loving and caring feelings ('water is poured in and out'). The social worker could describe their purpose as helping the child become less guarded ('break the seal') and finding a new family to give loving and caring feelings ('pour water from additional cups') (Wilson et al., 2008).

This skill of *'using a storyline'* is as useful for helping older children and teenagers understand the purpose of the work as it is younger children. Care must be taken to ensure that the language and analogies used are age-appropriate and sufficiently contemporary that the social worker does not appear completely out-of-touch with the everyday interests of young people. However, there is a corresponding danger in this of the social worker trying to be a teenager, which may cause a child's or young person's perception of the boundaries between adult and child to become blurred. A balance must be drawn. An example from the research study is of a social worker using a football team analogy to encourage Ravi, a 15-year-old avid Manchester United fan, to discuss how he could work with the social worker to plan changes in his education and relationships with extended family. She asked him to think about his life as if it were an important European Cup football game. She asked him to name who from his social network he would want in his team as 'key players'. She explained what her role would be in the team, what his role would be and the key positions and tactics available to all his key players. She detailed what one of her goals would be and asked what other goals might look like. To prepare for *'using this storyline'*, the social worker had researched the different tactics and rules of football, as well as ensuring she knew the names and key skills of all the current Manchester United footballers. As they talked, they sketched out his ideas on a sheet of paper in order to meet Ravi's needs for a more visual and symbolic medium of communication. This sketch provided a document of agreed work.

This illustration shows how the social worker communicated *'respect'* to the young person. First, she operated the specialist communication skill *'identify, validate and use the child's medium of communication'* in order to communicate in a way that was appropriate to Ravi's age and stage of cognitive and social development, and which was meaningful to him. Second, she was careful to ensure that she conveyed warmth and interest in Ravi's answers, seeking to demonstrate acceptance of his perspectives. Indeed, the background literature reminds us that young people have the right, through their developmental competence, to having their views respected and accounted for in decisions. Our practice example (5.2) similarly shows the social worker *'communicating respect'* to Danni.

Practice Example 5.2

Danni

Beginnings

Knock, knock. Danni opens the front door to the foster carer's home.

SOCIAL WORKER (SW): Hello Danni.

DANNI: Yeah.

SW: It's Paul. Can I come in, mate?

DANNI: Yeah.

SW: Is it all right if I sit down?

DANNI: Mmm.

SW: Oh, cool. I've come to see how you are getting on. How's things going, mate?

DANNI: All right. *(she looks down, pulls her baseball cap down over her face, curls her shoulders down almost into her lap)*

SW: So tell me how things are, Danni.

▶

DANNI: All right.

SW: So what sort of things are you not happy with?

DANNI: Dunno.

SW: I don't want you to be worried about talking to me. See what I want to do – we're in this situation, you're in this foster placement and don't want to be here. What I want to do, and with your help, is to try and make it easy and as good as it can be for you – and I need to listen to you – but if you're not talking, I can't listen.

(Social worker leans forward, opens his hands, palms up. Danni watches from under her cap.)

SW: What would be the main…give me the main thing that's cheesing you off.

DANNI: It's boring. *(sits up, cap still over eyes)*

SW: OK. In terms of … it's boring because of what?

DANNI: School's boring, here's boring.

SW: OK.

DANNI: It's just boring.

SW: Boring, tell me more …

DANNI: Umm … I just don't like it here. *(looks at social worker from under cap for the first time)*

In the dialogue, the social worker shows appreciation of the fact that he is entering Danni's home and that Danni has given up time to meet with him. He asks politely if he can enter and if he can be seated. The social worker goes on to communicate acceptance of Danni's communication, even though she is indicating feelings of ambivalence and mistrust about the social worker's presence and purpose of the work. An important aspect of this acceptance is that he calmly lets her *'take time'*. He does not rush into asking a series of questions, but positively affirms and immediately acknowledges Danni's answers with a simple 'OK', as well as using paraphrasing to demonstrate *'reflective listening'*. He then adapts his non-verbal communication to indicate that he would like Danni to expand upon her answers (*'social worker leans forward, opens his hands, palms up'*) and *'uses silences'*. He emphasises further how he is willing to *'take time'* as the dialogue proceeds in the subsequent practice example (5.3), by initiating an activity together (lunch at the cafe), and later highlights the point further by stating 'I want to spend as much time as I can with you today …'.

Practice Example 5.3

Danni

Work Phase

SW: Dan, Anywhere you want to go? I don't know this area, Dan. Do you know anywhere we can go for a drive?

DANNI: Not really.

SW: OK, let's go. How about we go to the greasy spoon cafe down the road? Probably, it will be quiet in there right now. Is that OK with you? It's better talking over a cup of tea and bacon sandwich!

DANNI: All right. *(smiles and stands up.)*

(They drive to the cafe, order food at the counter and sit down in a quiet corner.)

SW: Dan, you say that everything's boring. What's the placement like then?

DANNI: *(shrugs)* It's all right.

SW.   Is it? Is that boring as well?

DANNI: S'all right.

SW: So what are Fred and Jan like?

DANNI: He's all right.

SW: Fred? You see I don't know the guy, you know, he strikes me as nice enough. Is he…

DANNI: *(interrupts in irritated tone of voice)* Bloke doesn't really want me there. Prefers his kids.

SW: I'm sorry to hear that. *(pause)* Why do you say that, Danni?

DANNI: *(shrugs)* Don't know.

SW: Dan, listen, mate. I want to spend as much time as I can with you today, but I need to go and see your foster parent as well. Now you're telling me that there are some things that you're not happy with – now what I'd like to do is talk to your foster parent about that, but I need to get your ideas on this. Do you understand?

DANNI: Yeah.

SW: Yes? Tell me some of those things? I know you've been saying that some of the things are boring, and you've also said that you feel left out in favour of his children, but you need to give me a little bit more, because if we're going to work together on this, I need to know exactly, what and how you feel. Do you understand what I'm getting at? *(Danni nods slightly)* OK, so, if you are OK with this, can you tell me a little bit more?

▶

DANNI: I'm just a troubled kid, that's it.

(Silence from both of them.)

SW: You've had a hard life, but you're not a troubled kid. Your future's your own here, you can turn it which way you want, yeah. I can't do it for you and I'm not going to do it for you, but what we can do is, I could help you do it for yourself yeah? Your life hasn't ended – you've got every way you can go at the moment, and you've got to do something for yourself.

(Silence from both of them.)

DANNI: I want to go back with my mum and dad.

SW: OK. You know the reasons that you're with a foster carer at the moment do you?

DANNI: Yeah, but it was all right though. There I could do just what I want to do. Here, it's just: he's nagging me all the time. If one of his kids does something, it's all right, but if I do something, it's always my fault.

SW: And what needs to happen for you to go back and live with your mum and dad? It's not all down to you is it? It's down to your mum and dad as well, yeah? And what we need to do is work to get you back home, yeah? It doesn't have to be perfect for you at home, but it's got to be better and safer than it is now. What we've got to do is make the foster care as best as it can be for you, and then we can help, work to get you back home with mum and dad.

Undertaking an activity together achieves more than communicating willingness to *'take time'*. Some children and young people need to be engaged in a joint activity in order to feel comfortable to communicate to adults. There is less need for eye contact, less pressure to talk, and the opportunity for using toys or other props or analogies to express feelings in a more indirect manner, and at the child's own pace, which may feel more comfortable for the child. Wilson et al. (2008) call this specialist communication strategy *'the use of the third object'*.

Another aspect of *'communicating respect'* is *'giving choice'* to the young person. This requires explaining the rationale for the choice and the consequences that follow. In other words it should be an 'informed choice', to which the young person can give 'informed consent'. Our practice example (5.3) illustrates the social worker giving Danni the choice to be involved in the work.

SW: Dan, listen, mate. I want to spend as much time as I can with you today, but I need to go and see your foster parent as well. Now you're telling me that there are some things that you're not happy with – now what I'd like to do is talk to your foster parent about that, but I need to get your ideas on this. Do you understand?

DANNI: Yeah.

SW: Yes? Can you tell me some of those things? I know you've been saying that some of the things are boring, and you've also said that you feel left out in favour of his children, but you need to give me a little bit more, because if we're going to work together on this, I need to know exactly, what and how you feel. Do you understand what I'm getting at? (*Danni nods slightly*) OK, so, if you are OK with this, can tell me a little bit more?

The above dialogue communicates that the social worker genuinely wants to hear and understand Danni's point of view. He explains the benefit to Danni of her engaging in the work, and he makes clear what needs to happen – the boundaries or parameters – for the work to continue. If this verbal response was combined with specified non-verbal behaviours for helping someone manage their angry feelings (Koprowska, 2005), then the worker will have successfully challenged Danni to work with him. As such, I refer to this specialist communication strategy as *'challenging in a comfortable or non-threatening manner'*. Koprowska (2005: 149) recommends social workers include the following non-verbal behaviours in managing aggressive situations and containing angry feelings:

➤ ensure you are standing or seated at a slight angle and not 'square on', but at least a one-and-a-half arm distance away;

➤ look at the person's face, making frequent but not continuous eye contact;

➤ show an interested and relaxed facial expression, but do not smile;

➤ keep your arms relaxed, away from your hair, face or around your body (as this can be interpreted as being impatient, anxious, or seductive);

➤ keep your hands open and in view with palms up to indicate negotiation;

➤ keep the tone of your voice of low-register and calm.

Indeed, throughout the meeting the social worker must be emotionally attuned to the feelings that the immediate relationship with the child or young person will be arousing, demonstrating the aforementioned specialist communication skill *'containing a child's feelings by providing and being a 'safe place' in which feelings can be explored'*. The combined skills of *'reflective listening'* to narrative, tone of voice and attitude, and *'observing'* non-verbal behaviour through gesture and body position are critical in making sense of these feelings (see Chapter 3 for more discussion). Signs of incongruence between the verbal and non-verbal behaviour show the social worker that the child may not be comfortable with the shared agenda, and is demonstrating superficial compliance and passive involvement. The issues being uncovered may be too painful or difficult for the child to discuss. The child might be afraid to disclose their experiences of maltreatment for fear of repercussions.

In this chapter, therefore, I am using the skill *'observing'* to denote a specialist communication strategy. This extends its usual use as either an invaluable source of learning (Wilson et al., 2011; Le Riche and Tanner, 1998), or one of the essential methods for collecting information for social work assessment of children's developmental needs (Daniel, 2007). In the case of the former, observation as a learning experience allows the social worker to stand back from intervening and interpreting behaviour ('doing') to watching and feeling the experience and so becoming more aware of feelings that belong to the child and to 'self' ('being'). The 'art of being' and not 'doing' is considered a central process in achieving emotional engagement with a child (Kroll, 1995). In the case of the latter, observation as a method provides information about how a child functions within their social and physical world. This behaviour is appraised against stages of healthy development from child development theories. *'Observing'* as a communication skill requires the worker to take steps to prevent becoming immersed in the content of the narrative but simultaneously adopt some objective distance to watch and feel the interaction taking place. The participants in the research study underpinning this book found that this objective distancing was more easily achieved by the social worker slowing the flow of the conversation and having in mind questions like 'What is it that is really going on in the communication here?', 'What is the non-verbal communication telling me about this?', 'Does what I am feeling belong to me or the child?' and 'What does this tell me about whether there is an obstacle to this communication?'.

Practice Example 5.2 shows the social worker using *'observing'* to make sense of Danni's blunt, one word answers ('yeah', 'alright', 'dunno', 'boring') and body language *('she looks down, pulls her baseball cap down over her face, curls her shoulders down almost into her lap')*. The social worker identifies how Danni seems to be communicating feelings of ambivalence and mistrust about the social worker's presence and purpose of the work. There is an obstacle in the communication relating to the authority role, which would be attended to by the social worker *'showing empathy'* for these feelings and being more *'clear on purpose'*. He responds by making his body language more open and relaxed to demonstrate more warmth and receptiveness to feelings and views. He does this with his hands as he knows this is the only area that Danni can see from under her cap *('Social worker leans forward, opens his hands, palms up')*. As he does this, he uses the skill of *'putting feelings into words'* to empathise with Danni's feelings, followed by being *'clear on purpose'*:

> I don't want you to be worried about talking to me. See what I want to do – we're in this situation, you're in this foster placement and don't want to be here. What I want to do, and with your help, is to try and make it easy and as good as it can be for you – and I need to listen to you – but if you're not talking, I can't listen. ... What would be the main ... give me the main thing that's cheesing you off.

While Danni continues to respond with limited verbal narrative, her body language indicates to the social worker that she is more engaged. Immediately, we see that she *'sits up, cap still over eyes'*, and then a little later at the end of Practice Example 5.2, she *'looks at social worker from under her cap for the first time'*.

Another reason for Danni's limited verbal responses is that she may only know a small number of expressions to explain her thoughts and feelings. One of the main issues that arose from the research underpinning this book was that social workers found it difficult to help some children and young people to express feelings because they had a limited vocabulary of different feelings. We know from the literature that many children in contact with social workers are frequently unused to talking about feelings, particularly children who have suffered physical and emotional neglect. As children develop, they need to have someone explain the link between their senses and their feelings, and to have those feelings labelled. Often, neglected children have not had this experience. They could be confused about feelings, and indeed may use a different word to explain a feeling to the one used by the social worker. As stated earlier, disabled children are particularly vulnerable in this respect. Not only are they more susceptible to abuse than their non-disabled peers, but historically many of the communication systems that disabled people use do not have a wide range of words, signs or symbols to describe feelings, parts of the body (such as genitalia) or acts of maltreatment (Wilson et al., 2008). Thus, in order to communicate with any child about feelings and experiences, the social worker needs to *'establish a shared vocabulary of feelings'*. Ideally this specialist communication strategy should occur as early on in the working relationship as possible. The social worker should identify a range of feelings appropriate to the child's age and stage of cognitive and social development and discuss what and how those feelings mean to the child. This might range from a simple identification of 'happy' and 'sad' feelings, perhaps using two paper plates that reveal the two expressions, to a list or set of pictures of a hundred or more abstract feelings, such as 'overwhelmed', 'frustrated', 'excited' or 'delighted'. As before, the social worker needs to use the skill *'identify, validate and use the child's medium of communication'* in discussing the different feelings with a child or young person.

The background literature highlights that care should be taken in the way such exploration of feelings and gathering of facts takes place. Questions should be avoided where children do not have the cognitive ability to process and answer them. These questions tend to start with 'why' and 'how' as opposed to the easier, more factually based questions of 'what', 'where' and 'when' (Jones, 2003). Our practice example (5.3) illustrates the point well, when Danni struggles to answer the social worker's question about her relationship with one of her foster carers.

DANNI: Bloke doesn't really want me there. Prefers his kids.

SW: I'm sorry to hear that. (*Pause*) Why do you say that Danni?

DANNI: (*Shrugs*) Don't know.

The example shows that she finds it difficult to explain why she is finding it hard to get along with her carer. Conceptually, it is a higher-order term, and too difficult for her to grasp or find the words to explain. It would have been better for the social worker to seek clarification on her point by asking her to give examples of situations in which the issue has manifested itself through using questions beginning with 'what', 'where' and 'when'. As stated earlier, it is important that these questions are not 'leading' to ensure accuracy in information gathering. Leading questions indicate to the service user the answer that the social worker is expecting to hear. The service user may feel less inclined to give an authentic answer, but offer the expected response (Koprowska, 2005). Particular care must be taken to avoid this in communication with children as the power differential between children and adults means that children are even more inclined to give the answer that they think the speaker wants.

Finally, in Chapter 3 I described how basic good communication requires careful attention to endings. It is of particular importance in work with children and young people, as they need to be sensitive to a child's understanding and feelings about the separation and transition. Feelings about past separations might come to the fore and the child may seek to avoid facing those feelings. As such, it is important to prepare the child in advance for the ending of the working relationship. The child might need more than verbal communication both of the changes and achievements realised over the time period, as well as their value as a person within that relationship. A card or other token will help convey this message.

This chapter has described and discussed the capacity for, and application of, specialist social work communication that presumes the capacity of children to express their thoughts and feelings on central matters that affect their developmental wellbeing ('Knowing'). The onus is on the social worker to find the medium of communication that facilitates this expression ('Knowing' and 'Doing'). However, its success rests on the ability of the social worker to attend to the relationship dynamics in the working relationship, particularly those arising from the social worker's own experience of childhood relationships, and those that are structurally influenced by the social worker's authority role ('Being').

Mapping to the Professional Capability Framework

Qualifying Social Worker Level Capabilities

Please remember that these should be viewed as domains which overlap in an integrative manner rather than as a linear checklist.

'By the end of last placement/the completion of qualifying programmes newly qualified social workers should have demonstrated the Knowledge, Skills and Values to work with a range of user groups, and the ability to undertake a range of tasks at a foundation level, the capacity to work with more complex situations; they should be able to work more autonomously, whilst recognising that the final decision will still rest with their supervisor; they will seek appropriate support and supervision.
The Health Professions Council (the regulator of qualified social workers) and The College have mapped the Standards of Proficiency for Social Work (SOPs) against the PCF expectations for social work students at the end of their last placement. Whilst there are some differences in the way the standards and PCF are expressed, the overall expectations are the same.'

| Communication Capacity Domain – 'Knowing' (engaging with formal and informal knowledge in communication) | PCF 3 Diversity: Recognise diversity and apply anti-discriminatory and anti-oppressive principles in practice
➢ Understand how an individual's identity is informed by factors such as culture, economic status, family composition, life experiences and characteristics, and take account of these to understand their experiences, questioning assumptions where necessary
➢ With reference to current legislative requirements, recognise personal and organisational discrimination and oppression and with guidance make use of a range of approaches to challenge them |

PCF 5 Knowledge: Apply knowledge of social sciences, law and social work practice theory

➢ Demonstrate a critical understanding of the application to social work of research, theory and knowledge from sociology, social policy, psychology and health
➢ Demonstrate a critical understanding of the legal and policy frameworks and guidance that inform and mandate social work practice, recognising the scope for professional judgement
➢ Demonstrate and apply to practice a working knowledge of human growth and development throughout the life course
➢ Recognise the short and long term impact of psychological, socio-economic, environmental and physiological factors on people's lives, taking into account age and development, and how this informs practice
➢ Recognise how systemic approaches can be used to understand the person-in-the-environment and inform your practice
➢ Acknowledge the centrality of relationships for people and the key concepts of attachment, separation, loss, change and resilience
➢ Understand forms of harm and their impact on people, and the implications for practice, drawing on concepts of strength, resilience, vulnerability, risk and resistance, and apply to practice
➢ Demonstrate a critical knowledge of the range of theories and models for social work intervention with individuals, families, groups and communities, and the methods derived from them
➢ Value and take account of the expertise of service users, carers and professionals

KSS Adults (4): Safeguarding
Social workers must be able to recognise the risk indicators of different forms of abuse and neglect and their impact on individuals, their families or their support networks and should prioritise the protection of children and adults in vulnerable situations whenever necessary. This includes working with those who self-neglect. Social workers who work with adults must take an outcomes-focused, person-centred approach to safeguarding practice, recognising that people are experts in their own lives and working alongside them to identify person centred solutions to risk and harm.

KSS Adults (6): Effective Assessments and Outcome Based Support Planning
Social workers should demonstrate a good understanding of personalisation, the social model of disability and of human development throughout life and demonstrate a holistic approach to the identification of needs, circumstances, rights, strengths and risks. In particular, social workers need to understand the impact of trauma, loss and abuse, physical disability, physical ill health, learning disability, mental ill health, mental capacity, substance misuse, domestic abuse, aging and end of life issues on physical, cognitive, emotional and social development both for the individual and for the functioning of the family. They should recognise the roles and needs of informal or family carers and use holistic, systemic approaches to supporting individuals and carers. They should develop and maintain knowledge and good partnerships with local community resources in order to work effectively with individuals in connecting them with appropriate resources and support.

| Communication Capacity Domain – 'Doing' (the enactment of communication strategies in interaction) | **PCF 6 Critical Reflection and Analysis: Apply critical reflection and analysis to inform and provide a rationale for professional decision-making**
➢ Apply imagination, creativity and curiosity to practice
➢ Inform decision-making through the identification and gathering of information from multiple sources, actively seeking new sources
➢ With support, rigorously question and evaluate the reliability and validity of information from different sources
➢ Demonstrate a capacity for logical, systematic, critical and reflective reasoning and apply the theories and techniques of reflective practice
➢ Know how to formulate, test, evaluate, and review hypotheses in response to information available at the time and apply in practice
➢ Begin to formulate and make explicit, evidence-informed judgements and justifiable decisions

KSS Adults (8): Supervision, Critical Reflection and Analysis
Social workers should be able to make effective use of opportunities to discuss, reflect upon and test multiple hypotheses, the role of intuition and logic in decision making, the difference between opinion and fact, the role of evidence, how to address common bias in situations of uncertainty and the reasoning of any conclusions reached and recommendations made, particularly in relation to mental capacity, mental health and safeguarding situations.

Social workers should have a critical understanding of the difference between theory, research, evidence and expertise and the role of professional judgement. They should use practice evidence and research to inform the complex judgements and decisions needed to support, empower and protect their service users. They should apply imagination, creativity and curiosity to working in partnership with individuals and their carers, acknowledging the centrality of people's own expertise about their experience and needs.

KSS Children (2): Communication
Produce written case notes and reports, which are well argued, focused and jargon free. Present a clear analysis and a sound rationale for actions as well as any conclusions reached, so that all parties are well-informed. |
| | **PCF 7 Intervention and Skills: Use judgement and authority to intervene with individuals, families and communities to promote independence, provide support and prevent harm, neglect and abuse**
➢ Identify and apply a range of verbal, non-verbal and written methods of communication and adapt them in line with peoples' age, comprehension and culture
➢ Be able to communicate information, advice, instruction and professional opinion so as to advocate, influence and persuade
➢ Demonstrate the ability to engage with people, and build, manage, sustain and conclude compassionate and effective relationships
➢ Demonstrate skills in sharing information appropriately and respectfully |

➤ Recognise complexity, multiple factors, changing circumstances and uncertainty in people's lives, to be able to prioritise your intervention

➤ Understand the authority of the social work role and begin to use this appropriately as an accountable professional

➤ Recognise the factors that create or exacerbate risk to individuals, their families or carers, to the public or to professionals, including yourself, and contribute to the assessment and management of risk

KSS Adults (3): Person-centred Practice
They should work co-productively and innovatively with people, local communities, other professionals, agencies and services to promote self-determination, community capacity, personal and family reliance, cohesion, earlier intervention and active citizenship.

KSS Adults (4): Safeguarding
Social workers who work with adults must take an outcomes-focused, person-centred approach to safeguarding practice, recognising that people are experts in their own lives and working alongside them to identify person centred solutions to risk and harm. In situations where there is abuse or neglect or clear risk of those, social workers must work in a way that enhances involvement, choice and control as part of improving quality of life, wellbeing and safety.

KSS Adults (7): Direct Work with Individuals and Families
Social workers need to be able to work directly with individuals and their families through the professional use of self, using interpersonal skills and emotional intelligence to create relationships based on openness, transparency and empathy. They should know how to build purposeful, effective relationships underpinned by reciprocity. They should be able to communicate clearly, sensitively and effectively, applying a range of best evidence-based methods of written, oral and non-verbal communication and adapt these methods to match the person's age, comprehension and culture. Social workers should be capable of communicating effectively with people with specific communication needs, including those with learning disabilities, dementia, people who lack mental capacity and people with sensory impairment.

KSS Children (2): Communication
Communicate clearly and sensitively with children of different ages and abilities, their families and in a range of settings and circumstances. Use methods based on best evidence.
Create immediate rapport with people not previously known which facilitates engagement and motivation to participate in child protective enquiries, assessments and services.
Listen to the views, wishes and feelings of children and families and help parents and carers understand the ways in which their children communicate through their behaviour. Help them to understand how they might communicate more effectively with their children.
Promote speech, language and communication support, identifying those children and adults who are experiencing difficulties expressing themselves.

Communication Capacity Domain – 'Being' (the use of 'self')	**PCF 1 Professionalism: Identify and behave as a professional social worker, committed to professional development**
	➤ Be able to explain the role of the social worker in a range of contexts, and uphold the reputation of the profession ➤ Demonstrate professionalism in terms of presentation, demeanour, reliability, honesty and respectfulness ➤ Recognise the impact of self in interaction with others, making appropriate use of personal experience ➤ Be able to recognise and maintain personal and professional boundaries ➤ Recognise your professional limitations and how to seek advice ➤ Demonstrate a commitment to your continuing learning and development ➤ With support, take steps to manage and promote own safety, health, wellbeing and emotional resilience **KSS Adults (7): Direct work with individuals and families** Social workers should be capable of communicating effectively with people with specific communication needs, including those with learning disabilities, dementia, people who lack mental capacity and people with sensory impairment. They should do this in ways that are engaging, respectful, motivating and effective, even when dealing with conflict – whether perceived or actual – anger and resistance to change. **KSS Children (2): Communication** Act respectfully even when people are angry, hostile and resistant to change. Manage tensions between parents, carers and family members, in ways that show persistence, determination and professional confidence.
	PCF 2 Values and Ethics: Apply social work ethical principles and values to guide professional practice ➤ Recognise and, with support, manage the impact of own values on professional practice ➤ Manage potentially conflicting or competing values, and, with guidance, recognise, reflect on, and work with ethical dilemmas ➤ Demonstrate respectful partnership work with service users and carers, eliciting and respecting their needs and views, and promoting their participation in decision-making wherever possible ➤ Recognise and promote individuals' rights to autonomy and self-determination **KSS Adults (5): Mental Capacity** Social workers must model and lead a change of approach, away from that where the default setting is 'safety first', towards a person-centred culture where individual choice is encouraged and where the right of all individuals to express their own lifestyle choices is recognised and valued. In working with those where there is no concern over capacity, social workers should take all practicable steps to empower people to make their own decisions, recognising that people are experts in their own lives and working alongside them to identify person-centred solutions to risk and harm, recognising the individual's right to make 'unwise' decisions.

PCF 3 Diversity: Recognise diversity and apply anti-discriminatory and anti-oppressive principles in practice
(Appropriately placed in both 'Knowing' and 'Being')
➢ With reference to current legislative requirements, recognise personal and organisational discrimination and oppression and with guidance make use of a range of approaches to challenge them
➢ Recognise and manage the impact on people of the power invested in your role

KSS Adults (3): Person-centred Practice
They should coordinate and facilitate a wide range of practical and emotional support, and discharge legal duties to complement people's own resources and networks, so that all individuals (no matter their background, health status or mental capacity), carers and families can exercise choice and control, (supporting individuals to make their own decisions, especially where they may lack capacity) and meet their needs and aspirations in personalised, creative and often novel ways. They should work co-productively and innovatively with people, local communities, other professionals, agencies and services to promote self- determination, community capacity, personal and family reliance, cohesion, earlier intervention and active citizenship.

PCF 4 Rights, Justice and Economic Wellbeing: Advance human rights and promote social justice and economic wellbeing
➢ Understand, identify and apply in practice the principles of social justice, inclusion and equality
➢ Understand how legislation and guidance can advance or constrain people's rights and recognise how the law may be used to protect or advance their rights and entitlements
➢ Work within the principles of human and civil rights and equalities legislation, differentiating and beginning to work with absolute, qualified and competing rights and differing needs and perspectives
➢ Recognise the impact of poverty and social exclusion and promote enhanced economic status through access to education, work, housing, health services and welfare benefits

PCF 8 Contexts and Organisations: Engage with, inform, and adapt to changing contexts that shape practice. Operate effectively within own organisational frameworks and contribute to the development of services and organisations. Operate effectively within multi-agency and inter-professional partnerships and settings
➢ Recognise that social work operates within, and responds to, changing economic, social, political and organisational contexts
➢ Understand the roles and responsibilities of social workers in a range of organisations, lines of accountability and the boundaries of professional autonomy and discretion
➢ Understand legal obligations, structures and behaviours within organisations and how these impact on policy, procedure and practice
➢ Be able to work within an organisation's remit and contribute to its evaluation and development

| | **KSS Adults (9): Organisational Context**
They must understand and work effectively within financial and legal frameworks, obligations, structures and culture, in particular Human Rights and Equalities legislation, the Care Act, Mental Capacity Act, Mental Health Act and accompanying guidance and codes of practice. They must be able to operate successfully in their organisational context, demonstrating effective time management, caseload management and be capable of reconciling competing demands and embrace information, data and technology appropriate to their role. They should have access to regular quality supervision to support their professional resilience and emotional and physical wellbeing. |

6

Working with Young People with Offending Behaviour

Summary of Specialist Communication Skills in this Chapter

➢ developing early rapport

➢ defending the rights of the service user

➢ communicating consequences in a non-threatening manner

➢ listening for clues

➢ focused questioning

➢ assessing for truthfulness

➢ assessing for remorse and willingness to reform

➢ the avoidance of the 'why' and 'how' questions

➢ expressing empathy and understanding without necessarily signifying agreement

➢ giving choice

➢ reflective listening.

Policy and background literature

The measures introduced by the Crime and Disorder Act (1998) require that social workers work alongside representatives from the police, probation, health and education within local multi-agency Youth Offending Teams (YOTs). The statutory aim of this work is the targeted prevention of offending and reoffending by children and young people (Audit Commission, 2004). Literature highlights particular communication issues relevant to this setting in addition to those covered within the previous chapter on 'Working with Children'.

For young people who have offended, workers use a new structured assessment tool called AssetPlus. The tool replaces the previous assessment tools of Asset, Onset, SQIFA and SIFA. The development was a response to practitioner evaluations of its use and research developments around assessment practice and the youth offending context. Also, it reflected a wider practice perspective, heralded by the Munro (2011a; 2011b) review of child safeguarding practice, and favouring professional discretion and judgement in situations of complexity, uncertainty and risk (Baker, 2014). The consequence is that risk is considered in more dynamic and relational terms. As an example, as opposed to listing the occurrence of risk and protective factors experienced by a young person, the AssetPlus recognises that such factors interact with each other at different moments in a young person's life (Youth Justice Board, 2006; Youth Justice Board, 2008; Case, 2007; Baker et al., 2011). Moreover, such factors are considered to constitute different aspects of the totality of the young person in their situation, from the thoughts, feelings, beliefs and assumptions of their inner world, to the dynamics occurring in their family situation and peer network, and beyond to the structural influences of employment prospects, and human rights. These connections are considered (often) to relate to particular behaviours at particular times (Wikström and Sampson, 2009). For example, behaviours seeking to (illegally) gain material resources may be linked to a young person's perceived need to acquiring the economic assets to 'feel included' and 'prevent bullying' or 'gain employment'. As such, the connections highlight the importance of the social context to understanding behaviour; a new emphasis embodied within the AssetPlus framework for assessment (Baker, 2014). Thus, the purpose of AssetPlus is to identify the risk factors known to be associated with offending (criminogenic factors) as well as risk factors to welfare. The interactive influence of the social context means that the former cannot be considered without the latter. Moreover, in the light of this holistic approach to risk assessment, *AssetPlus* has been conceived to be applicable to, and completed with, all young people at different stages of the youth justice system. It is no longer relevant to just those subject to a 'Final Warning', or due to be sentenced to a custodial or community order.

The assessment process uses a number of structured tools to enable social workers (and other YOT workers) to understand the risks and needs of young offenders and identify intervention to reduce risks. The inclusion of the following elements give an indication of the communication issues arising in this practice setting:

> ➤ engaging the young person and their parents or carers to discuss and identify their needs, including assessing willingness to participate in interventions and exploration of areas of the young person's familial

and social life that might affect the prospect of achieving positive change; self-assessment tools are made available to the young person and parents;

➤ obtaining details on the seriousness and complexity of a young person's behaviour, including the detail of the offence, analysing differences between the young person's account and the Crown Prosecution Service's account, and the attitudes to offences and pattern of offending;

➤ analysing information from all sources to understand the reasons behind offending behaviour;

➤ identifying the risks of harm the young person may pose to themselves or the public;

➤ identifying the likelihood of the young person reoffending;

➤ a more strengths-orientated 'Foundations for Change' section that assesses the young person's resilience (including when faced with opportunities to offend), their life-goals and attitudes, with opportunities identified to enable the young person achieve positive outcomes; the level of engagement and participation, as well as factors affecting desistance (such as substance use) are brought into the assessment;

➤ deciding how the assessment informs intervention planning, such as pre-sentence reports for court or reports for youth offender panels.

It will be interesting to see whether the previously overriding concerns of determining 'desistance to offending' or 'risk of reoffending' diminish or continue to dominate practice in this setting and influence communication strategies. It is an issue which has come under heavy criticism from theorists who emphasise that the balance should be more towards a welfare rather than a punitive 'criminal justice' perspective (Armstrong, 2004; Case, 2007). Children and young people in contact with YOTs have been found to experience a number of difficulties that should be taken into account within communication, such as physical health needs, emotional/mental health needs, schooling difficulties or learning difficulties, with the statutory entitlement of 25 hours education being rarely achieved (HMI Probation, 2009). Problems often coexist, such as school achievement, attendance and substance misuse. The social worker needs to take account of these emotional issues and learning disabilities within their communication strategy. In particular, they need to respond to literature that has highlighted how autism and learning difficulties may affect the service user's communication of remorse or willingness to reform (Bishop, 2008).

Youth offending is often related to other familial problems, such as parental substance misuse and conflict. Indeed, in relation to identifying communication issues, the literature highlights the need to recognise the frequency of the young person having experienced stressful confrontations both from within their home, and often within school. The meeting with a social worker – as an adult with authority – is likely to reproduce further feelings of stress and uncertainty within a situation which is already stressful. Social work within YOTs can focus on improving parenting behaviour and the parenting environment, with the possibility of applying to the courts to obtain parenting orders to enforce the work on a compulsory basis.

Communication about issues of compulsion and control is also required when working with the high numbers of young people subject to remands in custody or sentenced to custody. Bail supervision and support are points of contact between a young person, the court and the YOT. These circumstances may raise particular communication issues relating to the social situation of the young person as being already involved in the wheels of the justice system and feeling disaffected from society. They may be feeling very fearful and alone (Sanford et al., 1981).

Finally, YOTs increasingly work with children and young people who have not yet offended but have been identified as being at risk of offending. The work seeks to help prevent them from being drawn into the youth justice system. The AssetPlus assessment is now equally applicable for these young people. It is used to identify whether a young person would benefit from participating in a prevention programme, as well as to identify and address their needs to reduce the likelihood of them engaging in offending behaviour. Clearly, the need to communicate about 'offending' to children and young people who have not offended, or been known to offend, presents more communication challenges for a worker.

Practice application

The breaking down of communication barriers between the service user and 'the system' – specifically social workers – by building rapport, is of paramount importance in this practice setting. Service users are already disaffected from society (particularly authority) as young offenders and there is a danger that communication between service user and social worker, will be mediated by the young person feeling that they are communicating with the social worker under duress or threat of punitive action. In fact, we might understand the major themes in specialist communication skills in this practice setting as falling largely into an umbrella category of building rapport and breaking down barriers.

Practice Example 6.1

Dean

Preparatory Stage

Dean is a 15-year-old youth living in an overcrowded city area. He describes his ethnicity as being black – his mother is white British and father is black British, of African descent. Both are employed. Over the past year Dean has rarely attended school. Previously, both Dean and his parents received social work services alongside two Youth Offending Team intervention programmes (a mentoring programme and a parenting programme), aimed at preventing his offending behaviour. Dean has committed four minor offences and one serious offence for which he received a reprimand and a warning. He has been involved with the police for three years now. Currently, Dean is estranged from his parents, and is 'sofa-surfing', spending nights on sofas in friends' homes. At this point, he has been to a Police Station and received a Final Warning. A member of the Youth Offending Team was present for that Final Warning and offered Dean the opportunity to work with them, using the AssetPlus assessment procedure, to design a programme to help prevent Dean from reoffending. Dean is now meeting with a different social worker from the Youth Offending Team to begin the work.

Practice Example 6.1 shows how social workers need to utilise specialist communication skills to develop rapport between the social worker and service user from the outset for productive and meaningful communication. Dean is meeting a social worker from the local Youth Offending Team to begin work on an AssetPlus assessment as part of the process involved in receiving a Final Warning for an offence in which it was alleged he had hit someone. Previously, both Dean and his parents received social work services aimed at preventing his offending behaviour. However, currently, Dean is estranged from his parents, and is 'sofa-surfing', spending nights on sofas in friends' homes. His representation of the world is in terms of 'them' (authority figures) and 'us' (young people). His disaffection and disengagement from society is palpable. Using a specialist communication skill of *'developing early rapport'* at the earliest stage of the interview is critical in seeking to overcome his previous negative experiences of social work.

'Phatic communication' has also been used within the communication literature as a term to describe the purpose and form of communication strategy that I am outlining here (Burnard, 2003; Koprowska, 2008). As a form of everyday communication, its purpose is to promote and maintain friendly relationships through demonstrating sociability as opposed to giving or seeking information. The use of this communication within professional relationships is considered to reduce service user anxiety. As Burnard (2003: 680) states:

> When we chat in this way, we are, perhaps, saying 'I am friendly, unhostile and I want to know you and acknowledge you!'

The communication that the social worker needs to transmit is that she is interested in Dean as a person, and that she, too, is a person and not an automated authority figure. At point 2 in Practice Example 6.2 we find the social worker achieving this through using the empathy skill of *'putting feelings into words'* to show understanding of Dean's ambivalence. She extends this skill by identifying how, as a human being, she may make errors but that she is genuinely seeking to be helpful. She emphasises this by stating her desire to receive his feedback on her usefulness. Most importantly, she seeks to demonstrate how she is drawing a line between this, her own approach and that of previous workers. In doing this, she is not inviting criticisms of those previous working practices, but looking ahead to how they might work together in a way that is more useful to Dean. I summarise this part of the social work communication approach at this earliest stage of the interview as operating a specialist communication skill of *'expressing empathy and understanding without necessarily signifying agreement'*. This skill is used later in the interview.

> I'm sure a lot of young people in your situation have felt that people don't care. But what I want to say is 'can we start afresh?' You've not worked with me before, I've not worked with you, so … if you don't think I'm doing something right, then please tell me, yeah? If you don't think I'm working or don't think I care, tell me, because I value your opinions. (*Dean shrugs, moves around in his seat, picks at something on his jacket*)

There is a second reason for building rapport at this early stage in the interview. This concerns the need to establish rapport to prepare for later exploratory questioning of potentially anxiety-provoking issues. These concern the factual circumstances of the offence, but also personal information surrounding attitudes, beliefs, psychosocial functioning and, particularly, the quality of familial relationships. Indeed, the requirements of the AssetPlus assessment in identifying the degree of victim empathy, extent of remorsefulness, motivation for change and socio-economic risk factors influencing the potential for change means that the level of personal information to be acquired increases as the interview proceeds. A social worker is more likely to be able to explore these increasingly personal issues if there is development of rapport throughout the interview which commences from the outset. Moreover, there is a view that early rapport improves the validity of the information being provided (Jones, 2003).

Further techniques for achieving this specialist communication skill of *'developing early rapport'* to prepare for later exploratory questioning include utlilising the specialist communication skills identified in the previous chapter on working with children and young people in relation to *'achieving a shared purpose'*. In this practice setting it is not only important to be clear on the role of the social worker and the purpose of the youth offending work, but ensure that the communication of this information is actually understood by the young person and agreed upon. In our practice example (6.2, points 3 to 5), the social worker seeks to explain the reasons for the meeting and completion of the AssetPlus assessment. She is completely transparent about the processes involved. Critically, she reminds Dean of the voluntary nature of his engagement in the work, while at the same time identifying that he will benefit from this work being done ('the final warning is voluntary – no one is gonna make you sit here and engage with the process'). In specifying the outcomes of the assessment she communicates to him that the work will have a use – not just empty words – and that she has belief in his potential to complete the work with her. In the last chapter we used the term *'giving choice'* to describe this kind of communication activity. In our practice example, the social worker does not continue with the interview until Dean actually states his agreement to engage with the work and achieve the outcomes (6.2, point 5).

Practice Example 6.2

Dean

Beginnings

Social Worker: knocks on the door.

[1] Dean: 'Yeah. Here'.

SW: 'Hi I'm Lorraine from the Youth Offending Team, are you alright?' *She shakes Dean's hand.* 'Nice to see you'. *She sits down.*

SW: How's it going?

Dean: Yeah.

SW: I understand that you were at the Police Station last week and received your final warning – how did you find that?

Dean: Well, it's one of those things, ain't it?

▶

◄

SW: Now I understand you met one of my colleagues when you were there who probably handed you some leaflets and told you about the Youth Offending Team. What I want to do, first of all, is explain to you the purpose of us getting together, if you like. And hopefully from there, plan work we can do in the future. We need to do an assessment today, aspects of your life and things that may affect your offending behaviour that we can work on together. But, do you know anything about the Youth Offending Team?

Dean: Stuff like a Social Worker, ain't it?

SW: Well, kind of. There are social workers in the Youth Offending Team. There are also police officers, probation officers, people from health, people from education. Basically we work as a team to try and prevent you from reoffending and stay out of trouble. Yeah? Does that make sense?

Dean: You gonna try to do what? I just wanna be left to do what I wanna do, you know what I mean?

SW: Well, we can talk about that.

Dean: You don't wanna talk about that though.

SW: Well, unfortunately once you've had a final warning we have to talk about it …

Dean: I tried to talk about it before, but no one ever listened did they? Now it's you lot. Social Services before – none of 'em are any better.

[2] SW: I'm sure a lot of young people in your situation have felt that people don't care. But what I want to say is 'can we start afresh?' You've not worked with me before, I've not worked with you, so ….if you don't think I'm doing something right, then please tell me, yeah? If you don't think I'm working or don't think I care, tell me, because I value your opinions. (*Dean shrugs, moves around in his seat, picks at something on his jacket.*)

[3] SW: Perhaps it will help if I explain a bit more about this work towards the final warning? (*Looks at Dean and allows a little silence*) I know that at the Police Station you said you would be prepared to do this work, but in my experience, there's often so much going on that people agree to things that they are not sure about, or forget what they have agreed to! Understandable, yeah? So, tell me, do you know about final warnings then?

Dean: Get locked up.

SW: Not exactly, not unless you do something really serious. Basically a final warning is kind of a second stage in the process of the Youth Justice system. Now, I understand you've had a reprimand up to now, yeah? The final warning stage is voluntary – no one is gonna make you sit here and engage with the process – but I'm kinda hoping you will because, at the end of the day, if you do and we work successfully together, then ideally it's gonna help stop you reoffending, yeah? If you don't or you choose not to engage

►

◀

	in the process, then I have to write down that this is where you have got to in the system. If you did go on to reoffend and appeared in court, then the Magistrate would actually be told you didn't engage in this process, yeah? Does that make sense?
Dean:	Yeah.
SW:	Here, if you were to reoffend, then you'd go to court and the police wouldn't be able to let you off with another final warning; and there's a range of options open to the courts. So that's why it's better to focus more on not reoffending again, yeah? As I say, we need to do an AssetPlus assessment – ask you some questions, to decide what should go into a programme to help stop you reoffending.
Dean:	So what kind of things are you gonna ask me?
[5] SW:	I'm going to be honest with you. Some of the questions are going to be very personal. They need to be if we are going to come up with a programme that is going to be as real and meaningful to you as possible. You need to be as honest as you can about those things. What you tell me is put on our database and we do share that with other people within the Youth Offending organisation. If you tell me something that shows you might be harmed in some way, then I will need to make sure you are protected, so I will tell people that can protect you, yeah? So, are we going to complete this AssetPlus assessment together?
Dean:	Yeah.
SW:	Yeah? Good.

In relation to this skill of *'giving choice'*, a key finding from the research study underpinning this book was that *'defending the rights of the service user'* was an important theme of specialist communication skills in working with young offenders. In this specific practice setting where the young person is faced with a punitive system, they felt that it was their role as a social worker to communicate the right of voluntary engagement, as they may not necessarily have been notified of it. This involved not just communicating to the service user that engagement is voluntary, but defending the right of the service user to refuse participation. Clearly, the theme of defending the rights of the service user contributes to *'develop early rapport'* by building trustworthiness of the social worker.

It all sounds rather 'heavy', but a key technique in achieving rapport, and indeed the aforementioned *'achieving a shared purpose'*, is to use humour and the service user's language. The use of humorous banter and slang is embedded in youth culture; therefore, use of banter and humour by social workers in their own discourse with the young offender helps to break down the view of the social worker as an authoritarian figure, by putting the social worker and service user on a more equal footing, through the medium of language. There is a danger of the social worker trying to be a teenager and, as stated in the previous chapter, this may create a distortion in the child's or young person's perception of the boundaries between adult and child. A balance must be drawn. Examples from the practice example include:

> ➤ 'SW: Probably what you call 'a little bit' and what I call 'a little bit' are different ... (*laughs*). Dean: You a light touch? Only one can? ...... *smiles*. SW: Yeah, that's true ... (*laughs*)' (6.3, point 8)

> ➤ 'So how were you feeling? Cos I think I'd be drunk and wiped –other people, like me, get drunk on anything. So how did you feel?' (6.3, point 10)

> ➤ 'Any history there of aggro between you guys?' (6.3, point 14)

> ➤ 'And had this bloke given you lip before?' (6.3, point 15)

> ➤ 'So the police came along, they all did a runner, but you got picked up? So what happened then?' (6.3, point 16)

In ethical terms, when *'giving choices'* to a young person about whether to engage in youth offending work, this should involve giving information about not only the processes involved once they have engaged in the work, but, importantly, also, the consequences for that young person if they do not engage in the work. It is about obtaining 'fully informed consent' or 'fully informed dissent'. The challenge for the social worker is to communicate the consequences of the situation to the service user in a manner that is non-threatening in order to continue to build rapport and maintain the quality of interaction achieved thus far.

There seem to be two aspects to this specialist communication skill of *'communicating consequences in a non-threatening manner'*. First, the social worker should avoid threat and judgement when communicating consequences. Using Practice Example 6.2 as an illustration, from points 3 to 5 the social worker explained to Dean the consequences of what would happen if he did not complete the AssetPlus assessment, but in a way that wasn't judging him. Rather, it simply gave him information. A key to this success was in the social worker not making the information too 'personal' by explaining that the process itself existed as something separate to him, i.e. it was not created by his actions as a punitive response to him personally. Significantly, it was crucial to frame the consequences as information-giving rather than a reprimand. Second, the social worker identified the trade off for compliance. This involved providing a balance to the information provided – identifying the positive consequences and belief in the potential for change and a different future. The social worker could have added 'if you do engage, maybe I'll never have to see you again and you can put this behind you. If you do reoffend, then the next step of the process is that you will go to court and the court can sentence you to any number of different measures'.

I want to emphasise that the operation of this communication skill is not as simple or obvious as it seems. The policy context to this practice setting is that of criminal (youth) justice, propounding a punitive system as opposed to a welfare system. This context places pressure on the social worker to stop the offending behaviour, which in turn has the potential to reinforce a zealous discourse with the service user about the consequences of reoffending. Indeed, the social work participants of the research study underpinning the book stated that this emphasis upon showing the service user the consequences of their offending behaviour was 'drummed into us'.

Practice Example 6.3

Dean

Work Phase

[6] SW: What I want to do to begin with is for you to tell me a little bit about the events. Exactly what happened?

Dean: Hanging with a few mates, smoking and …

SW: When you say a few mates, how many?

Dean: Four.

SW: Four, yeah, and what time of day was this?

Dean: About 6 in the evening.

[7] SW: So had you been drinking – you say you'd been smoking?

Dean: Yeah, a bit, but not loads.

[8] SW: Probably what you call 'a little bit' and what I call 'a little bit' are different … (*laughs*)

Dean: You a light touch? Only one can? … (*smiles*)

[9] SW: Yeah, that's true … (*laughs*) … So, you're there with 4 of your mates; early evening; couple of drinks – what classes as a couple of drinks?

Dean: Cans of cider, about 2 and a bit, then some vodka.

▶

◄

[10] SW: So how were you feeling? 'Cos I think I'd be drunk and wiped out – other people, like me, get drunk on anything. So, how did you feel?

[11] Dean: Alright, just a bit happy. But I was chilled out – we'd been smoking as well.

SW: So what were you smoking?

Dean: Weed. Just weed innit? My mate gets some good stuff.

[12] SW: Had you been smoking all day?

Dean: Just a couple of hours beforehand.

[13] SW: OK, so you're feeling merry. What happened then?

Dean: We got into a fight with these other lads – bit of shoving.

SW: What actually started the fight? I mean, where were you?

Dean: The park, innit? (*looks in a frustrated manner at social worker*)

SW: Yeah, whereabouts were you at the time, you know. Just thinking of location and where you were actually stood, sat?

Dean: Well you got the park and then there's the road next to it – then parked cars – and we were just by the park entrance and they was giving us some lip.

SW: So are you saying it was them that had started it?

Dean: They were just making fun and it ended up … a fight.

SW: OK, did you know any of the young people in the other group?

Dean: Yeah.

[14] SW: Any history there of aggro between you guys?

Dean: Yeah, aggro (*shrugs, hands up, smiles*). Know what I mean?

SW: Explain to me what you did.

Dean: They started it!

SW: OK. Where were you when this happened?

Dean: There was only a few of us. We all had a go … but it was unfortunate … they all kind of run off and I tripped and hurt my leg. One bloke had his nose broken.

SW: One of your group?

Dean: No, one of theirs.

SW: How did that happen?

Dean: They reckon it was my fault. That's why I'm here, ain't it?

►

◄

SW: Well, I'm interested in your views really.

Dean: They said if they get any of the others, they'd grass up our friends – I wouldn't do that. That's why I'm here.

SW: Had anything else been going on that day that had put you in a bad mood, frame of mind?

Dean: No, I was chilled out until they started being lippy like. Like, whatever, knock 'em out (*indicates fist on hand*).

[15] SW: And had this bloke given you lip before?

Dean: Yeah, always giving us grief. Like one of 'em was seeing my mate's girlfriend.

[16] SW: So there's history there then? So the police came along, they all did a runner, but you got picked up? So what happened then?

Dean: Got took to the police station, they started chatting … then 'the Social' turned up and give me grief.

SW: What, me?!

Dean: No, not you, but my friends and that.

SW: So we've just talked through what happened. We need to talk through some personal questions now, is that alright with you?

Dean nods his head.

SW: You don't mind? Right. (*Talks in a more quiet and gentle tone.*) Where are you currently living?

Dean: Staying at a friend's house.

SW: Staying at a friend's house, and how long have you been there?

Dean: A few weeks.

SW: A few weeks – is that someone you know well?

Dean: Yeah, I've been a school with 'em.

SW: You've been to school with them – a close friend. Do they know your family life? Are they known to your parents as well?

Dean: Yeah. I asked if I could stay there.

SW: Is it a quite busy household? Have you got lots of brothers and sisters?

Dean: A couple.

SW: Do you know if any are involved in any criminal activity at all? (*Dean is quiet and shrugs. Short silence.*) So you're living with these friends now, do you mind me asking where you were living before that?

►

◀

Dean: At home.

SW: At home, with your mum and dad, yeah? So what made you … what happened when you left home?

Dean: Just didn't get on.

SW: And do you still stay in contact with family?

Dean: Every now and then.

SW: Every now and then. So was it their choice or you choice that you move
out?

Dean: They don't like the stuff I do. They can't deal with it.

Practice Example 6.3 further illustrates how the communication skills for the assessment process are influenced by the youth justice context to the work. The model used for gathering information for the assessment is procedural. The social worker takes the role of expert asking the questions that he or she needs to complete the work. Criminal justice terms and jargon are evident throughout the practice example and all over the research transcripts. Communicating with a young person within the youth justice system appears to have some qualitative differences to that of communicating with a young person within the welfare system. This raises a significant ethical dilemma for social workers as the welfare needs of young people in contact with YOTs are significant. For example, our practice example (6.1) identifies Dean as a young person who is homeless and adrift. This entitles him to receive an assessment as a 'child in need', with resultant support services including accommodation under councils' section 20(1) duty of The Children Act 1989 to look after children whose parents or carers cannot accommodate them. The entitlement of welfare support for homeless youths has come under the spotlight with the House of Lords Judgement (2009) on the case R(G) v. London Borough of Southwark, which gave legal clarification concerning the way 16/17-year-olds who are in need of housing and support are managed. However, for the purposes of our discussion about communication here, the criminal justice–orientated context creates pressure for the social worker because the neglect, or separating out, of the welfare issue may inhibit 'tuning-in' and the development of emotional attunement for effective communication.

The first of these main differences in communicating with young people in the youth justice context appears to be that of 'listening for clues'. This involved actively listening for information emerging during the interview that might shed light on the determining or intervening factors giving rise to the offending behaviour. In most cases, the social worker would mentally note that information, and return to it later in the interview or at a subsequent date. In our practice example (6.3), we see that the social worker is *'listening for clues'* about whether Dean was drunk and, therefore, hypothesising whether the drinking of alcohol was a contributing factor in the offence taking place. The questions seek to ascertain how much alcohol Dean consumed at the time (to establish Dean's perspective of the circumstances of the offence) but also how much alcohol Dean regularly consumes (to establish whether alcohol consumption exists as a risk factor to Dean reoffending). The skill of *'listening for clues'* uses *'open questions'* (e.g. 6.3, point 9: 'what classes as a couple of drinks?') and *'closed questions'* (e.g. 6.3, point 10: 'So how were you feeling? 'Cos I think I'd be drunk and wiped out'). These skills are outlined in Chapter 4 as skills for gathering and exploring facts. It is not enough for the social worker to accept the information at face value but explore its relevance to offending. As such, in this practice setting I saw contextual information (either theoretical, or empirical research, or through victim statements) being used to introduce an issue that is likely to be difficult to uncover, such as where the information is embarrassing, or is potentially incriminating. In our practice example (6.3), the social worker uses their knowledge of how alcohol is a frequent antecedent contributory factor to violent offences to explore the circumstances of this alleged offence. She does not use an 'open question' in an indirect manner, such as 'what were you doing at the time?' Rather, she is more focused in the conversation by seeking to ascertain whether the young person had consumed alcohol 'So had you been drinking – you say you'd been smoking?'(6.3, point 7). Thus, we might understand this use of *'open questions'* and *'closed questions'* as *'focused questioning'*.

Another specialist communication skill for this practice setting that is different to that of Chapter 5 in working with children and young people is that of *'assessing for truthfulness'*. The social worker checks information provided by the victim statements and witnesses against what the service user is saying. Also, the social worker checks for quantity of detail in recalling the events (time, place, persons, objects, smells and other sensory information) and consistency of the dialogue taking place at this time. These are some of the common elements of the memory-based approach titled 'Statement Validity Analysis' to evaluate accuracy of accounts (or deceit) in a structured format during interviews with children (Wilson and Powell, 2001). Other elements include whether the child or young person shows motivation to be deceitful, and whether they express empathy or understanding of the motivation or behaviour of the other person. Skills from Chapters 4 and 5 are also important in terms of checking that the non-verbal behaviour is congruent with the verbal assertions. It is important to note that some social workers in the research study stated that they felt uncomfortable in assessing for truthfulness themselves. They stated that they prefer to present a report that states the service user's perspectives. In such instances, the judgement of truthfulness would take place at a subsequent date or event, when all the different sources of information would be compared. A quote from the research transcript illustrates this point:

Social worker 1:   I don't think it's my place to find out the truth. I don't think it's my place to record the discrepancy between the disclosures and what the young person's saying. I wouldn't say which is true. So whoever the report then goes to – the panel or the court – if they want to explore that then they can explore that.

Johanna: Ah, so you are looking for facts – getting the meat on the bones rather than digging around?

Social worker 2:   Rather than questioning the truth of it.

Johanna: So you are saying that questioning the truth doesn't happen in this situation – it happens with someone else; another time; outside the court?

Social worker 3:   Sometimes.

It seems to go without saying that it is important for social workers to have good basic communication skills for gathering facts and *'showing empathy'* (Chapter 4) in order to apply these specialist communication skills for this practice setting. The degree of mistrust of authority and disbelief in the potential of the social worker to be helpful means that the social worker must continually attend to the building of rapport and development of the working relationship throughout the interview. The ability to use non-verbal as well as verbal techniques to demonstrate *'reflective listening'* is central to this success. Body language needs to be 'open' and encourage the gathering of more information through nodding, sitting in a relaxed way (preferably without paper, pen and clipboard) and opening the arms as a way of indicating 'tell me more'. To achieve this it is important to convey *'respect'*, discussed in Chapter 5 and as relevant here in demonstrating acceptance of the young person. This operates the values of unconditional regard and identifying the service user as a person and not 'an object of concern'. Indeed, as the young person relates their account, information may emerge which is potentially distressing or anxiety-provoking for the social worker. Here, it is useful to use, again, the skill of *'expressing empathy and understanding without necessarily signifying agreement'*. Another quote from the research transcript illustrates the operation of these skills:

Social worker 3:	The social worker is establishing a rapport and getting a relationship and he's gathering information, he's getting information from him [the service user] by using humour.
Johanna:	He [the social worker] was moving his head and body side-to-side, was there non-verbal communication?
Social worker 4:	Yeah, he's using his hands quite a lot.
Johanna:	How is he using his hands?
Social worker 4:	He's using his hands like this (*lifts arms up, opens out wide and shakes about*). He's quite animated, he's not just sitting, writing. He's talking like to a person, not just a clipboard getting information, he's actually having a conversation. And by having a conversation he's gathering information. It doesn't feel like he's interviewing. He's actually having a chat.
Social worker 5:	When the service user was talking more freely about the offence, at the park, he was giving more eye contact; then he opened his legs; then he went like that (*opens arms wide*). Then, later, when he started talking about the police, he went like that (*opens up arms wide again … laughs …*).
Johanna:	I guess that is communicating that you are listening…The service user is saying some really quite contentious and dangerous things, and you're accepting what he's saying. Would other people struggle with that complete acceptance and maybe want to express a judgement like 'well you know that's dangerous' to them?

(*Social workers murmur disagreement.*)

The specialist communication skills for working with children and young people from Chapter 5 identify the importance of using a medium of communication that is familiar to the child and is appropriate to their age and stage of cognitive and social development in order to promote understanding of the issues under exploration. Certain types of questions are recommended to be avoided, as children do not have the cognitive ability to process and answer them. These questions tend to start with 'why' and 'how' as opposed to 'what', 'where' and 'when' (Jones, 2003). Young people in contact with YOTs tend to be in their teenage years, and also sensitive to any communication that seems childish or patronising. Yet, this specialist communication skill of *'avoiding the why and how questions'* is equally relevant to them. Indeed, the background literature indicates that young people in contact with YOTs often have developmental delay across all dimensions of child development, but particularly experience difficulties in relation to physical health, emotional/mental health, schooling and learning (HM Probation, 2009). It is unlikely, then, that talking alone is going to be sufficient in ensuring meaningful communication with many of these young people. Rather, use needs to be made of tools that use visual, symbolic and culturally relevant mediums of communication alongside the dialogue, such as drawing, or computer-based questionnaires.

I regard the need for social workers to communicate with young people in this practice setting using language and other mediums of communication that they can understand and utilise themselves as not just a matter of professional skill but a moral enterprise. Social workers are not only *'assessing for truthfulness'* in relation to the young person's version of events concerning the alleged offence, but also using that skill to explore the young person's attitudes and behaviour in relation to victim empathy and the extent of the desire to change their behaviour in response to their remorse. We might refer to this specialist skill as *'assessing for remorse and willingness to reform'*. Misunderstandings in the communication of this skill can have severe consequences for the young person, such as an increase in the severity of sanctions or a limit on the number and type of interventions made available to them. Yet, worryingly, the potential for misunderstandings to occur seems to be high. These issues of 'victim empathy', 'willingness to reform' and 'communicating truthfulness' are 'high-order' concepts that young people, particularly those with cognitive and psychosocial development delay, may find difficult to understand. Often, their own experience of relationships with parents, other family and peers is replete with instances of being rejected, neglected and devalued as a person. They might still be developing their ability to empathise with the emotional pain of another person, particularly if they have developed psychological defences to experiencing emotional pain themselves (Howe, 2005). Indeed, as stated earlier, literature highlights how social workers need to show awareness of the way autism and learning difficulties may affect the presentation of remorse or willingness to reform.

This chapter has described and discussed how the specialist social work communication strategies for youth offending work have some similarities but also differences to those used more widely with children and young people with significant welfare needs. The differences arise from the priority given within the social work role to preventing young people from offending or reoffending, and also the procedural context to the work with many technical concepts applied (reflecting domains of 'Being' and 'Knowing'). Key specialist communication skills involved gaining quick rapport with young people who are often disaffected from society in order to communicate and elicit understanding of the consequences of offending behaviour, and the degree of remorsefulness and willingness to reform ('Doing').

Mapping to the Professional Capability Framework

Qualifying Social Worker Level Capabilities

Please remember that these should be viewed as domains which overlap in an integrative manner rather than as a linear checklist.

'By the end of last placement/ the completion of qualifying programmes newly qualified social workers should have demonstrated the Knowledge, Skills and Values to work with a range of user groups, and the ability to undertake a range of tasks at a foundation level, the capacity to work with more complex situations; they should be able to work more autonomously, whilst recognising that the final decision will still rest with their supervisor; they will seek appropriate support and supervision.   The Health Professions Council (the regulator of qualified social workers) and The College have mapped the Standards of Proficiency for Social Work (SOPs) against the PCF expectations for social work students at the end of their last placement. Whilst there are some differences in the way the standards and PCF are expressed, the overall expectations are the same.'

Communication Capacity Domain – 'Knowing' (engaging with formal and informal knowledge in communication)	PCF 3 Diversity: Recognise diversity and apply anti-discriminatory and anti-oppressive principles in practice ➢ Understand how an individual's identity is informed by factors such as culture, economic status, family composition, life experiences and characteristics, and take account of these to understand their experiences, questioning assumptions where necessary ➢ With reference to current legislative requirements, recognise personal and organisational discrimination and oppression and with guidance make use of a range of approaches to challenge them
	PCF 5 Knowledge: Apply knowledge of social sciences, law and social work practice theory ➢ Demonstrate a critical understanding of the application to social work of research, theory and knowledge from sociology, social policy, psychology and health ➢ Demonstrate a critical understanding of the legal and policy frameworks and guidance that inform and mandate social work practice, recognising the scope for professional judgement ➢ Demonstrate and apply to practice a working knowledge of human growth and development throughout the life course

➢ Recognise the short and long term impact of psychological, socio-economic, environmental and physiological factors on people's lives, taking into account age and development, and how this informs practice

➢ Recognise how systemic approaches can be used to understand the person-in-the-environment and inform your practice

➢ Acknowledge the centrality of relationships for people and the key concepts of attachment, separation, loss, change and resilience

➢ Understand forms of harm and their impact on people, and the implications for practice, drawing on concepts of strength, resilience, vulnerability, risk and resistance, and apply to practice

➢ Demonstrate a critical knowledge of the range of theories and models for social work intervention with individuals, families, groups and communities, and the methods derived from them

➢ Value and take account of the expertise of service users, carers and professionals

KSS Adults (4): Safeguarding
Social workers must be able to recognise the risk indicators of different forms of abuse and neglect and their impact on individuals, their families or their support networks and should prioritise the protection of children and adults in vulnerable situations whenever necessary. This includes working with those who self-neglect. Social workers who work with adults must take an outcomes-focused, person-centred approach to safeguarding practice, recognising that people are experts in their own lives and working alongside them to identify person centred solutions to risk and harm.

KSS Adults (6): Effective Assessments and Outcome Based Support Planning
Social workers should demonstrate a good understanding of personalisation, the social model of disability and of human development throughout life and demonstrate a holistic approach to the identification of needs, circumstances, rights, strengths and risks. In particular, social workers need to understand the impact of trauma, loss and abuse, physical disability, physical ill health, learning disability, mental ill health, mental capacity, substance misuse, domestic abuse, aging and end of life issues on physical, cognitive, emotional and social development both for the individual and for the functioning of the family. They should recognise the roles and needs of informal or family carers and use holistic, systemic approaches to supporting individuals and carers. They should develop and maintain knowledge and good partnerships with local community resources in order to work effectively with individuals in connecting them with appropriate resources and support.

Communication Capacity Domain – 'Doing' (the enactment of communication strategies in interaction)	**PCF 6 Critical Reflection and Analysis: Apply critical reflection and analysis to inform and provide a rationale for professional decision-making**
	➢ Apply imagination, creativity and curiosity to practice
	➢ Inform decision-making through the identification and gathering of information from multiple sources, actively seeking new sources
	➢ With support, rigorously question and evaluate the reliability and validity of information from different sources
	➢ Demonstrate a capacity for logical, systematic, critical and reflective reasoning and apply the theories and techniques of reflective practice
	➢ Know how to formulate, test, evaluate, and review hypotheses in response to information available at the time and apply in practice
	➢ Begin to formulate and make explicit, evidence-informed judgements and justifiable decisions
	KSS Adults (8): Supervision, Critical Reflection and Analysis
	Social workers should be able to make effective use of opportunities to discuss, reflect upon and test multiple hypotheses, the role of intuition and logic in decision making, the difference between opinion and fact, the role of evidence, how to address common bias in situations of uncertainty and the reasoning of any conclusions reached and recommendations made, particularly in relation to mental capacity, mental health and safeguarding situations.
	Social workers should have a critical understanding of the difference between theory, research, evidence and expertise and the role of professional judgement. They should use practice evidence and research to inform the complex judgements and decisions needed to support, empower and protect their service users. They should apply imagination, creativity and curiosity to working in partnership with individuals and their carers, acknowledging the centrality of people's own expertise about their experience and needs.
	KSS Children (2): Communication
	Produce written case notes and reports, which are well argued, focused and jargon free. Present a clear analysis and a sound rationale for actions as well as any conclusions reached, so that all parties are well-informed.
	PCF 7 Intervention and Skills: Use judgement and authority to intervene with individuals, families and communities to promote independence, provide support and prevent harm, neglect and abuse
	➢ Identify and apply a range of verbal, non-verbal and written methods of communication and adapt them in line with peoples' age, comprehension and culture

➤ Be able to communicate information, advice, instruction and professional opinion so as to advocate, influence and persuade
➤ Demonstrate the ability to engage with people, and build, manage, sustain and conclude compassionate and effective relationships
➤ Demonstrate skills in sharing information appropriately and respectfully
➤ Recognise complexity, multiple factors, changing circumstances and uncertainty in people's lives, to be able to prioritise your intervention
➤ Understand the authority of the social work role and begin to use this appropriately as an accountable professional
➤ Recognise the factors that create or exacerbate risk to individuals, their families or carers, to the public or to professionals, including yourself, and contribute to the assessment and management of risk

KSS Adults (3): Person-centred Practice
They should work co-productively and innovatively with people, local communities, other professionals, agencies and services to promote self-determination, community capacity, personal and family reliance, cohesion, earlier intervention and active citizenship.

KSS Adults (4): Safeguarding
Social workers who work with adults must take an outcomes-focused, person-centred approach to safeguarding practice, recognising that people are experts in their own lives and working alongside them to identify person centred solutions to risk and harm. In situations where there is abuse or neglect or clear risk of those, social workers must work in a way that enhances involvement, choice and control as part of improving quality of life, wellbeing and safety.

KSS Adults (7): Direct Work with Individuals and Families
Social workers need to be able to work directly with individuals and their families through the professional use of self, using interpersonal skills and emotional intelligence to create relationships based on openness, transparency and empathy. They should know how to build purposeful, effective relationships underpinned by reciprocity. They should be able to communicate clearly, sensitively and effectively, applying a range of best evidence-based methods of written, oral and non-verbal communication and adapt these methods to match the person's age, comprehension and culture. Social workers should be capable of communicating effectively with people with specific communication needs, including those with learning disabilities, dementia, people who lack mental capacity and people with sensory impairment.

	KSS Children (2): Communication Communicate clearly and sensitively with children of different ages and abilities, their families and in a range of settings and circumstances. Use methods based on best evidence. Create immediate rapport with people not previously known which facilitates engagement and motivation to participate in child protective enquiries, assessments and services. Listen to the views, wishes and feelings of children and families and help parents and carers understand the ways in which their children communicate through their behaviour. Help them to understand how they might communicate more effectively with their children. Promote speech, language and communication support, identifying those children and adults who are experiencing difficulties expressing themselves.
Communication Capacity Domain – 'Being' (the use of 'self')	**PCF 1 Professionalism: Identify and behave as a professional social worker, committed to professional development** ➤ Be able to explain the role of the social worker in a range of contexts, and uphold the reputation of the profession ➤ Demonstrate professionalism in terms of presentation, demeanour, reliability, honesty and respectfulness ➤ Recognise the impact of self in interaction with others, making appropriate use of personal experience ➤ Be able to recognise and maintain personal and professional boundaries ➤ Recognise your professional limitations and how to seek advice ➤ Demonstrate a commitment to your continuing learning and development ➤ With support, take steps to manage and promote own safety, health, wellbeing and emotional resilience **KSS Adults (7): Direct work with individuals and families** Social workers should be capable of communicating effectively with people with specific communication needs, including those with learning disabilities, dementia, people who lack mental capacity and people with sensory impairment. They should do this in ways that are engaging, respectful, motivating and effective, even when dealing with conflict – whether perceived or actual – anger and resistance to change. **KSS Children (2): Communication** Act respectfully even when people are angry, hostile and resistant to change. Manage tensions between parents, carers and family members, in ways that show persistence, determination and professional confidence.

PCF 2 Values and Ethics: Apply social work ethical principles and values to guide professional practice
➤ Recognise and, with support, manage the impact of own values on professional practice
➤ Manage potentially conflicting or competing values, and, with guidance, recognise, reflect on, and work with ethical dilemmas
➤ Demonstrate respectful partnership work with service users and carers, eliciting and respecting their needs and views, and promoting their participation in decision-making wherever possible
➤ Recognise and promote individuals' rights to autonomy and self-determination

KSS Adults (5): Mental Capacity
Social workers must model and lead a change of approach, away from that where the default setting is 'safety first', towards a person-centred culture where individual choice is encouraged and where the right of all individuals to express their own lifestyle choices is recognised and valued.

In working with those where there is no concern over capacity, social workers should take all practicable steps to empower people to make their own decisions, recognising that people are experts in their own lives and working alongside them to identify person-centred solutions to risk and harm, recognising the individual's right to make 'unwise' decisions.

PCF 3 Diversity: Recognise diversity and apply anti-discriminatory and anti-oppressive principles in practice
(Appropriately placed in both 'Knowing' and 'Being')
➤ With reference to current legislative requirements, recognise personal and organisational discrimination and oppression and with guidance make use of a range of approaches to challenge them
➤ Recognise and manage the impact on people of the power invested in your role

KSS Adults (3): Person-centred Practice
They should coordinate and facilitate a wide range of practical and emotional support, and discharge legal duties to complement people's own resources and networks, so that all individuals (no matter their background, health status or mental capacity), carers and families can exercise choice and control, (supporting individuals to make their own decisions, especially where they may lack capacity) and meet their needs and aspirations in personalised, creative and often novel ways. They should work co-productively and innovatively with people, local communities, other professionals, agencies and services to promote self-determination, community capacity, personal and family reliance, cohesion, earlier intervention and active citizenship.

PCF 4 Rights, Justice and Economic Wellbeing: Advance human rights and promote social justice and economic wellbeing
- ➢ Understand, identify and apply in practice the principles of social justice, inclusion and equality
- ➢ Understand how legislation and guidance can advance or constrain people's rights and recognise how the law may be used to protect or advance their rights and entitlements
- ➢ Work within the principles of human and civil rights and equalities legislation, differentiating and beginning to work with absolute, qualified and competing rights and differing needs and perspectives
- ➢ Recognise the impact of poverty and social exclusion and promote enhanced economic status through access to education, work, housing, health services and welfare benefits

PCF 8 Contexts and Organisations: Engage with, inform, and adapt to changing contexts that shape practice. Operate effectively within own organisational frameworks and contribute to the development of services and organisations. Operate effectively within multi-agency and inter-professional partnerships and settings
- ➢ Recognise that social work operates within, and responds to, changing economic, social, political and organisational contexts
- ➢ Understand the roles and responsibilities of social workers in a range of organisations, lines of account-ability and the boundaries of professional autonomy and discretion
- ➢ Understand legal obligations, structures and behaviours within organisations and how these impact on policy, procedure and practice
- ➢ Be able to work within an organisation's remit and contribute to its evaluation and development

KSS Adults (9): Organisational Context
They must understand and work effectively within financial and legal frameworks, obligations, structures and culture, in particular Human Rights and Equalities legislation, the Care Act, Mental Capacity Act, Mental Health Act and accompanying guidance and codes of practice. They must be able to operate successfully in their organisational context, demonstrating effective time management, caseload management and be capable of reconciling competing demands and embrace information, data and technology appropriate to their role. They should have access to regular quality supervision to support their professional resilience and emotional and physical wellbeing.

7

Working with Parents

Summary of Specialist Communication Skills in this Chapter

➢ inquiring deeply and in practical terms about 'what works' in family interaction

➢ identifying a practical response of seeking to overcome the systemic barriers

➢ identifying social worker's personal attitudes and preconceptions of parenting

➢ positive framing of development than using negative deficits notions

➢ demonstrating knowledge of the individual child

➢ identifying, discussing and empathising with systemic barriers with parents.

Policy and background literature

Social work practice with children and their families is 'person-centred' and 'outcomes focused' (HM Government, 2015). Research for the government policy report, *Every Child Matters* (Department for Education and Skills, 2003) stated that all children should have the opportunity to fulfil their potential and grow up in secure, loving families, and set out five key outcomes:

➢ Being Healthy

➢ Staying Safe

➢ Enjoy and Achieve

➢ Making a Positive Contribution

➢ Economic Well being.

Legislation requires social workers to provide services to support parents to deliver these outcomes for their children and thereby safeguard and promote their welfare (The Children Acts 1989 and 2004; Children (Scotland) Act 1995; Children (Northern Ireland) Order, 1995). This is supported by Article 8 of the European Convention on Human Rights – the right to respect for family life.

This suggests that in communicating with parents, social workers should recognise how the legislation confirms that parents should have responsibility for, and a meaningful relationship with their children, with the important proviso that this is safe and in the child's best interests. Indeed, the core overriding principle, set out in the Children Act 1989, is that the child's welfare must be the paramount consideration in decisions concerning the child's upbringing. While the concept of welfare is not defined in the Children Act 1989, the aforementioned 'outcome factors' (as set in the *Every Child Matters* Outcomes Framework and remaining influential in policy) provides a guide, as well as those constituting the 'welfare checklist', which are used to assist a court in its determination of 'welfare':

➢ the ascertainable wishes and feelings of the child – in light of his or her age and understanding;

➢ the physical, emotional and educational needs of the child;

➢ the likely effect of any change on the child's circumstances;

➢ the age, sex, background and any other characteristics which the court considers to be relevant;

➢ any harm which the child has suffered or is at risk of suffering;

➢ how capable the child's parents (and/or any other relevant person) are of meeting the child's needs;

➢ the range of powers available to the court.

Within policy and current literature, parenting is considered to be a relationship which is multiply determined by a constellation of factors which impact and interact on and with each other (Belsky and Vondra 1989; Reder and Lucey, 1995; Department of Health, 2000a; Woodcock, 2003). Importantly, since the introduction of the Assessment Framework (*Working Together to Safeguard Children*, HM Government, 2015), there has been more policy attention given to both safeguarding *and promoting* the developmental welfare of children, where previously practice had centred exclusively upon establishing whether abusive behaviour had, or was likely, to occur (Department of Health, 1995; Department of Health, 2000a; HM Government, 2015). The role for the social worker in using the Framework is to establish and/or support the viability of the family, and indeed the capacity of the parent (in the context of the familial and wider social environment), to meet the needs of a child whose health and development may be impaired, or who is unable to meet a reasonable standard of health and development, or who is disabled. Given this, we should expect communication to focus on improving the parenting relationship, diminishing developmental risk to children and the vulnerability of the family, and seeking to establish protective factors (Rutter, 1985; Cleaver et al., 2011). Crucially, such protection might involve taking immediate safeguarding action by arranging the care of children within other families. Indeed, legislation confers upon social workers the duty to investigate and assess whether a child is at risk of significant harm, or likely to be at risk of significant harm (The Children Act 1989). Social workers have to be sufficiently nuanced in providing parenting support ('care') through identifying and building upon signs of strengths (protective factors) while also maintaining awareness of signs for compulsory protective action ('control').

An added dimension to this balancing of care and control is contained within the new legislative approaches to adult safeguarding (The Care Act 2014 in England, Wales and Northern Ireland; The Social Care (Self-directed support)(Scotland) Act 2013; The Social Services and Well-being (Wales) Act 2014). The legislation contains principles of empowering people to speak out and express informed choices in managing the risk encountered in their lives. Respecting the concepts of both dignity and quality of life, the emphasis is not upon risk avoidance but risk appraisal of the circumstances, history, personal preferences and lifestyle of the person concerned. The aim is not for overprotection but a proportionate response that can tolerate acceptable risks. Government guidance accompanying the Care Act specifies a more joined-up 'whole family approach' by drawing simultaneously upon the provisions of The Children and Families Act 2014 to assess and support families (Department of Health, 2015). A picture must be gained of the whole family context, and how preferred outcomes for one individual's wellbeing might impact positively or deleteriously upon another's. The matter is one of shared service user and professional judgement concerning 'proportionate intervention'. Children, young people and their parents and carers should be central actors in assessment and planning through person-centred processes of co-production, involvement and decision-making (The Children and Families Act 2014 (England, Wales and Northern Ireland)).

Communication within such collaborative practice will necessarily involve considerations of the influence and impact of 'self' upon parenting assessment (Wilson et al., 2011). One key aspect is the influence of the constructions of parenting held by the social worker. Such constructions can act as attitudinal barriers to the communication between a social worker and a parent. Feminist analysts have found social workers operating cultural stereotypes of the role of 'mothers' and 'caring', such as prescriptions to provide sensitive and responsive care regardless of social circumstances (Sheppard, 2000; Turney, 2000). Other research has emphasised how beliefs were influenced by workers' experiences of their own parenting and their own child's development pathways (Daniel, 2000; Holland, 2000; Woodcock, 2003).

Additional dynamics concerning the impact of 'self' can occur between the worker and service user, causing attitudinal communication barriers in parenting assessment. The first relates to the social worker looking for only confirmatory evidence of one, perhaps a favoured, hypothesis to describe the quality of the safeguarding behaviour of the parenting relationship under assessment. Dingwall (1986) first described this as the 'rule of optimism' and located it within practice which can be 'professionally dangerous'. Parton (1991: 55, cited in Kroll and Taylor, 2003) describes it as an approach which 'meant that the most favourable interpretation was put upon the behaviour of the parents and that anything that may question this was discounted or redefined'. He further linked the concept to the two dynamics of 'cultural relativism' and 'natural love'. Cultural relativism in its extreme form refers to professional assumptions that all values and behaviour are culture-specific and that they should only be appraised within the context of a particular culture. There are dangers in adopting this perspective that the values of another culture cannot be applied to another, particularly as regards human rights and the protection of children. One cannot appraise or allow parenting practices in terms of it being 'culturally relevant' to a particular culture, without simultaneously appraising it in the light of whether it is abusive or causes harm to all parties. Laird (2008) highlights the dangers of engaging in processes of cultural relativism when lacking knowledge or expertise in working with families of different ethnic and cultural backgrounds to one's own. Dominant stereotypes and normative assumptions about the cultural practices of people from different ethnic groups might be applied that do not account for individual differences in family forms, religious beliefs, lifestyle choices and outlooks.

In addition, the Peter Connolly tragedy (Laming, 2009) illustrates the relevance of Parton's dynamic called 'natural love'. 'Natural love' refers to the belief that all parents love their children because it is a natural or instinctive phenomenon. Parton says that when this belief is held, it is very difficult for practitioners to challenge it because it represents the origin of human behaviour. In Peter's case, the emphasis of the work was on family support than child protection. Workers gave more attention to evidence of Peter being a child receiving care from a loving mother, than a child whose injuries could potentially have been covered up. Social workers need to remember that not all parents love their children as an instinctual response. Children can hold all kinds of meanings to their parents on conscious and unconscious levels (Reder et al., 1993). For those interested, Kroll and Taylor (2003: 247–250) provide useful application of Parton's three concepts to social work practice with substance-using parents.

Howitt (1992) similarly suggests that social workers assess parental behaviour against societal and attitudinal templates, for example 'reasonable parenting'. He argues that this is a significant element in social work reasoning that can result in 'error-making' in social work decisions. Parton et al. (1997) also identify how social workers use common-sense reasoning devices to make decisions, usually in situations of uncertainty, such as in assessing risk of harm. This would involve clarifying the expected features of parenting in a situation and using the presence or absence of these features to judge the possibility of abuse occurring. In my earlier research on parenting assessment (Woodcock, 2003), I encouraged practitioners to move beyond their 'surface-static' perceptions of parenting behaviour as task-orientated and unchangeable, towards regarding parenting as fluid and variable over time and context due to the influences of social as well as individual factors. This all points to specialist communication capacity to recognise how, as a social worker, you influence the processes and outcome of any parenting assessment.

The literature highlights how social workers can find themselves caught in an aggressive and defensive communication pattern with a parent. Parents express a common concern when they come into contact with services – fear that their children will be 'taken away' (Buchanan and Young, 2002; Taylor and Kroll, 2004). The fear of initiation of child protection procedures can cause some parents to display erratic behaviour such as avoiding contact with social workers. Theorists from an attachment theory perspective (Howe, 2005) and systemic perspective (Reder et al., 1993; Reder and Lucey, 1995; Reder and Duncan, 2001) have proposed that parental difficulties in engagement can reflect long-standing interpersonal difficulties that can be traced back to severe adverse experiences in childhood. Reder and Duncan (1993; 2001) have explored how internal conflicts about care and control persist from childhood and are re-enacted in relationships as adults, including those with social workers. These may take the form of excessive or ambivalent dependency upon other people and sensitivity to feelings of loss even if this is threatened and not real. Another form is sensitivity to feeling controlled, manifested as 'fight or flight'. Indeed, a systems perspective is applied to describe how families operate boundaries along a continuum of 'openness and closedness' depending on the degree to which people within the system are allowed to share information or enter or leave the system. Parents in contact with social workers are often found to find the required changes and adaptations threatening and so closed off contact, whether in a direct way through unavailability, or a less direct way through passive resistance. In contrast, an open system has greater contact with other systems and is more flexible and capable of adapting to change. Thus, social workers are encouraged to consider whether the apparent openness that a parent might be presenting about willingness to change is congruent with actual or possible changes in the family dynamics or whether such openness is really disguised compliance.

The discussion relays the importance of skilled reflective work in the use of 'self'. It requires the social worker to hold back on only reacting to the concrete behaviours and to consider more deeply the thoughts, feelings and behaviours that lie beneath the immediate problem being presented. It not only requires attunement to the thoughts and feelings being enacted, but consideration of the circular patterns of interaction between members of the family and friend network. Different types and sources of evidence may reveal different or congruent contours to the interaction. Each type of evidence will need appraisal as to the accuracy and trustworthiness of the information provided. Knowledge sources should be drawn upon to make sense of the information, and these sources should be both formal (research evidence, theoretical frameworks, policy and practice guidance) as well as informal ('gut feeling', practice wisdom and experience). The reflexive work being described requires a capacity to 'tolerate uncertainty' in the face of risk (Wilson et al., 2011). This refers to a way of holding in mind the various emotional dynamics being played out, critically questioning the revelation of information, and allowing multiple hypotheses for the family's strengths and difficulties to come to the fore. This suggests a communication strategy which deliberately engages the 'use of self' to better understand and explore family dynamics, with regular self-examination about the veracity of the meanings being ascribed.

A way of practising that can 'tolerate uncertainty' and which looks for indications of strengths (protective factors) in the parenting relationship and wider social environment is considered more likely to produce safeguarding solutions which are 'proportionate' than risk-averse. Recently, the 'Signs of Safety' practice model has been proposed as offering one such approach (Bunn, 2013). This model has a solution-focused emphasis, seeking rigorous, sustainable everyday safety solutions in the child's actual home (Turnell and Edwards, 1999; Turnell et al., 2007; Turnell, 2012). It begins with a process of mapping the concrete everyday living circumstances surrounding a vulnerable child, seeking both strength and exploration of danger and risk. The approach seeks not to assert a definitive picture of the processes of risk but to ask probing, rigorous questions attentive to the four domains of worries, strengths, goals and judgement. Key questions to hold in mind when thinking about the situation facing a family are: *What are we worried about? What's working well? What needs to happen?* It involves a communication strategy of 'inquiring deeply and in practical terms about "what works" in family interaction'. Such inquiry is considered to be a motivating mechanism to enable discussion of dysfunctional behaviours and encourage change. The model claims to promote a balanced assessment of risk. Certainly, there have been criticisms raised of practice frameworks which have desisted from identifying deficits to parenting in order to promote strengths and support to families (Department for Children, Schools and Families, 2009). Equally, there are dangers for parenting assessment to become overly focused upon deficits in parenting capacity and for practitioners to be risk-averse. Findings of my earlier research concerning the parental assessment and provision of family support services to parents with children with developmental disabilities identified social workers as one of a number of professionals within a complex interagency network of services that tended to operate a negative deficit approach to their child's needs (Woodcock and Tregaskis, 2008). The parents identified frustration at the continual repetition of the child and family's history of problems. The lack of interaction between professionals was a constant theme, causing a multitude of practical obstacles. This highlights the perceived challenge of the well-informed service user, identifying again how social workers can find themselves caught in an aggressive and defensive communication pattern with a parent. When communicating with parents, social workers need to recognise how these parental feelings and behaviours are coping mechanisms – the result of experiencing structural barriers to their child receiving services, as well as dealing with the personal pain and trauma of their child's disability.

Practice application

The practice example (7.1) begins with a new social worker (Makemba) meeting with Ben and his mother, Maxine, to review whether the services being provided to Ben are promoting and safeguarding his developmental welfare needs. The social worker is seeking to support Maxine and her husband in their parenting of Ben, and where appropriate, offer services to facilitate this further.

The background literature highlighted that a number of societal barriers are likely to impact on the communication processes between the social worker and Maxine (Woodcock and Tregaskis, 2008). Of concern, at the outset, is that these barriers are likely to be located within the social worker himself as attitudes and behaviour (Marchant and Page, 2003). Indeed, in my earlier research of families of disabled children, I identify how social workers need to recognise how their own preconceived notions and cultural experiences shape their view of children's needs, particularly when the child has an impairment (Woodcock and Tregaskis, 2008). Some of the social workers that were described in the study were unprepared or unable to discuss the nature of the impairment, particularly individual differences specific to a child, preferring instead to adopt a generalised application from formal knowledge of the impairment. The social workers were reluctant to open themselves up to hearing parental 'private' (and therefore '*new*') knowledge about the individual characteristics of the impairment, and the individual way it affects family life. The fact that some professionals were either unable or unwilling to do this suggested that the problem lay with the social worker, and that particular communications skills were required to overcome this. A key suggestion was for social workers to purposively engage in a preparatory process of self-reflection to consider how they are bringing these obstacles to the situation.

This suggests that Shulman's (2009) communication skill of '*tuning-in*', as described in Chapter 4, is crucial for the worker to employ before he meets with Maxine. As a process of 'preparatory empathy', it will facilitate the worker to be ready to identify and address the obstacles to work and to be ready to listen and respond to Maxine's expression of feelings and thoughts, however direct or indirectly she expresses them. This preparatory empathy will be important because the background literature highlighted a high emotional content to communication with parents, particularly in relation to feelings of fear and apprehension at the authority role of the social worker in making decisions about parenting. The social worker has legislative duties to safeguard and promote the well-being of individuals, bringing an inevitable underpinning of compulsion or social control to the reason for the meeting. The fear and apprehension at this authority is exacerbated by the aforementioned negative stereotype of social workers as either 'busybodies poking their noses into private affairs', removing children or vulnerable adults from their homes without good evidence, or 'inadequate' by failing to protect children from harsh care-giving. In addition to these feelings of fear, my aforementioned research study of parents of disabled children identified that parents of disabled children often presented strong feelings of pain and frustration which were frequently related to the influence of systemic barriers in their lives (Woodcock and Tregaskis, 2008).

In applying these findings to our practice example (7.1), the social worker needs to prepare himself to discuss and contain such strong feelings, whether of pain and frustration and/or apprehension or fear during their meeting. The important consideration for the social worker is 'How might Maxine demonstrate these feelings?' He needs to consider as many alternatives as possible while ensuring that he is not completely assumptive or deterministic about those feelings when he meets with Maxine. The level of fear, apprehension, frustration and pain indicates that he might expect these feelings to be expressed verbally and non-verbally as ambivalence, resistance and aggression for the work taking place. Certainly the background literature highlights how these feelings emerge when parents are worried and ambivalent about the purpose of the work with a social worker. This reiterates the point made in Chapter 4, that the social worker must engage in a communication strategy which seeks a shared understanding of the purpose of the work and, crucially, how that work is beneficial to the child and parent within their situation. There needs to be an interactive process of introduction and negotiation to achieve a shared agenda for the work to take place. The social worker will need to encourage discussion about the parent and child's agenda and his own agenda and achieve agreement on how the agendas can be brought together in order to specify the purpose and processes for the ongoing work. I described this communication skill in Chapter 4 as *'achieving a shared purpose'*.

Perhaps for this practice setting ('working with parents'), over all others, it cannot be emphasised enough how important, yet difficult, it is to operate the communication skill required to *'achieve a shared purpose'*. First, the background literature highlights the myriad of issues for social workers in seeking a relationship-based approach with parents who may themselves have 'unresolved care and control conflicts', or an internal working model of relationships which is an 'insecure attachment style'. Not least, these relationship dynamics can cause a family to operate as a 'closed system', displaying overt avoidance to the social worker's interaction or covert, passive compliance. Second, the quality of social worker communication is almost certainly influenced by the current social, political and organisational context following the Inquiry Reports of the recent deaths of Victoria Climbie and Peter Connolly (Laming, 2003; Laming, 2009). Media and management scrutiny of individual practice against prescribed performance targets has resulted in increased workloads, increased applications for care orders, greater demand for resources, more time spent on administrative processes in front of a computer than spent interacting with service users and low staff morale among front-line social work staff. The emotional resources required of a social worker to analyse interpersonal communication dynamics and *'show empathy'* to 'hard to reach' parents are arguably harder to access within this context.

Yet, the social worker must recognise the degree to which communication is played out at the level of feeling and engage with it, if a service user is to feel really listened to and understood. As I explored in Chapter 2, rational thoughts are shaped by our emotions, and we often express our thoughts through our feelings (Ruch, 2009). The beginning of the practice example (7.1) illustrates this well.

Practice Example 7.1

Maxine and Ben

Preparatory Stage

Ben is approaching his fourth birthday. A new social worker (Makemba) is meeting Ben and his mother, Maxine, to review whether the services being provided to Ben are promoting and safeguarding his developmental welfare needs. Ben has Down's syndrome, and suffers with related heart problems. The extent of his learning disability is under review by the educational psychologist. The social worker is seeking to support Maxine and her husband in their parenting of Ben, and where appropriate, offer services to facilitate this further. The family are of White British ethnicity. Makemba is a black Zimbabwean man of 40 years, who qualified as a social worker in Zimbabwe and has been a social worker in the Joint Agency Team (JAT) for this authority for the past three years.

Beginnings

(The social worker rings the door bell. Maxine slides the door open.)

[1] Maxine: You've come to do Ben's review, right?

SW: Yes, we haven't met before. My name is Makemba. I have taken over from Janet. I have been a social worker for a few years in JAT, but not had the chance to meet you. Is your husband here too?

Maxine: No, he is working. There are so many meetings for Ben. He can't get to all of them. Come in. Do you want some coffee? Ben, be careful with that! Careful! Good boy. (*Ben crawls over to the doorway and bangs a toy against the door frame*)

SW: No, I'm OK, thank you. Hello, Ben. (*Crouches down to Ben's height and looks in his face. Smiles.*) Ben, I'm Makemba. What's that toy? (*Ben ignores him, turns around and returns to where he was sitting with his toys on the floor. He has a selection of brightly coloured trucks and pre-school educational toys which light up and make sounds. He moves the toys around, picking them up and banging them down. Maxine and Makemba follow Ben into the room and sit down on the sofa and accompanying arm chair*)

Maxine: Quietly, Ben. Quiet. Shush. (*Said in a quiet voice with a finger to her lips*)

[2] SW: He is happy with his toys there, isn't he? (*pause*) I expect it doesn't seem long since Ben's last review? What would you say has changed, or needs to happen within this review of his needs?

[3] Maxine: I just want to make sure that I can get the best for Ben. Of course I'm worried, but I want him to go into mainstream school. It's getting a bit frustrating ... (*silence for 5 seconds*)

▶

◄

[4] SW: Can you tell me a bit more about what your frustrations are and what your worries are?

Maxine: Well, you know, I'm concerned about making sure Ben's, you know, developing OK, but there's so many different services ... and they don't explain things fully ... and a lot of things go over my head and nothing seems to be getting done and it just seems to be getting delayed and delayed.

SW: What do you want to really happen?

Maxine: Nothing's happening.

SW: OK, I mean, what do *you* want to see happen?

Maxine: You know, I can't help worrying because I want to get Ben into mainstream school and at the moment, there's all these services but nothing seems to be happening. You have to put their name down at the school at this age but obviously, I can't ...

SW: And what exactly isn't happening?

Maxine: Well the fact that we're almost July and there's nothing set in stone, there's no structure. It's as though the services aren't following the same structure. I don't mean exactly the same structure because I know they have different reasons, but I still haven't been told whether, you know, the possibility of Ben getting into mainstream school. This has been going on for four or five months now and it just keeps getting delayed and delayed, so at the moment I think, what's the point of the meetings because we're going round and round ... it's a vicious circle!

SW: So what would you like to happen from here? Where would you like it to go?

Maxine: I'd like you to communicate more with each other.

[5] SW: It's natural to be really concerned about your child's development, and it would be really helpful if I spoke to some of the professionals that you've spoken to and see if I can coordinate some of the information that they have got. And I'll get back to you with it.

Maxine: Well that's been tried before. That's what I'm saying, you don't seem to communicate. They are not treated as individual cases, you know, my son is always talked about on the negative side, you know. I know he has certain needs. All children have certain needs. But I'm not getting told anything at all!

[6] SW: So how about if I give you an actual timescale when I would come back and talk to you? You know, next week, we'll actually make another date for a week's time and I'll get as much of that information together. Would that be helpful to you?

Maxine: Yeah, I want to get this sorted.

►

◄

> [7] SW: Then, if there's any gaps then, we can discuss those. We won't leave it for a long time because you are obviously concerned.
>
> Maxine: I don't want it to be left a long time.
>
> [8] SW: Well, I'll book a meeting with you today and I'll come back next Friday and I'll have gathered up as much information as I can and bring it back to you. (*Writes down the agreement in diary in view of Maxine*)

The social worker shows that he has previously *'tuned-in'* to the need to hear and respect parental 'private' knowledge about the individual characteristics of an impairment and the individual way it affects family life. He asks an *'open question'* to ascertain Maxine's perspectives (point 2: *'What would you say has changed, or needs to happen within this review of his needs?'*) Maxine responds by expressing feelings about her concerns for schooling and starts to hint at her negative experience of systemic barriers operating between agencies in respect of this (point 3: *'I just want to make sure that I can get the best for Ben. Of course I'm worried, but I want him to go into mainstream school. It's getting a bit frustrating.'*) The social worker demonstrates empathy for these feelings, perhaps showing that, again, he had previously *'tuned-in'* to the possibility of these feelings emerging during their meeting. The empathy is demonstrated by operating the communication skill described in Chapter 4 of *'putting feelings into words'* in the form of an *'open question'*: (point 4: *'Can you tell me a bit more about what your frustrations are and what your worries are?'*) He demonstrates, in doing so, that he has *'reflectively listened'* to Maxine's communication. Indeed, from this point onwards until point 8, Maxine unfolds more feelings of frustration at the systemic barriers that she is experiencing in obtaining information about Ben's developmental progress and a decision about his schooling.

This section of the dialogue raised two interesting issues for the social workers in the research study who were participating in the enactment of this role play as forum theatre. First, they stated that they felt Maxine's projection of frustration and anger within themselves. Processes of transference are considered useful and inevitable within social work communication with service users as the relationship exposes past experiences of relationships, particularly those relating to receiving help and care. 'Countertransference' has been used as a concept to describe the reaction set off in the worker as a result of being receptive to a service user's transferred feelings (Salzberger-Wittenberg, 1970). The social workers in our study seemed to be describing such processes of 'countertransference', but interestingly, their communication response was to seek to contain the feelings – those of the service user, but also those of themselves. Indeed, their own feelings were around feeling helpless in the face of knowledge deficit, and a desire to reassure and calm Maxine down. 'Containment' is described as an 'active process of struggling to "contain", understand and work through our own emotional responses in the hope that this will enable our clients to do the same for themselves' (Agass, 2002: 127). It is a communicative medium that enables people to feel understood, and in control of their emotional and social selves (Howe, 1998; Agass, 2002; Ruch, 2005b). The following extract from the research transcript describes how the social workers discussed using a practical response of 'getting the missing information' as a way of providing containment for the feelings of frustration being expressed by Maxine and helplessness experienced by themselves.

SW1:   The overriding thing is frustration. That's the thing that comes across. So you need to get at, to address that frustration right from the word 'go' and establish what that is.

SW2:   And establish an agenda. Obviously if she's got a different agenda from the social worker, who is there for a different reason, then you need to somehow deal with that.

SW3:   You could say, 'That's something I can help you with. I could make some enquiries about that possibility', couldn't you?

Johanna: Why would you want to do that? I'm not saying you are wrong. I just want to understand why you felt that was needed?

SW3:   She's so just kind of ... she's getting herself upset ... she's saying nothing is happening and, you know, you haven't got anything to give her, but there is a possibility that I may be able to make enquiries about that situation.

SW4:   I understand that this parent needs more information, but aren't we missing the point? This boy has such a special need that he might need to go to a special school and we're not actually addressing her fears around that.

SW3:   Well when I've gathered the information next week and that identifies that, then that's the discussion to have. But, I don't know that. Maybe she's not willing to offer up that [information] because she doesn't see her child as having a learning disability. She may not have dealt with that obstacle yet. That's my thinking. I've got to do some research on what's been said so far.

Thus, this decision to seek to show containment through operating specialist communication to 'identify a practical response of seeking to overcome the systemic barriers' through obtaining the missing information, essentially provides containment for the social workers' feelings of helplessness as much as the frustration expressed by Maxine. This poses a dilemma. If this skill is based as much on the social worker's felt responses as much as the service user's expressed feelings, then should it be given validity as a specialist communication skill? On the one hand, the skill can be criticised for reinforcing attitudinal barriers of a privileging of formal knowledge and 'professional explanations' over parental 'private' knowledge. Yet, on the other hand, service users told us that they felt more reassured by social workers who sought to overcome systemic barriers, who 'did what they said they would do', and who wrote down their agreed action. The important issue was that the social worker believed the service user, or even identified for themselves that there was a systemic issue causing difficulties in the first place.

The second issue raised by the social workers as part of the research study was that they stated that Maxine seemed to be emphasising schooling and social skills development rather than her relationship with her child. The parents of children with disabilities within my earlier research study were similarly perceived by social work analysts as prioritising their child's acquisition of social skills with peers in order to promote integration and reduce social isolation for their child over and above their relationship with the child (Woodcock and Tregaskis, 2008). The reason for the observation was that social workers, within their parenting assessments, are required to look for indications of prescribed social work dimensions of parenting, particularly those within the national policy document, *Working Together to Safeguard Children* (HM Government, 2015). One key dimension is to ascertain the warmth and reciprocity of the parenting relationship as a way of determining whether and how parents are responding to the developmental needs of their child. In the aforementioned study, I sought to understand why these parents communicated so strongly about aspects of child development. I found that while social workers sought to understand parenting behaviour in social terms, it was not sufficient, as it required the *social model of disability analysis* to recognise the reasons that this was about parental attempts to overcome systemic barriers to their child receiving effective help such as preparation for significant life stages (like going to school).

This discussion reiterates the need for social workers 'to *identify, discuss and empathise with systemic barriers with parents*' as a specialist communication strategy. An example of one such systemic barrier which is cited in this practice example (7.1) is the service failure to take the needs of Ben, Maxine and her husband, as an individual child and family into account, in favour of a 'one-size-fits-all' model. Another barrier alluded to by Maxine, concerned a failure to provide 'joined-up services' for individual needs. These barriers are considered to occur when services are developed primarily to meet the normative needs of the provider, and take insufficient account of the diverse needs of client groups (Barnes, 1991).

The dialogue demonstrates the social worker applying these skills through seeking to *'show empathy'* for the developmental concerns by *'putting feelings into words'*, and then operating the skill of *'identifying a practical response of seeking to overcome the systemic barriers'* by offering to obtain the missing information. (Practice Example 7.1, point 5: *'It's natural to be really concerned about your child's development and it would be really helpful if I spoke to some of the professionals that you've spoken to and see if I can coordinate some of the information that they have got. And I'll get back to you with it.'*)

Maxine responds with disbelief that this practical response will make any difference – perhaps understandably given the degree of difficulties she has faced with systemic barriers. The social worker then repeats the skill at points 6, 7 and 8 to attend to her disbelief and reinforce that he will do this information-gathering work. However, it is the non-verbal communication of actually writing the agreement and a future date in the diary that finally provides the containment for the feelings being expressed (Practice Example 7.1, point 8).

In Practice Example 7.2, the dialogue proceeds with the social worker seeking to simultaneously attend to the agendas required for this practice setting:

I. the need to hear and respect parental 'private' knowledge about the individual characteristics of an impairment and the individual way it affects family life;

II. looking for indications of prescribed social work dimensions of parenting, particularly those within the 'Assessment Framework' in the national policy document, *Working Together to Safeguard Children* (HM Government, 2015);

III. looking for signs of whether and how the child is being protected within his or her practical everyday life, holding in mind the questions: *What are we worried about? What's working well? What needs to happen?*

Practice Example 7.2

Maxine and Ben

Work Phase

[9]SW: You say you are concerned about Ben and different kinds of schools. What are your concerns? I'd like to understand your views on this situation.

[10]Maxine: Well, because all I ever hear from services such as yourself, education, psychology, health, is that I don't know the difference between, you know, an ordinary child, whatever that is, and I'm constantly being told that my child has learning difficulties, you know, disabilities. Now, that's all well and good, but I don't understand the difference with an ordinary child. Why is it being pinned on Ben so much? Is that the reason that nothing is happening, because services are going to actually presume that he won't go into mainstream school because 'oh no, he has a learning difficulty'? That is one thing me and my husband are livid about. I've asked that before. I don't see the need to pinpoint and pigeonhole people, particularly children. That's something I'm beyond frustrated about!

[11]SW: You're fed up with how professionals see Ben, as if he has deficits in different areas … and you don't like this label of disability used about him. *(Maxine looks at Makemba, sits still for about ten seconds and nods.)* So, how do you think Ben is developing at the moment? Is he doing the kinds of things you would expect? Have you got other children …

Maxine: No.

[12]SW: So you haven't got another child to compare...what about at playschool, does he play with other children? Is he talking?

[13]Maxine: Yes, the reports we received … the doctor said that development-wise Ben would be better off in a special educational needs school. But other services said that mainstream school would be OK for one or two times per week. That's what us as a family would really like to do because he is developing … I see him developing … He's probably going to be in a special education school, but I would like him to be in a mainstream school so he interacts. I don't want there to be such a distinction when he gets older; there's no life experience that way.

[14]SW: That's a really good way of doing it. A compromise … *(silence for five seconds)*

[15]SW: You know, you've told me what the professionals think. It's really important for me to hear what it's like for you and your son, you know, your family. What's a day in your life like for you and Ben?

▶

◀

Maxine: Right, OK. Well, my husband goes to work at 8.30 – he goes to work in the city. Then obviously breakfast with Ben, and then he goes to playgroup from 10.30 to 2.45pm.

SW: Do you stay with him, or do you leave him?

Maxine: No, I have stayed in the past but I do stuff at home as well … prepare for when he comes home … if that makes sense.

[16]SW: Gives you a bit of time.

Maxine: Yeah, not in a horrible way …

SW: But a bit of time.

Maxine: Yeah, it's demanding with children anyway.

[17]SW: So, how is he when you leave him at playgroup, does he like it?

Maxine: Yeah, he seems to enjoy it. He interacts well. It's a playgroup with a variety of children anyway – in the developmental process. So, I've stayed there, and I've watched him and played, just me and him, and other children have joined in as well.

[18]SW: Does he like the other children?

Maxine: Yeah, he's very funny. But it's nice because he interacts with children from all walks of life and problems and I think that's lovely … you know, that's probably why I want Ben to have both … not the best of both worlds, but …

SW: Opportunities? (*Maxine nods to this*) What happens at 2.45pm?

Maxine: Well, 2.45pm I go and pick him up and there's a park so we come back and go there, or just come straight home and he does lots of … pasting and things like that – nothing too obviously advanced, just … just lots of things …

[19]SW: Things that he enjoys?

Maxine: Yeah, yeah, yeah.

SW: Do you have a good relationship with him?

Maxine: Yeah, we laugh a lot.

SW: I'm really interested about where you're getting your support from. Do you have family or friends?

Maxine: Don't have many friends, but yeah, family.

SW: Are they supportive?

Maxine: Yeah. I would say so. Also, my husband's very supportive.

SW: What time does your husband get home? I would like to arrange a time when we can all meet.

[20]Maxine: He gets home about 7.

Communicating in a way that attends to this 'shared agenda' seems difficult and highly skilled. The degree of fear and apprehension surrounding the authority role of the social worker means that parents are likely to be alert and vigilant to the possibility of their child's developmental progress being misunderstood. As stated above, my earlier research identified parents describing fear that they were somehow inadvertently caring for their child inappropriately and fearing protective action might be taken (Woodcock and Tregaskis, 2008). In view of this, care needs to be taken to ensure that communication is focused on the individual developmental characteristics and progress of a child as opposed to identifying the general developmental milestones a child is not reaching. Parental resentment and upset at their child not being viewed as a child first with individual needs, but as a child with stereotypical features of a medical impairment is exemplified by Maxine's statement in Practice Example 7.2, point 10:

> Well, because all I ever hear from services such as yourself, education, psychology, health, is that I don't know the difference between, you know, an ordinary child, whatever that is, and I'm constantly being told that my child has learning difficulties, you know, disabilities. Now, that's all well and good but I don't understand the difference with an ordinary child. Why is it being pinned on Ben so much? Is that the reason that nothing is happening, because services are going to actually presume that he won't go into mainstream school because 'oh no, he has a learning difficulty?' That is one thing me and my husband are livid about. I've asked that before. I don't see the need to pinpoint and pigeon-hole people, particularly children. That's something I'm beyond frustrated about!

The social worker demonstrates *'reflective listening'* in responding empathically to this statement by Maxine. In doing so, he uses the basic communication skill described in Chapter 4 of *'summarising'*. (Practice Exercise 7.2, point 11: *'You're fed up with how professionals see Ben, as if he has deficits in different areas ... and you don't like this label of disability used about him.'*) Maxine's non-verbal communication, seen through her body language (sitting still and having eye contact with the social worker) and the resultant silence (possibly thinking and 'working' on the worker's statement), seems to indicate that her feelings about this have been contained. Unfortunately, the social worker ends the silence with a set of statements that do the opposite – he seeks to compare Ben's developmental progress with other children. This comparison approach presents a danger of describing Ben's development in negative terms, i.e. looking for deficits or differences across generalised developmental standards. Maxine's response to this is to return to being defensive. She repeats her desire for Ben's developmental progress to be regarded in individual terms by emphasising the fact that she sees notices small achievements in Ben's developmental progress regardless of expert opinion (Practice Example 7.2, point 13). These statements from Practice Example 7.2, points 11 and 14 are reproduced here:

[11]SW: So, how do you think Ben is developing at the moment? Is he doing the kinds of things you would expect? Have you got other children ...

Maxine: No.

[12]SW: So you haven't got another child to compare ... what about at playschool, does he play with other children? Is he talking?

[13]Maxine: Yes, the reports we received ... the doctor said that development-wise Ben would be better off in a special educational needs school. But other services said that mainstream school would be OK for one or two times per week. That's what us as a family would really like to do because he is developing ... I see him developing ... He's probably going to be in a special education school, but I would like him to be in a mainstream school so he interacts. I don't want there to be such a distinction when he gets older; there's no life experience that way.

[14]SW: That's a really good way of doing it. A compromise ... *(silence for five seconds)*

Thus the dialogue from the practice example and findings from the background literature illustrate how specialist communication capacity to *'positively frame development than using negative deficits notions'* and *'demonstrate knowledge of the individual child'* are clearly of paramount importance here. If this communication is not employed, then social workers are more likely to face strong emotions and opposition from parents. An approach which focuses in forensic detail upon successful rather than problematic, deficit behaviour is more likely to harness depth of response from parents and generate change. This is the aim of solution-focused approaches, such as promoted by the recent 'Signs of Safety' model (Turnell et al., 2007; Turnell, 2012). The communication strategy of 'inquiring deeply and in practical terms about "what works" in family interaction' may have been more useful in achieving the shared agenda to elicit protective factors in the everyday living environment and parenting relationship which diminish developmental risk and increase safety.

So why does the social worker seek to engage Maxine in a comparison of Ben's development with other children at this point? One answer lies in the background literature which tells us that in the face of knowledge deficits, social workers often rely on common-sense reasoning devices (Howitt, 1992; Parton et al., 1997; Woodcock, 2003). For example, Daniel's (2000), Holland's (2000) and Woodcock's (2003) studies emphasised how social work constructions of parenting were influenced by workers' experiences of their own parenting and their own child's development pathways. There are dangers with this. Indeed, Howitt (1992) identifies how in assessing parental behaviour against social and cultural templates, for example 'reasonable parenting', 'error-making' can occur in social work decisions. Parton et al. (1997) describe one such use of common-sense reasoning which could induce 'error-making' – the practice of clarifying the expected features of parenting in a situation and using the presence or absence of these features to judge the possibility of abuse occurring. I found the same practice occurring whereby parenting was assessed against a series of expectations of behaviour in my earlier research of parenting assessment (Woodcock, 2003).

A second answer might be that the social worker is once again responding to the parent's communication of strong feeling through processes of countertransference. Indeed, the social workers involved in the forum theatre for the research study discussed how, at this point in the dialogue, the social worker seemed, once again, to be keen to provide a practical response to contain Maxine's expression of feelings (Practice Example 7.2, point 14: *'That's a really good way of doing it. A compromise.'*) The social workers questioned whether and how this provision of a solution-focused response was appropriate. They were concerned that such a response might be imposing their own opinion onto the service user. In doing so, it might not have felt responsive to individual need. They also wondered whether the solution-focused response might have been used as a cover-up or as an avoidance tactic to sidestep having to deal with a potentially uncomfortable and difficult discussion concerning access to normative services. In so doing, the social worker could be construed as operating another dynamic that was identified in the background literature as potentially occurring between a social worker and service user in parenting assessment – the 'rule of optimism' (Dingwall, 1986; Parton, 1991). Prins (1999) described this dynamic in terms of a wish to see things moving forward, or improving, despite any evidence to suggest this is happening. Certainly the social worker is quick to apply a solution-focused response because it is deemed 'more acceptable' to the service user. There are dangers in this, for while the social worker might feel reassured that they have achieved a degree of engagement with the parent, the more difficult work of uncovering and challenging difficult feelings and decisions remains undone. The following extract from the research transcript illustrates these points:

Johanna: Why did you say 'it's a really good compromise'?

SW1:   I suppose because I just thought we hadn't heard the special needs bit before and that it might be a good place to start, I suppose ...

SW2:   But was that 'a really good compromise' from your point of view or her point of view?

SW1:   I don't know.

SW3:   But she seemed happy with it, like that was something she would agree to. She wasn't saying 'I don't want this.' She was sort of saying 'I've had this suggested to me ...'

SW2:   It just seems like its this classic thing that I sometimes do [where] it's a tricky situation and I'm out of my depth with knowledge ... which doesn't take very long! ... and I see a bit of an escape route and I think 'Oh this sounds really good.' I'm a bit of a Mr Fixit, so ... bang! I come in with a solution. It did sound a bit prescriptive, but, I mean, it's the sort of thing I do myself, that's why I recognise it. But I'm not sure whether it's what she wanted.

In summarising this set of points, the background literature and research transcript emphasises the degree to which a social worker influences the processes and outcomes of any parenting assessment. Thus a specialist communication skill which must be employed is that of *'identifying social worker's personal attitudes and preconceptions of parenting'*. The following questions might enable a social worker in fulfilling this:

➤ Am I operating a set of cultural and societal expectations about parenting behaviour?

➤ Am I viewing parenting as a relationship which is multiply determined and holistic?

➤ Am I viewing parenting in terms of promoting children's developmental welfare needs, and not just whether abuse and maltreatment is occurring?

➤ Am I seeking to support parenting as a means of safeguarding practice?

➤ Which of the factors influencing my judgements are to do with what's going on inside of me – the influence of my 'self'?

Point 15 of Practice Example 7.2 is a critical moment as the social worker recognises that he has fixated on his own agenda and concerns. He appears to recognise that work is not occurring between himself and Maxine, but rather it is, as Shulman puts it, 'the illusion of work'. Having recognised the illusion of work, he seeks to operate the skill of *'achieving a shared purpose'* once again (*'You know, you've told me what the professionals think. It's really important for me to hear what it's like for you and your son, you know, your family. What's a day in your life like for you and Ben?'*) This *'open question'* seeks elaboration, and again emphasises that he is prepared to hear and respect parental 'private' knowledge about the individual characteristics of an impairment and the individual way it affects family life. The rest of the dialogue demonstrates *'reflective listening'* through empathising with feelings (Practice Example 7.2, point 16: *'Gives you a bit of time.'*), but also, as importantly, by using *'open questions'* to ask for information about Ben's personality and individual response which is framed in positive language (Practice Example 7.2, point 17: *'How is he when you leave him at playgroup, does he like it?'*; point 18: *'Does he like the other children?'*; point 19: *'Things that he enjoys?'*). This again illustrates the importance of operating specialist communication skills of *'positive framing of development than using negative deficits notions'* and *'demonstrating knowledge of the individual child'*.

Conceptual ideas from systemic family therapy have been highlighted for work with families to make sense of the interconnections between parental problems, parenting, child wellbeing and other social factors in the familial environment. Kroll and Taylor (2003) particularly emphasise the usefulness of the systemic framework as a way of viewing how substance use operates as a part of the family system and impacts on everyone else. They recommend the use of genograms and ecomaps as visual, symbolic tools to gain information about the world of families as experienced by the different family members. Arguably, such an approach would work well with families with disabled children. *'Open questions'* and *'closed questions'* would need to draw out the quality of the relationship between the parent and child but also the relationship between each of them and the multitude of other social factors which coexist and interrelate with them. The systemic barriers experienced by parents would become easily identifiable, and it would be easier to operate the aforementioned specialist communication skill of *'identifying, discussing and empathising with systemic barriers with parents'*.

In summary, the specialist social work communication identified in this chapter has addressed the potential for misunderstanding and error-making in making judgements about parenting that emanate from within the 'self' and cultural and societal normative expectations of parenting ('Being'). Systemic barriers must be identified and communicated about ('Knowing' and 'Doing'). Second, the chapter has emphasised how important, yet difficult, it is to operate the specialist social work communication skills required to *'achieve a shared purpose'* with 'hard to reach' parents ('Doing'). Significant emotional resources are required of a social worker to analyse interpersonal communication dynamics and *'show empathy'* within this context ('Being' and 'Doing').

Mapping to the Professional Capability Framework and Knowledge and Skills Statements (KSS) for Adults and Children

Qualifying Social Worker Level Capabilities

Please remember that these should be viewed as domains which overlap in an integrative manner rather than as a linear checklist.

'By the end of last placement/ the completion of qualifying programmes newly qualified social workers should have demonstrated the Knowledge, Skills and Values to work with a range of user groups, and the ability to undertake a range of tasks at a foundation level, the capacity to work with more complex situations; they should be able to work more autonomously, whilst recognising that the final decision will still rest with their supervisor; they will seek appropriate support and supervision.
The Health Professions Council (the regulator of qualified social workers) and The College have mapped the Standards of Proficiency for Social Work (SOPs) against the PCF expectations for social work students at the end of their last placement. Whilst there are some differences in the way the standards and PCF are expressed, the overall expectations are the same.'

Communication Capacity Domain – 'Knowing' (engaging with formal and informal knowledge in communication)	**PCF 3 Diversity: Recognise diversity and apply anti-discriminatory and anti-oppressive principles in practice** ➢ Understand how an individual's identity is informed by factors such as culture, economic status, family composition, life experiences and characteristics, and take account of these to understand their experiences, questioning assumptions where necessary ➢ With reference to current legislative requirements, recognise personal and organisational discrimination and oppression and with guidance make use of a range of approaches to challenge them
	PCF 5 Knowledge: Apply knowledge of social sciences, law and social work practice theory ➢ Demonstrate a critical understanding of the application to social work of research, theory and knowledge from sociology, social policy, psychology and health ➢ Demonstrate a critical understanding of the legal and policy frameworks and guidance that inform and mandate social work practice, recognising the scope for professional judgement ➢ Demonstrate and apply to practice a working knowledge of human growth and development throughout the life course ➢ Recognise the short and long term impact of psychological, socio-economic, environmental and physiological factors on people's lives, taking into account age and development, and how this informs practice

| | ➢ Recognise how systemic approaches can be used to understand the person-in-the-environment and inform your practice
➢ Acknowledge the centrality of relationships for people and the key concepts of attachment, separation, loss, change and resilience
➢ Understand forms of harm and their impact on people, and the implications for practice, drawing on concepts of strength, resilience, vulnerability, risk and resistance, and apply to practice
➢ Demonstrate a critical knowledge of the range of theories and models for social work intervention with individuals, families, groups and communities, and the methods derived from them
➢ Value and take account of the expertise of service users, carers and professionals

KSS Adults (4): Safeguarding
Social workers must be able to recognise the risk indicators of different forms of abuse and neglect and their impact on individuals, their families or their support networks and should prioritise the protection of children and adults in vulnerable situations whenever necessary. This includes working with those who self-neglect. Social workers who work with adults must take an outcomes-focused, person-centred approach to safeguarding practice, recognising that people are experts in their own lives and working alongside them to identify person centred solutions to risk and harm.

KSS Adults (6): Effective Assessments and Outcome Based Support Planning
Social workers should demonstrate a good understanding of personalisation, the social model of disability and of human development throughout life and demonstrate a holistic approach to the identification of needs, circumstances, rights, strengths and risks. In particular, social workers need to understand the impact of trauma, loss and abuse, physical disability, physical ill health, learning disability, mental ill health, mental capacity, substance misuse, domestic abuse, aging and end of life issues on physical, cognitive, emotional and social development both for the individual and for the functioning of the family. They should recognise the roles and needs of informal or family carers and use holistic, systemic approaches to supporting individuals and carers. They should develop and maintain knowledge and good partnerships with local community resources in order to work effectively with individuals in connecting them with appropriate resources and support. |
| **Communication Capacity Domain – 'Doing'**
(the enactment of communication strategies in interaction) | **PCF 6 Critical Reflection and Analysis: Apply critical reflection and analysis to inform and provide a rationale for professional decision-making**
➢ Apply imagination, creativity and curiosity to practice
➢ Inform decision-making through the identification and gathering of information from multiple sources, actively seeking new sources
➢ With support, rigorously question and evaluate the reliability and validity of information from different sources
➢ Demonstrate a capacity for logical, systematic, critical and reflective reasoning and apply the theories and techniques of reflective practice |

➤ Know how to formulate, test, evaluate, and review hypotheses in response to information available at the time and apply in practice
➤ Begin to formulate and make explicit, evidence-informed judgements and justifiable decisions

KSS Adults (8): Supervision, Critical Reflection and Analysis
Social workers should be able to make effective use of opportunities to discuss, reflect upon and test multiple hypotheses, the role of intuition and logic in decision making, the difference between opinion and fact, the role of evidence, how to address common bias in situations of uncertainty and the reasoning of any conclusions reached and recommendations made, particularly in relation to mental capacity, mental health and safeguarding situations.

Social workers should have a critical understanding of the difference between theory, research, evidence and expertise and the role of professional judgement. They should use practice evidence and research to inform the complex judgements and decisions needed to support, empower and protect their service users. They should apply imagination, creativity and curiosity to working in partnership with individuals and their carers, acknowledging the centrality of people's own expertise about their experience and needs.

KSS Children (2): Communication
Produce written case notes and reports, which are well argued, focused and jargon free. Present a clear analysis and a sound rationale for actions as well as any conclusions reached, so that all parties are well-informed.

PCF 7 Intervention and Skills: Use judgement and authority to intervene with individuals, families and communities to promote independence, provide support and prevent harm, neglect and abuse
➤ Identify and apply a range of verbal, non-verbal and written methods of communication and adapt them in line with peoples' age, comprehension and culture
➤ Be able to communicate information, advice, instruction and professional opinion so as to advocate, influence and persuade
➤ Demonstrate the ability to engage with people, and build, manage, sustain and conclude compassionate and effective relationships
➤ Demonstrate skills in sharing information appropriately and respectfully
➤ Recognise complexity, multiple factors, changing circumstances and uncertainty in people's lives, to be able to prioritise your intervention
➤ Understand the authority of the social work role and begin to use this appropriately as an accountable professional
➤ Recognise the factors that create or exacerbate risk to individuals, their families or carers, to the public or to professionals, including yourself, and contribute to the assessment and management of risk

KSS Adults (3): Person-centred Practice

They should work co-productively and innovatively with people, local communities, other professionals, agencies and services to promote self- determination, community capacity, personal and family reliance, cohesion, earlier intervention and active citizenship.

KSS Adults (4): Safeguarding

Social workers who work with adults must take an outcomes-focused, person-centred approach to safeguarding practice, recognising that people are experts in their own lives and working alongside them to identify person centred solutions to risk and harm. In situations where there is abuse or neglect or clear risk of those, social workers must work in a way that enhances involvement, choice and control as part of improving quality of life, wellbeing and safety.

KSS Adults (7): Direct Work with Individuals and Families

Social workers need to be able to work directly with individuals and their families through the professional use of self, using interpersonal skills and emotional intelligence to create relationships based on openness, transparency and empathy. They should know how to build purposeful, effective relationships underpinned by reciprocity. They should be able to communicate clearly, sensitively and effectively, applying a range of best evidence-based methods of written, oral and non-verbal communication and adapt these methods to match the person's age, comprehension and culture. Social workers should be capable of communicating effectively with people with specific communication needs, including those with learning disabilities, dementia, people who lack mental capacity and people with sensory impairment.

KSS Children (2): Communication

Communicate clearly and sensitively with children of different ages and abilities, their families and in a range of settings and circumstances.
Use methods based on best evidence.
Create immediate rapport with people not previously known which facilitates engagement and motivation to participate in child protective enquiries, assessments and services.
Listen to the views, wishes and feelings of children and families and help parents and carers understand the ways in which their children communicate through their behaviour. Help them to understand how they might communicate more effectively with their children.
Promote speech, language and communication support, identifying those children and adults who are experiencing difficulties expressing themselves.

| Communication Capacity Domain – 'Being' (the use of 'self') | **PCF 1 Professionalism: Identify and behave as a professional social worker, committed to professional development**
➢ Be able to explain the role of the social worker in a range of contexts, and uphold the reputation of the profession
➢ Demonstrate professionalism in terms of presentation, demeanour, reliability, honesty and respectfulness
➢ Recognise the impact of self in interaction with others, making appropriate use of personal experience
➢ Be able to recognise and maintain personal and professional boundaries
➢ Recognise your professional limitations and how to seek advice
➢ Demonstrate a commitment to your continuing learning and development
➢ With support, take steps to manage and promote own safety, health, wellbeing and emotional resilience

KSS Adults (7): Direct work with individuals and families
Social workers should be capable of communicating effectively with people with specific communication needs, including those with learning disabilities, dementia, people who lack mental capacity and people with sensory impairment. They should do this in ways that are engaging, respectful, motivating and effective, even when dealing with conflict – whether perceived or actual – anger and resistance to change.

KSS Children (2): Communication
Act respectfully even when people are angry, hostile and resistant to change. Manage tensions between parents, carers and family members, in ways that show persistence, determination and professional confidence. |
| | **PCF 2 Values and Ethics: Apply social work ethical principles and values to guide professional practice**
➢ Recognise and, with support, manage the impact of own values on professional practice
➢ Manage potentially conflicting or competing values, and, with guidance, recognise, reflect on, and work with ethical dilemmas
➢ Demonstrate respectful partnership work with service users and carers, eliciting and respecting their needs and views, and promoting their participation in decision-making wherever possible
➢ Recognise and promote individuals' rights to autonomy and self-determination

KSS Adults (5): Mental Capacity
Social workers must model and lead a change of approach, away from that where the default setting is "safety first", towards a person-centred culture where individual choice is encouraged and where the right of all individuals to express their own lifestyle choices is recognised and valued. |

In working with those where there is no concern over capacity, social workers should take all practicable steps to empower people to make their own decisions, recognising that people are experts in their own lives and working alongside them to identify person-centred solutions to risk and harm, recognising the individual's right to make 'unwise' decisions.

PCF 3 Diversity: Recognise diversity and apply anti-discriminatory and anti-oppressive principles in practice
(Appropriately placed in both 'Knowing' and 'Being')
➢ With reference to current legislative requirements, recognise personal and organisational discrimination and oppression and with guidance make use of a range of approaches to challenge them
➢ Recognise and manage the impact on people of the power invested in your role

KSS Adults (3): Person-centred Practice
They should coordinate and facilitate a wide range of practical and emotional support, and discharge legal duties to complement people's own resources and networks, so that all individuals (no matter their background, health status or mental capacity), carers and families can exercise choice and control, (supporting individuals to make their own decisions, especially where they may lack capacity) and meet their needs and aspirations in personalised, creative and often novel ways. They should work co-productively and innovatively with people, local communities, other professionals, agencies and services to promote self-determination, community capacity, personal and family reliance, cohesion, earlier intervention and active citizenship.

PCF 4 Rights, Justice and Economic Wellbeing: Advance human rights and promote social justice and economic wellbeing
➢ Understand, identify and apply in practice the principles of social justice, inclusion and equality
➢ Understand how legislation and guidance can advance or constrain people's rights and recognise how the law may be used to protect or advance their rights and entitlements
➢ Work within the principles of human and civil rights and equalities legislation, differentiating and beginning to work with absolute, qualified and competing rights and differing needs and perspectives
➢ Recognise the impact of poverty and social exclusion and promote enhanced economic status through access to education, work, housing, health services and welfare benefits

PCF 8 Contexts and Organisations: Engage with, inform, and adapt to changing contexts that shape practice. Operate effectively within own organisational frameworks and contribute to the development of services and organisations. Operate effectively within multi-agency and inter-professional partnerships and settings
➢ Recognise that social work operates within, and responds to, changing economic, social, political and organisational contexts

> Understand the roles and responsibilities of social workers in a range of organisations, lines of accountability and the boundaries of professional autonomy and discretion
> Understand legal obligations, structures and behaviours within organisations and how these impact on policy, procedure and practice
> Be able to work within an organisation's remit and contribute to its evaluation and development

KSS Adults (9): Organisational Context
They must understand and work effectively within financial and legal frameworks, obligations, structures and culture, in particular Human Rights and Equalities legislation, the Care Act, Mental Capacity Act, Mental Health Act and accompanying guidance and codes of practice. They must be able to operate successfully in their organisational context, demonstrating effective time management, caseload management and be capable of reconciling competing demands and embrace information, data and technology appropriate to their role. They should have access to regular quality supervision to support their professional resilience and emotional and physical wellbeing.

8

Working with People with Problematic Substance Use

Summary of Specialist Communication Skills in this Chapter

➢ tuning in to social worker's personal attitudes and preconceptions of people who use substances

➢ identify social worker's personal attitudes and preconceptions of parenting

➢ enter the world of substance-using families

➢ make the child visible

➢ addressing service user fears of stigmatisation

➢ avoid exhortations to change

➢ motivate service users to decide to make changes, including components of:
  ➢ provide affirmation
  ➢ encourage service user recognition of the divergence between their values or goals and the reality of their current behaviour
  ➢ provide all options to encourage feelings of self-efficacy.

Policy and background literature

Recent clarity has been given to the roles and associated capabilities of social workers for knowing what to do in supporting individuals and families negatively affected by substance use (Galvani, 2015). A development group of leading social work organisations in England has specified the three key roles as (Galvani, 2015: 7):

1. To engage with the topic of substance use as part of their duty of care to support their service users, their families and dependents.

2. To motivate people to consider changing their problematic substance-using behaviour and support them (and their families and carers) in their efforts to do so.

3. To support people in their efforts to make and maintain changes in their substance use.

The capabilities for fulfilling these social work roles have been cross-referenced to social work's Professional Capabilities Framework (PCF). This is in terms of capability within and across the domains of capability, but also in terms of level of developing capability, with knowledge and skill accumulating as experience increases (see Galvani, 2015 for more detail of the mapping). The need for professionals to 'promote effective communication for and about individuals' (Drug and Alcohol National Occupational Standards (DANOS), 2012) is considered to be core within each of the roles. Social workers in Scotland are encouraged to consider the cross-mapping in relation to the document 'Supporting the development of Scotland's Alcohol and Drug Workforce'.

The social work key roles (Galvani, 2015) emphasise that the topic of substance use should be actively engaged with during communication. The Drug and Alcohol National Occupational Standards (DANOS, 2012) highlight that such 'engaged communication' should be about the use and its associated risks at a time, level and pace appropriate to the individual in order to maximise the likelihood of the individual understanding it. Guidance, support and advice should be given to service users on ways in which methods of substance use and activities affected by it can be practised more safely.

People who use substances often have poor self-image, very negative outlooks on life and find little things overwhelming. Physical addiction is only part of the problem, and difficult to entangle from emotional, psychological and social elements (Kroll and Taylor, 2003; Forrester and Harwin, 2011). Indeed, it is important for social workers working with substance users to recognise the social factors that are contained within the aetiology, progression and maintenance of substance use. These concern developmental issues, effects of stress and role of social support, peer group and other cultural influences, social exclusion and cultural stereotypes, prevention and treatment models (Skills for Care and Development, 2008).

When I was undertaking the work of identifying how these themes from within the literature related to specialist communication skills, I found many to be relevant, but two key issues were particularly significant. These concerned: (i) the degree of stigmatisation and (ii) the levels of secrecy and denial involved in substance use.

It is considered critical to understand how processes of 'denial' influence understanding of levels and the impact of substance use upon wellbeing and also influence the dynamics of the working relationship with a service user (Taylor, 1999). Denial is considered to come out from conflicted emotions between the desire to continue to be emotionally connected or 'attached' to a substance and the distress resulting from the behaviour and other consequences caused by the substance (Orford, 2001). If the conflicting emotions cannot be resolved, then confusion, panic and despair will set in (Taylor, 1999). Thus the psychological operation of denial comes in to prevent the conflicting emotions coming to the surface. Orford (2001) also points out how processes of denial operate in not just an internal way, but also through an increased secrecy about the behaviour externally, such as within relationships with friends, family and support workers. As Kroll and Taylor (2003: 96) summarise, 'denial is a natural and self-protective response to pain', which when employed as a survival strategy resists demands to change. Unfortunately, in maintaining levels of secrecy and denial, other significant relationships become ignored, with family members and particularly dependent children rendered 'invisible' (Kroll and Taylor, 2003). Continual relationship breakdown is a common feature and one which is likely to impact upon the communication processes within the relationship with the social worker (Woodcock and Sheppard, 2002; Galvani and Forrester, 2011).

Social workers' professional judgements concerning problematic substance use can be influenced by personal attitudes and negative cultural stereotypes based on 'moral panics' (Forrester and Harwin, 2004; Forrester and Harwin, 2011). There is considerable stigma accorded to people who have problems using drugs and alcohol, resulting in marginalisation from society. The stigma exists despite the reality of drug use embracing legal as well as illegal activity, including recreational drug use, experimental drug use and prescribed drug use. Substance or chemical use is a feature of everyday life for most people. Alcohol is a frequent part of celebrations or relaxation, and many people take prescribed or unprescribed drugs for medical conditions. In any of these situations, a person could lose control over their substance use, creating a number of risks to their health and safety, and that of their friends and family (Paylor, 2008; Paylor et al., 2012). The terminology used by practitioners about substance use can reflect such personal, cultural and practice-derived preconceptions. Galvani (2012) identifies how there have been changes in the substance use field in regard to terminology, with a recent favouring of 'recovery concepts' from policy. Similarly, in relation to alcohol consumption, there is a preference for the idea of levels of risk to all individuals consuming alcohol than identifying hazardous, harmful and dependent behaviours. When viewed from a more social model, terms are used such as 'problematic substance use' or 'substance problem' or 'intervention' than the medical conceptualisation of 'alcoholic' and 'drug addict' and 'treatment'. Thus, for Galvani, an important aspect of skilled communication is for social workers to reflect upon their language-in-use, both in terms of the way it is expressed and the meanings behind it. Her point highlights the importance for specialist communication of attention to anti-oppressive practice involving reflexive consideration of personal and professional values and beliefs.

Literature highlights the importance of achieving an empowering relationship in which the social worker shows willingness to listen, to actively engage with the topic of substance use, and not judge (Galvani, 2015). It is within this supportive relational context that a social worker can encourage processes of change in substance-misusing behaviour (Prochaska and DiClemente,1983; Prochaska et al., 1992; Velleman, 2001; Barber, 2002; Kroll and Taylor, 2003). As an example, Velleman's process of 'enabling change' has six stages: 'developing trust'; 'exploring the problem'; 'helping clients to set goals'; 'empowering clients to take action'; 'helping them to maintain changes'; and 'agreeing with them when the time comes to end the counselling relationship'. DiClemente and Velasquez's (2002) model of change describes five key motivational stages that are often represented as a turning circle to indicate how a person may not pass through the stages in a particular order. These stages comprise: Precontemplation, Contemplation, Preparation, Action and Maintenance. Barber (2002) notes in operating the Prochaska and DiClemente (1983) model that workers must treat the individual with respect, take time and not be judgemental – 'not beating over the head with "you must change". Communication with 'precontemplators' of change will focus on reducing the value of substance use. If ambivalence or desire to change is evident, then the focus of communication should change as the service user is within the 'contemplation' stage. Communication skills will be directed at eliciting individual decision-making. The social worker's role in supporting the change process does not end at 'contemplation', but is equally about supporting the maintenance of the change in the short, medium and long term. As Galvani (2015) highlights, people recovering from problematic substance use often cite 'maintenance' as the most challenging part. It involves learning new coping skills, new everyday routines and new ways of relating to people within (often) new social networks. Previously fractured relationships with friends and family often have to be strengthened and trust rebuilt. Social work communication should focus upon providing encouragement and signalling past successful strategies and strengths. Probably it will also involve communication with other professionals to advocate for connections to health, employment and education services. It could also include challenging potential stigmatising assumptions that may be occluding access.

When turning to the literature concerning parental substance use, I identified a number of practice dilemmas relevant to specialist communication. First, professional and cultural preconceptions exist about parental substance use, such as assuming that all parents who use drugs or alcohol will be a danger to their children (Cleaver et al., 1999; Cleaver et al., 2011). Substance-using parents do not constitute a homogenous group (Taylor and Kroll, 2004). Many parents use alcohol and chemical substances and parent effectively (SCODA, 1997; Harbin and Murphy, 2000; Buchanan and Young, 2002). However, there is an increasing body of evidence that parental substance use is linked to problems in child development and child maltreatment (Cleaver et al., 1999; Cleaver et al., 2011; ACMD, 2003).

Second, the organisational context has been found to impact upon effectiveness in assessing and treating parental substance misuse. This occurs despite all agencies who engage substance-using parents being given a duty from the Children Acts (1989 and 2004 in England and Wales, and 1995 in Scotland) to assess the needs of children whose health and development may be at risk of being harmed. This duty was emphasised by the policy initiative 'Hidden Harm' (Scottish Executive, 2004). Historically, problem substance use and child protection systems have developed separately and with different orientations, which have caused barriers for collaborative working (Taylor and Kroll, 2004). An organisational orientation towards child welfare has tended to prioritise children's safeguarding needs over parental needs. In contrast, substance users have tended to be viewed as the primary focus of intervention if the professional orientation is substance use treatment (Taylor and Kroll, 2004). The separation of organisational systems and orientations has meant that social workers, in general, lack training and confidence in working with combined issues of substance use and parenting (Forrester and Harwin, 2004; Paylor, 2008).

Third, drug users have been found to express a common concern when they come into contact with services – fear that their children will be 'taken away' (Buchanan and Young, 2002; Taylor and Kroll, 2004). The fear of initiation of child protection procedures can cause some parents to display erratic behaviour such as avoiding contact with social workers. Taylor and Kroll (2004) identified that many of the difficulties that professionals faced in gaining trust to achieve authentic information about lifestyle centred on secrecy and denial. Fear about how the agency might act on disclosed information caused parents to deny the reality of the impact of their substance use on their child, as well as failing to sustain engagement.

Finally, social work perceptions about parental substance use are inevitably influenced by perceptions of parenting more generally. Literature has focused on the influence of the constructions of parenting held by social workers themselves (Daniel, 2000; Holland, 2000; Woodcock, 2003). Feminist analyses have identified how workers make judgements about the role of 'mothers' and 'caring' resulting in the phenomenon of 'mother-blaming' (Turney, 2000). The interactive dynamic between the worker and the service user is also given attention by theoretical considerations of 'reflexivity' (Sheppard, 1998). Reflexivity exemplifies that parenting assessment is not just a technical activity but involves various underlying factors that influence practice, including beliefs and values about what is 'good enough' or 'not good enough'. Daniel's (2000) study particularly emphasised how beliefs were influenced by workers' experiences of their own parenting and their own child's development pathways. Howitt (1992) similarly suggested that workers assess parental behaviour against social templates (for example 'reasonable parenting') resulting in 'error making' in social work decisions. Some of my own earlier research (Woodcock, 2003) confirmed that of Parton et al. (1997) in finding social workers using common-sense reasoning devices to make decisions, usually in situations of uncertainty, such as in assessing risk of harm. In my research study this involved clarifying the expected features of parenting in a situation and using the presence or absence of these features to judge the possibility of abuse occurring. Clearly, if any social worker leaves his or her personal attitudes about parenting unexamined, then he or she may reinforce the marginalisation already experienced by service users.

Practice application

Practice Examples 8.1 and 8.2 focus on the communication between a social worker (Iona) and two substance-using parents, Karen and John.

Practice Example 8.1

The Collins-Evans Family

Preparatory stage

Yesterday, John Collins (28 years old) and Karen Evans (25 years old), both describing themselves as 'white Welsh' ethnic origin, received a telephone call from a social worker from the city's Children's Services (Local Authority) to arrange an appointment to visit them and their three children: Caris (8 years), Natasha (5) and Josh (18 months). A teacher from the children's school had contacted the social work team with a number of concerns about the wellbeing of Caris and Natasha. These included: the children being frequently late for school; the children being overtired with poor concentration; the eldest child (Caris) being quiet and withdrawn, and overly mature

▶

◀

for her years such that she appears to parent Natasha. Two parents have told Caris's teacher, in confidence, that their father has a drug addiction which is out of control, and their mother has approached them for money to meet the household bills. The social worker wants to meet with the whole family as part of her initial assessment of the children's safety and wellbeing.

The family live in a recently built local authority housing estate, located in a socially deprived area of a medium-sized city in the UK. The general practitioner notes that Karen has a history of depression and that she received advice about the dangers of alcohol consumption during her pregnancy with Josh. The couple's relationship has broken down on a number of occasions in the past. Karen has a strained relationship with her mother who lives locally. Her mother looks after the children for one evening per week to give Karen a break. John lost contact with his family when he began using street drugs five years ago.

Practice Example 8.2

The Collins-Evans Family

Beginnings

Dialogue begins with the social worker visiting the family home, having telephoned to make an appointment to meet with the whole family the previous day.

SW:	Ms Evans? (*Karen nods slightly*) Hello, I'm Iona. We spoke on the phone yesterday (smiles and *offers to shake her hand*). It's good to meet you.
[1]Karen:	Hello. Come in. Just in there (*gestures with her hand towards the living room where the rest of the family are sitting on sofas, then turns towards her partner, John*) Get your feet off there! (*Karen waves her hand in an agitated manner at John*) This is John.
[2]SW:	Hello John, I'm Iona (*offers to shake John's hand*). These your girls, Caris and Natasha? Hello. And Josh? *(smiles at Josh, who is sat on Caris's lap on the sofa).* Is it OK for me to sit down? Here OK? Thanks. As I said on the phone, I'm a social worker from Children's Services. I'm here to discuss the referral. I guess you've probably been wondering why I'm coming. Maybe worried. I really believe in being open and honest and working alongside people. *(pause)* Can we discuss the concerns that the school have raised in the referral together? *(pause)* I'm wondering … have the children got some toys that they could play with just while we talk?
Karen:	Caris, take Natasha and Josh out to the garden to play.
Caris:	Can we take some crisps? (*Karen nods and the children all leave*)

▶

◄

SW:	Thanks, Caris … Do you know anything about the referral? Has the school discussed it with you?
Karen:	The school phoned me today.
SW:	What did the school say?
Karen:	Well just generally …
[3]John:	(*interrupts in a loud voice*) Look, what they said is I'm a druggie…got a problem with me! I'm not doing anything that's affecting my kids.
[4]SW:	OK. So they are saying you are using drugs. OK. What are they saying are their concerns about your use specifically?
John:	Don't know.
[5]SW:	You see, my experience is that people who use drugs do it in different ways and different issues come up for people, and sometimes problems come up.
[6]Karen:	It's about him taking drugs and keeping the kids off school.
SW:	They're not getting to school …
[7]Karen:	I can't do everything. Getting them up, getting them to school. Tash can be a right one in the mornings …
SW:	John, do you have any care of them? Do you take them to school?
John:	From time to time.
SW:	So, Karen, it sounds like you feel that you are left with the care of the children and you find it hard to get everyone up in the morning to get them to school. Are they quite overtired in the morning?
Karen:	They don't seem to get tired in the evening and it takes ages to get them to bed. They're not out playing like the other kids round here. They don't use up their energy.
John:	That's 'cos they get bullied.
Karen:	I'm not surprised! They say their dad's a druggie! He spends £400 on it.
[8]SW:	What are your thoughts and feelings about that, John?
John:	They're just kids saying it at the end of the day.
[9]SW:	John, it would help me understand more if you tell me what kinds of drugs are you using (*gestures with hands for John to say more*).
[10]John:	Smack.
[11]SW:	Have you got some support to help you manage your drug-taking safely?
[12]Karen:	We've tried before for John to stop but it hasn't worked. Look, my kids are OK. I don't do anything.

►

◀

[13]SW: I can see you're worried about me asking all these questions about the children. The reason I'm asking you and John these things is to try and work out what impact your drug use has on your parenting. I'm not judging you for taking drugs, but I will need to know more about the drugs you are taking and what happens to you when you take them. Where I can, I want to support you both and work out how to support the children, so they are not affected in their daily lives by the drug use. Things like, are they upset by it? Are they missing school? Are you getting the income you need? Have you got friends to support you or are you lonely and tired? If you are not going to address your drug use, then we will need to provide much more help and support to the children. How does that sound to you? Can we work on this together?

[14]Karen: OK. We'll have to sort this out.

SW: That's really positive, Karen ... you know ... that you want to think about this. First, John, I need to find out more about your drug use. Do you mind speaking here with Karen or would you prefer to be on your own? I could arrange for you to meet with a specialist drugs and alcohol worker to talk through the issues?

The background literature highlighted how social workers' professional judgements concerning problematic substance use can be influenced by personal attitudes and negative cultural stereotypes (Forrester and Harwin, 2004). *'Tuning in to social worker's personal attitudes and preconceptions of people who use substances'* is a crucial first specialist communication skill for the social worker in preparing to become attuned to the ways in which Karen and John might express their emotions during the meeting. There is a danger of the social worker assuming that Karen and John will inevitably be a danger to their children because they use drugs or alcohol. It is important to remember that the problematic substance use itself may not cause significant harm but the particular way that it impacts upon parenting and the child's wellbeing needs identification (Cleaver et al., 1999). An attitude that sees all drug use as dangerous will fail to distinguish between recreational use and problematic dependence. The social worker needs to prepare herself for not over-reacting or under-reacting to both types of use, whether relating this to Karen's use of alcohol or John's use of drugs (Gilman, 2000).

The social worker needs to tune in to how her personal attitudes might be orientated towards a particular model of addiction. An individualised (medical) model would view the parents' problematic substance use as being due to biological or emotional disposition or sickness. In this instance, the social worker will inevitably only perceive that the service users are at less risk of harming their health and wellbeing if they abstain from using substances. This attitude, while commonly and often unconsciously held, will fail to take into account the number of environmental factors existing within the practice scenario. Indeed, abstinence is very difficult to maintain, and so the social worker might feel fairly pessimistic about its success. These attitudes of 'individual responsibility to abstain', individually based treatment and negativity or feelings of hopelessness about success will influence how well the social worker empathises with the service users' communication.

Personal attitudes might be orientated towards another dominant model – that of viewing drug use as the development of patterns of habitual behaviour that have become dysfunctional and unsafe due to triggers that are psychological or within the social environment (Paylor, 2008). Social workers operating this set of attitudes will seek to see changes in the social environment, with the individual seeking to utilise harm reduction strategies and terminate the dysfunctional behavioural patterns. This attitude also propagates 'individual responsibility', but the focus is on the service user managing drug use through improvements in the psychosocial situation. The sheer number and complexity of different psychosocial factors within this practice scenario may cause similar feelings of pessimism about success, which could influence the communication. Clearly, if any social worker leaves his or her own feelings and knowledge about substance use unchecked, then he or she may exacerbate the marginalisation already experienced by service users.

This is not just a meeting to discuss substance use in isolation, but to work out the impact of the substance use upon parenting and the children's welfare. The background literature identified how parenting assessments can be influenced by social worker's personal constructions of parenting. Thus, at this preparatory stage of 'tuning in', the social worker needs to use the specialist communication skill of *'identifying social worker's personal attitudes and preconceptions of parenting'*. In particular, the social worker needs to guard against operating a set of societal expectations about parenting behaviour as opposed to a multiply determined, holistic model, such as set out within the Assessment Framework (HM Government, 2015) or SCODA guidelines (Forrester and Harwin, 2004). Indeed, although in many areas women have achieved greater equality, oppressive gender stereotypes still pervade women's lives in relation to parenting. Cultural prescriptions of 'good parenting' expect mothers to know how to parent and to always provide 'sensitive and responsive' care regardless of social circumstance (Sheppard, 2000; Woodcock, 2003). Karen, as an alcohol-using mother in receipt of social work services, is doubly vulnerable to 'mother-blaming'. As Paylor (2008: 603) states: 'The female alcohol/drug user can be portrayed as a morally inadequate person failing to fulfill their duty as a "decent woman"'.

In addition to *'tuning in to personal attitudes and preconceptions'*, the social worker should seek to *'tune in'* to the way in which the service users might express their emotions to her during their meeting together. The background literature highlighted that drug users frequently expressed fear that their children will be 'taken away', which was evidenced through avoidance and other strategies of secrecy and denial (Buchanan and Young, 2002; Taylor and Kroll, 2004). In our practice example (8.2, point 3), we see John communicating fear about how the social worker might act on disclosed information through his reticence to become involved in the communication and then angrily outburst that his substance use is having no effect on the children ('John interrupts in a loud voice: "Look, what they said is I'm a druggie...got a problem with me! I'm not doing anything that's affecting my kids.') Karen communicates the same fear, but in a less confrontational manner, such as emphasising how the demands of the care are particularly high and her children are thriving (Practice Example 8.2, points 7 and 12). In drawing on the basic communication skills described in Chapter 4, the social worker will need to achieve and communicate empathy for these fears when they arise in order to enable the service users to feel understood, if they are to engage and retain them (Paylor, 2008).

The social worker needs to *'tune in'* to the likelihood that Karen and John have experienced multiple relationship breakdowns, and that, subsequently, they will bring insecure relationship templates to their relationships and, indeed, communication with her. Modern attachment theorists have explored the way the mind processes interpersonal information to use as a psychosocial template for relationships (Howe, 2005). Relationships can confirm or disconfirm those internal relationship models at any point across the lifespan. People with an insecure-ambivalent attachment relationship model will feel only conditionally worthwhile, uncertain of whether they will be understood and valued, and therefore constantly seek to test out the emotional and physical availability of the social worker. Alternatively, they might provide responses that 'seek to please' as opposed to risking any indication of their true feelings. People with an insecure-avoidant relationship model, however, bring to the communication their experience of having their needs consistently ignored. They are mistrustful of the potential of the social worker to be helpful, preferring to rely on their own coping strategies, which generally involves keeping emotionally detached to avoid inevitable rejection. Their self-esteem is often very low – feeling unlovable and without worth. In *'tuning in'*, the social worker could hypothesise from the number of relationship breakdowns that Karen and John may have developed either type of inse-cure relationship pattern and anticipate them communicating reluctance to exploring their difficulties due to their mistrust of adults who are sup-posed to care for them. As before, the social worker will need to prepare to achieve and communicate empathy for this anxiety.

When first meeting with the family, the social worker must employ the four parts of the basic communication skill from Chapter 4 of *'achieving a shared purpose'*, i.e. *'being clear on role'*; *'being clear on purpose'*; *'reach for feedback'*; and *'showing empathy'*. As stated above, the authority that the social worker brings through their legislative role can cause significant fear and mistrust which can dramatically influence the communication. Consequently, the social worker must ensure that they *'show empathy'* to those feelings immediately as they arise in order to enable Karen and John to feel understood, and in control of their emotional and social selves (Howe, 1998; Agass, 2002; Ruch, 2005b). Immediately at point 1 of our practice example (8.2), we see Karen potentially communicating this fear non-verbally through her agitated behaviour, and John demonstrates fear through his silent observation of events. The social worker *'shows empa-thy'* for these anticipated feelings within her opening statement (Practice Example 8.2, point 2).

> As I said on the phone, I'm a social worker from Children's Services. I'm here to discuss the referral with you. I guess you've probably been wondering why I'm coming. Maybe worried. I really believe in being open and honest and work-ing alongside people. *(pause)* Can we discuss the concerns that the school have raised in the referral together? *(pause)* I'm wondering ... have the children got some toys that they could play with just while we talk?

The social worker immediately goes on to demonstrate that the open-ing statement, including the demonstration of empathy, is not just an empty promise of honesty and openness in collaborative working. She emphasises that she wants to share the referral information with the par-ents, and, more than this, she wants to ensure that they have an equal understanding of the concerns being raised. The data from the research transcripts called attention to this practice as a way of communicating a desire for partnership working. It constituted an expression of seeking to 'work with' as opposed to 'doing to' service users, and was considered part of a dynamic that would alleviate anxiety about the social worker's authority role.

> Johanna: In your experience of this practice setting, is 'are you going to take my children away' said straightaway? No? So you think this is at the back of their minds ... being worried?

SW: Yeah, if this is a new referral, referred by education about their con-
            cerns, then that conversation could be ameliorated by actually say-
            ing to them, the parents, that the reason we have come to see you is
            to actually hear your views about the referral … that … you know …
            we are not coming to judge you. We are coming because a) it's your
            right to know we've had a referral and b) to get your views … I can
            hear that you are anxious …

It may be that a demonstration of such collaborative working will encourage service users to give their feedback to the social worker's beginning
attempts at *'achieving a shared purpose'*. This enables movement towards
achieving a shared agenda for work to occur. Certainly, in our practice
example, the supportiveness of the statement could have precipitated
John's revelation about his substance use and expression of feeling
(Practice Example 8.2, point 3). His communication of denial about the
impact of substance use on his children's welfare could be understood as
further communication of fear of the social worker acting on any disclosed
information. However, in drawing on the background literature concerning the dominance of issues of secrecy and denial, it could also be understood as an early indication of John denying the existence of a substance
use problem for himself or his family generally. Indeed, the presence of
the social worker may be causing the aforementioned internal intrapsy-
chic conflict about his substance-using behaviour to come to the fore.
Certainly his tone is angry, suggesting he is struggling with his emotions.

This instance in the dialogue provides a good illustration of how the
social worker needs to simultaneously adopt some objective distance as
well as achieving emotional attunement to the thoughts and feelings being
expressed. In Chapter 4, we referred to this objective distancing as operating a 'third ear', or a 'second head', with the social worker having in mind
questions like 'What is it that is really going on in the communication
here?', or, 'Is the problem that she or he is describing the most immediate problem or is there something more worrying?' In this situation, if the
social worker considers the communication to be predominately about fear
of her authority role, then it would seem useful to *'use immediacy'*, one of
the basic communication skills discussed in Chapter 4, to allow the social
worker to comment honestly and directly on what is occurring within the
process between the social worker and the service user. An example of this is:
'You know, John, I wonder if you are feeling worried about me being a social
worker and whether you can trust me, and this means you are reluctant to
share your concerns with me. What do you think, can we talk about this?'

However, the dialogue shows the social worker implementing the alternative interpretation – that John is showing early evidence of denial of
his problem substance use. The worker responds with *'reflective listening'*

through *'paraphrasing'* John's statement, but in a calm, accepting and non-judgemental way (*'OK. So they are saying you are using drugs. OK. What are their concerns about your use specifically?'*) In so doing, she establishes a reality of the drug use and potential effects, as opposed to collaborating with any denial of it existing.

The social worker's legal duty is to make sense of the way that the drug use is affecting the lives of all members of the family, the parenting being provided to the children and the children's wellbeing. The multiplicity and interaction of the problems experienced, such as mental health, finances or lack of emotional support network, means that it is not easy to make connections between the substance use and the parenting and the social circumstances. A holistic approach to understanding is vital. Also, it means that it is important to consider each family situation individually. When *'being clear on purpose'*, the social worker needs to communicate how and why she is taking a holistic and individual approach to the family situation. In naming this specialist communication skill, I have chosen to adopt a phrase used by Aldridge (1999) for describing what a social worker should do to fully understand parental substance use, which is *'to enter the world of substance-using families'*.

I hope that the articulation of this skill will help social workers to be clearer about their purpose of work with the substance-using parents and families with whom they work. The background literature indicated that this lack of clarity of purpose has its roots in the problematic organisational context, in terms of the separation of organisational systems and orientations of being child welfare focused or substance use focused. These organisational separations have impacted upon social workers' knowledge and confidence in working with combined issues of substance use and parenting (Forrester and Harwin, 2004; Paylor, 2008). Indeed, this theme was evident within the forum theatre for the research study underpinning the book. The research transcript showed that social workers struggled with ways of describing their purpose within this setting. The following excerpt illustrates this confusion:

SW1:   Wouldn't you just introduce yourself as the social worker and say you are 'the one you spoke to the other day on the telephone and I've come to discuss the call we had, and to sit down and talk to you about this, and hear your views. Is this OK with you? Can we sit down and talk somewhere?' Then talk about the obstacle – 'We've had a referral from education, regarding your substance use. Have you heard from them?'

SW2:   I would do that a bit differently, though, because the referral was about the child. I wouldn't say 'the concerns are about your substance use' but about 'the parenting capacity'. The concerns are about the impact of the substance use upon the child.

Johanna: So how are you going to phrase it?

SW2:   Yeah, I don't know.

A helpful way of communicating a preparedness *'to enter the world of substance-using families'* is to adopt conceptual ideas from systemic family therapy that have been highlighted for work with families to make sense of the interconnections between substance use, parenting, child wellbeing and other social factors in the familial environment (Kroll and Taylor, 2003). The systemic framework provides a way of viewing how the substance operates as a part of the family system and impacts on everyone else. Different levels of responsibility between family members can be identified, although care should be taken not to emphasise blame, or reinforce power or gender imbalances. Kroll and Taylor (2003) recommend the use of genograms and ecomaps as visual, symbolic tools to gain information about the world of families as experienced by the different family members. The tools address three of the main issues from the background literature about parental substance use. First, communicating in a way that *'makes the child visible'* is critical for this practice setting. The placing of children upon the genogram and ecomap as part of the family system ensures that they are visible and not hidden behind parental or professional preoccupations with the substance. Second, the significance of the relationship between the substance and the parent, and the consequential relationship between the children and the substance needs to be given attention in the communication. The mapping of all family members upon the ecomap, including the substance as a 'family member', enables the quality of relationships to be explored. *'Open questions'* and *'closed questions'* would need to draw out the quality of the relationship between the parent and child but also the relationship between each of them and the substance. Finally, the use of the visual tools enables exploration of the role of the multitude of other social factors which co-exist and interrelate with the substance use. For example, intergenerational patterns and significant life events can be explored within a genogram and sources of support or tension within the extended family, friends and wider community can be investigated within an ecomap.

Communication which demonstrates that professional interest is of the totality of the family experience and support of family members, as opposed to apportioning blame to one or more individuals, is more likely to address service user fears of stigmatisation. There is considerable self-disapproval as well as social disapproval in the use of the label 'alcoholic' or 'drug addict'. As such, it is important to communicate in a way that does not attribute this label. The practice example (8.2) illustrates the social worker operating this specialist communication of *'addressing service user fears of stigmatisation'*. At point 5, the social worker emphasises to the service user how her perspective of substance use is that it is not necessarily problematic, and that people who use substances are not just one homogenous group but that each person and situation has individual characteristics ('You see, my experience is that people who use drugs do it in different ways and different issues come up for people, and sometimes problems come up.') She goes on to highlight her own non-judgemental attitude about drug use by exploring whether his drug use is 'managed' and 'safe' as opposed to a closed attitude of establishing if it occurs or not ('Have you got some support to help you manage your drug-taking safely?'). At point 13, the social worker goes about *'addressing service user fears of stigmatisation'* by directly stating that she will not judge the service user for taking drugs ('I'm not judging you for taking drugs but I will need to know more about the drugs you are taking and what happens to you when you take them'). As before, she does not rely on empty words but gives illustrations of the types of issues she needs to consider with the parents in order to support them and the children.

Communication must go beyond non-attributing a label, to the positive emphasis of personal choice and individual responsibility for deciding future behaviour (Miller and Rollnick, 2002). The premise underpinning motivational interviewing, identified in the background literature as a dominant approach in addiction treatment, is that the service user and social worker should identify how much of a problem the service user and family is having with the substance use, and whether or not to change. While social workers may wish to confront parents with the reality or truth of the problem substance use and the impact of that problem usage on the welfare of their children, the strategies of confrontation are more likely to cause a response of denial and/or be perceived as argumentative (Barber, 2002). As such, a key specialist communication skill for the social worker to adopt is to *'avoid exhortations to change'*.

It is better if service users come to their own conclusions through social workers drawing the arguments for or against change from the service users themselves. I have chosen to refer to this as a specialist communication strategy of *'motivating service users to decide to make changes'*. The three themes that Barber considers to be interwoven through motivational interviewing would seem to be central components of this strategy. The first theme is for the social worker to *'provide affirmation'* of the service user's statements and feelings. This is best achieved through using the basic non-verbal and verbal communication skills outlined in Chapter 4 of *'reflective listening'* and demonstration of empathy through skills such as *'putting feelings into words'*, *'reach for feeling'* and *'use of silences'* (Shulman, 2009). Barber (2002: 96) recommends a strategic use of these skills. While the social worker should demonstrate acceptance and 'a sense of being' for the service user, he or she should carefully select which service user statements to reflect and explore. Of these statements it is important to show positive confirmation about the need for change.

The practice example (8.2, point 4) illustrates this specialist communication of *'providing affirmation'* for change. As stated earlier, the social worker *'paraphrases'* John's statement that he is 'a druggie', and that his usage has no effect on his children, in a calm, accepting and non-judgemental way that establishes a reality of the drug use existing along with possible difficulties in that usage. She does not collaborate with any denial of it existing (*'OK. So they are saying you are using drugs. OK. What are their concerns about your use specifically?'*) At point 5, the social worker offers information that the drug use can affect people's lives in a negative way, but then asks an open question about John's usage. In so doing, she avoids showing any judgement about his behaviour but begins to introduce the idea that John might benefit from considering how his drug-taking is potentially problematic. Barber refers to this type of open questioning as 'affirmative questioning'.

The second of Barber's themes can be summarised as *'encouraging service user recognition of the divergence between their values or goals and the reality of their current behaviour'*. This requires the social worker to help the service user clarify their life goals as well as specific goals about substance use. *'Open questions'* are important for enabling exploration of the service user's own perspectives. The social worker should provide feedback, in an individualised, empathic and non-judgemental manner about how the substance use is not conducive to those goals (Paylor, 2008). Finally, Barber specifies that social workers should seek to *'provide all options to encourage feelings of self-efficacy'* to promote motivation. The service user needs to believe that there is a realistic possibility for change and that they have the capacity to solve the problem. This will mean that the social worker and service user should discuss all the different options that are available. Communication skills from Chapter 4 of *'summarising'* and *'paraphrasing'* will be useful in drawing information together to achieve more focus (and therefore more motivation) within this discussion.

The background literature suggests that the success of this specialist communication strategy of *'motivating service users to decide to make changes'* is also dependent upon the stage that a person has reached within a process of change. In applying the cycle of change model (Prochaska et al., 1992) to our practice example, it is possible to identify that Karen is at a stage of wanting to change the situation for the family. While she has not yet engaged in a discussion of her own alcohol use, she has made a clear statement that the substance use and parenting difficulties need to be addressed (Practice Example 8.2, point 14). Also, she has continually shown through the dialogue that she is unhappy with John's drug use, and is prepared to discuss the level of the use and the way it impacts upon the children's lives. She is moving through the 'contemplation' stage. Barber highlights that communication at this stage needs to focus on maintaining service user cooperation and his or her own vision of the problematic aspects of the substance use (whether, in this example, it relates to her own or her partner's use) and the options and capacity she has to make changes for the safety of each of the family members. John's communication indicates that he is a 'precontemplator' of change, showing neither ambivalence about his drug use nor a desire to change. In applying Barber's model, communication with John as a 'precontemplator' needs to focus on reducing the value of substance use, and working with Karen and the wider social network to reduce the stresses within the environment to reduce the value of the drug-taking behaviour to John.

This chapter has identified how social work communication with substance users is influenced by wider tensions in society concerning problematising and stigmatising attitudes to substance use which have caused marginalisation for individual substance users and their families ('Knowing'). The specialist social work communication skills identified and discussed within the chapter seek to provide a balance between 'care' and 'control' ('Being'). These can be summarised as communication that represents authority and making supportive challenges for work, but at the same time attends to welfare concerns of promoting safety and wellbeing for all family members, and preventing marginalisation ('Being' and 'Doing').

Mapping to the Professional Capability Framework

Qualifying Social Worker Level Capabilities

Please remember that these should be viewed as domains which overlap in an integrative manner rather than as a linear checklist.

> 'By the end of last placement/ the completion of qualifying programmes newly qualified social workers should have demonstrated the Knowledge, Skills and Values to work with a range of user groups, and the ability to undertake a range of tasks at a foundation level, the capacity to work with more complex situations; they should be able to work more autonomously, whilst recognising that the final decision will still rest with their supervisor; they will seek appropriate support and supervision.
>
> The Health Professions Council (the regulator of qualified social workers) and The College have mapped the Standards of Proficiency for Social Work (SOPs) against the PCF expectations for social work students at the end of their last placement. Whilst there are some differences in the way the standards and PCF are expressed, the overall expectations are the same.'

Communication Capacity Domain – 'Knowing' (engaging with formal and informal knowledge in communication)	**PCF 3 Diversity: Recognise diversity and apply anti-discriminatory and anti-oppressive principles in practice** ➢ Understand how an individual's identity is informed by factors such as culture, economic status, family composition, life experiences and characteristics, and take account of these to understand their experiences, questioning assumptions where necessary ➢ With reference to current legislative requirements, recognise personal and organisational discrimination and oppression and with guidance make use of a range of approaches to challenge them
	PCF 5 Knowledge: Apply knowledge of social sciences, law and social work practice theory ➢ Demonstrate a critical understanding of the application to social work of research, theory and knowledge from sociology, social policy, psychology and health ➢ Demonstrate a critical understanding of the legal and policy frameworks and guidance that inform and mandate social work practice, recognising the scope for professional judgement ➢ Demonstrate and apply to practice a working knowledge of human growth and development throughout the life course ➢ Recognise the short and long term impact of psychological, socio-economic, environmental and physiological factors on people's lives, taking into account age and development, and how this informs practice ➢ Recognise how systemic approaches can be used to understand the person-in-the-environment and inform your practice ➢ Acknowledge the centrality of relationships for people and the key concepts of attachment, separation, loss, change and resilience ➢ Understand forms of harm and their impact on people, and the implications for practice, drawing on concepts of strength, resilience, vulnerability, risk and resistance, and apply to practice ➢ Demonstrate a critical knowledge of the range of theories and models for social work intervention with individuals, families, groups and communities, and the methods derived from them ➢ Value and take account of the expertise of service users, carers and professionals **KSS Adults (4): Safeguarding** Social workers must be able to recognise the risk indicators of different forms of abuse and neglect and their impact on individuals, their families or their support networks and should prioritise the protection of children and adults in vulnerable situations whenever necessary. This includes working with those who self-neglect. Social workers who work with adults must take an outcomes-focused, person-centred approach to safeguarding practice, recognising that people are experts in their own lives and working alongside them to identify person centred solutions to risk and harm.

	KSS Adults (6): Effective Assessments and Outcome Based Support Planning Social workers should demonstrate a good understanding of personalisation, the social model of disability and of human development throughout life and demonstrate a holistic approach to the identification of needs, circumstances, rights, strengths and risks. In particular, social workers need to understand the impact of trauma, loss and abuse, physical disability, physical ill health, learning disability, mental ill health, mental capacity, substance misuse, domestic abuse, aging and end of life issues on physical, cognitive, emotional and social development both for the individual and for the functioning of the family. They should recognise the roles and needs of informal or family carers and use holistic, systemic approaches to supporting individuals and carers. They should develop and maintain knowledge and good partnerships with local community resources in order to work effectively with individuals in connecting them with appropriate resources and support. **Roles and Capabilities of Social Workers in Relation to Substance Use (Role 1): To Engage People who Use Substances** To understand why people use substances and may develop problems and develop a critical understanding of the social context of substance use, e.g. poverty, abuse. Have an awareness of the range of effects substances might have on a person or others around them, including children and other dependents. To understand the challenges people, and their families/carers, face in trying to change their problematic use. **Roles and Capabilities of Social Workers in Relation to Substance Use (Role 2): To Motivate People to Consider Changing their Problematic Substance Using Behaviour and Support Them** Identify substance use and problematic substance use. Have knowledge of the general impact of substances on mental and physical health and well being. Understand the law and wider policy in relation to substance use, e.g. Mental Capacity Act 2005, the Care Act 2014, Mental Health Act 1983 (amended 2007). Actively engage with the research agenda and evidence base in relation to substance use.
Communication Capacity Domain – 'Doing' (the enactment of communication strategies in interaction)	**PCF 6 Critical Reflection and Analysis: Apply critical reflection and analysis to inform and provide a rationale for professional decision-making** ➤ Apply imagination, creativity and curiosity to practice ➤ Inform decision-making through the identification and gathering of information from multiple sources, actively seeking new sources ➤ With support, rigorously question and evaluate the reliability and validity of information from different sources

➢ Demonstrate a capacity for logical, systematic, critical and
reflective reasoning and apply the theories and techniques of
reflective practice
➢ Know how to formulate, test, evaluate, and review hypotheses
in response to information available at the time and apply in
practice
➢ Begin to formulate and make explicit, evidence-informed
judgements and justifiable decisions

**KSS Adults (8): Supervision, Critical Reflection and
Analysis**
Social workers should be able to make effective use of
opportunities to discuss, reflect upon and test multiple
hypotheses, the role of intuition and logic in decision making,
the difference between opinion and fact, the role of evidence,
how to address common bias in situations of uncertainty and
the reasoning of any conclusions reached and recommendations
made, particularly in relation to mental capacity, mental health
and safeguarding situations.

Social workers should have a critical understanding of the
difference between theory, research, evidence and expertise and
the role of professional judgement. They should use practice
evidence and research to inform the complex judgements and
decisions needed to support, empower and protect their service
users. They should apply imagination, creativity and curiosity
to working in partnership with individuals and their carers,
acknowledging the centrality of people's own expertise about
their experience and needs.

KSS Children (2): Communication
Produce written case notes and reports, which are well argued,
focused and jargon free. Present a clear analysis and a sound
rationale for actions as well as any conclusions reached, so that
all parties are well-informed.

**Roles and Capabilities of Social Workers in Relation
to Substance Use (Role 1): To Engage People who Use
Substances**
Be willing to acknowledge their own views and experiences
in relation to substance use and how they could impact on
practice.
Be willing to identify and respond to substance use, for example,
ask questions about substance use routinely.
Be willing to undertake formal substance use assessments
requiring developed knowledge, use of reference materials,
capacity to use validated assessment tools (where appropriate).
To demonstrate a commitment to routinely raise and discuss
substance use issues in supervision and management roles.
To encourage staff to reflect on risks, ethics of care, and
attitudes relating to substance use and people with substance
problems.

PCF 7 Intervention and Skills: Use judgement and authority to intervene with individuals, families and communities to promote independence, provide support and prevent harm, neglect and abuse

➤ Identify and apply a range of verbal, non-verbal and written methods of communication and adapt them in line with peoples' age, comprehension and culture

➤ Be able to communicate information, advice, instruction and professional opinion so as to advocate, influence and persuade

➤ Demonstrate the ability to engage with people, and build, manage, sustain and conclude compassionate and effective relationships

➤ Demonstrate skills in sharing information appropriately and respectfully

➤ Recognise complexity, multiple factors, changing circumstances and uncertainty in people's lives, to be able to prioritise your intervention

➤ Understand the authority of the social work role and begin to use this appropriately as an accountable professional

➤ Recognise the factors that create or exacerbate risk to individuals, their families or carers, to the public or to professionals, including yourself, and contribute to the assessment and management of risk

KSS Adults (3): Person-centred Practice
They should work co-productively and innovatively with people, local communities, other professionals, agencies and services to promote self-determination, community capacity, personal and family reliance, cohesion, earlier intervention and active citizenship.

KSS Adults (4): Safeguarding
Social workers who work with adults must take an outcomes-focused, person-centred approach to safeguarding practice, recognising that people are experts in their own lives and working alongside them to identify person centred solutions to risk and harm. In situations where there is abuse or neglect or clear risk of those, social workers must work in a way that enhances involvement, choice and control as part of improving quality of life, wellbeing and safety.

KSS Adults (7): Direct Work with Individuals and Families
Social workers need to be able to work directly with individuals and their families through the professional use of self, using interpersonal skills and emotional intelligence to create relationships based on openness, transparency and empathy. They should know how to build purposeful, effective relationships underpinned by reciprocity. They should be able to communicate clearly, sensitively and effectively, applying a range of best evidence-based methods of written, oral and non-verbal communication and adapt these methods to match the person's age, comprehension and culture. Social workers should be capable of communicating effectively with people with specific communication needs, including those with learning disabilities, dementia, people who lack mental capacity and people with sensory impairment.

KSS Children (2): Communication

Communicate clearly and sensitively with children of different ages and abilities, their families and in a range of settings and circumstances.

Use methods based on best evidence.

Create immediate rapport with people not previously known which facilitates engagement and motivation to participate in child protective enquiries, assessments and services.

Listen to the views, wishes and feelings of children and families and help parents and carers understand the ways in which their children communicate through their behaviour. Help them to understand how they might communicate more effectively with their children.

Promote speech, language and communication support, identifying those children and adults who are experiencing difficulties expressing themselves.

Roles and Capabilities of Social Workers in Relation to Substance Use (Role 2): To Motivate People to Consider Changing their Problematic Substance Using Behaviour and Support Them

Identify substance use and problematic substance use.

Determine level of motivation for change through skilled listening and communication.

Assess risk to self, risk to family members (including unborn children), and risk to others, from the person's substance use.

Assess the person's substance use sensitively and effectively, e.g. know what to ask, how and when to ask it. Have a conversation.

Take action on any risks identified and decide whether safeguarding action is needed or education/advice provided.

Provide information and support to children/family members/ partners/carers (both independently in their own right and as part of the family/group) or refer to more appropriate service.

Identify strengths and positive support in the person's life.

Roles and Capabilities of Social Workers in Relation to Substance Use (Role 3): To Support People in their Efforts to Make and Maintain Changes in their Substance Use

Provide continuing support for people who enter formal treatment settings and those who choose not to.

Provide on going support for children and family members, particularly in terms of supporting them to rebuild relationships.

Work in partnership with the individual, their children and family members to develop a maintenance and relapse prevention plan.

Conduct ongoing risk assessment to ensure they and any dependents are supported if substance use increases and if any reduction in substance use has not reduced the risks to self or others.

Provide practical assistance as needed to ensure the post intervention care plan meets the needs of all concerned.

Review and amend the post intervention care plan.

Communication Capacity Domain – 'Being' (the use of 'self')	**PCF 1 Professionalism: Identify and behave as a professional social worker, committed to professional development**
	➤ Be able to explain the role of the social worker in a range of contexts, and uphold the reputation of the profession
	➤ Demonstrate professionalism in terms of presentation, demeanour, reliability, honesty and respectfulness
	➤ Recognise the impact of self in interaction with others, making appropriate use of personal experience
	➤ Be able to recognise and maintain personal and professional boundaries
	➤ Recognise your professional limitations and how to seek advice
	➤ Demonstrate a commitment to your continuing learning and development
	➤ With support, take steps to manage and promote own safety, health, wellbeing and emotional resilience
	KSS Adults (7): Direct work with individuals and families
	Social workers should be capable of communicating effectively with people with specific communication needs, including those with learning disabilities, dementia, people who lack mental capacity and people with sensory impairment. They should do this in ways that are engaging, respectful, motivating and effective, even when dealing with conflict – whether perceived or actual – anger and resistance to change.
	KSS Children (2): Communication
	Act respectfully even when people are angry, hostile and resistant to change. Manage tensions between parents, carers and family members, in ways that show persistence, determination and professional confidence.
	Roles and Capabilities of Social Workers in Relation to Substance Use (Role 1): To Engage People who Use Substances
	Understand that working with substance use is part of social work practice.
	Be willing to acknowledge their own views and experiences of substance use and how this might impact upon practice.
	Be willing to learn and fill gaps in substance use knowledge and skills.
	Be willing to work in partnership with substance use services including mutual exchange of knowledge about service models, confidentiality, duties and boundaries of care.
	Be willing to undertake formal substance use assessments requiring developed knowledge, use of reference materials, capacity to use validated assessment tools (where appropriate).
	Roles and Capabilities of Social Workers in Relation to Substance Use (Role 2): To Motivate People to Consider Changing their Problematic Substance Using Behaviour and Support Them
	Work in partnership with specialist substance use colleagues and any other health and social care professionals involved in the person's care.

Make an informed referral to a relevant substance use service and actively support the service user to attend wherever possible.
Seek feedback from service users regarding the effectiveness of, and impact of, the service they received.

PCF 2 Values and Ethics: Apply social work ethical principles and values to guide professional practice
➤ Recognise and, with support, manage the impact of own values on professional practice
➤ Manage potentially conflicting or competing values, and, with guidance, recognise, reflect on, and work with ethical dilemmas
➤ Demonstrate respectful partnership work with service users and carers, eliciting and respecting their needs and views, and promoting their participation in decision-making wherever possible
➤ Recognise and promote individuals' rights to autonomy and self-determination

KSS Adults (5): Mental Capacity
Social workers must model and lead a change of approach, away from that where the default setting is 'safety first', towards a person-centred culture where individual choice is encouraged and where the right of all individuals to express their own lifestyle choices is recognised and valued.

In working with those where there is no concern over capacity, social workers should take all practicable steps to empower people to make their own decisions, recognising that people are experts in their own lives and working alongside them to identify person-centred solutions to risk and harm, recognising the individual's right to make 'unwise' decisions.

Roles and Capabilities of Social Workers in Relation to Substance Use (Role 1): To Engage People who Use Substances
Understand that working with substance use is part of social work practice.
Be willing to acknowledge their own views and experiences of substance use and how this might impact upon practice.
Be willing to identify and respond to substance use, for example, ask questions about substance use routinely.
Be willing to identify and respond to risks to self and others posed by substance use.
Be willing to engage carers, children and family members in discussion around their own support needs and how they can support the individual using substances.

PCF 3 Diversity: Recognise diversity and apply anti-discriminatory and anti-oppressive principles in practice
(Appropriately placed in both 'Knowing' and 'Being')
➤ With reference to current legislative requirements, recognise personal and organisational discrimination and oppression and with guidance make use of a range of approaches to challenge them
➤ Recognise and manage the impact on people of the power invested in your role

KSS Adults (3): Person-centred Practice
They should coordinate and facilitate a wide range of
practical and emotional support, and discharge legal duties
to complement people's own resources and networks, so that
all individuals (no matter their background, health status or
mental capacity), carers and families can exercise choice and
control, (supporting individuals to make their own decisions,
especially where they may lack capacity) and meet their needs
and aspirations in personalised, creative and often novel ways.
They should work co-productively and innovatively with people,
local communities, other professionals, agencies and services
to promote self- determination, community capacity, personal
and family reliance, cohesion, earlier intervention and active
citizenship.

**Roles and Capabilities of Social Workers in Relation
to Substance Use (Role 1): To Engage People who Use
Substances**
Be willing to challenge others' negative views in relation to
people using substances.
To understand the challenges people, and their families/carers,
face in trying to change their problematic use.
To recognise the stigma people with problematic substance use
face and commit to non-judgemental practice, including positive
language and an inclusionary approach.

**Roles and Capabilities of Social Workers in Relation to
Substance Use (Role 3): To Support People in their Efforts to
Make and Maintain Changes in their Substance Use**
Provide a holistic approach to support recognising the
environmental risk factors for relapse.

**PCF 4 Rights, Justice and Economic Wellbeing: Advance
human rights and promote social justice and economic
wellbeing**
➤ Understand, identify and apply in practice the principles of
   social justice, inclusion and equality
➤ Understand how legislation and guidance can advance
   or constrain people's rights and recognise how the law
   may be used to protect or advance their rights and
   entitlements
➤ Work within the principles of human and civil rights and
   equalities legislation, differentiating and beginning to work
   with absolute, qualified and competing rights and differing
   needs and perspectives
➤ Recognise the impact of poverty and social exclusion and
   promote enhanced economic status through access to education, work, housing, health services and welfare benefits

**Roles and Capabilities of Social Workers in Relation
to Substance Use (Role 1): To Engage People who Use
Substances**
A willingness to empower and advocate on behalf of people with
problematic substance use.

	To recognise the stigma people with problematic substance use face and commit to non-judgemental practice, including positive language and an inclusionary approach. **Roles and Capabilities of Social Workers in Relation to Substance Use (Role 2): To Motivate People to Consider Changing their Problematic Substance Using Behaviour and Support Them** Advocate for service users and families through the referral and intervention process. **Roles and Capabilities of Social Workers in Relation to Substance Use (Role 3): To Support People in their Efforts to Make and Maintain Changes in their Substance Use** Advocate for the individual, their children and family members as needed including access to practical and financial resources.
	PCF 8 Contexts and Organisations: Engage with, inform, and adapt to changing contexts that shape practice. Operate effectively within own organisational frameworks and contribute to the development of services and organisations. Operate effectively within multi-agency and inter-professional partnerships and settings ➤ Recognise that social work operates within, and responds to, changing economic, social, political and organisational contexts ➤ Understand the roles and responsibilities of social workers in a range of organisations, lines of accountability and the boundaries of professional autonomy and discretion ➤ Understand legal obligations, structures and behaviours within organisations and how these impact on policy, procedure and practice ➤ Be able to work within an organisation's remit and contribute to its evaluation and development **KSS Adults (9): Organisational Context** They must understand and work effectively within financial and legal frameworks, obligations, structures and culture, in particular Human Rights and Equalities legislation, the Care Act, Mental Capacity Act, Mental Health Act and accompanying guidance and codes of practice. They must be able to operate successfully in their organisational context, demonstrating effective time management, caseload management and be capable of reconciling competing demands and embrace information, data and technology appropriate to their role. They should have access to regular quality supervision to support their professional resilience and emotional and physical wellbeing. **Roles and Capabilities of Social Workers in Relation to Substance Use (Role 1): To Engage People who Use Substances** Be willing to work in partnership with substance use services including mutual exchange of knowledge about service models, confidentiality, duties and boundaries of care.

	Roles and Capabilities of Social Workers in Relation to Substance Use (Role 2): To Motivate People to Consider Changing their Problematic Substance Using Behaviour and Support Them Have knowledge of local services, their referral processes and waiting list times, and knowledge of range and type of specialist substance use intervention. Actively develop local links with substance use services. **Roles and Capabilities of Social Workers in Relation to Substance Use (Role 3): To Support People in their Efforts to Make and Maintain Changes in their Substance Use** Consult, liaise and work in partnership with addictions specialists which may include specialist treatment services. Help develop and support mutual aid and peer led support networks or group activity. Make referrals/re-referrals to other agencies or helping professions as needed.

9

Working with Adults with Disabilities

Summary of Specialist Communication Skills in this Chapter

➤ use the whole communication spectrum

➤ actively look for the channels of communication that the person is using

➤ validate and recognise 'private' knowledge of the individual nuances of the impairment as applied to a person

➤ communicating empathy for the experience of systemic barriers

➤ taking time.

Policy and background literature

New legislation has strengthened the person-centred approach as a policy and practice agenda (The Care Act 2014 in England, Wales and Northern Ireland; The Social Care (Self-directed support) (Scotland) Act 2013; The Social Services and Well-being (Wales) Act 2014). This has amplified existing policy exhortations for augmented skills in communication ('Valuing People (2001)'; 'Independence, Well-being and Choice' (2005); Disability Discrimination Act (2005); 'Our Health, Our Care, Our Say' (2006b), Disability Discrimination (Northern Ireland) Order, 2006). The reforms go beyond the previous 'good practice' person-centred principles of involving service users as expert participants, treating people with dignity, as individuals, and enabling choice about care to maximise independence (Department of Health, 2001; Department of Health, 2005; Department of Health, 2006b). While these developments had already built upon the Direct Payment Schemes of the 1990s to the use of 'Individual Budgets', 'self-assessed need' and 'self-directed support', progress was slow (Boxall et al., 2009; Sapey, 2009). Now social workers are required to elicit the personal views and wishes of each service user of how to address their health and wellbeing to meet outcomes and goals deemed most important to them. It is a deliberate movement away from the care management process-driven, tick-box practice of considering what service to fit a service user into. Social workers must adopt a flexible, relational, individualised approach to have a 'genuine conversation'. Using their knowledge and skills, they must create a co-produced assessment of the care and support needs that matter most to the person concerned. This active involvement and/or 'co-productive' approach cannot occur without effective communication. Social workers must identify service users' communication needs, particularly where service users might have substantial difficulty in engaging with the assessment and planning processes. These include difficulties in understanding and retaining information, as well as difficulties in weighing up information to consider and express preferences, alongside difficulties in communicating their views, wishes and feelings. The legislation goes hand in hand with principles underpinning the Mental Capacity Act (2005), which beholds social workers to presume that a service user has the capacity to make decisions unless it has been established that they lack that capacity. This indicates the need for social workers to use particular communication skills to explore issues of 'decision-making capacity'. Indeed, one of the items within the functional test that is applied to ascertain capacity for decision-making concerns the ability of the service user to communicate and understand their decision effectively, both through their words and everyday actions. This means that the social worker needs to be alert to all the different forms and channels of communication that a service user may be using, or be encouraged or enabled to use. Thus social workers must show communication capacity to display sensitivity while managing such complex and difficult conversations. Indeed, the new Care Act (2014) expects social workers to consider the emotional and physical impact of the assessment when planning interventions upon service user wellbeing, taking steps to mitigate this within their communication approach.

The requirement for social workers to facilitate a safe relationship from which to explore feelings and opinions concerning choice, risk and protection is also underlined by the new approaches to adult safeguarding within the new legislation (The Care Act 2014). Identifying and addressing the abuse of adults at risk continues to be a priority, with new duties for safeguarding introduced. These include making or causing enquiries to be made where there is a safeguarding concern; hosting safeguarding adults boards; and carrying out safeguarding adults reviews. The Social Care Institute of Excellence (SCIE, 2015) has identified the following types of abuse, recognising that signs may be hard to detect and that different types may occur at the same time:

➤ Physical abuse

➤ Domestic violence or abuse

➤ Sexual abuse

➤ Psychological or emotional abuse

➤ Financial or material abuse

➤ Modern slavery

➤ Discriminatory abuse

➤ Organisational or institutional abuse

➤ Neglect or acts of omission

➤ Self-neglect.

The legislation places a responsibility upon the social worker to investigate and take action when a vulnerable adult is believed to be suffering abuse at the hands of carers or other people in their social environment. The new safeguarding approach within the legislation is to prevent abuse and reduce risk, but to respond proportionately, without taking control away from the individual. 'Proportionality' is understood as the 'proportionate and least intrusive response appropriate to the risk presented' (Department of Health, 2011). Within this, social workers must ensure that they use the least restrictive options for freedom of action, complying with the Human Rights Act (1998) and the Mental Capacity Act (2005). It involves the use of professional judgement and the management of risk, rather than the removal of risk. Risk-taking and managing risk is recognised as a normal part of everyday life for anyone. Skills for Care (2015) provide a useful summary:

> There must be an emphasis on sensible risk appraisal, not risk avoidance, which takes into account individuals' preferences, histories, circumstances and life-styles to achieve a proportionate tolerance of acceptable risks. In the words of Lord Justice Munby 'what good is it making someone safer if it merely makes them miserable?'

Previous research, however, has found that while (some) staff working with people with disabilities recognise risk management as an essential aspect of normal life, these views tended to conflict with parents or carers (and indeed some staff) who wanted the person to be protected from such daily dangers (Mitchell and Glendinning, 2007). Carers' perspectives are not always consistent with those of the service user. Moreover, the Care Act 2014 takes a more 'joined-up' approach to considering the care and support needs of carers themselves. A picture must be gained of the whole family context, and how preferred outcomes for one individual's wellbeing might impact positively or deleteriously upon another's. Skilled communication is needed to attain this level of shared information gathering and shared judgement in order to achieve proportionate solutions for safety and support which facilitate the 'best interests' of the individual (Mental Capacity Act, 2005).

The literature points to the need for social workers to operate with an appropriate theoretical model of disability – 'the social model of disability' – where the assumption of impairment is that of normalcy. This stands opposed to a focus on the physical limitations of impairment, which is often accompanied by a desire to promote adjustment to a perceived 'normal' world occupied by the able-bodied (Oliver and Sapey, 1999; 2006). The social model of disability argues that such attitudes constitute barriers which when a) internalised, b) are reproduced behaviourally and c) become institutionalised create disabling psychosocial and structural interrelationships and environments for people with impairments (Thomas, 2007; Sapey, 2009). In relation to communication, society places a high value upon the written and spoken word. However, the more appropriate social model of disability recognises the importance of not framing communication strategies on the basis of this privileged reality but respecting how the other person senses, perceives and communicates about their world. The Disability Discrimination Act (2005) places a duty upon organisations and professional workers to be proactive in activating this 'positive communication'.

'Valuing People' (Department of Health, 2001) identified that people with learning and/or sensory disabilities do not have one recognised set of language tools but are dependent on professionals to use individually tailored communication technologies using additional forms of communication like objects, pictures, signs, gestures and symbols. In addition, the policy and other literature supports the need for workers to use a 'common language' or 'total communication system' that utilises a range of communication mediums to encourage inclusion in communication at any level or point of professional encounter with a service user.

Research surrounding communicating with people with aphasia similarly emphasises an attitude to interaction which is 'authentic' with people prepared to engage with each other, and to find mutually intelligible and accessible forms of communication (Parr et al., 2004). This literature identifies how people need additional time to process information; formulate and express ideas; and negotiate choice and decisions. Workers often displayed ignorance in how to react to a communication disability or language impairment, yet changes to structures and processes make a difference, such as timing a meeting to a time when an individual is most alert; providing paper to explore ideas pictorially; or ensuring quiet and minimising distractions (Parr et al., 2004).

The literature suggests that the social worker should prepare to empathise with the social barriers faced by people with impairments and their carers (Barnes, 1991). In my previous published research of specialist communication with parents of children with disabilities I found that while social workers sought to understand parenting behaviour in social terms, it was not sufficient, as it required the *social model of disability analysis* to emphasise the influence of systemic barriers on families' ability to function in their social environment (Woodcock and Tregaskis, 2008). By 'adding on' a practical application of the social model of disability approach, I achieved greater appreciation of the ecological context of the everyday living environment. Moreover, the research revealed that social workers needed to be prepared to discuss and contain strong feelings of pain and frustration being presented by service users with disabilities due to the influence of those systemic barriers in their lives. There was a high emotional content to the discourse, with a resulting impact on the listener. Systemic barriers included a service failure to take the specific needs of an individual and families into account, in favour of a 'one size fits all' model. Another service failure was to provide 'joined-up services' for individual needs. For example, one child was recommended activities by a speech therapist which involved sitting upright, but the child could not sit up independently and occupational therapy would not supply the chair needed because the child was not on their list. Barnes (1991) would explain these systemic barriers as occurring because services are developed primarily to meet the normative needs of the provider, and take insufficient account of the diverse needs of client groups. The effect of such normative provision on disabled people's lives is described more extensively in Barnes (1991).

Practice application

Drawing on the social model of disability, a key issue for the social worker (in Practice Example 9.1) is to identify the barriers in society which are impacting on his communication with Sue, and seek to overcome them.

Practice Example 9.1

Sue and Steve Preston

Preparatory Stage

Our practice example shows a number of meetings between Sue, a 32-year-old woman, her husband Steve (35 years old) and their new social worker. Sue survived a stroke two years ago. The stroke caused a lasting impairment to her brain function and speech. Since the stroke she tires more easily when moving around the home. Steve has become a full-time carer for his wife. The last review of Sue's care was six months ago. Steve is described by the various health professionals involved in Sue's life as being very protective of his wife and essentially operates a gate-keeping role in relation to visitors and professionals, from a well-meaning position of seeking to shield Sue from getting upset. Both Sue and Steve are distressed about the impact of the impairment upon their lives. Sue was very young to have suffered a stroke. Their loss at not fulfilling the hopes and plans they had made together is palpable. There is an air of pessimism about the future.

A first step is to acknowledge that barriers are likely to be located within himself as attitudes and behaviour (Marchant and Page, 2003). The social worker must start from an attitudinal position which is that Sue has a right to be communicated with and be facilitated to express decisions concerning her life (Wilson et al., 2008). The social worker needs to find out as much as he can about the way in which Sue communicates, and value that means of communication. Importantly, it is the responsibility of the social worker to determine it (Morris, 2002; Wilson et al., 2008). This suggests another attitudinal position, summarised by Wilson et al. (2008: 323) as 'a point where we believe the person has something to say and then think creatively about how this can be achieved.' Communication could use different methods and formats beyond that of verbalisation such as body language but also pictures, symbols, signs and media packages. Moreover, the background literature identified how the use of several methods in tandem encouraged a more thorough understanding for both parties – 'a total communication system'. Given this, I have chosen to refer to two skills for this specialist communication strategy: *'actively look for the channels of communication that the person is using'* and *'using the whole communication spectrum'*. The social worker in the practice example needs to ensure he has the knowledge and skills to use the different methods of communication. Thus, planning his communication strategy at this preparatory stage will be essential in increasing his confidence and skill.

In promoting Sue's right to be communicated with and facilitating expression of her thoughts and feelings, the social worker must consider how he will respond if Sue's carer, in this case her husband Steve, communicates for her. In addition to attending to her right for privacy and to be communicated with in her own right, the background literature identified how carers' perspectives are not always consistent with those of the service user. The social worker needs to be both confident and empathic in dealing with the likelihood of Steve communicating for Sue. This will include recognising how his behaviour might be a response to the experience of systemic barriers in their lives. As opposed to seeing Steve's 'gate-keeping' behaviour as over-protectiveness, a social model of disability approach would consider if this was about his attempts to overcome systemic barriers to his wife receiving effective help such as reducing her feelings of depression, or preparation for significant life changes (like leaving familiar surroundings to go for rehabilitation or treatment). The basic communication skill of *'tuning-in'* will enable preparation for delivering an empathic and challenging response to his communication should it arise. In Chapter 4, I described how Shulman (2009) identifies *'tuning-in'* as a vital communication skill for identifying and attending to thoughts and feelings, particularly if indirectly expressed, to enable service users to feel 'listened to' and understood.

Thus, when first meeting with the family, the social worker must employ the four parts of the basic communication skills listed in Chapter 4: 'achieving a shared purpose', that is:

➤ *'being clear on role'*

➤ *'being clear on purpose'*

➤ *'reach for feedback'*

➤ *'showing empathy'*.

Practice Example 9.2, points 1–4 begins with the social worker seeking to be 'clear on purpose' with Sue's husband, Steve.

While the social worker had sought to meet with Sue first, as anticipated, Steve is seeking communication with the social worker ahead of his wife. He is communicating anxiety about whether this new social worker will be able to effect any positive changes in his wife's situation and, related to this, whether any communication with his wife will simply cause her further upset. The way Steve communicates this is indirect,

Practice Example 9.2

Sue and Steve Preston

Beginnings

[1]SW: Hello. Mr Preston?

Steve: Yes.

SW: Great. I'm Ewan Jones, a social worker. I wrote to your wife to arrange an appointment today. You wrote to us saying that a review of services was needed for your wife. I'd like to get a bit of an understanding from you both of what it's like for her and you at the moment...starting with your wife and then both of you. Can I come in?

[2]Steve: Yes, in here. Thanks. You can sit down here. Right, OK. (*They both sit down on settees at right angles to each other. Social worker looks for Mrs Preston in order to begin. Mr Preston sits forward, rubbing his hands in an agitated manner, waiting for the social worker to start talking.*) What is it that you need to know then?

[3]SW: Uh, what I want to do is see if the situation of six months ago is still the same today. I'm just going to try and get some up-to-date information from you and your wife about how your wife's recovery is going, and how she is managing the various things in everyday life at the moment.

Steve: Are you going to make a change then?

SW: What we need to do together, what we need to work on, is find out from your wife, and from you, what are the things that are affecting you both, and what we can do is see if we can actually help with your wife's situation, okay?

Steve: What? So how do you want to help?

[4]SW: (*leans forward in chair, puts elbows on thighs and opens hands out, palms showing*) Yes, I'd like to help...I can see you are worried about your wife. Well, it would be finding out things like 'What's the impact of your wife's condition at the moment?' and 'What's going well or not going well day-to-day?' and 'Are the services working out for her?'

Steve: Well, she gets tired more easily, um, she enjoys kind of going out for walks and that, but since the incident a few weeks ago she's not too sure about that now, so she's, uh you know, she used to be really extrovert, but now she's just kind of really going back into herself. You know, not being able to go out much. It's really difficult for her to communicate as well, as it's really affected her speech.

[5]SW: You know, Mr Preston, is your wife around? It really feels like we should have her here too. It just feels as if we're talking about her and her views are, like, really the most central.

▶

◀

Steve: She's sleeping. She gets tired, you know, she gets tired a lot. You know, it's so difficult to arrange a time for people to come around, and when she's feeling well enough to talk, and you know, we're both around. When she goes to sleep, I try to go to sleep as well. It's the only time I've got. Or, I'm catching up on everything else that needs to be done in the house, um, so it's really kind of, it's really tricky, so ... you know, all different people, like nurses and that, they talk to me and ... yeah, treat me like I'm an expert and I'm meant to know every-thing about the whole illness, and to be honest, I don't know how my wife is reacting, and I don't know what to do, but I do my best.

[6]SW: I'm sure you do. (*pause*) Is there a particular time of day that's better for your wife when we could meet, you know, sometimes when people have had a stroke they find that they have a bit more energy at a par-ticular time of the day.

Steve: Yeah, kind of, early afternoon is alright, you know, but it depends, you know, it changes from day-to-day. I mean, it tends to be kind of early afternoon she's alright. First thing in the morning she's not great. She's taken her medication so it's got to have time to kick in. She doesn't, you know, since she's not been out she's not comfortable talking in front of too many people. Certainly not talking to many people for any length of time. She's aware of her disability, and she knows that other people are aware of that and, you know, I don't know how that makes her feel. I can only imagine. And then people ask me questions you know, I can only second guess.

[7]SW: How do you find it best to communicate with your wife? I'll try to do the same ...

Steve: Well, we can, you know, we can talk to each other, but it is a lot ... it's drawn out a lot more. Her words are slurred a lot, so it's really difficult sometimes to grasp what she's saying. I mean, I know you get better at it. You know, it's been two years now, but I'm still kind of starting to understand her more now. It's just, you know, where she gets really bad days, and I'm really stressed, that we don't talk so well.

[8]SW: OK, so I must make sure I have plenty of time. What about writing things down or drawing things ... does that help?

[9]Steve: Sometimes. You could try, but she's not stupid. It's an injury. She's not mentally ill. She's brain damaged through a stroke, and not... you know ... her behaviour's been affected because of brain injury, but it's not a mental health problem.

[10]SW: No, I promise you Mr Preston, I will not speak to your wife like she is stupid. It's just that it's important that she contributes as much as she can to the meeting. I want to make sure that I do everything I can to communicate as well as possible. *(Silence for ten seconds)* You know, you have a right to an assessment as a carer too. You are doing so

▶

◀

much here. Would it be OK for us to meet up on our own too, after we have met with your wife?

Steve: Um ... I don't know ... obviously if you ask me the same questions in front of her then, you know, it makes it really difficult for me. I know you need to talk to her, but I don't want to be put in the situation where I have to lie in front of my wife. You know, I've got my feelings, but you know, I don't want her getting more upset when ...

SW: If there's anything you find particularly difficult to raise when she's there, then perhaps it would be good if we can meet up again after that to talk about your needs so that we can support you?

Steve: No, I'm okay, I'm fine, but I need to make sure that she's getting the best, you know, that's all we need to do, we just need to start with that. Like I say, I don't want to be put in the situation where she finds out how difficult it is for me and you know, how tough it can be trying to keep everything together. I know she knows, but I don't trust myself emotionally, you know, to try and keep it together in front of her, and you know, that's tough ... so ... I can see what you're saying ... I can see where you're coming from, but um, I don't know. Maybe if you spoke to her and I came in at the end, that might make me feel better.

[11]SW: OK. Great, then that gives your wife the opportunity to talk to me on her own. I have to make sure that that happens. When I come, we'll just see if your wife is happy with those arrangements as well. Can we arrange a date at this stage to come back and meet your wife?

Steve: Yeah, this week or ...?

SW: Yes, this week if it's convenient

Steve: Okay, uh ... Thursday's quite good, usually ... I would say about half twelve. She won't be able to ... any earlier on. Can I tell Sue that things are going to get sorted? Are you guys gonna get on top of it now?

SW: Well that's the plan, obviously to come along find out what she actually wants in the future, to see what we can actually do. But obviously if she's not feeling well on that day ... Well, what I'll do is I'll give you a ring and see how she's feeling about a quarter of an hour before I'm due to come over. Is that OK?

Steve: Are you actually going to turn up?

[12]SW: Yes I will, yeah (*writes appointment in diary*)

Steve: But there's so many workers who are coming but just don't turn up. They expect us to deal with all this stuff, you know.

[13]SW: I can only apologise for the sort of experiences you've had, but I certainly will.

both through seeking clarification and reassurance of the social worker's purpose and method for working and non-verbally such as agitated body language. The relevant section from the dialogue (Practice Example 9.2, points 3–4) is provided here:

SW: Uh, what I want to do is see if the situation of six months ago is still the same today. I'm just going to try and get some up-to-date information from you and your wife about how your wife's recovery is going, and how she is managing the various things in everyday life at the moment.

Steve: Are you going to make a change then?

SW: What we need to do together, what we need to work on, is find out from your wife, and from you, what are the things that are affecting you both, and what we can do is see if we can actually help with your wife's situation, okay?

Steve: What? So how do you want to help?

SW: (*leans forward in chair, puts elbows on thighs and opens hands out, palms showing*) Yes, I'd like to help … I can see you are worried about your wife. Well, it would be finding out things like 'What's the impact of your wife's condition at the moment?' and 'What's going well or not going well day-to-day?' and 'Are the services working out for her?'

In this section we see how the social worker recognises that Steve's communication could relate to his experience of systemic barriers. He takes time to explain the purpose of his work, and through using the basic communication skill (from Chapter 4) of *'putting feelings into words'* he demonstrates that he has *'reflectively listened'* to Steve's worries about his wife's emotional wellbeing. ('Yes, I'd like to help … I can see you are worried about your wife.') His statement is mirrored by his body language changing to a more 'open' and receptive position, which emphasises a wish to engage with him on that matter ('leans forward in chair, puts elbows on thighs and opens hands out, palms showing'). This seems to constitute a specialist communication skill of *'communicating empathy for the experience of systemic barriers'*.

While the social worker recognises that Steve's communication could relate to his experience of systemic barriers, he must not become so focused on this particular explanation that he fails to see the possibility of others. One explanation for Steve's reluctance for the social worker and other professionals to see Sue on her own is that he might be worried that she may disclose information that he is causing her significant harm. The aforementioned policy guidance concerning safeguarding vulnerable adults emphasises that social workers must recognise that people with disabilities are particularly vulnerable to abuse whether by strangers or by carers. Physical impairment and/or learning difficulties can render a person more vulnerable to being exploited as victims of physical, emotional or sexual violence. Furthermore, historically, many of the communication systems that disabled people use do not have a wide range of words, signs or symbols to describe feelings, parts of the body (such as genitalia) or acts of maltreatment (Wilson et al., 2008).

The social worker seeks to ensure that he attends to Sue's rights to dignity and to be communicated with about her needs by refusing to take the conversation any further without her being present. He follows the aforementioned policy guidance concerning safeguarding vulnerable adults and mental capacity to make sure Sue has the opportunity to express how she feels about her life situation, particularly whether she feels safe from harm (Practice Example 9.2, point 5: 'You know, Mr Preston, is your wife around? It really feels like we should have her here too. It just feels as if we're talking about her and her views are, like, really the most central' and point 11: 'Great, then that gives your wife the opportunity to talk to me on her own. I have to make sure that that happens.')

In arranging the subsequent meeting with Sue, the social worker uses the opportunity to uncover the best communication method for communicating with her (Practice Example 9.2, points 7–8). He asks Steve for his perspective on what works best in communication with Sue. In so doing, the worker operates the aforementioned specialist communication skill of *'actively look for the channels of communication that the person is using'*. Furthermore, he initiates the idea of using non-verbal forms of communication, demonstrating that he is willing to apply the principles of 'total communication' and think more creatively about the different media he could use in addition to verbalisation. This demonstrates the specialist communication in *'using the whole communication spectrum'*.

SW: How do you find it best to communicate with your wife? I'll try to do the same ...

SU: Well, we can, you know, we can talk to each other, but it is a lot ... it's drawn out a lot more. Her words are slurred a lot, so it's really difficult sometimes to grasp what she's saying. I mean, I know you get better at it. You know, it's been two years now, but I'm still kind of starting to understand her more now. It's just you know, where she gets really bad days, and I'm really stressed, that we don't talk so well.

SW: OK, so I must make sure I have plenty of time. What about writing things down or drawing things ... does that help?

Another aspect to this section of the dialogue is the social worker's preparedness to discuss the impairment in a frank and more individualised manner, rather than a generalised application from formal knowledge of the impairment. The social worker demonstrates the same communication strategy when he draws on his formal knowledge about the impairment to identify that medication may cause particular times of the day to be more difficult for Sue to concentrate, but he does not assume that this is necessarily the case for Sue. Rather he seeks to understand the way the impairment may impact upon Sue in an individual way (Practice Example 9.2, point 6: 'Is there a particular time of day that's better for your wife when we could meet, you know, sometimes when people have had a stroke they find that they have a bit more energy at a particular time of the day.')

In my aforementioned earlier research with parents of disabled children, I indicated that it will be felt as more supportive to service users, through being more inclusive to their individual need, if a specialist communication approach is taken that seeks to *'validate and recognise "private" knowledge of the individual nuances of the impairment as applied to a person'* (Woodcock and Tregaskis, 2008). Social workers need to open themselves up to hearing *new* knowledge about the individual characteristics of an impairment, and the individual way it affects family life. My research found that some professionals were either unable or unwilling to do this, which suggested that the problem lay with the disabling attitudes of the professionals concerned. This presents another example of the way barriers in society impact on communication with people with impairments.

This specialist communication theme of *'validate and recognise "private" knowledge of the individual nuances of the impairment'* was dominant within the research transcripts of the forum theatre undertaken for this practice setting for this book. The qualifying social workers showed continued respect for the service user's expert knowledge in relation to their own impairment or disability. They acknowledged that their understanding of an impairment or specific disability was likely to be fairly low-level, and, as disability affects each individual uniquely, that the only people who could truly have an in-depth and longitudinal understanding of the minutiae of the situation were the service users. As such, partnership emerged as such a strong theme throughout the research of communication in this practice setting. Recognition of the service user expertise meant that the service user was consulted about the appropriateness of all possible actions throughout a meeting.

The third dominant theme arising from the research transcripts for the book concerned the way in which *promises* were used in this practice setting. Although the issue of commitment emerged in other practice settings, the social workers demonstrated the skill of recognising the need for a more personally meaningful commitment to service users with disabilities who were feeling let down by social care and social work services. While the social workers did not use the term 'systemic barriers' to describe the use of promises to empathise with feelings of disappointment, the aforementioned specialist communication skill of *'communicating empathy for the experience of systemic barriers'* did seem to be what they were describing. An illustration of the use of promises in this way is within our practice example (9.2) at the point where the social worker seeks to empathise with Steve's worries that his wife might be distressed by his communication (as seen at point 9), while simultaneously emphasising that he will treat Sue with dignity and respect (Practice Example 9.2, point 10: *'No, I promise you Mr. Preston, I will not speak to your wife like she is stupid.'*) Also, at the end of the practice example, he responds to Steve's communication of mistrust that he might be 'like all the others' and 'let them down' by promising that he is different to the previous workers (Practice Example 9.2, point 13: *'I can only apologise for the sort of experiences you've had, but I certainly will.'*) He uses non-verbal communication to additionally emphasise the point through immediately writing the appointment in the diary in full observation by Steve (Practice Example 9.2, point 12). The qualifying social workers in the study for the book noted that promises carried weight and therefore should not be given lightly, but if used appropriately would build trust and rapport with the service user. There were two aspects to this theme: making realistic promises to build trust and the importance of not making promises that cannot be kept.

In Practice Example 9.3 the social worker is meeting with Sue. He seeks to create an atmosphere for the communication of thoughts and feelings by engaging in *'reflective listening'*. In Chapter 4 I described how *'reflective listening'* conveys the assurance of warmth and concern while paying attention to the service user's communication, whether through narrative or those non-verbal instances of feeling that illuminate their perception of, and response to, their difficulties and situation. This helps that person feel able to disclose information or worries without fearing blame or misunderstanding. The social worker begins by ensuring that he is sat opposite Sue, so that both can see each other's faces clearly and pick up any non-verbal communication to aid understanding (Practice Example 9.3, point 15). As part of the basic communication skill described in Chapter 4 of *'achieving a shared purpose'*, he states that he recognises that Sue might wish to have Steve present to provide communication support, but also explains why he would like to speak to her on her own in order to hear her own perspective of her situation. He uses short sentences and allows for pauses to give Sue time to mentally process the content of what he is saying, and time to formulate her answers (Practice Example 9.3, points 14–16). This specialist communication skill of *'taking time'* is vital to gaining shared understandings. The skill gives Sue confidence that she will not need Steve present to aid her communication for the meeting, and so it proceeds.

Practice Example 9.3

Sue Preston

Work Phase

SW:	Hello again, Mr Preston.
Steve:	Hello. Come in. Sue's in the living room. Do you want a cup of tea, or …?
SW:	Tea would be great. Milk and sugar, thanks. Shall I go on in to see Sue?
Steve:	Yes, hang on (*walks past the social worker and leads him into the living room. He walks over to Sue and waves his hand towards the social worker*) Sue, the social worker's here … er … Ewan …
[14]SW:	Yes, Ewan Jones (*smiles and walks towards Sue*). Good to meet you. Are you happy for us to meet here together this afternoon?
Sue:	(*Nods her head*) Yes.
SW:	I have come to talk to you about how to help you and your husband. He wrote to me saying you wanted a review of services.
Sue:	(*Nods her head*) Yes.
[15]SW:	I'd like to talk with you on your own first. I need to hear your views. (*pause*) Steve said he would join us later on. Is that OK with you? (*Sits down opposite Sue. Looks directly at Sue's face.*)
Sue:	(*Nods her head*) Yes.
Steve:	(*Comes in with two cups of tea and places them on the table next to Sue.*) I'll be in the kitchen for a bit, getting dinner ready. I'll come back when you are done.
SW:	Thanks. Uh, Mrs Preston … Sue, is that OK? (*Looks at Sue's face and she nods*) I know you had the stroke two years ago. It must have been a tough time. (*Sue nods her head. Silence for about 5 seconds*) Tell me what things you feel you need help with at the moment.
Sue:	Uh, moving … (*waves arm, gesturing around the room*) … going out.
SW:	You mean getting around the house? Going outside?
[16]Sue:	Yes … uh … (*sighs*)
[17]SW:	Erm, Sue, I've got these flash cards with me in my bag here. They are really good … helps us to talk about problems you may have. Look, they have pictures, see? (*pause*) If I show you them one at a time, perhaps you could tell me if the picture shows something you would like help with? (*pause*) Have you seen them before?
Sue:	No. (*Leans forward, looks interested*)

▶

◄

SW:	OK, look at this, what about walking? (*shows a card*)
Sue:	(*nods*) Yes, slow. Steve.
SW:	Steve helps you? (*Sue nods*) It's slow, but you walk without problems? (*Sue nods*) OK, so not great, and I can see that it's worrying you.
SW:	(*shows a second card*) What about getting up and washing?
Sue:	No. Steve.
SW:	Steve helps you to get up and washed in the morning? Are you OK with that, or would you like someone else to come and help you?
Sue:	No. Steve.
SW:	OK. You would prefer Steve to help.
[18]Sue:	Yes. Steve ... (*Sue becomes tearful*) Helps me ... housework.
[19]SW:	You're upset. Sue, tell me, what's wrong?
Sue:	Steve ...

(Sue cries quietly. Silence for 20 seconds. Social worker sits quietly.)

[20]SW:	Sue, you're really sad ... Can we talk about it? Look at these cards. Do any of those pictures show why you are upset?
Sue:	(*Picks picture of man and woman smiling and hugging*) Steve.
[21]SW:	Does this show you being happy with Steve?
Sue:	(*nods*) Yes.
SW:	Do you want me to get Steve?
Sue:	(*nods*)
[22]SW:	OK. I'll just get him. Look, our tea's getting cold! Here you are.

(Gives Sue the cup of tea and then goes out to the kitchen.)

SW:	Steve, erm, Sue's got a bit upset. She would like you to come back in. Is that OK?
Steve:	Yeah. Upset? She does get tearful. It's frustrating for her.

(They walk back to the living room.)

As the meeting unfolds it becomes apparent to the social worker that Sue is becoming frustrated by being unable to explain the different issues she is experiencing in her life (Practice Example 9.3, point 16). At this point, the worker introduces the flash cards as an additional medium for their communication. In so doing, he operates the aforementioned specialist communication skill of *'using the whole communication spectrum'* (Practice Example 9.3, point 17: 'Erm … Sue, I've got these flash cards with me in my bag here. They are really good … helps us to talk about problems you may have. Look, they have pictures, see? *(pause)* If I show you them one at a time, perhaps you could tell me if the picture shows something you would like help with? *(pause)* Have you seen them before?') The social worker goes on to utilise this 'total communication' while maintaining an adult style of interaction. He makes use of *'closed questions'* other than *'open questions'*, as he has seen how Sue finds it easier to respond with 'yes' or 'no' answers (Practice Example 9.3, points 17–18). This demonstrates the importance of *'actively looking for the channels of communication that the person is using'*.

The specialist communication strategy appears to have some success in facilitating Sue's expression of thoughts and feelings. At point 18 of the dialogue, she communicates strong feelings of distress and frustration.

Sue: Steve … (*Sue becomes tearful*) Helps me … housework.

SW: You're upset. Sue, tell me, what's wrong?

Sue: Steve … (*Sue cries quietly. Silence for 20 seconds. Social worker sits quietly*)

SW: Sue, you're really sad … Can we talk about it? Look at these cards. Do any of those pictures show why you are upset?

At this point the worker shoes empathy for her distress by *'putting feelings into words'* and asks an *'open question'* to seek clarification on why she is feeling that way (Practice Example 9.3, point 19: 'You're upset. Sue, tell me, what's wrong?') He uses an *'open question'* because he is aware that there could be many reasons for her distress, including that of being in danger of harm. Policy guidance for safeguarding adults warns against the use of questions that could be construed as being 'leading'. It is apparent, however, that Sue needs additional communication support to explain and explore her distress. The social worker offers the flash cards again, which contain a number of different scenarios, including different pictures of a person being intimidated or harmed by another person (Practice Example 9.3, point 20). Arguably, the cards could still be considered as being 'leading' through offering only a selection of possible responses. Certainly, there are these limitations to the method. However, the cards do offer Sue a wider vocabulary then she currently has access to. In this event she chooses a card that indicates an expression of love between a man and a woman. The worker is careful not to assume that the scenario depicted on the card has the same meaning for Sue as it does for him. The picture could still have been interpreted as a scene of exploitation.

Again, he uses *'closed questions'* to check with Sue about the meaning of the scenario to her (Practice Example 9.3, point 21:'Does this show you being happy with Steve?').

This chapter has identified specialist communication skills required by the social worker for working as an effective partner to service users in determining very complex issues and ethical dilemmas about safeguarding and the protection of adults at risk, choice and independence ('Being'). Consideration was given to how barriers to communication can be caused by individual life experiences and dominant cultural expectations and beliefs about disability in society ('Knowing' and 'Being'). A key element of the specialist social work communication strategy was to use language that identified and addressed these societal and systemic barriers and focused on the individual nuances of an impairment for a person in their life situation ('Doing').

Mapping to the Professional Capability Framework

Qualifying Social Worker Level Capabilities

Please remember that these should be viewed as domains which overlap in an integrative manner rather than as a linear checklist.

'By the end of last placement/ the completion of qualifying programmes newly qualified social workers should have demonstrated the Knowledge, Skills and Values to work with a range of user groups, and the ability to undertake a range of tasks at a foundation level, the capacity to work with more complex situations; they should be able to work more autonomously, whilst recognising that the final decision will still rest with their supervisor; they will seek appropriate support and supervision.

The Health Professions Council (the regulator of qualified social workers) and The College have mapped the Standards of Proficiency for Social Work (SOPs) against the PCF expectations for social work students at the end of their last placement. Whilst there are some differences in the way the standards and PCF are expressed, the overall expectations are the same.'

Communication Capacity Domain – **'Knowing'** (engaging with formal and informal knowledge in communication)	**PCF 3 Diversity: Recognise diversity and apply anti-discriminatory and anti-oppressive principles in practice** ➢ Understand how an individual's identity is informed by factors such as culture, economic status, family composition, life experiences and characteristics, and take account of these to understand their experiences, questioning assumptions where necessary ➢ With reference to current legislative requirements, recognise personal and organisational discrimination and oppression and with guidance make use of a range of approaches to challenge them

PCF 5 Knowledge: Apply knowledge of social sciences, law and social work practice theory

➢ Demonstrate a critical understanding of the application to social work of research, theory and knowledge from sociology, social policy, psychology and health

➢ Demonstrate a critical understanding of the legal and policy frameworks and guidance that inform and mandate social work practice, recognising the scope for professional judgement

➢ Demonstrate and apply to practice a working knowledge of human growth and development throughout the life course

➢ Recognise the short and long term impact of psychological, socio-economic, environmental and physiological factors on people's lives, taking into account age and development, and how this informs practice

➢ Recognise how systemic approaches can be used to understand the person-in-the-environment and inform your practice

➢ Acknowledge the centrality of relationships for people and the key concepts of attachment, separation, loss, change and resilience

➢ Understand forms of harm and their impact on people, and the implications for practice, drawing on concepts of strength, resilience, vulnerability, risk and resistance, and apply to practice

➢ Demonstrate a critical knowledge of the range of theories and models for social work intervention with individuals, families, groups and communities, and the methods derived from them

➢ Value and take account of the expertise of service users, carers and professionals

KSS Adults (4): Safeguarding

Social workers must be able to recognise the risk indicators of different forms of abuse and neglect and their impact on individuals, their families or their support networks and should prioritise the protection of children and adults in vulnerable situations whenever necessary. This includes working with those who self-neglect. Social workers who work with adults must take an outcomes-focused, person-centred approach to safeguarding practice, recognising that people are experts in their own lives and working alongside them to identify person centred solutions to risk and harm.

KSS Adults (6): Effective Assessments and Outcome Based Support Planning

Social workers should demonstrate a good understanding of personalisation, the social model of disability and of human development throughout life and demonstrate a holistic approach to the identification of needs, circumstances, rights, strengths and risks. In particular, social workers need to understand the impact of trauma, loss and abuse, physical disability, physical ill health, learning disability, mental ill health, mental capacity, substance misuse, domestic abuse, aging and end of life issues

	on physical, cognitive, emotional and social development both for the individual and for the functioning of the family. They should recognise the roles and needs of informal or family carers and use holistic, systemic approaches to supporting individuals and carers. They should develop and maintain knowledge and good partnerships with local community resources in order to work effectively with individuals in connecting them with appropriate resources and support.
Communication Capacity Domain – 'Doing' (the enactment of communication strategies in interaction)	**PCF 6 Critical Reflection and Analysis: Apply critical reflection and analysis to inform and provide a rationale for professional decision-making** ➢ Apply imagination, creativity and curiosity to practice ➢ Inform decision-making through the identification and gathering of information from multiple sources, actively seeking new sources ➢ With support, rigorously question and evaluate the reliability and validity of information from different sources ➢ Demonstrate a capacity for logical, systematic, critical and reflective reasoning and apply the theories and techniques of reflective practice ➢ Know how to formulate, test, evaluate, and review hypotheses in response to information available at the time and apply in practice ➢ Begin to formulate and make explicit, evidence-informed judgements and justifiable decisions **KSS Adults (8): Supervision, Critical Reflection and Analysis** Social workers should be able to make effective use of opportunities to discuss, reflect upon and test multiple hypotheses, the role of intuition and logic in decision making, the difference between opinion and fact, the role of evidence, how to address common bias in situations of uncertainty and the reasoning of any conclusions reached and recommendations made, particularly in relation to mental capacity, mental health and safeguarding situations. Social workers should have a critical understanding of the difference between theory, research, evidence and expertise and the role of professional judgement. They should use practice evidence and research to inform the complex judgements and decisions needed to support, empower and protect their service users. They should apply imagination, creativity and curiosity to working in partnership with individuals and their carers, acknowledging the centrality of people's own expertise about their experience and needs. **KSS Children (2): Communication** Produce written case notes and reports, which are well argued, focused and jargon free. Present a clear analysis and a sound rationale for actions as well as any conclusions reached, so that all parties are well-informed.

PCF 7 Intervention and Skills: Use judgement and authority to intervene with individuals, families and communities to promote independence, provide support and prevent harm, neglect and abuse

➤ Identify and apply a range of verbal, non-verbal and written methods of communication and adapt them in line with peoples' age, comprehension and culture

➤ Be able to communicate information, advice, instruction and professional opinion so as to advocate, influence and persuade

➤ Demonstrate the ability to engage with people, and build, manage, sustain and conclude compassionate and effective relationships

➤ Demonstrate skills in sharing information appropriately and respectfully

➤ Recognise complexity, multiple factors, changing circumstances and uncertainty in people's lives, to be able to prioritise your intervention

➤ Understand the authority of the social work role and begin to use this appropriately as an accountable professional

➤ Recognise the factors that create or exacerbate risk to individuals, their families or carers, to the public or to professionals, including yourself, and contribute to the assessment and management of risk

KSS Adults (3): Person-centred Practice
They should work co-productively and innovatively with people, local communities, other professionals, agencies and services to promote self-determination, community capacity, personal and family reliance, cohesion, earlier intervention and active citizenship.

KSS Adults (4): Safeguarding
Social workers who work with adults must take an outcomes-focused, person-centred approach to safeguarding practice, recognising that people are experts in their own lives and working alongside them to identify person centred solutions to risk and harm. In situations where there is abuse or neglect or clear risk of those, social workers must work in a way that enhances involvement, choice and control as part of improving quality of life, wellbeing and safety.

KSS Adults (7): Direct Work with Individuals and Families
Social workers need to be able to work directly with individuals and their families through the professional use of self, using interpersonal skills and emotional intelligence to create relationships based on openness, transparency and empathy. They should know how to build purposeful, effective relationships underpinned by reciprocity. They should be able to communicate clearly, sensitively and effectively, applying a range of best evidence-based methods of written, oral and non-verbal communication and adapt these methods to match the person's age, comprehension and culture. Social workers should be

	capable of communicating effectively with people with specific communication needs, including those with learning disabilities, dementia, people who lack mental capacity and people with sensory impairment. **KSS Children (2): Communication** Communicate clearly and sensitively with children of different ages and abilities, their families and in a range of settings and circumstances. Use methods based on best evidence. Create immediate rapport with people not previously known which facilitates engagement and motivation to participate in child protective enquiries, assessments and services. Listen to the views, wishes and feelings of children and families and help parents and carers understand the ways in which their children communicate through their behaviour. Help them to understand how they might communicate more effectively with their children. Promote speech, language and communication support, identifying those children and adults who are experiencing difficulties expressing themselves.
Communication Capacity Domain – 'Being' (the use of 'self')	**PCF 1 Professionalism: Identify and behave as a professional social worker, committed to professional development** ➤ Be able to explain the role of the social worker in a range of contexts, and uphold the reputation of the profession ➤ Demonstrate professionalism in terms of presentation, demeanour, reliability, honesty and respectfulness ➤ Recognise the impact of self in interaction with others, making appropriate use of personal experience ➤ Be able to recognise and maintain personal and professional boundaries ➤ Recognise your professional limitations and how to seek advice ➤ Demonstrate a commitment to your continuing learning and development ➤ With support, take steps to manage and promote own safety, health, wellbeing and emotional resilience **KSS Adults (7): Direct work with individuals and families** Social workers should be capable of communicating effectively with people with specific communication needs, including those with learning disabilities, dementia, people who lack mental capacity and people with sensory impairment. They should do this in ways that are engaging, respectful, motivating and effective, even when dealing with conflict – whether perceived or actual – anger and resistance to change. **KSS Children (2): Communication** Act respectfully even when people are angry, hostile and resistant to change. Manage tensions between parents, carers and family members, in ways that show persistence, determination and professional confidence.

PCF 2 Values and Ethics: Apply social work ethical principles and values to guide professional practice
- ➢ Recognise and, with support, manage the impact of own values on professional practice
- ➢ Manage potentially conflicting or competing values, and, with guidance, recognise, reflect on, and work with ethical dilemmas
- ➢ Demonstrate respectful partnership work with service users and carers, eliciting and respecting their needs and views, and promoting their participation in decision-making wherever possible
- ➢ Recognise and promote individuals' rights to autonomy and self-determination

KSS Adults (5): Mental Capacity
Social workers must model and lead a change of approach, away from that where the default setting is 'safety first', towards a person-centred culture where individual choice is encouraged and where the right of all individuals to express their own lifestyle choices is recognised and valued.

In working with those where there is no concern over capacity, social workers should take all practicable steps to empower people to make their own decisions, recognising that people are experts in their own lives and working alongside them to identify person-centred solutions to risk and harm, recognising the individual's right to make 'unwise' decisions.

PCF 3 Diversity: Recognise diversity and apply anti-discriminatory and anti-oppressive principles in practice
(Appropriately placed in both 'Knowing' and 'Being')
- ➢ With reference to current legislative requirements, recognise personal and organisational discrimination and oppression and with guidance make use of a range of approaches to challenge them
- ➢ Recognise and manage the impact on people of the power invested in your role

KSS Adults (3): Person-centred Practice
They should coordinate and facilitate a wide range of practical and emotional support, and discharge legal duties to complement people's own resources and networks, so that all individuals (no matter their background, health status or mental capacity), carers and families can exercise choice and control, (supporting individuals to make their own decisions, especially where they may lack capacity) and meet their needs and aspirations in personalised, creative and often novel ways. They should work co-productively and innovatively with people, local communities, other professionals, agencies and services to promote self- determination, community capacity, personal and family reliance, cohesion, earlier intervention and active citizenship.

	PCF 4 Rights, Justice and Economic Wellbeing: Advance human rights and promote social justice and economic wellbeing ➤ Understand, identify and apply in practice the principles of social justice, inclusion and equality ➤ Understand how legislation and guidance can advance or constrain people's rights and recognise how the law may be used to protect or advance their rights and entitlements ➤ Work within the principles of human and civil rights and equalities legislation, differentiating and beginning to work with absolute, qualified and competing rights and differing needs and perspectives ➤ Recognise the impact of poverty and social exclusion and promote enhanced economic status through access to education, work, housing, health services and welfare benefits
	PCF 8 Contexts and Organisations: Engage with, inform, and adapt to changing contexts that shape practice. Operate effectively within own organisational frameworks and contribute to the development of services and organisations. Operate effectively within multi-agency and inter-professional partnerships and settings ➤ Recognise that social work operates within, and responds to, changing economic, social, political and organisational contexts ➤ Understand the roles and responsibilities of social workers in a range of organisations, lines of accountability and the boundaries of professional autonomy and discretion ➤ Understand legal obligations, structures and behaviours within organisations and how these impact on policy, procedure and practice ➤ Be able to work within an organisation's remit and contribute to its evaluation and development **KSS Adults (9): Organisational Context** They must understand and work effectively within financial and legal frameworks, obligations, structures and culture, in particular Human Rights and Equalities legislation, the Care Act, Mental Capacity Act, Mental Health Act and accompanying guidance and codes of practice. They must be able to operate successfully in their organisational context, demonstrating effective time management, caseload management and be capable of reconciling competing demands and embrace information, data and technology appropriate to their role. They should have access to regular quality supervision to support their professional resilience and emotional and physical wellbeing.

10

Working with People with Mental Health Problems

Summary of Specialist Communication Skills in this Chapter

➢ promoting understanding of links between experiences and symptoms

➢ tuning-in to experience the individual experience of mental 'distress'

➢ being open to communication at all levels

➢ use of silences

➢ gives time to process thoughts or feelings and respond

➢ maintains a non-threatening body position.

Policy and background literature

Social workers are the core of the Approved Mental Health Professional (AMHP) workforce in England and Wales and undertake the role of Mental Health Officers in Scotland. In this complex and challenging area of practice, social workers work within complicated legal frameworks to operate a rights-based practice for protection when decisions have to be taken for people to receive interventions (The Mental Health Act, 1983 and 2007 (England and Wales); The Mental Health (Care and Treatment) (Scotland) Act, 2000). Social workers balance competing rights to optimise involvement in decisions and ensure that the least restrictive and invasive measures are taken to secure wellbeing. Yet, while mental health social workers are considered to have advanced relationship-based skills to engage in this complex work (Allen, 2014), policy and practice guidance gives a very limited message about social work communication skills (Department of Health, 1999; Department of Health, 2012). It could be argued that this is a reflection of a lack of attention and clarity to the roles of professionals in this sector. Recent years have seen significant organisational change as local government social service departments integrated within Health and/or Social Care Trusts, and change through the creation of new roles for mental health professionals. There were concerns that the knowledge and skills from the socially informed training of ASWs was potentially being insufficiently recognised and that the place of social interventions might be compromised by a health perspective (Bowl, 2009). Interestingly, however, although current government policy is emphasising even more integration of health and social care to meet principles of person-centred practice, prevention and wellbeing (the Care Act 2014), attention has been given to the vital role of social workers for working in partnership with service users to harness informal support systems and challenge barriers to inclusion (Allen, 2014). Two key areas of mental health social work expertise are highlighted: i) the social perspective to mental health which challenges illness-based medical models and promotes recovery and service user perspectives of lived experience, and ii) the rights-based approach which challenges discrimination and stigmatisation. I should note that the measures within the Care Act (2014) for adult safeguarding are equally applicable to this practice area, and as such, readers should read the previous chapter about working with adults with disability.

Within this integrated 'joined-up' health and social orientation, policy has sought to balance the status of mental health services with services for physical health (Department of Health, 2012). The rhetoric builds on policy which has required a more positive emphasis towards mental health as being concerned with health and developmental wellbeing and not just illness (Department of Health, 1999; Department of Health, 2004a). Mental health should be viewed as recovery, not as a deficit static state, but as a state of developmental wellness, dependent on several factors that can change over time (Health Advisory Service, 1995; Mental Health Foundation, 1999; World Health Organization, 2001). Thus, 'mental health' is no longer just the province of specialist mental health workers operating within multidisciplinary community and primary-care settings offering assessment, consultation and outreach to identify severe, complex need, or specialised services for severe, complex and enduring conditions. The broader definition of mental health services includes primary care professionals promoting mental health and initiating early intervention, and this includes social workers located within any practice setting. We conclude that, in terms of communication strategies, these should include increased positive emphasis and openness to mental health and wellbeing at every level of intervention.

Yet, entrenched derogatory Western stereotypes of mental health persist (Royal College of Psychiatrists, 1998; World Health Organization, 2001; World Health Organization, 2005). The inequality and discrimination faced by people with mental health problems has been highlighted by many policy documents in this area (Department of Health, 1999; National Institute for Clinical Excellence, 2002; Crisis, 2003; Department of Health, 2006b; Department of Health, 2012). Unfortunately, professionals can perpetuate stigmatisation through feelings of fear of perceived unpredictability and aggression, or through an unwillingness to consider mental health as operating along a continuum of 'normal' human experience and clinical disorder, for fear of acknowledging their own vulnerability to such problems (Dogra et al., 2002). As opposed to embracing the positivity behind the term 'mental health', it is still perceived as a derogatory term, with a tendency to avoid its use (Dogra et al., 2002).

Many people find coming to terms with mental distress and diagnosis a long and difficult process. Their experience of stigmatising attitudes, home or financial insecurity and loss of relationships causes isolation and social withdrawal. Fear concerning emotional and physical safety is pervading (Mental Health Foundation, 2000). Research (Mental Health Foundation, 1997) highlights how the actions of 'seeking and achieving acceptance from others' is a vital element of survival because it provides a means of achieving self-acceptance. Many people with mental distress seek out and create their own 'accepting communities' to achieve shared experience and shared identity because they felt alone in their own experiences and fearful. Indeed, as an illustration, social work research has repeatedly identified the importance of the role of 'supportive confidante' for depressed mothers. Thus, social workers need to communicate emotional support as 'being there for the service user', not just in terms of a physical presence, but a sense of safety and security for the person in distress and a sense of being unconditionally accepted. Service users cite the importance of their relationships with social workers as achieving a level of depth and consistency not achieved with other professionals (Mental Health Foundation, 2000; Bowl, 2009).

An orientation towards 'recovery' as opposed to becoming 'symptom-free' has been propounded by the service user movement (and now taken up by government policy) as a way of dealing with the stigma of having a 'mental illness' and labelled as being a 'mental patient' (National Institute for Mental Health England, 2005; Bowl, 2009; HM Government, 2012). This entails focusing on strengths and encouraging inclusion through participation in social and occupational activities, such as attending leisure centres. Communication needs to be about developing strengths and abilities to build resilience while sustaining an optimistic perspective (Scottish Executive, 2006a; Scottish Executive, 2006b). An aspect of this person-centred perspective is for communication to be culturally sensitive, such as using phrases and idioms which are ethnospecific; attending to the relevance of traditional and cultural healing systems; and taking into account gender relations and the placing of individuals in their families

(Al-Krenawi and Graham, 2000). Religious faith and spiritual beliefs are often cited by people with mental health problems as a helpful factor by giving meaning in their lives and a reason to continue through deep mental distress (Mental Health Foundation, 2000).

Mental distress frequently coexists and interacts with other problems in everyday living, such as repeated relationship breakdown, problems in substance use, social exclusion and criminal activity. Problems are likely to be multiple and compounding. From the research underpinning this book, an important communication issue for the social worker seems to be that of 'promoting understanding of links between experiences and symptoms' – both in terms of how past experiences affect current behaviour and symptoms, and also how the problems in everyday living impact upon symptoms. If these everyday problems could be attended to, then the symptoms could improve. Such complex and potentially dangerous situations require social workers to evaluate risk of the person causing significant harm to themselves and others, whether they need safeguarding from exploitation or harm, and whether they have the capacity to give informed consent to services and treatment (Mental Capacity Act, 2005). They have to judge appropriate limits to confidentiality. Sometimes compulsory powers are exercised to enforce detention. Communication skills are needed to obtain the information to make these judgements within the context of dealing with challenging and/or aggressive behaviour. Social workers need to be aware that their feelings about managing uncertainty and being 'agents of social control' could impact upon the communication processes with a service user.

The day-to-day lives of people with severe and enduring mental health problems are made harder by poor physical health, which only serves to increase the social exclusion they already experience. Life chances in education, employment, housing and social networks are all affected. A particular concern is that much of this illness goes undetected. This is in part due to social exclusion and to the tendency for physical health symptoms to be confused with mental health symptoms allowing serious problems to remain untreated (Phelan et al., 2001). This masking of symptoms can be caused by assumptions made by health and social care staff involved in caring for people with severe and enduring mental health problems. For instance, complaints of ill health such as lethargy and tiredness can be assumed to be what are termed the negative symptoms of psychotic illness but are also indicators of many of the physical health problems common among people with mental health problems. Similarly, staff can make inaccurate assumptions about the attitudes of people with mental health problems towards their own physical health. These commonly include that people with mental health problems are not concerned about weight gain, or do not have high levels of commitment to stopping smoking, eating healthily or engaging in physical exercise programmes. There is good research evidence to show that people with mental health problems are in fact at least as concerned about their physical wellbeing as anyone (Osborn et al., 2003). People experiencing severe mental ill health have themselves complained that insufficient attention was paid to their physical health (Petit-Zeman et al., 2002).

Literature also highlights inadequate recognition of mental health needs of people with physical impairments and disabilities even though they are even more likely to be users of mental health services, and people with mental health difficulties are more likely to have physical impairments as a consequence of accidents (Morris, 2004). Service users report how not getting an appropriate response for mental health needs causes fear; for example, staff interacted with them differently on discovering mental health difficulties, and/or medication for physical conditions had negative effects on mental health and vice versa. Through the 'Choosing Health' policy, the previous Labour government required workers to adopt 'a new approach' to the physical healthcare of people with mental health problems through tackling health and social inequalities (Department of Health, 2004b). Social workers need to ensure that their communication attends to both mental health needs and physical health and impairment.

In relation to working with older service users with mental health needs, there is a wider literature for working with people with dementia and other cognitive impairments, and this is covered in more detail in Chapter 12 concerning 'Working with Older People'. Put simply, a person's basic tools of communication, such as speech and memory, may be impaired, so people with dementia often have some difficulty communicating through language because they feel a lot of pressure in having to think quickly, particularly where higher-order concepts are employed (Tibbs, 2001; Reid et al., 2001; Proctor, 2001). There is a need for social workers to obtain as much factual information as possible before the visit, and to be clear on the purpose of the visit in terms that make sense to the user and carer. Generally it is better to make a number of short visits rather than a long one. Research by the Joseph Rowntree Foundation (Allan, 2001) emphasises how a range of communication techniques and approaches (e.g. pictures, word cards) should help workers understand client views and preferences.

Practice Application

The background literature indicated that overarching emotions of fear, distress and anger have a significant role in this practice setting, with the corresponding need for social workers to tread carefully and sensitively to avoid scaring and alienating service users. Suspicion and mistrust may not only be born of negative marginalisation from society and services but may also be a symptom of the mental distress itself. It is distressing, frightening and isolating to experience mental pain. The social workers from the research study identified that these constitute barriers to overcome at the inception of any communication with individuals suffering mental distress.

Preparing to demonstrate empathy for that communication of feeling, through operating the basic communication skill of 'tuning-in', is therefore vital (see Chapter 4 for discussion). Indeed, Wilson et al. (2008: 318) state that social workers must not only be 'emotionally available' to communication by service users of their mental pain, but expect that communication to occur at a number of levels, including internally within the social worker. Thus, within this area of specialist practice, when operating the skill of 'tuning-in' the social worker needs to engage with concepts from the psychoanalytic and psychodynamic literature concerning projection, transference and countertransference (see Chapter 4 for explanation). 'Tuning-in' will facilitate the first stage of a meaningful 'person-centred' communication, as opposed to 'illness-focused' communication with service users (Bowl, 2009). Service users have stated that this approach builds relationships, as it demonstrates the social worker being interested in the service user's needs as a person and not an 'object of concern' (Cree and Davis, 2007). As such, I have decided to call this early specialist communication skill 'tuning-in to experience the individual experience of mental distress'.

Practice Example 10.1

Preparatory Stage

Graeme

Graeme is a single, homeless man of 36 years, who presented at the drop-in of a local community mental health centre a week ago. Such was his mental distress and physical condition that he could hardly speak. He was cold and hungry. He simply handed over a sheet of paper that had his name written on it with the address for the centre. The approved mental health professional on duty immediately provided a hot drink and a sandwich. Short-term accommodation was arranged for Graeme at a local charity-run homeless shelter. Graeme appeared fearful and mistrusting of staff at the shelter. He stayed in his room and spoke very little. Graeme has not seen his general practitioner for several years as he finds the surgery environment difficult to manage. He says that he will attend an appointment next week. His general practitioner has treated him for anxiety and severe depression in the past.

▶

◄

The approved mental health professional that arranged the accommodation for Graeme is a male social worker of 48 years called Dave Smith. Dave has visited Graeme at the shelter on one previous occasion this week, and found him to be highly anxious. Today he is visiting to continue assessing Graeme's mental wellbeing and vulnerability. He has to begin to make medium term plans with Graeme, both for Graeme's immediate treatment and accommodation, and also the form of future support services, whether informal or formal in nature.

A central dimension to this specialist skill is to engage in reflexive processes by 'tuning-in' to 'self'. This requires the social worker to reflect on how well they might receive the feelings being transferred by the service user, and whether any barriers might be in the way. Crucially, for this practice setting, the social worker must seek to identify how their own preconceived notions and cultural stereotypes (based on their own experiences and biography) of 'mental health problems' might influence their judgement or, indeed, their behaviour in tolerating painful feelings to be shared and the service user's personality to come forward. Indeed, the background literature highlighted that professionals can perpetuate stigmatisation through feelings of fear of perceived unpredictability and aggression, or through an unwillingness to consider mental health as operating along a continuum of 'normal' human experience and clinical disorder. This might occur due to fear of acknowledging their own vulnerability to such problems (Dogra et al., 2002). Questions should be brought to mind like 'Who, where or what did they, themselves, experience when they suffered their most troubled, anxious experiences?' Identifying and recalling their own feelings will help the social worker identify with some of the difficult feelings that Graeme is likely to transfer. Wilson et al. (2008: 318–319) neatly summarise the point:

> Think – perhaps there have been times when you have felt so worried and anxious you really could not 'hear' what anyone else had to say; or times when you felt so emotionally low that reassurance and encouragement just had no effect on you; or even times when you were so convinced that everyone disliked and hated you that you 'snapped their heads off' when they tried to come close. Now think again – suppose that such a state of mind were deeper and much more lasting than the experience you had. Perhaps that brings us closer to understanding part of what it is to 'have a mental health problem', and what the particular challenges are in terms of communication.

Having 'tuned-in', we find, at the beginning of the practice example (10.2), the social worker giving his opening statement – part of the basic communication skill from Chapter 4 of 'achieving a shared purpose.'

Practice Example 10.2

Graeme

Beginnings

The social worker, Dave, is meeting with Graeme in one of the consultation rooms in the homeless shelter. This is the third time that Graeme has met Dave this week, but the first time that Graeme has been able to talk with Dave about his wellbeing. Earlier in the week, Graeme had presented a lot of mental distress, and he was hungry, cold and sleep deprived.

[1]SW: Hello Graeme. Good to see you again. It's been a week since we last spoke. Shall we sit here? *(Social worker moves one of the chairs at about a 45-degree angle, and at about a metre away to the other chair, possibly so he could look into Graeme's face more. Graeme is silent and sits down.)*

SW: How are you doing today?

Graeme: OK.

[2]SW: Do you feel like you are recovering a bit? *(Graeme nods.)* That's good. We need to talk, the two of us, about how to help you in the situation that you are in ... help you feel better ... you know ... For us to do that, I need to understand more about you ... what you might need. Are you OK with that?

Graeme: You want to ask questions?

[3]SW: Well, yes, I guess it might be hard, but if you can talk to me about what's going on for you in your life, how you feel about it, then I might be able to understand and help you. I won't judge you in any way.

Graeme: What do you want to know?

SW: The other day you said you were struggling to find food when you were on the streets.

Graeme: Just rummaging through bins, Sunday roast, chicken sandwich ... just anything I could find really.

SW: So how long were you doing that for?

[4]Graeme: *(shakes his head)* About 10 months. Well, it was alright at first. I had a bit of money, you know. I just didn't want to live in a house. I wanted to get away from things.

SW: What did you want to get away from?

Graeme: Life.

SW: Any particular part of life?

▶

◄

[5]Graeme: I don't know where to start.

[6]SW: Wherever you want to start. *(Silence for about 10 seconds. Graeme is leaning forward, head down, and hands rubbing over the back of his head. Social worker is sitting with legs apart, arms resting on knees but hands clasped, slightly leaning back.)*

Graeme: Every day there was trouble. Always fighting and arguing. I just wanted to get away from it.

SW: Fighting and arguing. Was it someone in particular or in general?

Graeme: Just everyone.

SW: Everyone. Family? Friends? People you know?

[7]Graeme: Family. I was drinking to get away from all the arguing. I thought that by walking every night it would be alright and better. But then you realise that you are constantly looking over your back. It's not as safe as you think.

[8]SW: It sounds like it's quite painful ... and that when you are walking, checking over your shoulder, is it like you are running away from something? *(Motions with hands.)*

[9]Graeme: *(Puts his hands up to cover his eyes, rocks forward and back in his seat)* I don't run from anything. *(Silence. Social worker sits still.)* You'll never understand me.

[10]SW: The more you talk about it, the more I can try and understand. You seem upset and angry. If you don't want to talk to me about it, then that is fine. It's completely your choice. *(pause)* But, I can try to get to know you and get to know the situation better.

Graeme: So now you want to be my friend. I come here off the streets. Tell you my deepest, darkest secrets? *(Sits back and looks social worker in the eye.)*

SW: I'm a social worker. You've been talking about strained relationships, being without a home ... Hopefully, in talking to me about your life at the moment, you can have a better understanding of what's going on for yourself, and what you need to happen for things to be better.

Graeme: Oh, I understand what's going on because I've had to live with it all my life! And then you come in and you try to take it over! *(Moves around on his chair. He looks directly at the social worker. Social worker sits quietly and still in the same position.)*

SW: Do you think I'm taking it over? Taking control?

Graeme: What do you need to know about me? You need to know nothing about me. *(Silence. Graeme sits forward with his hands running over his head. Silence continues.)*

►

◄

Graeme:	Spent 18 months drinking. I don't want to think. I drink to stop think-ing. I walk to stop thinking. So why would I come in here to think about everything I want to forget?
SW:	*(Moves forward. Puts hands clasped together in front of his legs.)* It's obviously upsetting and painful. Graeme, I don't want you to feel pressurised in any way. Do you want some space now? Look, I'm at the centre most mornings. You can always contact me whenever you feel you want or need to talk. I want to be helpful to you. I guess it's too soon today.

The service user immediately responds with dialogue which seems to be communicating the anticipated fear about what information to reveal ('You want to ask questions?'). The social worker immediately 'shows empathy' for this fear by using the basic communication skill 'putting feelings into words' ('Well, yes, I guess it might be hard') but also empha-sising that he will be non-judgemental about the information that the service user might put forward ('I won't judge you in any way.') In doing this, he attends to a potential obstacle that might have arisen concern-ing service user fear of stigma and mistrust of this worker. Shulman's (1998, 2009) name for an obstacle about trust is the 'intimacy obstacle'. Attending to the obstacle in this direct but empathic way means that there is a greater chance of a shared agenda for the rest of the communication. Certainly the rest of the social worker's opening statement seeks to show the service user the benefits of doing the work together with the social worker, and as such tries to create the right kinds of conditions for work to occur ('Well, yes, I guess it might be hard, but if you can talk to me about what's going on for you in your life, how you feel about it then I might be able to understand and help you. I won't judge you in any way.')

The social worker then goes on to try and make sense of Graeme's state of mind through carefully listening to the way Graeme describes his expe-rience of his everyday life. Skills in good 'reflective listening' are usefully employed. In this instance, the social worker uses 'open questions' along-side 'paraphrasing', such as:

Graeme: I wanted to get away from things.

SW: What did you want to get away from?

Graeme: Life.

SW: Any particular part of life?

The social worker uses several of the service user's own words as part of the paraphrasing, and it seems to have some success in showing that the social worker is listening and accepting of the service user's perspectives. The 'open questions' seek clarification in order to check for shared meanings and obtain further details. Often this use of the service user's own words is called 'reflecting back' or 'mirroring'.

Graeme: Every day there was trouble. Always fighting and arguing. I just wanted to get away from it.

SW: Fighting and arguing. Was it someone in particular or in general?

Graeme: Just everyone.

SW: Everyone. Family? Friends? People you know?

Graeme: Family. I was drinking to get away from all the arguing.

'Reflective listening' involves receiving thoughts and feelings made evident by the narrative but also revealed through tone of voice and attitude, and non-verbally through gesture and body position. Thus, 'listening' needs to be carried out in tandem with 'observing' non-verbal behaviour, as well as internally experiencing the thoughts and feelings to fully attend to the service user's total communication. Whatever the channel of communication ('listening', 'observing', 'feeling') or level of communication ('internally' or 'interaction' or 'structurally'), the social worker needs to receive these feelings in an open, warm and receptive manner.

By way of illustration, a critical point in our practice example is when we see the social worker communicating empathy for the anxiety and anger communicated by Graeme as a result of his painful feelings becoming difficult to control (Practice Example 10.2, points 7–10). The empathy is needed in order to enable Graeme to feel understood, and in control of his emotional and social self (Howe, 1998; Agass, 2002; Ruch, 2005b). In Chapter 4, I considered how Bion's (1962) concept of 'containment' is frequently used to describe this process, summarised by Agass (2002: 127) as, 'not simply putting up with or absorbing whatever unpleasant or uncomfortable feelings the client stirs up in us. It is a much more active process of struggling to "contain", understand and work through our own emotional responses in the hope that this will enable our clients to do the same for themselves.' The availability of this communication medium is critical for service users seeking to communicate their mental pain, as they may find that their thoughts and feelings might be 'crowding in' and dominating consciousness to the extent that ordinary communication may be difficult (Wilson et al., 2008). 'Being open to communication at all levels' is therefore an important specialist communication skill.

Herein, Wilson et al. (2008) recommend that social workers are sensitive to the particular, and often complex, ways a service user might use to communicate their states of mind. For example, metaphors and images may be used. In our practice example, Graeme uses an image of him walking the streets to 'get away' from his painful thoughts. The social worker picks up on the image being used and asks Graeme to explain a little more about what he is 'running from'. Graeme denies 'running away' verbally, but his body language tells the social worker that whatever it is he is 'running from', it is emotionally painful for Graeme and he is trying to hide it. It is an image that they might both use at a later time.

The social worker appears unabashed by Graeme's anger. His demonstration of 'containment' is evident in the way he communicates non-verbally, such as his 'use of silences', the way he 'gives time to process thoughts or feelings and respond', and the way he 'maintains a non-threatening body position' by remaining still and open. Each of these constitutes a specialist communication skill for this practice setting and will be considered in turn.

The skill of 'using silences', regardless of how difficult and uncomfortable the communication may have been, is important for developing a working relationship with a service user with mental health problems. Sitting alongside and just 'being' with the service user demonstrates support and acceptance. 'Being' gives respect by allowing difficult thoughts to remain undisclosed until an appropriate time for the service user, whereas 'doing' demands work to be done on those feelings when the service user is unwilling or unable to do so (Wilson et al., 2008). Often social workers need to practice 'the art of being' as they are used to interpreting situations and problem-solving (Kroll, 1995). Holding back and giving the service user choice and control over what to work upon attends to person-centred rights for dignity, consideration and rationality.

Also, silences enable the social worker to 'give time to process thoughts or feelings and respond'. This thinking time might be required by the service user or the social worker. Indeed, the social worker must take steps to prevent becoming so immersed in the content of the narrative that they fail to engage the aforementioned specialist communication skill of 'being open to communication at all levels'. They might miss seeing the feelings that are being unconsciously revealed by attitude, gesture or tone of voice as the service user pursues their line of thought. A short period of silence can enable what I referred to in Chapter 4 as operating a 'third ear' or 'second head' to simultaneously adopt some objective distance as well as achieving emotional attunement to the thoughts and feelings being expressed. Questions to enable analysis of the interaction could be held in mind like 'What is it that is really going on in the communication here?', 'Is the problem that she or he is describing the most immediate problem or is there something more worrying?', 'What is the nature of the obstacle in our communication?' and 'What skill should I use next?'

'Maintaining a non-threatening body position' is critical in situations where service users are demonstrating anger and a loss of self-control. Koprowska (2005: 149) recommends social workers include the following non-verbal behaviours in managing aggressive situations and containing angry feelings. These were considered in Chapter 4 but are repeated here to emphasise their usefulness within these situations:

➢ Ensure you are standing or seated at a slight angle and not 'square on', but at least a one-and-a-half arm distance away.

➢ Look at the person's face, making frequent but not continuous eye-contact.

➢ Show an interested and relaxed facial expression, but do not smile.

➢ Keep your arms relaxed, away from your hair, face or around your body (as this can be interpreted as being impatient, anxious, or seductive).

➢ Keep your hands open and in view with palms up to indicate negotiation.

➢ Keep the tone of your voice of low-register and calm.

It does not matter that there was not a lot spoken about during the meeting. The fact that the social worker stayed with Graeme, and accepted his behaviour as displayed, and feelings as communicated, gave Graeme an important message about how Dave will not reject his difficulties and pain. The consistency of the relationship between service user and social worker is considered vital if service users are to reveal deeply hidden reasons for mental distress (Bowl, 2009). Service users have reported how their relationships with social workers achieve a level of depth and consistency not achieved with other professionals.

In summary, the specialist social work communication skills in this chapter have focused on the social worker achieving a level of emotional attunement sufficient to 'hear', and demonstrate empathy for, the service user's communication of mental pain ('Being' and 'Doing'). Crucial to this were specialist communication skills to overcome obstacles that might arise concerning service user fear of stigma and mistrust of the social worker. These skills communicated acceptance and support, as well as helping the service user to link how past experiences affect current behaviour and symptoms, and also how the problems in everyday living impact upon symptoms ('Knowing' and 'Doing').

Mapping to the Professional Capability Framework

Qualifying Social Worker Level Capabilities

Please remember that these should be viewed as domains which overlap in an integrative manner rather than as a linear checklist.

'By the end of last placement/ the completion of qualifying programmes newly qualified social workers should have demonstrated the Knowledge, Skills and Values to work with a range of user groups, and the ability to undertake a range of tasks at a foundation level, the capacity to work with more complex situations; they should be able to work more autonomously, whilst recognising that the final decision will still rest with their supervisor; they will seek appropriate support and supervision.

The Health Professions Council (the regulator of qualified social workers) and The College have mapped the Standards of Proficiency for Social Work (SOPs) against the PCF expectations for social work students at the end of their last placement. Whilst there are some differences in the way the standards and PCF are expressed, the overall expectations are the same.'

Communication Capacity Domain – 'Knowing' (engaging with formal and informal knowledge in communication)	**PCF 3 Diversity: Recognise diversity and apply anti-discriminatory and anti-oppressive principles in practice** ➢ Understand how an individual's identity is informed by factors such as culture, economic status, family composition, life experiences and characteristics, and take account of these to understand their experiences, questioning assumptions where necessary ➢ With reference to current legislative requirements, recognise personal and organisational discrimination and oppression and with guidance make use of a range of approaches to challenge them
	PCF 5 Knowledge: Apply knowledge of social sciences, law and social work practice theory ➢ Demonstrate a critical understanding of the application to social work of research, theory and knowledge from sociology, social policy, psychology and health ➢ Demonstrate a critical understanding of the legal and policy frameworks and guidance that inform and mandate social work practice, recognising the scope for professional judgement ➢ Demonstrate and apply to practice a working knowledge of human growth and development throughout the life course ➢ Recognise the short and long term impact of psychological, socio-economic, environmental and physiological factors on people's lives, taking into account age and development, and how this informs practice ➢ Recognise how systemic approaches can be used to understand the person-in-the-environment and inform your practice ➢ Acknowledge the centrality of relationships for people and the key concepts of attachment, separation, loss, change and resilience ➢ Understand forms of harm and their impact on people, and the implications for practice, drawing on concepts of strength, resilience, vulnerability, risk and resistance, and apply to practice

	➢ Demonstrate a critical knowledge of the range of theories and models for social work intervention with individuals, families, groups and communities, and the methods derived from them ➢ Value and take account of the expertise of service users, carers and professionals
	KSS Adults (4): Safeguarding Social workers must be able to recognise the risk indicators of different forms of abuse and neglect and their impact on individuals, their families or their support networks and should prioritise the protection of children and adults in vulnerable situations whenever necessary. This includes working with those who self-neglect. Social workers who work with adults must take an outcomes-focused, person-centred approach to safeguarding practice, recognising that people are experts in their own lives and working alongside them to identify person centred solutions to risk and harm. **KSS Adults (6): Effective Assessments and Outcome Based Support Planning** Social workers should demonstrate a good understanding of personalisation, the social model of disability and of human development throughout life and demonstrate a holistic approach to the identification of needs, circumstances, rights, strengths and risks. In particular, social workers need to understand the impact of trauma, loss and abuse, physical disability, physical ill health, learning disability, mental ill health, mental capacity, substance misuse, domestic abuse, aging and end of life issues on physical, cognitive, emotional and social development both for the individual and for the functioning of the family. They should recognise the roles and needs of informal or family carers and use holistic, systemic approaches to supporting individuals and carers. They should develop and maintain knowledge and good partnerships with local community resources in order to work effectively with individuals in connecting them with appropriate resources and support.
Communication Capacity Domain – 'Doing' (the enactment of communication strategies in interaction)	**PCF 6 Critical Reflection and Analysis: Apply critical reflection and analysis to inform and provide a rationale for professional decision-making** ➢ Apply imagination, creativity and curiosity to practice ➢ Inform decision-making through the identification and gathering of information from multiple sources, actively seeking new sources ➢ With support, rigorously question and evaluate the reliability and validity of information from different sources ➢ Demonstrate a capacity for logical, systematic, critical and reflective reasoning and apply the theories and techniques of reflective practice ➢ Know how to formulate, test, evaluate, and review hypotheses in response to information available at the time and apply in practice ➢ Begin to formulate and make explicit, evidence-informed judgements and justifiable decisions

KSS Adults (8): Supervision, Critical Reflection and Analysis
Social workers should be able to make effective use of opportunities to discuss, reflect upon and test multiple hypotheses, the role of intuition and logic in decision making, the difference between opinion and fact, the role of evidence, how to address common bias in situations of uncertainty and the reasoning of any conclusions reached and recommendations made, particularly in relation to mental capacity, mental health and safeguarding situations.

Social workers should have a critical understanding of the difference between theory, research, evidence and expertise and the role of professional judgement. They should use practice evidence and research to inform the complex judgements and decisions needed to support, empower and protect their service users. They should apply imagination, creativity and curiosity to working in partnership with individuals and their carers, acknowledging the centrality of people's own expertise about their experience and needs.

KSS Children (2): Communication
Produce written case notes and reports, which are well argued, focused and jargon free. Present a clear analysis and a sound rationale for actions as well as any conclusions reached, so that all parties are well-informed.

PCF 7 Intervention and Skills: Use judgement and authority to intervene with individuals, families and communities to promote independence, provide support and prevent harm, neglect and abuse
➤ Identify and apply a range of verbal, non-verbal and written methods of communication and adapt them in line with peoples' age, comprehension and culture
➤ Be able to communicate information, advice, instruction and professional opinion so as to advocate, influence and persuade
➤ Demonstrate the ability to engage with people, and build, manage, sustain and conclude compassionate and effective relationships
➤ Demonstrate skills in sharing information appropriately and respectfully
➤ Recognise complexity, multiple factors, changing circumstances and uncertainty in people's lives, to be able to prioritise your intervention
➤ Understand the authority of the social work role and begin to use this appropriately as an accountable professional
➤ Recognise the factors that create or exacerbate risk to individuals, their families or carers, to the public or to professionals, including yourself, and contribute to the assessment and management of risk

KSS Adults (3): Person-centred Practice
They should work co-productively and innovatively with people, local communities, other professionals, agencies and services to promote self-determination, community capacity, personal and family reliance, cohesion, earlier intervention and active citizenship.

	KSS Adults (4): Safeguarding Social workers who work with adults must take an outcomes-focused, person-centred approach to safeguarding practice, recognising that people are experts in their own lives and working alongside them to identify person centred solutions to risk and harm. In situations where there is abuse or neglect or clear risk of those, social workers must work in a way that enhances involvement, choice and control as part of improving quality of life, wellbeing and safety. **KSS Adults (7): Direct Work with Individuals and Families** Social workers need to be able to work directly with individuals and their families through the professional use of self, using interpersonal skills and emotional intelligence to create relationships based on openness, transparency and empathy. They should know how to build purposeful, effective relationships underpinned by reciprocity. They should be able to communicate clearly, sensitively and effectively, applying a range of best evidence-based methods of written, oral and non-verbal communication and adapt these methods to match the person's age, comprehension and culture. Social workers should be capable of communicating effectively with people with specific communication needs, including those with learning disabilities, dementia, people who lack mental capacity and people with sensory impairment. **KSS Children (2): Communication** Communicate clearly and sensitively with children of different ages and abilities, their families and in a range of settings and circumstances. Use methods based on best evidence. Create immediate rapport with people not previously known which facilitates engagement and motivation to participate in child protective enquiries, assessments and services. Listen to the views, wishes and feelings of children and families and help parents and carers understand the ways in which their children communicate through their behaviour. Help them to understand how they might communicate more effectively with their children. Promote speech, language and communication support, identifying those children and adults who are experiencing difficulties expressing themselves.
Communication Capacity Domain – 'Being' (the use of 'self')	**PCF 1 Professionalism: Identify and behave as a professional social worker, committed to professional development** ➢ Be able to explain the role of the social worker in a range of contexts, and uphold the reputation of the profession ➢ Demonstrate professionalism in terms of presentation, demeanour, reliability, honesty and respectfulness ➢ Recognise the impact of self in interaction with others, making appropriate use of personal experience ➢ Be able to recognise and maintain personal and professional boundaries ➢ Recognise your professional limitations and how to seek advice ➢ Demonstrate a commitment to your continuing learning and development ➢ With support, take steps to manage and promote own safety, health, wellbeing and emotional resilience

KSS Adults (7): Direct work with individuals and families
Social workers should be capable of communicating effectively with people with specific communication needs, including those with learning disabilities, dementia, people who lack mental capacity and people with sensory impairment. They should do this in ways that are engaging, respectful, motivating and effective, even when dealing with conflict – whether perceived or actual – anger and resistance to change.

KSS Children (2): Communication
Act respectfully even when people are angry, hostile and resistant to change. Manage tensions between parents, carers and family members, in ways that show persistence, determination and professional confidence.

PCF 2 Values and Ethics: Apply social work ethical principles and values to guide professional practice
> Recognise and, with support, manage the impact of own values on professional practice
> Manage potentially conflicting or competing values, and, with guidance, recognise, reflect on, and work with ethical dilemmas
> Demonstrate respectful partnership work with service users and carers, eliciting and respecting their needs and views, and promoting their participation in decision-making wherever possible
> Recognise and promote individuals' rights to autonomy and self-determination

KSS Adults (5): Mental Capacity
Social workers must model and lead a change of approach, away from that where the default setting is 'safety first', towards a person-centred culture where individual choice is encouraged and where the right of all individuals to express their own lifestyle choices is recognised and valued.

In working with those where there is no concern over capacity, social workers should take all practicable steps to empower people to make their own decisions, recognising that people are experts in their own lives and working alongside them to identify person-centred solutions to risk and harm, recognising the individual's right to make 'unwise' decisions.

PCF 3 Diversity: Recognise diversity and apply anti-discriminatory and anti-oppressive principles in practice
(Appropriately placed in both 'Knowing' and 'Being')
> With reference to current legislative requirements, recognise personal and organisational discrimination and oppression and with guidance make use of a range of approaches to challenge them
> Recognise and manage the impact on people of the power invested in your role

KSS Adults (3): Person-centred Practice
They should coordinate and facilitate a wide range of practical and emotional support, and discharge legal duties to complement people's own resources and networks, so that all individuals (no matter their background, health status or mental capacity), carers

and families can exercise choice and control, (supporting individuals to make their own decisions, especially where they may lack capacity) and meet their needs and aspirations in personalised, creative and often novel ways. They should work co-productively and innovatively with people, local communities, other professionals, agencies and services to promote self- determination, community capacity, personal and family reliance, cohesion, earlier intervention and active citizenship.

PCF 4 Rights, Justice and Economic Wellbeing: Advance human rights and promote social justice and economic wellbeing
➢ Understand, identify and apply in practice the principles of social justice, inclusion and equality
➢ Understand how legislation and guidance can advance or con-strain people's rights and recognise how the law may be used to protect or advance their rights and entitlements
➢ Work within the principles of human and civil rights and equalities legislation, differentiating and beginning to work with absolute, qualified and competing rights and differing needs and perspectives
➢ Recognise the impact of poverty and social exclusion and pro-mote enhanced economic status through access to education, work, housing, health services and welfare benefits

PCF 8 Contexts and Organisations: Engage with, inform, and adapt to changing contexts that shape practice. Operate effectively within own organisational frameworks and contribute to the development of services and organisations. Operate effectively within multi-agency and inter-professional partnerships and settings
➢ Recognise that social work operates within, and responds to, changing economic, social, political and organisational contexts
➢ Understand the roles and responsibilities of social workers in a range of organisations, lines of accountability and the boundaries of professional autonomy and discretion
➢ Understand legal obligations, structures and behaviours within organisations and how these impact on policy, procedure and practice
➢ Be able to work within an organisation's remit and contribute to its evaluation and development

KSS Adults (9): Organisational Context
They must understand and work effectively within financial and legal frameworks, obligations, structures and culture, in particular Human Rights and Equalities legislation, the Care Act, Mental Capacity Act, Mental Health Act and accompanying guidance and codes of practice. They must be able to operate successfully in their organisational context, demonstrating effective time management, caseload management and be capable of reconciling competing demands and embrace information, data and technology appropriate to their role. They should have access to regular quality supervision to support their professional resilience and emotional and physical wellbeing.

11

Working with Older People

Summary of Specialist Communication Skills in this Chapter

➤ use the whole communication spectrum

➤ actively looking for the channels of communication that the person is using

➤ validation

➤ mirroring

➤ emphasising or exaggerating non-verbal communication without being patronising

➤ taking time

➤ using short, simple sentences.

Policy and background literature

The changing UK national policy agenda of the past decade, originating with the modernising social services agenda (Department of Health, 1998; Scottish Office, 1999) and developed by the 'National Services Framework for Older People' (Department of Health, 2001; Welsh Assembly Government, 2006), has culminated in new legislation cementing the person-centred approach within social work practice (The Care Act 2014 in England, Wales and Northern Ireland; The Social Care (Self-directed support) (Scotland) Act 2013; The Social Services and Well-being (Wales) Act 2014). The 'new philosophy' of social care provision brought about by these changes requires social workers to engage particular communication skills. Indeed, the policy requires social workers to elicit the personal views and wishes of each service user of how to address their health and wellbeing to meet outcomes and goals deemed most important to them. Through adopting a flexible, individualised approach, social workers should seek to have a 'genuine conversation' to create a co-produced assessment of the care and support needs that matter most to the person concerned. This active involvement and/or 'co-productive' approach necessitates the identification of service users' communication needs, particularly where service users might have *'substantial difficulty'* in engaging with the assessment and planning processes. These include difficulties in understanding and retaining information, as well as difficulties in weighing up information to consider and express preferences, alongside difficulties in communicating their views, wishes and feelings. Social workers must also consider the emotional and physical impact of the assessment when planning interventions upon service user wellbeing, taking steps to mitigate this within their communication approach. Thus their communication strategy must be 'person-centred', achieved through treating service users with dignity, as individuals, and enabling choice about care. Indeed, the principles underpinning the Mental Capacity Act (2005) behold social workers to presume a service user has the capacity to make decisions unless it has been established that they lack that capacity. This indicates the need for social workers to use particular communication skills to explore issues of 'decision-making capacity'.

New approaches to adult safeguarding within the Care Act 2014 echo these same principles of empowering people to speak out and express informed choices in managing the risk encountered in their lives. Respecting the concepts of both dignity and quality of life, the emphasis is not upon risk avoidance but risk appraisal of the circumstances, history, personal preferences and lifestyle of the person concerned. The aim is not for overprotection but a proportionate response that can tolerate acceptable risks. Within this, social workers must ensure that they use the least restrictive options for freedom of action, complying with the Human Rights Act (1998) and the Mental Capacity Act (2005). Skilled communication is needed to attain this level of shared information gathering and shared judgement in order to achieve proportionate solutions for safety and support. The indication is for social workers to ensure that their communication is not exclusively geared towards obtaining tangible outcomes such as service referral but facilitating a safe relationship from which to explore feelings and opinions.

A central underpinning principle is that of combating ageism. Standard one of the National Service Framework expects social work and social care staff to meet a minimum standard of 'rooting out age discrimination' (Department of Health, 2001). This was reinforced by European legislation to prevent age discrimination within employment, which came into force in the UK in 2006 (Directive 2000/78/EC). The social work literature emphasises how social workers must actively resist ageism, both in terms of their own attitudes and from other sources. An often quoted definition of ageism is 'the social process through which negative images of and attitudes towards older people, based solely on the characteristics of old age itself, result in discrimination' (Hughes and Mtejuka in Thompson, 1995).

The wider literature relating to communication with older people almost entirely relates to working with people with dementia, people who have experienced a stroke, or those who have developed loss of sight and/ or hearing. The themes identify particular communication challenges and skills necessary to promote collaborative, person-centred work with a person whose vision and/or hearing and/or cognitive abilities are becoming progressively diminished.

A common theme from across the literature was to recognise that it can take a person considerable effort to concentrate on verbal information being provided and then to put a sentence together (Buijssen, 2005). A repeated theme was to 'give the person time', as the person is likely to need more time to process information and formulate a response. Similarly, it is better to engage in frequent, shorter meetings than one long, protracted meeting. Also, the use of short and simple questions and statements helps concentration and clarity (Buijssen, 2005).

A second common theme from across the literature was to recognise that as the use of language becomes difficult, there is a need for communication to occur in ways that do not solely involve words but use the whole communication spectrum. The onset of dementia or sensory impairment is usually gradual, and not always recognised by the service user or social worker. As such, the service user may already be relying on non-verbal communication and not actually identify that they are doing so. Thus social workers need to show skill in emphasising or exaggerating non-verbal communication without being patronising (Bender et al., 1987). For example, social workers need to check that their body language, such as facial gestures, reflect the content of what they are saying (Bounds and Hepburn, 1996). They need to be ready to write things down. They need to ensure that the physical environment does not provide a distraction, such as ensuring good light, sitting close and 'face on' to the service user in order that their lips and, indeed, their facial expression can be read (Bounds and Hepburn, 1996).

A related theme across the literature concerned the importance of physical contact to older people. The literature highlights how many older people do not experience much physical contact, and a light touch on the arm, or a hand being squeezed, can be a useful and emotionally powerful means of non-verbal communication (Bender et al., 1987). Equally, it is important to attend to cultural difference and cultural conventions, as a person may find aspects of the non-verbal communication, such as physical contact or eye contact, to be intrusive or disrespectful (Bender, 1987; Alibhai-Brown, 1998). Indeed, the potential for cultural misunderstanding is a repeated theme across the literature. As opposed to adopting ageist attitudes, some cultural groups see old age as inevitable and to be valued (Alibhai-Brown, 1998). It is important for social workers to learn the formalities that are important to different cultural groups, such as respect to minority ethnic elders, but also the more subtle, understated forms of communication, which a worker could misread as a lack of concern (Alibhai-Brown, 1998). There may be culturally based attitudinal differences to problems. For example, the use of the term 'dementia', and/or the care and treatment for it, is not shared and agreed across all cultural groups. Indeed, in this respect, Bowes and Dar (2000) refer to the need for workers to develop 'linguistic and cultural communication'.

Over and above these communication issues, the literature identifies further skills in working with people with dementia. As people move through phases of dementia with their cognitive and language skills altering in different ways, they develop a heightened awareness of non-verbal communication, and experience a particular preoccupation with the emotional aspects of their lives (Kitwood, 1997; Killick and Allan, 2001; Buijssen, 2005). Thus, there is a need for social workers to actively look for the channels of communication that the person is using – to look for the feeling that is being articulated, even though the words may not be making any sense to the worker (Buijssen, 2005; Bounds and Hepburn, 1996). This skill of seeing everything that a person with dementia does as meaningful is described by Chapman et al. (1994) as 'validation' and is contained within the 'care mapping approach'. It requires the worker to actively listen and watch the communication; to try and understand the feeling; and then to find a way to communicate with that person about the feeling. Herein the literature points to three additional skills that can help a worker to achieve this. The first is 'mirroring' (Killick and Allan, 2001). This involves focusing on movements and reflecting back what the person does in the style that they used. Frequently this might involve physical contact, such as squeezing a hand, or giving a hug (Killick and Allan, 2001; Burnside 1986). The second is the use of 'reminiscence' or 'biography' (Chapman et al., 1994). Memories in the past are stored longer than the present. Through evoking some of these memories, it is possible to 'gain contact' with the person and 'put them at ease' (Buijssen, 2005). The third is to make use of creative arts, as these provide a medium for the expression of wishes and feelings in a way that does not involve words (Killick and Allan, 2001). On a more day-to-day contact level, research by the Joseph Rowntree Foundation emphasises how a range of communication techniques and approaches (e.g. pictures, word cards) should help workers understand client views and preferences (Macer et al., 2009). Indeed, people with dementia can experience a lot of additional frustration and upset because others do not take the time to communicate effectively with them. Often this can lead to an increase in either apathy and depression, or the kind of non-verbal communication that is often described as 'challenging behaviour'. Dementia does not remove capacity to have opinions or preferences, or capacity for feelings and emotions.

Practice application

At the beginning of our practice example (11.1), we find the social worker 'tuning-in' to Doug as an adult at risk. This begins with the social worker writing to the service user, Doug, to arrange a visit and also tele-phoning to ensure that the service user has the information. Furthermore, the social worker telephones an hour before the visit to remind him of her imminent arrival. These seem mundane, and not extraordinary, steps but they are important in terms of service user safety on two levels. First, the service user needs to be assured that it is the social worker and not a stranger at their door. Crimes against vulnerable older people on their own doorstep, such as mugging, theft and violence, have increased in recent years, creating fear of the 'knock on the door'. Second, the social worker needs to begin facilitating a safe relationship from which to explore feelings and opinions, as the social worker has the responsibility to investigate and take action when an adult at risk is believed to be suffer-ing abuse. Moreover, it is about treating the service user with dignity and respect as an individual through creating a relationship for the service user to be an active participant, enabling choice in decisions. Trust is unlikely to develop if the service user is unable to differentiate the social worker from any of the other care professionals involved in the service user's life. Hence, it is important to ensure that the service user is clear about the social worker's name and role in advance of their visit; just prior to their arrival; and upon their arrival. The provision of ID at the door is a critical part of that process (as it is within any practice situation with any service user).

This point concerning the confusion experienced by service users of the numbers of different care professionals in their lives and the parameters of their differing roles is illustrated throughout our Practice Example 11.1 (points 2–5). Doug comments that the care professionals 'just turn up'. He is unsure of what each professional actually does, except that 'they' obtain his pension. Importantly, this communicates not only the aforementioned confusion concerning number and role of profession-als but also a degree of vulnerability concerning his own safety. In fact, the dialogue goes on to reveal that he gains some reassurance of the legiti-macy of their presence by their behaviour in sharing a cup of tea with him. He seeks to do the same with the social worker. Indeed, the social workers within our research study identified the need for the social worker to pick up on this non-verbal communication cue for reassurance. The need for social workers to *'actively look for the channels of communication that the person is using'* – to look for the feeling that is being articulated – is a point backed up by the background literature, and as such constitutes a specialist communication skill in this setting. If, as Chapman et al. (1994) state, the social worker 'validates' this communication as being as meaningful as a verbal expression of wishes and feelings, then the social worker must not only actively listen and watch the communication to try and understand the feeling, but then find a way to communicate with that person about the feeling. *'Validation'*, therefore, becomes an important specialist communication skill. In our practice example, the social worker uses this skill by going to buy some milk and making a cup of tea to share with the service user. This is a crude and basic illustration of the skill of *'mirroring'*, with the social worker focusing on behaviour and reflecting back what the person does in the style that they use. Killick and Allan (2001) and Burnside (1986) note that *'mirroring'* more frequently involves physical contact, such as squeezing a hand, or giving a hug.

Practice Example 11.1

Doug

Preparatory Stage

Doug is a 76-year-old white Eastern European man who lives on his own in a block of flats within an inner-city residential area. The social worker is about to visit Doug in order to review his care plan with him. Doug has limited mobility and so receives home care services on a weekly basis (shopping and cleaning). He enjoys volunteering at the local day centre, and arranges transport to participate in this. Doug has infrequent contact with his family. The social worker, Claire, is 45 years old, white British, and has recently moved to the area from London.

Beginnings

(Social worker knocks at door. Doug walks slowly towards the door, gradually placing one step in front of the other, and opens the door.)

Doug: Ooh, hello (*friendly tone*).

[1]SW: Hello there, Doug, it's Claire, the social worker. Remember? I phoned today to say I was coming. Do you need to see my ID before we go in? (*offers ID card to Doug*)

▶

◄

Doug: Oh, er, come in. (*Doug walks slowly towards the living room, gradually placing one step in front of the other.*)

SW: Need any help there or are you OK?

[2]Doug: No, I'll manage. I would make you a cup of tea, but I haven't any milk.

SW: No, I've just had one.

Doug: Silly of me, really. I'm dying for a cup.

SW: Is there anyone who can help you get some milk?

Doug: No, not really, I asked this young care worker who comes around, I said to her, 'can she go and get any' and she said no. Silly. I don't understand it.

SW: So you asked her to go and get some stuff for you and she wasn't happy to do that?

Doug: Something to do with the Council, she said. I don't understand what she means.

SW: So you're doing without a food shop at the moment?

Doug: I've got a few bits in. Don't need much. I could do with a cup of tea, though.

SW: Want me to make you a quick cup of tea? You haven't got milk though. OK without milk?

Doug: No, urgh!

SW: I'm going to get you some milk. If I go out to get it, will you be alright to get up and let me in again, or do you want to give me your key, just to let myself in?

Doug: Here's the key. Thank you. Good of you. (*Social worker leaves and returns with milk.*)

[3]SW: Hello Doug (*walks over to Doug*). Is it OK to change my mind and have a cup with you? (*Walks past Doug to kitchen. Brings tea cups over to Doug and sits down across from him.*)

SW: So, how are things going for you at the moment?

Doug: Fine. You don't want to moan too much do you?

SW: That's what I'm here for: to listen to any moans you've got at the moment.

Doug: Where do I start?

SW: Let's go back to that care worker who's not able to get milk and bread for you. What's she doing for you?

►

◀

Doug:	I don't know, she turns up, she sits down for ten minutes and then she goes out, you know. She is allowed to get my pension … which helps … but I can't get to the shops.
SW:	So she goes and gets your pension, but not any milk? What else does she do?
Doug:	Don't know. To do with the Council. Ridiculous though, isn't it, you don't expect it! (*voice gets louder, tone agitated*)
SW:	Doesn't sound sensible. Maybe it's something she thinks she can't do but really she can. You happy for me to have a word with her?
Doug:	You are in the same department … I don't know why you can't just talk to each other? (*voice still sounding louder, starts rocking forwards and backwards, agitated*)
SW:	Actually, I don't work in the same department, but I am happy to have a word with them.
Doug:	I don't know, do I? Expect you two know what you're doing. No one talks to each other. (*louder voice*) It's silly. (*said more quietly*)
SW:	I can understand that. I'm happy to go back and have a word.
Doug:	Yes, that's what I need. These are things I need. (*silence for a few seconds*)
SW:	Doug, you may remember … a previous social worker drew up a care plan with you. I had a look at a copy of it before I came. It says what the care worker should do.
Doug:	(*Looks down at piles of papers down by his feet*) So many papers. I try to keep it as organised as I can.
[4]SW:	I can see you looking for it now. Don't worry. What would help me would be if I could have an idea of what happens during the week. Who comes to see you? What do they do for you?
Doug:	They just turn up (*still looking down*).
SW:	Every day?
Doug:	Once a week if I'm lucky.
SW:	On the care plan it says once a week to pick up the pension.
Doug:	(*Looks up, but not at social worker*) Kids come round. Got their own families now. It's difficult for them.
SW:	They probably still care what happens to you though?
Doug:	You'd think so, but kids these days … It all changes (*looks down again*)
[5]SW:	(*Reaches across to Doug and touches his shoulder. Silence for a minute.*)

As our practice example (11.1) unravels it becomes evident that Doug is demonstrating diminished cognitive abilities. When the social worker asks questions about the responsiveness of the service he is receiving from the care professionals, Doug becomes agitated, frustrated and cross (Practice Example 11.1, between points 3 and 4: 'Don't know. To do with the Council. Ridiculous though, isn't it, you don't expect it! *(voice gets louder, tone agitated)*'; 'You are in the same department...I don't know why you can't just talk to each other? *(voice still sounding louder, starts rocking forwards and backwards, agitated)*'; 'I don't know, do I? Expect you two know what you're doing. No one talks to each other *(louder voice)*. It's silly *(said more quietly).*') Doug is confused by the role and tasks of those different professionals, and probably just as confused about the role and purpose of the social worker sitting in front of him. The background literature identifies that in moving through phases of dementia with cognitive and language skills altering in different ways, people develop a heightened awareness of non-verbal communication, and experience a particular preoccupation with the emotional aspects of their lives (Kitwood, 1997; Killick and Allan, 2001; Buijssen, 2005). Potentially, this explains why the detail of the work carried out by the care professionals is not relayed by Doug. The information he provides to the social worker about the work carried out for him in his home is that of the feeling he gets when the care professionals share a cup of tea with him. Retaining knowledge about the detail of those services is less important to him. Hence, he becomes frustrated with the social worker questioning him about his knowledge of those services.

Information provided by Doug later in the interview also sheds light on the communication behind his agitated behaviour at this beginning stage. Doug states he has received social work services in the past. This relates to his childhood experiences of living in a children's home due to parental neglect and physical abuse. We know from the background literature that memories in the past are stored longer than the present. Doug's memories of those events may have been evoked by the social worker visiting. The feelings aroused by those memories may be causing him emotional pain. His agitation and anger may be an external demonstration of a psychological defensive response to the evocation of those memories and associated feelings. Certainly, between points 4 and 5 (Practice Example 11.1) Doug becomes quiet and contemplative, disengaging with the social worker through closed body language.

SW: What would help me would be if I could have an idea of what happens during the week. Who comes to see you? What do they do for you?

Doug: They just turn up *(still looking down)*.

SW: Every day?

Doug: Once a week if I'm lucky.

SW: On the care plan it says once a week to pick up the pension.

Doug: (*Looks up, but not at social worker*) Kids come round. Got their own families now. It's difficult for them.

SW: They probably still care what happens to you though?

Doug: You'd think so, but kids these days … It all changes (*looks down again*).

Interestingly, the social workers in our research study, who were participating in the enactment of this role play as forum theatre, found this point in the communication to be critical. Although at this stage of the interview they had no knowledge of his childhood experiences, they felt the projection of anxiety, fear and pain within themselves. In Chapter 4, I identified how social workers need to attend to such transference processes occurring between the service user and social worker. The feelings being evoked within the social worker give clues to the communication of the service user. Moreover, in attending to those feelings, the social worker can provide understanding and containment. In our practice example, however, it may not be sufficient or appropriate to simply utilise the basic communication skill of 'putting feelings into words' (such as, 'Are you worried about me being here, Doug?'). Rather, in acknowledging Doug's potentially heightened awareness of non-verbal communication, it is important for the social worker to check that her body language, such as her facial gestures, reflects the content of what she is saying. A specialist communication skill, in this respect, is therefore that of *'emphasising or exaggerating non-verbal communication without being patronising'*. In our Practice Example 11.1 (point 5), the social worker did this through reaching across to Doug and lightly touching his shoulder. In doing so, she again uses the skill of *'validation'* to acknowledge the feelings being communicated and sought a way to communicate with that person about the feeling.

The qualifying social workers within the research study highlighted that the decision whether to have physical contact with the service user was important, as it may have considerable bearing on successful communication with the service user. On the one hand, the qualifying social workers recognised that the demonstration of physical comfort can communicate with the service user in a way that words cannot. However, they also stated that touching the service user would put them in a very vulnerable position concerning possible allegations of inappropriate behaviour. For some, this was not something that they were prepared to risk. Clearly some service users would be offended by such a gesture. Some qualifying social workers were less absolute in their decision about this issue. Evidently, personal decisions have to be made regarding where to draw the line in one's own individual practice. It seems important to note that the service users we interviewed for the research study told us that they missed having physical contact with another person, and that they wished that sometimes a social worker would just give them a hug. This position is supported by the background literature which highlighted how, for an older person who does not experience much physical contact, a light touch on the arm, or a hand being squeezed, can be a useful and powerful means of non-verbal communication (Bender, 1987).

Thus, even at this early beginning stage, Practice Example 11.1 illustrates significant importance in the social worker allocating sufficient time to promote communication occurring in ways that do not solely involve words but use the whole communication spectrum. This suggests two specialist communication skills: the importance of *'taking time'* and the need to *'use the whole communication spectrum'*.

The specialist communication skill of *'taking time'* was found to be crucial within the second part of our practice example (11.2), mainly because the unfolding communication showed the negative consequences of 'not taking enough time'! From points 7 to 10, we find lengthy dense dialogue, with Doug becoming increasingly agitated. Unfortunately, the social worker starts to rely solely on verbal communication as opposed to continuing the skill of *'actively looking for the channels of communication that the person is using'*. The pace of each retort becomes faster and faster, until at point 8 the social worker interrupts Doug and at point 10 it becomes evident that there are two agendas to the meeting, as opposed to a 'shared agenda' ('Doug, I did make an appointment with you. I don't want to get into an argument with you. What I'm trying to do is find out what we can do to make things better for you.') In Chapter 4, I identified that in situations where two agendas seem to operating, it is important for the social worker to ask themselves the questions 'is there an obstacle present?' and 'what kind of obstacle is it?' Having identified the obstacle, they can try and address it. In this way, the communication channels will be clearer and the work more purposeful.

In this instance, the obstacle seems to stem from both parties experiencing increasing frustration at being misunderstood. It is probably the case that Doug experiences this frustration frequently within a number of conversations. Hence the frustration and anger rises quickly. This is an example of communication which is so often labelled 'challenging behaviour'. Interestingly, this point in the communication presented another point at which the qualifying social workers in the research study, participating in the enactment of this role play as forum theatre, felt projection

Practice Example 11.2

Doug

Work Phase

[6]SW: Doug, you seem a little anxious about me being here. Is there anything that's worrying you about me being here?

Doug: No, we worry about a lot of things, don't we? (*silence for about 10 seconds*) I'd like to get out more. There's only my volunteering. Got to be back ... people coming round and ... well ...

SW: What do you do with your volunteering?

Doug: I go down to the Help the Aged place. It's great down there. It's really good.

SW: So how many days a week is that?

Doug: It's only once a week. Gets me out of the house.

SW: Sounds like you enjoy it. Would you like to do more of that?

Doug: It's finding it ... the hours aren't a problem ... hard to get out of the house. I get a couple of hours, but the rest of the time I'm stuck in. Not nice.

SW: So, the volunteer that helps you to get to Help the Aged ... could we help you to get more support for more days at Help the Aged? It helps to get out and chat to people, doesn't it?

Doug: It's your independence back. It's so important. You get used to having independence and when you can't do small things, it's difficult. (*silence for 10 seconds*)

SW: Is there anything else that's worrying you at the moment?

Doug: Bit of tidying up. I can't bend down either ... and then it's difficult to get back up (*laughs*). It's tough, really tough.

[7]SW: How would you feel if someone gave you a hand with the tidying up?

Doug: Don't want people moving all my stuff around. You know, it's not ... (*waves his arms at the papers at his feet*).

SW: But if you gave them directions?

Doug: They don't listen. They move, walk around and 'they've got to do it'. Oh no. More hassle than it's worth sometimes.

SW: Anything you particularly need them to do? (*silence for 10 seconds*) I understand that you don't want your things moved because they are personal, but do they cause you any problems when you are getting around?

▶

◀

Doug: No, they're alright.

SW: Have you had any falls or anything ...

Doug: No, I'm still alright. I can still manoeuvre around the house. It's when you go outside. Pavements are not even flat these days, it's ...

[8]SW: (*interrupts*) Back to the papers. I understand you don't want a carer ... but what about if your family helped you to move them aside?

Doug: No, they're very busy. Sometimes can't get round each week. It's not something ... it's my place. I want things left as they are. They will be alright. I don't want things moved around.

SW: I'm sorry. I understand that. I didn't mean to tell you where to put them and if I did, I apologise.

Doug: You wait for weeks for an appointment. Someone just turns up. You open the door and there's someone new standing there. I don't even remember about you coming round today. Did you tell me?

SW: I did tell you. Yes. You've obviously forgotten, but it really doesn't matter.

[9]Doug: Well, I don't forget everything. People think that as you get older your brain goes. I still know what I mean. Every now and then you forget the odd word. Things don't fit into place as they used to. (*silence for a minute*)

SW: What would be the one thing that we could do to help you with at home?

Doug: People just telling me when they're coming round. Not just turning up. More regular visits. People don't come round. They turn up when they want to.

SW: At the moment you have someone round once a week to get your pension for you?

Doug: She's useless. Just sits there ... drinks my tea and then doesn't get anymore.

SW: One person gets your pension for you. You're saying that you need someone else to get your bread, milk and tea for you. A more regular shop?

Doug: Yes, that would help.

SW: How often would you need that? How many days a week?

Doug: Every couple of days ... and it gets so lonely up here. Would be nice if someone could take me out. All I hear is departments shifting ...

SW: You're saying you want to get out more?

▶

◀

Doug: Yes, been trying to say that … get people to do that for ages. No one ever seems to listen to me.

SW: I'm trying to listen to you now. What I'm trying to say is … not take you here, there and everywhere, but find out where you …

Doug: Don't want to go here, there and everywhere! Just up the road is fine.

SW: Where's 'up the road'?

Doug: Walk round the block, going out for lunch and things. No one seems to care. 'Got too many people on the books', that's all I get.

SW: I don't think it's 'too many people on the books'. It's that your circumstances have changed in the last few weeks.

Doug: Don't understand why people come round … don't make appointments … and when they come round, they can't do anything! It's silly, isn't it!

[10]SW: Doug, I did make an appointment with you. I don't want to get into an argument with you. What I'm trying to do is find out what we can do to make things better for you.

Doug: I've said, haven't I? Not just to you but to other people who come round.

SW: What you've said to me is you want to get out up the road, to have a walk round. I need to find out how we manage that, whether it's us that gets someone to do that, or whether there's someone you'd like to do that with you … friends or family?

Doug: Family are not around. They are very busy people. I thought Social Services are there to help. Then you come round, want to move my stuff, get my family, volunteers to come round …

SW: I'm not saying to bring volunteers round. What I'm saying is, who would you like to come round? If you'd like family and you'd like me to speak to them, that's fine. If not family, then that's fine. I need to find out who you'd like to do that.

Doug: What about the carer that comes round, can't she take me out? No. She doesn't come back with bread and milk. It's silly. Wouldn't trust her.

SW: Well, I'm going to go back to the office to sort that out and make sure what she's supposed to be doing, she's doing. If you don't get on with that carer, then she wouldn't be the right person to do it. (*silence for about a minute*)

SW: Doug, it's obviously difficult at this time to decide what to do. What about if I come back tomorrow?

Doug: You actually going to come back tomorrow? Because they say they'll come and then they don't.

▶

◄

SW:	Is 11 o'clock alright?
Doug:	Yes, OK.
SW:	I'll phone 15 minutes beforehand to say I'm on my way.

THE NEXT DAY

SW:	Hello, Doug. It's Claire. (*offers ID card*)
Doug:	Yes, come in. (*Doug walks slowly towards the living room, gradually placing one step in front of the other.*)
SW:	Since yesterday, have you had any thoughts on who you'd like to come round and take you out?
Doug:	Still don't know why you can't come round. You're here now.
SW:	We can go for a walk now if you want?
Doug:	Yes, could go now. How long you got? (*social worker picks up her coat ...*)

of anxiety, fear and pain within themselves. Surprisingly, projection seemed to come from both directions, with the social workers empathising with the frustration and anger of both Doug and the social worker. We might understand the feelings being projected from the social worker as 'countertransference'. In Chapter 4, I outlined how countertransference has been used to describe the reaction set off in the worker as a result of being receptive to a service user's transferred feelings. These emotions are considered to be a helpful guide to understanding transferred feelings which are unexpressed. Equally, though, the reaction could be negative. The social worker could be transferring feelings from their own past experiences and inappropriately applying them to the service user or their problem. The social worker needs to check whether their responses are valid according to what the service user is communicating, or whether it is the social worker reacting to what they are bringing to the situation.

The specialist communication skill of *'taking time'* will contribute in lessening Doug's frustration and facilitating his understanding, if combined with the skill of *'using short, simple sentences'*. While the social worker's questions sought to show respect, they were often very long, included more than one sentence at a time and used higher-order concepts. Questions that start with 'why' and 'how' create difficulties for service users with diminished language and cognitive skills as these type of questions require detailed, lengthy, explanative responses. It would take that person great effort to concentrate on how to put such a response together and then deliver it (Buijssen, 2005).

I would argue that there exists a second related obstacle at this point. This concerns a statement frequently repeated by Doug throughout the dialogue (Practice Example 11.2), for example at point 9: 'Well, I don't forget everything. People think that as you get older your brain goes. I still know what I mean. Every now and then you forget the odd word. Things don't fit into place as they used to.' Whenever a statement is repeated, it should become clear to the social worker that it is important to the service user. Doug seems to want to communicate to the social worker that his diminishing cognitive ability is a concern to him. Indeed, the theme appears in a less direct way when he states that 'people just turn up' and expresses anger, vulnerability and confusion at their 'sudden appearance' at his door. The awareness that one's cognitive skills are diminishing is a frightening feeling and could be understood as a communication obstacle surrounding a societal taboo area of diminishing cognitive ability. Drawing on the basic communication skills from Chapter 4, the social worker needs to attend to the obstacle through doing what Seden (2005: 26) refers to as 'listening to the base line (what is not openly said but possibly is being felt)'. Verbal communication using Shulman's (2009) skills of *'reach for feeling'* and *'putting feelings into words',* alongside my aforementioned specialist communication skill *'emphasising or exaggerating non-verbal communication without being patronising'*, will be useful for drawing out these feelings which are not immediately at the surface or are difficult for Doug to express. This will provide *'validation'* of Doug's repeated concerns, which he raised as indirect cues and hidden communication throughout the practice example.

The background literature suggests that the non-verbal techniques should extend to writing things down or using flash cards. The specialist communication strategy should be to *'use the whole communication spectrum'*. The social worker in Practice Example 11.2 does not use such examples of visual communication alongside the verbal communication. However, at the end of the practice example we find the social worker using non-verbal communication to achieve rapport and trust in the relationship by offering to go for a walk with Doug. In so doing, she returns to the skill of *'actively looking for the channels of communication that the person is using'*. The action shows that she has listened to Doug's wishes to go out, but also that she has responded to his anxiety about whether he can make his communication understood. Thus, once again, the specialist communication skill of *'validation'* is supremely important.

In summary, social workers who work with vulnerable older people, particularly in the statutory sector, do so in the context of agency pressure that prioritises task-orientated, outcome-focused practice within tight timescales. This provides a challenging environment in which to enact person-centred practice. In this chapter, I have identified how social work communication with vulnerable older people is complex and emotionally challenging ('Being'). The focus must be on the processes of the work and not just outcomes ('Being'). Herein, a specialist communication strategy that actively looks for, and validates the meaning provided by, different forms, mediums, channels and content of communication by a service user is critical ('Knowing' and 'Doing').

Mapping to the Professional Capability Framework

Qualifying Social Worker Level Capabilities

Please remember that these should be viewed as domains which overlap in an integrative manner rather than as a linear checklist.

'By the end of last placement/ the completion of qualifying programmes newly qualified social workers should have demonstrated the Knowledge, Skills and Values to work with a range of user groups, and the ability to undertake a range of tasks at a foundation level, the capacity to work with more complex situations; they should be able to work more autonomously, whilst recognising that the final decision will still rest with their supervisor; they will seek appropriate support and supervision.
The Health Professions Council (the regulator of qualified social workers) and The College have mapped the Standards of Proficiency for Social Work (SOPs) against the PCF expectations for social work students at the end of their last placement. Whilst there are some differences in the way the standards and PCF are expressed, the overall expectations are the same.'

Communication Capacity Domain – 'Knowing' (engaging with formal and informal knowledge in communication)	PCF 3 Diversity: Recognise diversity and apply anti-discriminatory and anti-oppressive principles in practice ➢ Understand how an individual's identity is informed by factors such as culture, economic status, family composition, life experiences and characteristics, and take account of these to understand their experiences, questioning assumptions where necessary ➢ With reference to current legislative requirements, recognise personal and organisational discrimination and oppression and with guidance make use of a range of approaches to challenge them
	PCF 5 Knowledge: Apply knowledge of social sciences, law and social work practice theory ➢ Demonstrate a critical understanding of the application to social work of research, theory and knowledge from sociology, social policy, psychology and health ➢ Demonstrate a critical understanding of the legal and policy frameworks and guidance that inform and mandate social work practice, recognising the scope for professional judgement

> Demonstrate and apply to practice a working knowledge of human growth and development throughout the life course
> Recognise the short and long term impact of psychological, socio-economic, environmental and physiological factors on people's lives, taking into account age and development, and how this informs practice
> Recognise how systemic approaches can be used to understand the person-in-the-environment and inform your practice
> Acknowledge the centrality of relationships for people and the key concepts of attachment, separation, loss, change and resilience
> Understand forms of harm and their impact on people, and the implications for practice, drawing on concepts of strength, resilience, vulnerability, risk and resistance, and apply to practice
> Demonstrate a critical knowledge of the range of theories and models for social work intervention with individuals, families, groups and communities, and the methods derived from them
> Value and take account of the expertise of service users, carers and professionals

KSS Adults (4): Safeguarding
Social workers must be able to recognise the risk indicators of different forms of abuse and neglect and their impact on individuals, their families or their support networks and should prioritise the protection of children and adults in vulnerable situations whenever necessary. This includes working with those who self-neglect. Social workers who work with adults must take an outcomes-focused, person-centred approach to safeguarding practice, recognising that people are experts in their own lives and working alongside them to identify person centred solutions to risk and harm.

KSS Adults (6): Effective Assessments and Outcome Based Support Planning
Social workers should demonstrate a good understanding of personalisation, the social model of disability and of human development throughout life and demonstrate a holistic approach to the identification of needs, circumstances, rights, strengths and risks. In particular, social workers need to understand the impact of trauma, loss and abuse, physical disability, physical ill health, learning disability, mental ill health, mental capacity, substance misuse, domestic abuse, aging and end of life issues on physical, cognitive, emotional and social development both for the individual and for the functioning of the family. They should recognise the roles and needs of informal or family carers and use holistic, systemic approaches to supporting individuals and carers. They should develop and maintain knowledge and good partnerships with local community resources in order to work effectively with individuals in connecting them with appropriate resources and support.

| Communication Capacity Domain – 'Doing' (the enactment of communication strategies in interaction) | **PCF 6 Critical Reflection and Analysis: Apply critical reflection and analysis to inform and provide a rationale for professional decision-making**
➢ Apply imagination, creativity and curiosity to practice
➢ Inform decision-making through the identification and gathering of information from multiple sources, actively seeking new sources
➢ With support, rigorously question and evaluate the reliability and validity of information from different sources
➢ Demonstrate a capacity for logical, systematic, critical and reflective reasoning and apply the theories and techniques of reflective practice
➢ Know how to formulate, test, evaluate, and review hypotheses in response to information available at the time and apply in practice
➢ Begin to formulate and make explicit, evidence-informed judgements and justifiable decisions

KSS Adults (8): Supervision, Critical Reflection and Analysis
Social workers should be able to make effective use of opportunities to discuss, reflect upon and test multiple hypotheses, the role of intuition and logic in decision making, the difference between opinion and fact, the role of evidence, how to address common bias in situations of uncertainty and the reasoning of any conclusions reached and recommendations made, particularly in relation to mental capacity, mental health and safeguarding situations.

Social workers should have a critical understanding of the difference between theory, research, evidence and expertise and the role of professional judgement. They should use practice evidence and research to inform the complex judgements and decisions needed to support, empower and protect their service users. They should apply imagination, creativity and curiosity to working in partnership with individuals and their carers, acknowledging the centrality of people's own expertise about their experience and needs.

KSS Children (2): Communication
Produce written case notes and reports, which are well argued, focused and jargon free. Present a clear analysis and a sound rationale for actions as well as any conclusions reached, so that all parties are well-informed. |
| | **PCF 7 Intervention and Skills: Use judgement and authority to intervene with individuals, families and communities to promote independence, provide support and prevent harm, neglect and abuse**
➢ Identify and apply a range of verbal, non-verbal and written methods of communication and adapt them in line with peoples' age, comprehension and culture
➢ Be able to communicate information, advice, instruction and professional opinion so as to advocate, influence and persuade |

➢ Demonstrate the ability to engage with people, and build, manage, sustain and conclude compassionate and effective relationships

➢ Demonstrate skills in sharing information appropriately and respectfully

➢ Recognise complexity, multiple factors, changing circumstances and uncertainty in people's lives, to be able to prioritise your intervention

➢ Understand the authority of the social work role and begin to use this appropriately as an accountable professional

➢ Recognise the factors that create or exacerbate risk to individuals, their families or carers, to the public or to professionals, including yourself, and contribute to the assessment and management of risk

KSS Adults (3): Person-centred Practice

They should work co-productively and innovatively with people, local communities, other professionals, agencies and services to promote self-determination, community capacity, personal and family reliance, cohesion, earlier intervention and active citizenship.

KSS Adults (4): Safeguarding

Social workers who work with adults must take an outcomes-focused, person-centred approach to safeguarding practice, recognising that people are experts in their own lives and working alongside them to identify person centred solutions to risk and harm. In situations where there is abuse or neglect or clear risk of those, social workers must work in a way that enhances involvement, choice and control as part of improving quality of life, wellbeing and safety.

KSS Adults (7): Direct Work with Individuals and Families

Social workers need to be able to work directly with individuals and their families through the professional use of self, using interpersonal skills and emotional intelligence to create relationships based on openness, transparency and empathy. They should know how to build purposeful, effective relationships underpinned by reciprocity. They should be able to communicate clearly, sensitively and effectively, applying a range of best evidence-based methods of written, oral and non-verbal communication and adapt these methods to match the person's age, comprehension and culture. Social workers should be capable of communicating effectively with people with specific communication needs, including those with learning disabilities, dementia, people who lack mental capacity and people with sensory impairment.

KSS Children (2): Communication

Communicate clearly and sensitively with children of different ages and abilities, their families and in a range of settings and circumstances.

Use methods based on best evidence.

	Create immediate rapport with people not previously known which facilitates engagement and motivation to participate in child protective enquiries, assessments and services. Listen to the views, wishes and feelings of children and families and help parents and carers understand the ways in which their children communicate through their behaviour. Help them to understand how they might communicate more effectively with their children. Promote speech, language and communication support, identifying those children and adults who are experiencing difficulties expressing themselves.
Communication Capacity Domain – 'Being' (the use of 'self')	**PCF 1 Professionalism: Identify and behave as a professional social worker, committed to professional development** ➤ Be able to explain the role of the social worker in a range of contexts, and uphold the reputation of the profession ➤ Demonstrate professionalism in terms of presentation, demeanour, reliability, honesty and respectfulness ➤ Recognise the impact of self in interaction with others, making appropriate use of personal experience ➤ Be able to recognise and maintain personal and professional boundaries ➤ Recognise your professional limitations and how to seek advice ➤ Demonstrate a commitment to your continuing learning and development ➤ With support, take steps to manage and promote own safety, health, wellbeing and emotional resilience **KSS Adults (7): Direct work with individuals and families** Social workers should be capable of communicating effectively with people with specific communication needs, including those with learning disabilities, dementia, people who lack mental capacity and people with sensory impairment. They should do this in ways that are engaging, respectful, motivating and effective, even when dealing with conflict – whether perceived or actual – anger and resistance to change. **KSS Children (2): Communication** Act respectfully even when people are angry, hostile and resistant to change. Manage tensions between parents, carers and family members, in ways that show persistence, determination and professional confidence.
	PCF 2 Values and Ethics: Apply social work ethical principles and values to guide professional practice ➤ Recognise and, with support, manage the impact of own values on professional practice ➤ Manage potentially conflicting or competing values, and, with guidance, recognise, reflect on, and work with ethical dilemmas ➤ Demonstrate respectful partnership work with service users and carers, eliciting and respecting their needs and views, and promoting their participation in decision-making wherever possible ➤ Recognise and promote individuals' rights to autonomy and self-determination

KSS Adults (5): Mental Capacity
Social workers must model and lead a change of approach, away from that where the default setting is 'safety first', towards a person-centred culture where individual choice is encouraged and where the right of all individuals to express their own lifestyle choices is recognised and valued.

In working with those where there is no concern over capacity, social workers should take all practicable steps to empower people to make their own decisions, recognising that people are experts in their own lives and working alongside them to identify person-centred solutions to risk and harm, recognising the individual's right to make 'unwise' decisions.

PCF 3 Diversity: Recognise diversity and apply anti-discriminatory and anti-oppressive principles in practice
(Appropriately placed in both 'Knowing' and 'Being')
➢ With reference to current legislative requirements, recognise personal and organisational discrimination and oppression and with guidance make use of a range of approaches to challenge them
➢ Recognise and manage the impact on people of the power invested in your role

KSS Adults (3): Person-centred Practice
They should coordinate and facilitate a wide range of practical and emotional support, and discharge legal duties to complement people's own resources and networks, so that all individuals (no matter their background, health status or mental capacity), carers and families can exercise choice and control, (supporting individuals to make their own decisions, especially where they may lack capacity) and meet their needs and aspirations in personalised, creative and often novel ways. They should work co-productively and innovatively with people, local communities, other professionals, agencies and services to promote self-determination, community capacity, personal and family reliance, cohesion, earlier intervention and active citizenship.

PCF 4 Rights, Justice and Economic Wellbeing: Advance human rights and promote social justice and economic wellbeing
➢ Understand, identify and apply in practice the principles of social justice, inclusion and equality
➢ Understand how legislation and guidance can advance or constrain people's rights and recognise how the law may be used to protect or advance their rights and entitlements
➢ Work within the principles of human and civil rights and equalities legislation, differentiating and beginning to work with absolute, qualified and competing rights and differing needs and perspectives
➢ Recognise the impact of poverty and social exclusion and promote enhanced economic status through access to education, work, housing, health services and welfare benefits

PCF 8 Contexts and Organisations: Engage with, inform, and adapt to changing contexts that shape practice. Operate effectively within own organisational frameworks and contribute to the development of services and organisations. Operate effectively within multi-agency and inter-professional partnerships and settings

➤ Recognise that social work operates within, and responds to, changing economic, social, political and organisational contexts

➤ Understand the roles and responsibilities of social workers in a range of organisations, lines of accountability and the boundaries of professional autonomy and discretion

➤ Understand legal obligations, structures and behaviours within organisations and how these impact on policy, procedure and practice

➤ Be able to work within an organisation's remit and contribute to its evaluation and development

KSS Adults (9): Organisational Context

They must understand and work effectively within financial and legal frameworks, obligations, structures and culture, in particular Human Rights and Equalities legislation, the Care Act, Mental Capacity Act, Mental Health Act and accompanying guidance and codes of practice. They must be able to operate successfully in their organisational context, demonstrating effective time management, caseload management and be capable of reconciling competing demands and embrace information, data and technology appropriate to their role. They should have access to regular quality supervision to support their professional resilience and emotional and physical wellbeing.

12
Working with Refugees and Asylum Seekers

Summary of Specialist Communication Skills in this Chapter

➢ experiencing service user feelings

➢ using the whole communication spectrum

➢ tuning-in to the fear and uncertainty over citizenship

➢ demonstrating cultural acceptance.

Policy and background literature

At the time of writing, the 'migrant crisis' is high on the policy agenda. Vast numbers of people are fleeing the war-torn countries of Syria, Iraq, Afghanistan and certain African nations to seek asylum in Europe. The provision of support to people seeking asylum and those gaining refugee status is now an established area of social work practice, where the role of the state in assessing asylum and the cultural climate within the UK of racist attitudes regarding egalitarian coexistence presents particular communication issues for social workers. In communicating with asylum seekers, social workers need to recognise the pervasiveness of the legal framework within their lives, whereby they live within an atmosphere of fear, anxiety, control and uncertainty caused by the role of the state in assessing their application for asylum (Fell, 2004). Their overriding concern is to prove that their 'case' meets the 1957 UN Convention requirements.

The psychological distress that asylum seekers experience as a result of their traumatic pre-migrating experiences, such as rape, torture, mourning and bereavement (Parker, 2000; Kohli, 2006), will also affect communication processes. For unaccompanied minors, this psychological distress is particularly severe and often communicated through problematic behaviour. The literature points to a compounding number of stressors experienced by asylum seekers and those granted refugee status: isolation, insecurity, fear and a struggle to cope with unsettlement, often related to the aforementioned asylum process (Daycare Trust, 1995; Rutter, 2003). The experience of racist attacks often causes social withdrawal. Economic hardship and confusion, combined with wariness about from whom to seek advice and help regarding housing and schooling, is frequent.

These issues point to a need for communication to help asylum seekers feel less marginalised and gain some degree of inclusion (Fell, 2004). Central to this is overcoming issues of trust and the reluctance to approach professionals for help for fear that it might be reflected back to the Home Office and prejudice their application for asylum. Active listening, availability and the ability to be a stable point of contact is recognised as important in relation to establishing trust (Comley, 1998; Fell, 2004). The use of more comprehensive communication strategies other than simple verbal language in conveying warmth, understanding and acceptance is significant (Morales and Sheafor, 2001; Koprowska, 2005). Where verbal communication takes place, it needs to be at a slower pace, avoiding complex or ambiguous grammar, and with repeated checks for understanding (Koprowska, 2005). Cultural awareness and sensitivity is significant within these strategies. Definitions of family and change are not necessarily the same as that of the host (Fell, 2004; Devore, 2001). Indeed, it is critical to guard against any stereotyping of values or practices of members of ethnic groups (Parker, 2000; Jones, 2003). Warnings surrounding 'cultural relativism' within social work practice are well-versed and relevant here (see Chapter 2 for further discussion).

Access to English language support and interpreters is important, yet the literature also points to the conflict and potential dangers inherent within the role of both formal and informal interpreters. Green et al. (2005) highlight that although there have been improvements in the availability and quality of interpreting services across health and social care, many service users rely on informal sources to make contact, appointments and attend consultations and meetings. Studies identify that informal interpreters are often preferred by families because they offer emotional and practical support, they are readily available and provide greater understanding of the service user (Rhodes and Nocon, 2003, Green et al., 2005). Yet, the majority of the literature focuses on the inappropriateness and potentially ineffectiveness of informal interpreters, particularly child interpreters (Ebden et al., 1988, Flores et al., 2003). The reasons cited are that children may not have sufficient sophistication within the languages to interpret accurately, and they may lack emotional maturity to manage sensitive and distressing information about health problems. However, Cohen et al. (1999) and Green et al. (2005) identify normative ideology underpinning this perspective concerning the social construction of childhood in Western societies and relative inappropriateness for children to 'take on' such adult responsibility. Green et al.'s study of the perspectives of child interpreters found that the children rarely considered themselves as 'exploited' or that their translation was 'inadequate'. Rather, they saw themselves as skilled mediators, bridging the communication between two adults. The contribution that they made to their family gave them a sense of self-esteem. Difficulties arose when there were differences in the normative expectations of their role in the family, such as young men being asked to translate about their mothers' reproductive health problems, or young women being asked to investigate whether their parents are being compliant with medication instructions.

Care needs to be taken to establish the 'ethnic reality or experience' of the individual concerned (Devore, 2001). Indeed, an important aspect of communication seems to be that of a readiness to listen and validate asylum seekers' and refugees' accounts of their past experiences (Parker, 2000; Devore, 2001; Fell, 2004). The preparedness of the social worker to emotionally attend to these accounts, but at the same time be able to communicate about help with practical issues, such as schooling, appropriate housing and finance seems to be successful within work with refugees (Parker, 2000; Fell, 2004). Related to this, literature supports the importance of social workers addressing racism and racist experiences (Fanning, 2004; Dominelli, 1992). Social workers are expected to have learned ways of countering unfair discrimination, racism, poverty, disadvantage and injustice. However, literature highlights that professionals avoid attending to issues of race and culture, finding the issues uncomfortable to discuss (Abney, 2002; Alexander-Floyd, 2008). Given that this area of practice is replete with instances and attitudes of hostility, social workers need to develop strategies to counter such racism at interpersonal and structural levels.

Practice application

The background literature states that the overriding concern for asylum seekers is to move from non-citizenship to greater citizenship by being recognised as a refugee under the 1951 UN Convention (Fell, 2004). Thus, a central concern for the social worker in our practice example (12.1) should be to identify how societal barriers relating to this uncertainty over citizenship impact on her communication with Maria, and to seek to overcome them. To this end, it is important for the worker to recognise that a significant barrier is likely to be an atmosphere of fear, anxiety, control and uncertainty caused by the role of the state in assessing her application for asylum. Maria is likely to meet the social worker with suspicion and trepidation that she might be an official from the Home Office, fearing that any disclosed information might be referred to the Home Office and affect her asylum claim. Thus, it is important for the social worker to engage in 'tuning-in' to prepare to 'show empathy' for the way in which Maria might express these feelings in their meeting. In so doing, the worker will be more able to demonstrate that she is not adopting a role that is controlling or hostile but seeking to be accepting, available and willing to listen and understand Maria's thoughts and feelings. So critical is this preparatory empathy for this practice setting, that it seems important to emphasise the specialist communication strategy as being one of 'tuning-in to the fear and uncertainty over citizenship'.

Practice Example 12.1

Maria

Preparatory Stage

Maria (aged 32 years) and her two children (Milosh, aged 13 years and Gordana, aged 10 years) are a Roma family from Kosovo who came to the UK seven months ago seeking asylum. With Maria's permission, her general practitioner referred the family to the duty social worker of the local Advice and Assessment (Intake) Social Work Team. The general practitioner is treating Maria for depression. He feels that the victimisation that she is experiencing from neighbours, alongside the problematic behaviour of her eldest son and negative reports from school, is exacerbating Maria's mental health. The general practitioner feels that urgent social work intervention is needed to support the family functioning and prevent further deterioration of Maria's mental health.

Maria, her husband and two young children were among the 120 000 Roma people who had to leave Kosovo as a consequence of the Yugoslav wars in the late 1990s. Over the last few years, Roma people who fled to neighbouring countries of Hungary, Slovakia and the Czech Republic have been attacked with firebombs, stabbings and beatings. Many of the attacks have been aimed at families and children. There are lingering feelings of hostility among the majority population in Kosovo in relation to Roma people, as they often speak Serbian and are accused as having collaborated with Serbian forces.

A specialist communication strategy of 'demonstrating cultural accept-ance' is significantly important given that the aforementioned legal framework reflects a more general cultural climate within the UK of rac-ist attitudes regarding egalitarian coexistence. There are regular reports of racist discrimination, stigma and disadvantage being experienced by asylum seekers, refugee groups and other migrant workers and families of minority ethnic groups (Cohen, 1994; Parker, 2000). Where appropriate, the social worker must be prepared to discuss instances of racism and atti-tudes of hostility that Maria may have experienced and believes to impact upon the safety of her family and home situation. Clearly though, she should not assume that racism is a necessary element of Maria's situation, as to do so would be racist in itself (Jones, 2003). However, being aware about and sensitive to cultural differences among the people that a social worker serves is considered to be a vital element of cultural competence (Compton et al., 2005). This involves recognising that all cultures can sup-ply strength to people and, equally, can oppress or create liberation for their members.

Given that the background literature highlighted that professionals often find issues of race and culture uncomfortable to discuss (Abney, 2002; Alexander-Floyd, 2008), it is important that the social worker reviews her own deficits in knowledge and skills in relation to cultural competence at this preparatory stage (Devore, 2001). Devore (2001:36) cites Miley et al. (1998: 39) in identifying how such self-examination should cover the four areas of personal identity, spiritual beliefs, knowl-edge of others and cross-cultural skills. She highlights the following ques-tions as helpful within this analysis:

➢ Have I been a racist or recipient of racist attacks?

➢ What privileges do I accrue because of my ethnicity or gender?

➢ Am I religious?

➢ What ethnic dispositions influence my identity?

➢ What am I doing to increase my knowledge about people in other eth-nic groups?

Answering such questions will be essential in increasing social worker confidence and skill in 'demonstrating cultural acceptance'. Social workers will learn about themselves as members of an ethnic group and accompanying cultural norms and values, as well as increasing knowledge about other groups (Devore, 2001). Thus, in relation to this example, as part of this preparatory self-examination, the social worker should iden-tify the cultural norms and values that frequently exist among Roma populations from Central Europe. Examples of such norms include the respect shown to traditional purity laws. Women often wear long skirts to cover their bodies from the waist-down, as these parts of the body are considered more private and 'less pure'. Times of menstruation, childbirth and postpartum periods are similarly considered impure, with cleanliness rituals adopted and women withdrawing from collective gatherings at these times. Men and women tend to adopt gender roles, with women being the primary caregivers and homemakers. Marriage tends to occur at an earlier age, and with other members of the Roma population. Sexual relationships before marriage are generally forbidden. Roma people tend to adopt the religion of the majority population in which they are living, and in Central Europe this is frequently the Christian or Muslim faith.

Having an awareness of these cultural norms and values will prepare the social worker to be sensitive to cultural differences and variations in patterns and styles of communication with Maria. While many Europeans experience eye contact as signalling openness, trust and honesty in communication, those who are Muslim women sometimes find such direct eye contact to be insulting. If Maria is a practising Muslim, then she may avoid appointments coinciding with appointed times of prayer. If Maria adopts the traditional Roma norms and values concerning purity and gender roles, then she may be offended by the social worker being dressed in clothes which accord her body far less covering. Depending on whether it is a time of less purity, she may be unable to leave the house to attend an appointment, or indeed avoid touching the social worker, such as shaking hands. However, it is equally important that the social worker recognises that these norms, values and patterns of communication may not be replicated within Maria's family. In 'demonstrating cultural acceptance', she must not assume homogeneity in the values and practices of any ethnic group (Parker, 2000). For example, Maria and/or her children may have chosen to adopt some or all of the cultural norms of the majority ethnic population of the country or region in which she and her children now live. As Compton et al. (2005: 190) state: 'we are born into some cultures and we may adopt others... many [service users] routinely draw from several cultures and multiple roles'. They consider communication to improve when social workers view cultural identification as being not being just primarily about race, ethnicity and religion, but seek to hear from service users about what they believe to be the most important contributing factors to their personal and cultural identity.

The social worker needs to 'tune-in' to another societal barrier that impacts upon communication, and that concerns the way in which society places a high value upon the written and spoken word. This creates a disadvantage for people who do not speak the language of the majority population as their first language. In the case of our practice example, the social worker must start from an attitudinal position, which is that Maria and her children have a right to be communicated with in their first language and be facilitated to express decisions concerning their lives. Arguably the use of an interpreter is crucial in enabling Maria to express her thoughts and feelings more accurately. However, the background literature has highlighted that the use of interpreters is not without its difficulties. Indeed, while interpreters are used far more extensively within social work practice, there are many instances where it is not possible to obtain the services of an interpreter, such as in emergency or unplanned situations, or where it is difficult to match the dialect of a language, or where the service user declines the service. Moreover, it is important to recognise that communication strategies with Maria should not just be framed on the basis of written and spoken word, but respect how Maria senses, perceives and communicates about her experiences. Communication could use different methods and formats beyond that of verbalisation such as body language and also pictures, symbols and signs. As with so many of the practice settings within this book, adopting a specialist communication strategy that *'uses the whole communication spectrum'* will help overcome the societal barriers to communication.

Practice Example 12.2 shows the social worker employing the four parts of the basic communication skill from Chapter 4 of 'achieving a shared purpose', i.e. 'being clear on role'; 'being clear on purpose'; 'reaching for feedback' and 'showing empathy'.

Practice Example 12.2

Maria

Beginnings

(Social worker knocks at the door. Maria calls through the door.)

[1]Maria: Who is that?

SW: Er, Mrs Kovac. My name's Angela Moore. I phoned you this morning.

Maria: Phoned? Who are you?

SW: Angela Moore *(bends down to letter box to speak more quietly)*. I telephoned you this morning. *(says more quietly)* I'm the social worker.

Maria: Social Worker. Come in. *(opens the door)*

▶

◄

SW:	Hello, Mrs Kovac? (raises her hand in a gesture of greeting) ... Nice to meet you. I'm Angela, from the social work office at Central Hall, a social worker. Um ... Your doctor was worried about you. I might be able to help. Do you mind if I call you Maria?
Maria:	Yes, Maria.
SW:	Where shall we sit? (*They sit down on two dining room chairs. The social worker moves her chair more towards Maria and Maria looks into her face.*)
SW:	Maria ... do you know why I've come to see you today?
Maria:	Um (*points to left*) um ... my roof?
[2]SW:	(*maintains eye contact, speaks slowly and clearly*) We can look at the roof, but first, it's about how you are ... and how your children are ... and whether we can help you in any way ... okay?
[3]Maria:	Okay (*nods slowly in nervous way*).
[4]SW:	(*continues to speak slowly and clearly*) You seem a bit worried ... I want you to know that I'm not from the Home Office, okay? And I'm not from the police ... I'm from Social Services ... do you understand Social Services?
Maria:	No.
[5]SW:	It's um ... we try to help people ... all sorts of people ... not just people from other countries. We have older people, younger people ... so lots ... lots of people we try to help ... okay? And what I want to do is see what help you need today.
Maria:	Mmm.
SW:	The doctor is worried about you Maria ... The doctor said you were very sad ... finding it difficult ... Can we talk about it? (*Pause*) Is that okay?
Maria:	Mmm.
[6]SW:	Your English is very good, but you probably need a little bit more help with your English? (*pause for 10 seconds*) Maybe an interpreter is a good idea?
[7]Maria:	Well, no, my children ... they help me.
SW:	They help you. Your children ... how old are they? (*Social worker indicates differences in height with hand.*)
Maria:	At school ... thirteen. Ten.
SW:	Their English ... they have learned it at school?
Maria:	Yes.
SW:	And your English ... how have you learned your English?

►

◀

Maria:	Through my children.
SW:	Through your children?
Maria:	Yes, and speaking …
SW:	And speaking in this country?
Maria:	Yes.
SW:	And you've been here for seven months?
Maria:	Yes.
SW:	And how do you like this country?
Maria:	It is good.
SW:	It is good?
Maria:	Yes.
SW:	What do you not like about this country? (*shaking head*)
Maria:	(*tilts head indicating that she does not understand*)
[8]SW:	What do you not like about this country? (*shaking head and making negative hand gestures*) What is bad with this country?
Maria:	Um … Home Office?
SW:	The Home Office? You don't like them?
Maria:	No.
SW:	You're waiting to hear from the Home Office whether you can stay?
Maria:	(*nods*) Yes … yes
SW:	You would like to do that? (*nodding*) You would like to stay here?
[9]Maria:	Yes … Um … (*waves arm…face reddens…she appears upset, tearful*) My husband …
[10]SW:	(*leaning forward*) It's okay … (*silence for 10 seconds*) Is it difficult for you to talk about that? (*Maria nods, silence for another 10 seconds*)
SW:	Do you want to talk to me about that? (*pause*)
Maria:	(*nods – is upset*) I am … a little … (*silence for 20 seconds*)
SW:	Your husband? Is he back in Kosovo?
Maria:	Yes. (*nodding and crying*)
[11]SW:	That must be very painful for you (*reaches out and touches Maria's arm*) and your children to be in a strange country. Are you missing your husband? (*Maria nods and is very tearful*)
SW:	Do you want a tissue? (*Maria shakes head*) Would you like to talk about that now … or later, perhaps?

As anticipated, Maria seems to be communicating feelings of apprehension at speaking to the social worker. The 'tuning-in' activity revealed that this is likely to be due to the authority that the social worker brings through her legislative role and professional status. Maria's body language shows anxiety (Practice Example 12.2, point 3: *'nods slowly in nervous way'*), and her answers seem confused about the exact role and purpose for the visit. The social worker uses the skill from Chapter 4 of 'putting feelings into words' to 'show empathy' for Maria's feelings of apprehension, and also begins to find a way of better *'clarifying her role'* by asking Maria to provide her understanding of the work of a social worker (Practice Example 12.2, point 4: 'You seem a bit worried ... I want you to know that I'm not from the Home Office, okay? And I'm not from the police ... I'm from Social Services ... do you understand Social Services?') It is likely that the social worker will need to continue to 'show empathy' for these feelings throughout their meeting. This will continue to demonstrate that she is not adopting a role that is controlling or hostile but seeking to be accepting, available and willing to listen and understand Maria's thoughts and feelings.

Point 5 of Practice Example 12.2 illustrates the difficulty in explaining the role of a social worker in circumstances where there is no equivalent welfare system within the cultural experience of the other person. The language difference and difficulties between Maria and the social worker compound the problem in achieving a shared meaning. The opportunity for misunderstanding and miscommunication is great. Indeed, it is frightening enough for Maria to speak to a person in authority about her mental health and social situation, without the additional demands of communicating in a second language with the accompanying worry over misunderstanding. The social worker quickly realises this and offers to arrange for an interpreter for a subsequent meeting (Practice Example 12.2, point 6). Maria refuses this offer, preferring to involve her children as interpreters (Practice Example 12.2, point 7). The matter of seeking translation services through informal sources such as bilingual children, extended family, friends or other members of the cultural community caused considerable debate among the social workers involved in the research study for this book. Indeed, the same debate occurs in the background literature, which was summarised earlier. The social worker needs to ensure that she is conversant with the advantages and disadvantages of using formal and informal interpreters. This should include recognising that an immediate aversion to allowing Maria's children to interpret might reflect an attitude rooted in normative ideology concerning the social construction of childhood in Western societies and relative inappropriateness for children to 'take on' such adult responsibility. It is important that the social worker takes into account the specific cultural and social role definitions that influence Maria in making this decision about requesting her children be interpreters. It may be viewed as an expected part of the usual set of economic and social relations of the family, which frequently gives the children self-esteem and a sense of pride to the family. However, it would be wrong to consider these values and family norms solely within the context of Maria's culture. This would constitute an extreme form of cultural relativism (Compton et al., 2005). The decision must also be made on the basis of whether the behaviour meets the legal conditions set out within The Children Acts 1989 and 2004 and The Children and Families Act 2014 to safeguard and promote the welfare of children in need, including ascertaining their perspectives on those decisions in their own right.

In the research transcripts for the study underpinning the book, the theme of non-verbal communication, while present in all other transcripts, came very much to the fore; similarly, the role of feelings emerged as significant. While in most of the other practice settings, non-verbal communication skills play a supporting role for what is communicated linguistically, when working with this particular service user whose spoken English was limited, spoken word took a lesser role and the importance of non-verbal communication skills emerged. The social workers identified that where language is perhaps a barrier, the use of non-verbal techniques can offer support, encouragement and facilitate communication. Aside from non-verbal communication, the qualifying social workers also highlighted other ways of trying to adapt verbal communication to make it easier for the service user to understand, such as using short, non-complex sentences and repetition. This repeated check for understanding demonstrates basic communication skills discussed in Chapter 4 of 'reflective listening', which describes how a social worker in attending to the service user's narrative and non-verbal communication of thoughts and feelings with warmth and concern, might encourage that person to feel more able to disclose information or worries without fearing blame or misunderstanding. Points 7 to 9 of Practice Example 12.2 illustrate this communication strategy. 'Closed questions' which are short and non-complex allow Maria time to process the information and formulate the appropriate answer ('Your children... how old are they?', 'And you've been here for seven months?') The social worker uses occasional 'open questions' but keeps the questions short and avoids using higher-order concepts or grammatically ambiguous words ('How have you learned your English?', 'What is bad with this country?').

The specialist communication strategy appears to have some success in facilitating Maria's expression of thoughts and feelings. At point 9 of the dialogue (Practice Example 12.2), she communicates strong feelings of distress through her body language. This continues until point 12.

[9]Maria: Yes ... Um ... (*waves arm ... face reddens ... she appears upset, tearful*) My husband ...

[10]SW: (*leaning forward*) It's okay ... (*silence for 10 seconds*) Is it difficult for you to talk about that? (*Maria nods, silence for another 10 seconds*)

[11]SW: Do you want to talk to me about that? (*pause*)

Maria: (*nods – is upset*) I am ... a little ... (*silence for 20 seconds*)

SW: Your husband? Is he back in Kosovo?

Maria: Yes. (*nodding and crying*)

[12]SW: That must be very painful for you (*reaches out and touches Maria's arm*) and your children to be in a strange country. Are you missing your husband? (*Maria nods and is very tearful*)

[13]SW: Do you want a tissue? (Maria shakes head) Would you like to talk about that now ... or later, perhaps?

At point 10, the social worker 'shows empathy' for her distress in non-verbal ways through 'using silences' and verbally providing reassurance that she will support Maria with these feelings ('It's okay', 'Is it difficult for you to talk about that?'). In Chapter 8, I described how the skill of *'using silences'* is important for developing a working relationship with a service user expressing mental distress. Sitting alongside and just 'being' with the service user demonstrates support and acceptance. 'Being' gives respect by allowing difficult thoughts to remain undisclosed until an appropriate time for the service user, whereas 'doing' demands work to be done on those feelings when the service user is unwilling or unable to do so (Wilson et al., 2011). Conceptually, the process provides 'containment' of painful feelings which have become difficult to control. Containment is described as an active process by which the social worker experiences the difficult feelings transferred by the service user and then seeks to work on those feelings in order to help the service user feel more understood, more 'in control' and less isolated (Agass, 2002).

Interestingly, the qualifying social workers in our research study, who were participating in the enactment of this role play as forum theatre, found this point in the communication to be critical. Although at this stage of the interview they had no knowledge of Maria's pre-migration experiences or those relating to settlement, they felt her projection of sadness and pain within themselves. Feelings emerged as a larger theme within this practice setting than others considered for the book. It is likely that this is because this service user was being victimised, isolated and was visibly upset and emotional. The social workers noted the importance primarily of helping this person to feel less sad and scared, with practical assistance as almost a secondary consideration (although still vital). As this service user had also a limited ability to communicate and was scared, the social workers identified a feeling in themselves of their own helplessness coupled with tremendous empathy for the service user. The theme of 'experiencing service user feelings' can be classified as a specialist communication skill because the empathy for the service user in their role as social worker (especially when the limits of what they could do in their role were felt as helplessness) was clearly contributing to the development of reflexive practitioners.

The impact of this transference meant that at point 12, when the social worker uses Shulman's (2009) skill of 'putting feelings into words' to verbally demonstrate empathy for Maria's feelings (Practice Example 12.2, point 12: 'That must be very painful for you and your children to be in a strange country') some of the qualifying social workers (within the forum theatre) encouraged the use of non-verbal communication to further emphasise the demonstration of empathy (Practice Example 12.2, point 12: '*(reaches out and touches Maria's arm)*'). They constantly debated the decision whether or not to have physical contact or not with the service user, as it may considerably influence successful communication. As stated earlier, the cultural norms and values of some cultural groups indicate that some service users would be offended by such a gesture. Indeed, some social workers were not prepared to risk any allegations of inappropriate behaviour.

Repeatedly, the social worker uses an 'open question' to encourage Maria to talk to her about her feelings because she is aware that there could be many reasons for her distress, including that of being in danger of harm from racist violence in a variety of forms (Practice Example 12.2, point 11: 'Do you want to talk to me about that?'; point 13: 'Would you like to talk about that now ... or later, perhaps?')

The background literature identified how asylum seekers experience psychological distress as a result of their traumatic pre-migrating experiences, such as rape, torture, mourning and bereavement (Parker, 2000), as well as isolation, insecurity, fear and stress in coping with unsettlement, which is often related to the aforementioned asylum process (Daycare Trust, 1995; Rutter, 2003). An important aspect of specialist communication seems to be that of a readiness to listen and validate asylum seekers' and refugees' accounts of their past experiences (Parker, 2000; Devore, 2001; Fell, 2004). The worker in our practice example should demonstrate acceptance of Maria's 'world view' or 'private voice' of her experiences.

Fell (2004: 119) makes the point that social workers, who have the privilege of cultural and economic capital, professional status and citizenship, will find it difficult to envisage ever being able to empathise with 'those who have suffered more than we may ever have to'. We are outsiders to those personal stories, and as such, we should give validity to personal accounts and learn from them.

In summary, this chapter has highlighted the degree to which the wider social and political context in which social work communication occurs can cause barriers that impede the effectiveness of that communication ('Knowing'). I have identified how a specialist social work communication strategy of attending to service users' fear and uncertainty over citizenship is crucial ('Being' and 'Doing'). Of equal importance is that of communication which demonstrates cultural acceptance and validity to lived experiences, given that the aforementioned legal framework reflects a more general cultural climate within the UK of racist attitudes regarding egalitarian coexistence ('Knowing', 'Being' and 'Doing').

Mapping to the Professional Capability Framework

Qualifying Social Worker Level Capabilities

Please remember that these should be viewed as domains which overlap in an integrative manner rather than as a linear checklist.

'By the end of last placement/ the completion of qualifying programmes newly qualified social workers should have demonstrated the Knowledge, Skills and Values to work with a range of user groups, and the ability to undertake a range of tasks at a foundation level, the capacity to work with more complex situations; they should be able to work more autonomously, whilst recognising that the final decision will still rest with their supervisor; they will seek appropriate support and supervision.
The Health Professions Council (the regulator of qualified social workers) and The College have mapped the Standards of Proficiency for Social Work (SOPs) against the PCF expectations for social work students at the end of their last placement. Whilst there are some differences in the way the standards and PCF are expressed, the overall expectations are the same.'

Communication Capacity Domain – 'Knowing' (engaging with formal and informal knowledge in communication)	**PCF 3 Diversity: Recognise diversity and apply anti-discriminatory and anti-oppressive principles in practice**
	➤ Understand how an individual's identity is informed by factors such as culture, economic status, family composition, life experiences and characteristics, and take account of these to understand their experiences, questioning assumptions where necessary
	➤ With reference to current legislative requirements, recognise personal and organisational discrimination and oppression and with guidance make use of a range of approaches to challenge them

PCF 5 Knowledge: Apply knowledge of social sciences, law and social work practice theory

➢ Demonstrate a critical understanding of the application to social work of research, theory and knowledge from sociology, social policy, psychology and health

➢ Demonstrate a critical understanding of the legal and policy frameworks and guidance that inform and mandate social work practice, recognising the scope for professional judgement

➢ Demonstrate and apply to practice a working knowledge of human growth and development throughout the life course

➢ Recognise the short and long term impact of psychological, socio-economic, environmental and physiological factors on people's lives, taking into account age and development, and how this informs practice

➢ Recognise how systemic approaches can be used to understand the person-in-the-environment and inform your practice

➢ Acknowledge the centrality of relationships for people and the key concepts of attachment, separation, loss, change and resilience

➢ Understand forms of harm and their impact on people, and the implications for practice, drawing on concepts of strength, resilience, vulnerability, risk and resistance, and apply to practice

➢ Demonstrate a critical knowledge of the range of theories and models for social work intervention with individuals, families, groups and communities, and the methods derived from them

➢ Value and take account of the expertise of service users, carers and professionals

KSS Adults (4): Safeguarding

Social workers must be able to recognise the risk indicators of different forms of abuse and neglect and their impact on individuals, their families or their support networks and should prioritise the protection of children and adults in vulnerable situations whenever necessary. This includes working with those who self-neglect. Social workers who work with adults must take an outcomes-focused, person-centred approach to safeguarding practice, recognising that people are experts in their own lives and working alongside them to identify person centred solutions to risk and harm.

KSS Adults (6): Effective Assessments and Outcome Based Support Planning

Social workers should demonstrate a good understanding of personalisation, the social model of disability and of human development throughout life and demonstrate a holistic approach to the identification of needs, circumstances, rights, strengths and risks. In particular, social workers need to understand the impact of trauma, loss and abuse, physical disability, physical ill health, learning disability, mental ill health, mental capacity, substance misuse, domestic abuse, aging and end of life issues on physical,

	cognitive, emotional and social development both for the individual and for the functioning of the family. They should recognise the roles and needs of informal or family carers and use holistic, systemic approaches to supporting individuals and carers. They should develop and maintain knowledge and good partnerships with local community resources in order to work effectively with individuals in connecting them with appropriate resources and support.
Communication Capacity Domain – 'Doing' (the enactment of communication strategies in interaction)	**PCF 6 Critical Reflection and Analysis: Apply critical reflection and analysis to inform and provide a rationale for professional decision-making** ➢ Apply imagination, creativity and curiosity to practice ➢ Inform decision-making through the identification and gathering of information from multiple sources, actively seeking new sources ➢ With support, rigorously question and evaluate the reliability and validity of information from different sources ➢ Demonstrate a capacity for logical, systematic, critical and reflective reasoning and apply the theories and techniques of reflective practice ➢ Know how to formulate, test, evaluate, and review hypotheses in response to information available at the time and apply in practice ➢ Begin to formulate and make explicit, evidence-informed judgements and justifiable decisions **KSS Adults (8): Supervision, Critical Reflection and Analysis** Social workers should be able to make effective use of opportunities to discuss, reflect upon and test multiple hypotheses, the role of intuition and logic in decision making, the difference between opinion and fact, the role of evidence, how to address common bias in situations of uncertainty and the reasoning of any conclusions reached and recommendations made, particularly in relation to mental capacity, mental health and safeguarding situations. Social workers should have a critical understanding of the difference between theory, research, evidence and expertise and the role of professional judgement. They should use practice evidence and research to inform the complex judgements and decisions needed to support, empower and protect their service users. They should apply imagination, creativity and curiosity to working in partnership with individuals and their carers, acknowledging the centrality of people's own expertise about their experience and needs. **KSS Children (2): Communication** Produce written case notes and reports, which are well argued, focused and jargon free. Present a clear analysis and a sound rationale for actions as well as any conclusions reached, so that all parties are well-informed.

PCF 7 Intervention and Skills: Use judgement and authority to intervene with individuals, families and communities to promote independence, provide support and prevent harm, neglect and abuse

➢ Identify and apply a range of verbal, non-verbal and written methods of communication and adapt them in line with peoples' age, comprehension and culture

➢ Be able to communicate information, advice, instruction and professional opinion so as to advocate, influence and persuade

➢ Demonstrate the ability to engage with people, and build, manage, sustain and conclude compassionate and effective relationships

➢ Demonstrate skills in sharing information appropriately and respectfully

➢ Recognise complexity, multiple factors, changing circumstances and uncertainty in people's lives, to be able to prioritise your intervention

➢ Understand the authority of the social work role and begin to use this appropriately as an accountable professional

➢ Recognise the factors that create or exacerbate risk to individuals, their families or carers, to the public or to professionals, including yourself, and contribute to the assessment and management of risk

KSS Adults (3): Person-centred Practice
They should work co-productively and innovatively with people, local communities, other professionals, agencies and services to promote self-determination, community capacity, personal and family reliance, cohesion, earlier intervention and active citizenship.

KSS Adults (4): Safeguarding
Social workers who work with adults must take an outcomes-focused, person-centred approach to safeguarding practice, recognising that people are experts in their own lives and working alongside them to identify person centred solutions to risk and harm. In situations where there is abuse or neglect or clear risk of those, social workers must work in a way that enhances involvement, choice and control as part of improving quality of life, wellbeing and safety.

KSS Adults (7): Direct Work with Individuals and Families
Social workers need to be able to work directly with individuals and their families through the professional use of self, using interpersonal skills and emotional intelligence to create relationships based on openness, transparency and empathy. They should know how to build purposeful, effective relationships underpinned by reciprocity. They should be able to communicate clearly, sensitively and effectively, applying a range of best evidence-based methods of written, oral and non-verbal communication and adapt these methods to match the person's age, comprehension and culture. Social workers should be capable of communicating effectively with people with specific communication needs, including those with learning disabilities, dementia, people who lack mental capacity and people with sensory impairment.

	KSS Children (2): Communication Communicate clearly and sensitively with children of different ages and abilities, their families and in a range of settings and circumstances. Use methods based on best evidence. Create immediate rapport with people not previously known which facilitates engagement and motivation to participate in child protective enquiries, assessments and services. Listen to the views, wishes and feelings of children and families and help parents and carers understand the ways in which their children communicate through their behaviour. Help them to understand how they might communicate more effectively with their children. Promote speech, language and communication support, identifying those children and adults who are experiencing difficulties expressing themselves.
Communication Capacity Domain – 'Being' (the use of 'self')	**PCF 1 Professionalism: Identify and behave as a professional social worker, committed to professional development** ➤ Be able to explain the role of the social worker in a range of contexts, and uphold the reputation of the profession ➤ Demonstrate professionalism in terms of presentation, demeanour, reliability, honesty and respectfulness ➤ Recognise the impact of self in interaction with others, making appropriate use of personal experience ➤ Be able to recognise and maintain personal and professional boundaries ➤ Recognise your professional limitations and how to seek advice ➤ Demonstrate a commitment to your continuing learning and development ➤ With support, take steps to manage and promote own safety, health, wellbeing and emotional resilience **KSS Adults (7): Direct work with individuals and families** Social workers should be capable of communicating effectively with people with specific communication needs, including those with learning disabilities, dementia, people who lack mental capacity and people with sensory impairment. They should do this in ways that are engaging, respectful, motivating and effective, even when dealing with conflict – whether perceived or actual – anger and resistance to change. **KSS Children (2): Communication** Act respectfully even when people are angry, hostile and resistant to change. Manage tensions between parents, carers and family members, in ways that show persistence, determination and professional confidence.
	PCF 2 Values and Ethics: Apply social work ethical principles and values to guide professional practice ➤ Recognise and, with support, manage the impact of own values on professional practice ➤ Manage potentially conflicting or competing values, and, with guidance, recognise, reflect on, and work with ethical dilemmas

> Demonstrate respectful partnership work with service users and carers, eliciting and respecting their needs and views, and promoting their participation in decision-making wherever possible
> Recognise and promote individuals' rights to autonomy and self-determination

KSS Adults (5): Mental Capacity
Social workers must model and lead a change of approach, away from that where the default setting is 'safety first', towards a person-centred culture where individual choice is encouraged and where the right of all individuals to express their own lifestyle choices is recognised and valued.

In working with those where there is no concern over capacity, social workers should take all practicable steps to empower people to make their own decisions, recognising that people are experts in their own lives and working alongside them to identify person-centred solutions to risk and harm, recognising the individual's right to make 'unwise' decisions.

PCF 3 Diversity: Recognise diversity and apply anti-discriminatory and anti-oppressive principles in practice
(Appropriately placed in both 'Knowing' and 'Being')
> With reference to current legislative requirements, recognise personal and organisational discrimination and oppression and with guidance make use of a range of approaches to challenge them
> Recognise and manage the impact on people of the power invested in your role

KSS Adults (3): Person-centred Practice
They should coordinate and facilitate a wide range of practical and emotional support, and discharge legal duties to complement people's own resources and networks, so that all individuals (no matter their background, health status or mental capacity), carers and families can exercise choice and control, (supporting individuals to make their own decisions, especially where they may lack capacity) and meet their needs and aspirations in personalised, creative and often novel ways. They should work co-productively and innovatively with people, local communities, other professionals, agencies and services to promote self-determination, community capacity, personal and family reliance, cohesion, earlier intervention and active citizenship.

PCF 4 Rights, Justice and Economic Wellbeing: Advance human rights and promote social justice and economic wellbeing
> Understand, identify and apply in practice the principles of social justice, inclusion and equality
> Understand how legislation and guidance can advance or constrain people's rights and recognise how the law may be used to protect or advance their rights and entitlements

➤ Work within the principles of human and civil rights and equalities legislation, differentiating and beginning to work with absolute, qualified and competing rights and differing needs and perspectives

➤ Recognise the impact of poverty and social exclusion and promote enhanced economic status through access to education, work, housing, health services and welfare benefits

PCF 8 Contexts and Organisations: Engage with, inform, and adapt to changing contexts that shape practice. Operate effectively within own organisational frameworks and contribute to the development of services and organisations. Operate effectively within multi-agency and inter-professional partnerships and settings

➤ Recognise that social work operates within, and responds to, changing economic, social, political and organisational contexts

➤ Understand the roles and responsibilities of social workers in a range of organisations, lines of accountability and the boundaries of professional autonomy and discretion

➤ Understand legal obligations, structures and behaviours within organisations and how these impact on policy, procedure and practice

➤ Be able to work within an organisation's remit and contribute to its evaluation and development

KSS Adults (9): Organisational Context
They must understand and work effectively within financial and legal frameworks, obligations, structures and culture, in particular Human Rights and Equalities legislation, the Care Act, Mental Capacity Act, Mental Health Act and accompanying guidance and codes of practice. They must be able to operate successfully in their organisational context, demonstrating effective time management, caseload management and be capable of reconciling competing demands and embrace information, data and technology appropriate to their role. They should have access to regular quality supervision to support their professional resilience and emotional and physical wellbeing.

Conclusion

The recent reforms to social work in the UK have given significant attention to social workers building upon a generalist knowledge and skills base and developing their specialist knowledge and skills as a characteristic of their continuing professional development (Trevithick, 2012). A key measure from the Social Work Reform Board (2010) was to link the learning of specialist practice approaches with increasing expertise and career progression. The Professional Capabilities Framework (PCF) signified a 'single, nationally recognised career structure', aspiring to 'set out, for the first time, consistent expectations of social workers at every point of their career' (Social Work Reform Board, 2010: 3). Social workers are expected to 'extend and deepen' their specialist skills and knowledge as they engage within increasingly complex and demanding situations, actions for which they are individually responsible and held professionally accountable.

The extent to which the learning of specialist practice approaches should have its roots in generalist skills and knowledge learned at qualifying graduate level and transferred to the demands of specialist settings has been placed under scrutiny. On the one hand, the PCF's developmental and holistic model to increasing knowledge and skills development is considered to be more aligned to the broader vision of the social work role in society favoured by many European states (Higgins, 2015). This is reflected by the greater attention given by the 'domains' of the PCF to the knowledge base of social work and of its commitment to social justice, democratic rights and values (Humphrey, 2006; Marthinsen and Julkunen, 2012; Goodyer and Higgins, 2013; Higgins, 2015). Herein, there are considered to be connections between the nine domains of the PCF and the International Federation of Social Workers (2000) definition of social work (Higgins, 2015). This is most evidenced in the 'transformational' and 'sociopolitical awareness' language of the PCF. At the same time, commentators have challenged the PCF for being so broadly focused that it is overly 'rhetorical', and as such unable to reclaim the professional artistry and ethical integrity found wanting in the bureaucratic managerialism of the UK's statutory social work model (Higgins, 2015). While social work in the UK is not solely practised from the statutory local authority model, being practised across the statutory and independent sector with tasks addressing equally high levels of risk and complexity, government-driven reviews and consultation documents appear to have situated the statutory local authority role as the dominant paradigm in UK social work (Higgins, 2015). The experience of the statutory local authority model is not of prevention, nor inclusion, nor advocacy and political challenge but rescue and protection (Bates et al., 2010; Jack and Donnellan, 2010; Goodyer and Higgins, 2013). As such, the statutory local authority role is regarded as a more narrow vision to the social work role than encapsulated by the PCF (Higgins, 2015).

The government's most recent review of qualifying education in children's social work (Narey, 2014) is indicative of the dominance being given to the statutory local authority model. In that review, Martin Narey identified 18 recommendations for improving qualifying education, arguing for the need for specialism in children's work within qualifying education, including an allowance for undergraduates to complete both their assessed placements within statutory children's settings. In his view, generalist approaches did not adequately prepare newly qualified social workers for the demands faced at the frontline of statutory local authority practice. Moreover, he sought for the Chief Social Worker for Children to produce a definition of what a newly qualified social worker should be able to understand and do within that setting. Definitions of the key knowledge and skills required by newly qualified social workers in statutory children's settings and in adult social care settings have since been issued by the Chief Social Worker for Children (Isabelle Trowler) and Chief Social Worker for Adults (Lyn Romero). Framed as the Knowledge and Skills Statements (KSS), with one set for children and one set for adults, the KSS 'strengthens and enhances' the PCF by defining the expectation of 'specialist knowledge and skills' for all newly qualified social workers. As they commence their Assessed and Supported Year, qualifying social workers are expected to demonstrate generic knowledge (in all aspects) but develop those relevant to the employment setting. Essentially, the KSS are mapped onto the PCF for that level of capability. Thus, while qualifying social work education is required to provide a generalist education and assessment, the impact of the KSS is that employers are looking for capacity for specialist knowledge and skills at an earlier stage for qualifying students. This is particularly the case for those within the graduate fast-track, employer-based qualifying social work training (Frontline, Step-Up, Think Ahead), however, all qualifying students are now required to show a similar explicit awareness of the KSS at the qualifying level. This occurs despite capacity for such knowledge and skills being already embedded within the PCF.

The accent upon developing capacity for specialist knowledge and skills within qualifying education – as promoted by the KSS – does not mean that the PCF is redundant. Social work practice with adults continues to require a joint mapping of the PCF with the KSS for adults at qualifying level. The broader vision of the PCF for a holistic 'think family' perspective within person-centred planning continues to be emphasised, a matter made all the more apparent by the prominence of person-centred approaches within new legislation (The Care Act 2014 in England, Wales and Northern Ireland; The Social Care (Self-directed support) (Scotland) Act 2013; The Social Services and Well-being (Wales) Act 2014; and The Children and Families Act, 2013) to assess and support families (Department of Health et al., 2015). Even children's services specify that employers may jointly cite the PCF and the KSS, with mapping across the two. Indeed, there are arguments against specialisation coming too early within qualification. A generalist foundation, which is research-based and refined through repeated observation, reflection and assessment, can present powerful generalist knowledge and skills which can be transferred to the individual demands of differing situations (Trevithick, 2012). A broader, generalist knowledge can 'open up' a greater number of hypotheses for understanding what might be going on within complex situations, and how to intervene within those circumstances. Indeed, as Trevithick notes, even as a specialist, one often employs generalist skills to enact specialist interventions.

The discussion here, and indeed shown in the developing argument of the book, is that the capacity to develop specialist skills and knowledge has become a feature of qualifying education seeking to equip newly qualified social workers for the challenges of particular settings. The challenge for educators and students alike is to make the links between where the roots of those specialist skills lie in the generalist foundation and where they are to be developed further, and on what theoretical basis such linkages can be made. It is my contention that it is in turning to the demands of the context and the voice of the service users within that context that theoretical linkages for specialist practice might be identified. In this regard, specialist practice might justifiably be considered as 'superior knowledge and skill'. Indeed, I concur with Trevithick (2012) in drawing upon Parsloe (2000: 145) in conceptualising 'superior knowledge and skill' for distinguishing generalist approaches from specialist practice:

> Specialist practice ... can mean either a division of labour or superior knowledge and skill about a client group, problem area, methods or settings. The specialist practitioner can be at the frontline or specialism can extend up the organisation.

The way in which I have conceptualised the superior knowledge and skill development of communication capacity is not confined by the narrow definition of a statutory local authority social work role which seeks to manage the complexity and risk of service users lives through the bureaucratic procedures of stringent eligibility criteria, risk averse performance indicators and quantifiable outcomes. This is not a role that social workers (whether in statutory or non-statutory settings) aspire to in operating either the PCF or the KSS – well, not rhetorically, anyway. Certainly it is not one that can comprehensively promote the legislative principles for person-centred practice and proportionality in risk management within the Care Act (2014). Rather, I have responded to the person-centred policy and practice agenda more wholeheartedly, utilising interrelational frameworks that focus upon respect, independence, choice and co-production with service users. Thus, my conceptualisation of communication capacity is through the idea of the embodied enactment of practical wisdom, grounded in a relationship-based approach. The social worker has the capacity to employ his or her 'holistic self' constituting personal and professional experiences and expertise encompassing knowledge which is both formal and informal in nature (Wilson et al., 2011). The embodied action is not only intrapersonal (internal world of thoughts and feelings) but also reflects an interplay with structural forces in which sociocultural symbols, conventions, assumptions and stereotypes can serve to give meaning to, but also possibly obstruct, shared understandings. It is about learning to practice in a way which maximises relational and interpersonal dimensions, but which equally has regard to structural obstacles and opportunities arising from differing practice contexts. To achieve such integration, and respond to constantly changing and increasingly complex contexts, involves critical, active thinking ('capacity'). Throughout the chapters, I have drawn upon Lefevre (2012) and Barnett and Coate (2005) to consider a model or tool for conceptualising such integration and progressive professional development: the 'Knowing', 'Being', 'Doing' model. This consists of three domains constituting the 'Doing' of communication action, alongside the 'Knowing' of what knowledge to draw upon to rationalise the approach and the personal attributes brought ('Being') to enact it in a particular manner.

It is through such integrative work that the book has endeavoured to equip social work learners to engage with the realities of practice across some of the different practice settings that social workers find themselves working within. Thus, within each of the eight chapters relating to eight different social work practice settings, an attempt has been made to make theoretical linkages between:

a) the communication issues identified by social work service users as central for effective communication;

b) the communication issues identified by policy and dominant themes within the existing literature for that setting;

c) the communication strategies uncovered by social workers as responding effectively to those issues.

In the case of a) and c), existing literature on communication skills was used to augment the author's own empirical research. Carried out using two research studies, this research purposefully sought to identify social workers' communication skills from the first base of the reality of their practice actions and practice learning. Experiential learning (Schön, 1983) was used as a research methodology, with forum theatre methods used to observe and analyse social worker communication while they were 'in action', as well as collating their critical reflections 'on action' immediately after it occurred. It was crucial to both studies for the knowledge sought through the 'reflection-in-action' to be embodied and not solely derived through abstract thought. I was as interested in how the social workers were feeling, in a physical sense, in response to service user communication and the requirements of the practice setting, as well as their thinking processes.

If student learning is now understood as the continuous, progressive development of increasing capacity, then the development of communication capacity can be considered as a continuous process of seeking whether and how a student makes links between their 'Knowing' of what to do, and the personal attributes they bring ('Being') to enact it using particular skills and interactions ('Doing'). Indeed, the recognition of connection between thoughts and feelings ('Thinking' and 'Being') is a repeated theme within the discussion of specialist social work communication skills throughout the book. This was perhaps unsurprising given that a relationship-based theoretical approach was taken to these discussions. A major premise of this approach is that social workers must be attuned to the ways in which feelings might be expressed, because as complex beings, we find that our rational thoughts are shaped by our emotions, and we often express our thoughts through our feelings (Wilson et al., 2011; Ruch, 2009). In relation to each different practice setting, particular basic 'universal' communication skills were utilised to prepare social workers to expect feelings to be a medium of communication and to prepare for the manifestation of those feelings in the particular ways that those feelings might be communicated within a specific practice setting. 'Tuning-in' (Shulman, 2009) was a skill found to be relevant to all settings in this respect. However, the background literature and service user perspectives identified that particular emphasis needed to be given to this component of communication skill in certain practice settings. The required emphasis upon the operation of this skill within these settings meant that a more specific label was given to the skill that summarised the purposes for its use. In this respect, it moved from being a basic communication skill to being a specialist communication skill in certain settings. Thus 'tuning in to experience the child's world' was identified for working with children, 'tuning in to social worker's personal attitudes and preconceptions of people who use substances' was highly relevant for substance users, and 'tuning in to experience the individual experience of mental distress' was highlighted as essential for working with people with mental health problems.

A second theoretical position adopted by the book is that until both thoughts and feelings are identified (and often actually 'felt' in an affective sense through transference), those perspectives will not be 'heard' or understood by social workers. As psychodynamic processes of 'containment' are considered crucial for achieving this attention to thoughts and feelings (Bower, 2005; Ruch, 2009), there was discussion and illustration of its use within each of the chapters pertaining to the different practice settings. Again, some settings seemed to require more discussion and application of its use than others. In some instances, this finding emanated from the analysis of the background literature which strongly emphasised a particular theoretical approach or issue affecting or likely to affect communication of containment. In these instances, a label was applied to the specialist skill to depict this. Thus, in working with children, the specialist skill of 'containing a child's feelings by providing and being a safe place in which feelings can be explored' was highlighted. In the case of work with substance users, social workers will need to 'address service user fears of stigmatisation', and when working with people with mental distress there is a need for 'being open to communication at all levels'. However, in some practice settings, specialist communication skills for containment were identified following processes of transference within the classroom itself in response to the feelings being elicited within the qualifying and qualified social workers by the forum theatre. An example of this learning and identification process was in relation to working with refugees and asylum seekers where the specialist skill of 'experiencing service user feelings' was identified.

The policy requirements to 'think person-centred' in terms of finding out from the person's perspective what is important to them and how to live their life, places a demand for greater clarity in generating the aims and purposes of social work assessment and ongoing intervention. Co-production of those aims and purposes should be sought wherever possible. Communication skills for 'achieving a shared purpose' for the social worker and service user meeting were operated within each of the practice settings. The background literature and service user perspectives for each of the different practice settings identified that the authority that the social worker brings through social and legal mandates for safeguarding causes a power differential and barrier to communication that needs to be overcome. In some settings, this authority role caused particular dynamics within the communication, with specific communication skills identified to deal with them. Thus, in relation to working with children, there was need for a 'child-centred contract' to ensure shared understanding of social work role and purpose. Two practice settings demonstrated particular communication dynamics of secrecy and denial in response to the authority role of the social worker. First, work with young people engaging in offending behaviour was considered to require specialist skills of: 'communicating consequences in a non-threatening manner'; 'developing early rapport'; and 'defending service user rights' to overcome authority obstacles. Second, in relation to work with substance using parents, it was identified as vital to 'enter the world of substance-using families'.

One core premise to the book was that a practical application of the social model of disability approach provides greater appreciation of the impact upon communication of obstacles relating to normative expectations and required social work communication strategies than achieved by the relationship-based approach alone. Person-centred approaches may fail without attending to such obstacles. A repeated theme within all the practice settings was that communication skills are needed to address attitudinal barriers within the social worker themselves. Frequently this should involve taking an attitude that: a) does not privilege expert knowledge but seeks to validate private perspectives wherever reasonable, and b) does not privilege particular forms and mediums of communication. Thus, in working with people with disabilities, specialist communication skills were identified concerning the need to 'validate and recognise private knowledge of the individual nuances of the impairment as applied to a person', and use a 'totality of communication – on a number of levels using a number of methods'. On a similar theme, working with children and young people required the need to 'identify, validate and use the child's medium of communication', and when working with older people specialist communication involved skills of 'actively looking for the channels of communication that the service user is using', 'validation' and 'using the whole communication spectrum'. 'Taking time' was a specialist skill across many practice settings, but in work with children and young people it was identified as a sub-skill of 'showing respect'. These communication strategies underpin the increasingly popular structured tools to support person-centred planning and overcome authority obstacles, such as the 'Three Houses' technique, the 'Outcomes Star' and 'One Page Profiles'. Indeed, structured tools such as eco-maps and genograms, when carried out collaboratively with service users, can enable the exploration of systemic barriers encountered by service users within their lives. The background literature and service user perspectives of some practice settings particularly identified how social workers need to find a communication mechanism whereby they identify and discuss such systemic barriers with service users, expecting such communication in direct and indirect ways. This was a particular feature of working with parents, where the following specialist communication skills were considered relevant: 'identifying social worker's personal attitudes and preconceptions of parenting'; 'identify, discuss and empathise with systemic barriers with parents'; 'identify a practical response of seeking to overcome systemic barriers'; 'positive framing of development than using deficit notions' and 'demonstrating knowledge of the individual child'.

It is important not to be uncritical about the claims to knowledge made here in the book. This second edition continues my excavation of the theoretical linkages between service user perspectives, policy, key theoretical concerns and practice strategies that affect communication in different practice settings. It is not possible to claim that all the aspects of the diversity of social work practice and service user experiences have been explored here. The individuality of service users in relation to gender, ethnicity, class, age, personality and other important characteristics that might impact upon communication processes is missing. Related to this, I have located the specialist communication skills around administrative bureaucratic categories of social work agencies and policy literature as opposed to the self-definitions that service users may use. In a book of this size, I have only been able to highlight key issues using the policy, existing literature and research study as a guide. The empirical studies themselves examined the communication practice strategies of a limited number of social workers, some with many years of experience and some at the point of qualification from social work degree programmes in England. They volunteered their time and, as such, we might expect them to be sufficiently comfortable with research procedures to present a bias to this preference in their insights. Thus, it is not possible to make claims that the research findings can be generalised to all social worker–service user meetings within a particular type of practice setting.

Readers are encouraged to view the findings as tentative theoretical insights within a developing conceptual practice area concerning social work communication capacity. The analysis, in linking the different sources of information, sought to gain a more holistic understanding of the specialist social work communication skills and issues. Pawson et al. (2003) identify that social workers can only make judgements on the 'best evidence' that is available, ensuring that this evidence is integrated with the personal accounts of service users of their situations. By making the research and analytic processes clear, including providing illustrative examples of the application of the skills to practice, I hope to have achieved the potential for some degree of 'transferability' (Lincoln and Guba, 1985) for readers to decide whether theoretical concepts can be transferred to their particular social work practice context.

The business of teaching qualified and qualifying social workers to practice in a way which maximises relational and interpersonal dimensions, but which has equal regard to structural obstacles and opportunities arising from differing practice contexts, is not easy. It is a challenge for educators as much as it is for students. Yet, professional capacity is arguably encapsulated by our social workers striving for and achieving such integration, involving continual responsiveness to constantly changing and increasingly complex contexts, and engagement of critical, active thinking. It is my hope that this book can be seen as an attempt to achieve such integrative, 'active-thinking work' in relation to developing capacity for specialist communication for social workers.

Research Appendix

Background

This research responds to the challenge for educators to: a) better integrate communication skills training with practice learning in order to prepare social workers for the real-life challenges of practice, b) begin to bridge the knowledge gap of relevant 'specialist social work communication skills' for those real-life challenges in different practice settings and c) increase service user involvement in the design and delivery of such work (Diggins, 2004; Trevithick et al., 2004). The content draws partly upon empirical findings from an innovative research methodology and teaching method that I used to elicit the practice learning of qualifying social workers of 'specialist communication skills' for the first edition, and which I have since repeated and updated for the purposes of my current doctoral research concerning communication with parents.

Innovatively, I felt that qualifying social work students at the very point of qualification (the original study) and combined groups of qualifying and qualified social workers (my doctoral study) could be supported to bridge the aforementioned knowledge gap themselves by using a 'bottom-up' method to learning, with the participants actively discerning theoretical linkages to the real-life challenges and actions of their practice learning settings. This meant observing and analysing their communication while they were 'in action', as well as collating their critical reflections 'on action' immediately after it occurred. Experiential learning (Schön, 1983) was explicitly used as a research methodology, with Forum Theatre methods used to gather this 'reflection-in-action' in a way that paid as much attention to how the social workers were feeling, in a physical sense, in response to service user communication and the requirements of the practice setting, in addition to their abstract thinking processes.

Boal's (1979) method of Forum Theatre is rarely reported in social work (Houston et al., 2001), but ideally suited in facilitating conscious recognition of collective problems (in this case, identifying specialist communication) and developing realistic and dialogical strategies for action. Indeed, the method, which involves the dynamic involvement of the audience with three main characters in an unfolding drama sketch, provides a space in which debate can take place. The three main characters usually consist of a protagonist whose role is to represent the experience of the group, an antagonist who embodies an oppressor role, and a 'facilitator' who acts as a link between the actors and audience by providing commentary on the unfolding drama and inviting response and intervention. For the purposes here, the delineation between the social worker (as oppressor) and service user (as oppressed) was not so strictly drawn, as, clearly, social workers seek to fulfil requirements to be anti-oppressive. Yet, the roles *were* useful in aiding identification of how practice actions (i.e. communication strategies) might be experienced as oppressive and unhelpful. An additional important component of the method was to facilitate comparison of social work perceptions with service user perceptions of the type and nature of communication skills required. This draws on recent research findings by the author (Woodcock and Tregaskis, 2008) that using a combined model – in seeking both a social work perspective and service user 'insider' (social model) perspective of relevant communication skills in differing settings – was found to produce a more holistic and ecological analysis as issues were considered at personal, cultural and structural levels, and drew on data from both parties of the communication process.

Methods

In the original study, a group of qualifying (Stage 3) undergraduate social work students (n=55) were divided and assigned to one or more Specialist Social Work Communication Skills workshops corresponding to eight different practice settings in which they were undertaking their practice learning: children; parents; older people; adults with disabilities and their carers; people with mental health difficulties; asylum seekers and refugees; young offenders; and people who misuse substances. In my recent doctoral study, a combined group of qualified social workers alongside qualifying undergraduate (Stage 3) and graduate (MA) social work students (n=31) engaged in one Specialist Social Work Communication Skills workshop focusing upon the practice setting of parenting assessment. It was the function of these workshops (two-hour duration) to engage the students and practitioners in the Forum Theatre method. Attendance was good, not least for the reason that the students were seeking to make use of the data as part of their professional development.

The method involved two paid, experienced actors performing a scripted role play to the audience of participants within each workshop. In addition, a third person acting as facilitator invited students to interact with the actors, ensuring that: a) interaction and discussion occurred with the role play and b) that the discussion focused on communication issues, and the type and nature of communication skills relevant for particular settings. Such prompts included: 'why was that issue mentioned', 'what's going on', 'what's going well and why', 'what's not going well and why' and 'do you want to ask them anything'. Different scripts were written to reflect the 'typical' 'everyday' issues of communication between a service user and a social worker within different practice settings. The scripts were written by one of the actors and the author, in consultation with volunteers recruited from Service User Consultative Groups, recruited by three Universities in the South of England. This service user involvement was important, as the author wanted the data yielded by the method to encompass both service user and practitioner perspectives. The debates were recorded using a camcorder to capture the detail of the verbal articulation of the communication issues and skills raised, and any non-verbal communication arising during the role-play interaction. The recording was transcribed, analysed and sent to all students in order that they could use the information in writing their assessment.

Outcome measures of effectiveness

Effectiveness was measured in relation to how far and in what way participants evidenced the following outcome measures in a) the transcript of the workshop session, b) the detail of their summative assessment (original study only) and c) responses to a semi-structured questionnaire at pre and post stages of the intervention/method:

i. identified specialist communication skills for different social work practice settings;

ii. identified the differences and similarities between service user and social work perceptions of issues of communication and the type and nature of communication skills required;

iii. used theory, research evidence and practice experience to analyse the role-play of real-life illustrations of the dilemmas and challenges in communication between social workers and service users;

iv. engaged in reflective processes about their practice learning experiences concerning communication skills (evidenced by consideration of what went well, what didn't go well and where improvements might be made).

The short, semi-structured questionnaire contained a combination of closed and open-ended questions to facilitate student reflection of issues of communication and the type and nature of communication skills required by their practice setting. Participants received and responded to it before the workshop. After the workshop, participants were presented with a copy of their completed questionnaire with additional questions seeking their perspective on whether and how their understanding of 'specialist communication skills' and their theoretical underpinning had improved, and the way and extent to which the teaching method helped this. They were then asked to revisit their answers in light of this analysis.

Analytic tactics of Constant Comparative Analysis (Woodcock and Tregaskis, 2008) were used to identify and compare 'instances', which demonstrated experiences, definitions or perspectives of communication issues and skills as they appeared at any point across the four data sources. This involved categorising and labelling ('open coding': Strauss and Corbin, 1990) potentially theoretically relevant concepts and relationships, then questioning emergent themes by making connections between service user concerns and (student) social workers' concerns and responses, seeking to elicit the range and dimensions of the categories and relationships ('axial coding': Strauss and Corbin, 1990). The participants gave independent and anonymous feedback of their perspectives of the usefulness of the Forum Theatre method for helping them to elicit specialist social work communication skills in their practice settings.

Ethical considerations

The author attended the Service User Consultative Group meetings at the three universities to allow discussion of information and engender trust and stake in the project. An information sheet was emailed and handed out to all participants explaining the project process, right to withdraw, details for contacting the author and an undertaking that participants' names would be confidential to the research team and that all information relating to service users considered in the students' work would be sufficiently anonymized so that identification could not occur. It was stated that where information revealed a person being at risk of significant harm, then that information would be passed on to relevant social work personnel. A consent form was used. As Forum Theatre is a dynamic and emotive learning experience, participants could have been left with some unresolved feelings, and, as such, contact details for counselling services were provided at each workshop.

Bibliography

Abney, V. (2002) 'Cultural competency in the field of child maltreatment' in J. Myers, L. Berliner and J. Briere (eds)*The APSAC Handbook on Child Maltreatment*, London: Sage.

ACMD (2003) *Hidden Harm: Responding to the Needs of Children of Problem Drug Users. Report of an Inquiry by the Advisory Council on the Misuse of Drugs*, London: The Home Office.

Aldridge, T. (1999) 'Family values: rethinking children's needs living with drug-using parents', *Druglink* 14: 8–11.

Agazarian, Y. A. (1997) *System-Centred Group Psychotherapy*, New York: Guilford Press.

Agass, D. (2002) 'Countertransference, supervision and the reflection process', *Journal of Social Work Practice* 16: 125–133.

Aldgate, J. and Bradley, M. (1999) *Supporting Families Through Short Term Fostering*, London: The Stationery Office.

Al-Krenawi, A. and Graham, J. R. (2000) 'Culturally sensitive social work practice with Arab clients in mental health settings', *Health and Social Work* 25: 9–22.

Alibhai-Brown, Y. (1998) *Caring for Ethnic Minority Elders: A Guide*, London, Age Concern.

All Party Parliamentary Group on Social Work (2013) *Inquiry into the State of Social Work Report*, Birmingham: British Association of Social Workers, available from: http://cdn.basw.co.uk/upload/basw_90352-5.pdf, accessed 31.01.2016.

Allan, K. (2001) *Exploring Ways for Staff to Consult People with Dementia about Services*, Bristol: Joseph Rowntree Foundation.

Allen, R. (2014) *The Role of the Social Worker in Mental Health Services*, London: The College of Social Work, available from www.basw.co.uk, accessed 10.6.2016.

Alexander-Floyd, N. (2008) 'Critical race pedagogy: teaching about race and racism through legal learning strategies', *Political Science & Politics* 41(1): 183–188.

Archer, M. (1995) *Realist Social Theory: The Morphogenetic Approach*, Cambridge: Cambridge University Press.

Archer, M. S. (2003) *Structure, Agency and the Internal Conversation*, Cambridge: Cambridge University Press.

Armstrong, D. (2004) 'A risky business? Research, policy, governmentality and youth offending', *Youth Justice* 4(2): 100–116.

Armstrong, K. L., Fraser, J. A., Dads, M. R. and Morris, J. (2000) 'Promoting secure attachment, maternal mood and child health in a vulnerable population: A randomized controlled trial', *Journal of Paediatric Child Health* 36: 555–562.

Ash, A. (2013) 'A cognitive mask? Camouflaging dilemmas in street-level policy implementation to safeguard older people from abuse', *British Journal of Social Work* 43, 1: 99–115.

Audit Commission (2004) *Youth Justice 2004: A Review of the Reformed Youth Justice System*, London: Audit Commission.

Baker, K. (2014) *AssetPlus Rationale*, London: Youth Justice Board, available from www.gov.uk, accessed 26.2.2016.

Banks, S. (2001) *Ethics and Values in Social Work*, Basingstoke: Palgrave Macmillan.

Barber, J. G. (2002) *Social Work with Addictions* (2nd edition), Basingstoke: BASW /Palgrave.

Barlow, J. and Scott, J. (2010) *Safeguarding in the 21st Century – Where to Now?*, Dartington: Research in Practice.

Barn, R. (2007) '"Race", Ethnicity and Child Welfare: A Fine Balancing Act', *British Journal of Social Work* 37: 1425–1434.

Barnes, C. (1991) *Disabled People in Britain and Discrimination: A Case for Anti-discrimination Legislation*, London: Hurst and Co.

Barnett, R. and Coate, K. (2005) *Engaging the Curriculum in Higher Education*, Maidenhead: SRHE/Open University Press.

BASW/TCSW (2012) *Research on Supervision in Social Work, with particular reference to supervision practice in multi disciplinary teams (England Document)*, London: BASW, available from: http://cdn.basw.co.uk/upload/basw_13955-1.pdf, accessed 1.3.2016.

Bates, N., Immins, T., Parker, J., Keen, S., Rutter, L., Brown, K. and Zsigo, Z. (2010) '"Baptism of fire": The first year in the life of a newly qualified social worker', *Social Work Education* 29(2); 152–170.

Beddoe, L. (2010) 'Surveillance or Reflection: Professional Supervision in the "Risk Society"', *British Journal of Social Work* 40(4):1279–1296.

Bell, M. (1999) 'Working in Partnership in Child Protection: The Conflicts', *British Journal of Social Work* 29(3): 437–455.

Belsky, J. and Vondra, J. (1989) 'Lessons from abuse: The determinants of parenting' in D. Cichetti and V. Carlson (eds) *Child Maltreatment: Theory and Research on the Causes and Consequences of Child Abuse and Neglect,* Cambridge: Cambridge University Press.

Bender, M., Norris, A. and Bauckham, P. (1987) *Groupwork with the Elderly: Principles and Practice*, Oxon: Winslow Press.

Beresford, P., Branfield, F., Lalani, M., Maslen, B., Sartori, A., Jenny, Maggie and Manny (2007) 'Partnership working: service users and social workers learning and working together' in M. Lymbery and K. Postle (eds) *Social Work: A Companion for Learning*, London: Sage.

Biggs, J. (2003) *Teaching for Quality. Learning at University* (2nd edition), Buckingham: Society for Research into Higher Education /Open University Press.

Biggs, J. (2007) *Teaching for Quality Learning at University: What the Student Does*, Buckingham: SHRE and OU.

Bion, W. (1962) *Learning from Experience*, London: Heinemann.

Bishop, D. (2008) 'An Examination of the Links Between Autistic Spectrum Disorders and Offending Behaviour in Young People', *Internet Journal of Criminology*, available from: http://www.internetjournalofcriminology.com/Bishop%20-%20 Autistic%20Spectrum%20Disorders%20and%20Offending%20Behaviour%20 in%20Young%20People.pdf, accessed 26.2.2016.

Blom-Cooper, L. (1985) *A Child in Trust: The Report of the Panel of Inquiry into the Circumstances of the Death of Jasmine Beckford*, Brent: London Borough of Brent.

Boal, A. (1979) *Theatre of the Oppressed*, London: Pluto Press.

Bogo, M., Paterson, J., Tufford, L. and King, R. (2011a) 'Supporting front-line practitioners' professional development and job satisfaction in mental health and addiction', *Journal of Interprofessional Care* 25(3): 209–214.

Bogo, M., Paterson, J., Tufford, L. and King, R. (2011b) 'Interprofessional clinical supervision in mental health and addiction: toward identifying common elements', *Clinical Supervisor* 30(1): 124–140.

Bondi, L., Carr, D., Clark, C., and Clegg, C. (eds) (2011) *Towards Professional Wisdom: Practical Deliberation in the 'People Professions'*, Farnham: Ashgate.

Bounds, J. and Hepburn, H. (1996) *Empowerment and Older People*, Birmingham: Pepar Publications.

Bourn, D. and Hafford-Letchfield, T. (2011) 'The role of social work professional supervision in conditions of uncertainty', *The International Journal of Knowledge, Culture and Change Management* 10(9): 41–56.

Bower, M. (2005) *Psychoanalytic Theory for Social Work Practice: Thinking Under Fire*, London: Routledge.

Bowes, A. M. and Dar, N. S. (2000) 'Researching social care for minority ethnic older people: implications of some Scottish research', *British Journal of Social Work* 30: 305–321.

Bowl, R. (2009) 'PQ social work practice in mental health' in P. Higham (ed) *Post-Qualifying Social Work Practice*, London: Sage Publications.

Bowlby, J. (1962) 'Preface' in M. L. Ferard and N. K. Hunnybun (1962) *The Caseworker's Use of Relationships*, London: Tavistock Publications.

Boxall, K. and Speakup Self Advocacy and Eastwood Action Group (2009) 'Learning disability' in P. Higham (ed) *Post-Qualifying Social Work Practice*, London: Sage Publications.

Brandon, M., Thoburn, J., Lewis, A. and Way, A. (1999) *Safeguarding Children with the Children Act 1989*, London: The Stationery Office.

Brandon, M., Howe, A., Dagley, V., Salter, C. and Warren, C. (2006) 'What appears to be helping or hindering practitioners in implementing the Common Assessment Framework and Lead Professional Working?', *Child Abuse Review* 15(6): 396–413.

Bray, M. (2007) *Sexual Abuse: The Child's Voice: Poppies on the Rubbish Heap*, London: Jessica Kingsley.

British Agencies for Adoption and Fostering (1984) *In Touch with Children*, London: BAAF.

British Agencies for Adoption and Fostering (1986) *Working with Children*, London: BAAF.

Broadhurst, K., Hall, C., Wastell, D., White, S. and Pithouse, A. (2010) 'Risk, Instrumentalism and the Humane Project in Social Work: Identifying the Informal Logics of Risk Management in Children's Statutory Services', *British Journal of Social Work* 40(4): 1046–1064.

Bronfenbrenner, U. (1979) *The Ecology of Human Development: Experiments by Nature and Design*, Cambridge, MA: Harvard University Press.

Brookfield, S. (1987) *Developing Critical Thinkers*, Milton Keynes: Open University Press.

Brown, G. and Harris, T. (1978) *Social Origins of Depression: A Study of Psychiatric Disorder in Women*, London: Tavistock Publications.

Buchanan, J. and Young, J. (2002) 'Child protection: Social worker's views' in H. Klee, M. Jackson and S. Lewis (eds) *Drug issue and Motherhood*, Routledge: London.

Buckley, H. (2000) 'Child protection: An unreflective practice', *Social Work Education* 19: 253–263.

Buijssen, H. (2005) *The Simplicity of Dementia*, London: Jessica Kingsley.

Bunn, A. (2013) *Signs of Safety® in England: An NSPCC commissioned report on the Signs of Safety model in child protection*, available from: www.nspcc.org.uk, accessed 31.1.2016.

Burnard, P. (2003) 'Ordinary chat and therapeutic conversation: Phatic communication and mental health nursing', *Journal of Psychiatric and Mental Health Nursing* 10: 678–682.

Burnside, J. (1986) *Working with the Elderly: Group Process and Techniques*, Boston, MA: Jones and Bartlett Publications.

Butler-Sloss, E. (1988) *Report of the Inquiry into Child Abuse in Cleveland 1987*, London: HMSO.

Cameron, H. (2008) *The Counselling Interview: A Guide for the Helping Professions*, Basingstoke: Palgrave Macmillan.

Case, S. (2007) 'Questioning the "Evidence" of Risk that Underpins Evidence-led Youth Justice Interventions', *Youth Justice* 7: 91–105.

Chand, A. (2000) 'The over-representation of black children in the child protection system: Possible causes, consequences and solutions', *Child and Family Social Work* 5: 67–77.

Chapman, A., Jacques, A. and Marshall, M. (1994) *Dementia Care: A Handbook for Residential and Day Care*, London: Age Concern England.

Clark, C. and Volz, F. R. (2012) 'Professional ethics as the interpretation of life praxis' in J. Lishman (ed) *Social Work Education and Training*, London: Jessica Kingsley Publishers.

Cleaver, H., Unell, I., and Aldgate, J. (1999) *Children's Needs, Parenting Capacity: The Impact of Parental Mental Illness, Problem Alcohol and Drug Use and Domestic Violence on Children's Development*, London: The Stationery Office.

Cleaver, H., Unell, I. and Aldgate, J. (2011) *Children's Needs – Parenting Capacity. Child Abuse: Parental mental illness, learning disability, substance misuse and domestic violence* (2nd edition), available from: www.official-documents.gov.uk.

Cohen, P. (1994) 'Adding insult to injury', *Community Care* 6 October 1994: 14–15.

Cohen, S., Moran-Ellis, J. and Smaje, C. (1999) 'Children as informal interpreters in GP consultations: pragmatics and ideology', *Sociology of Health and Illness* 21: 163–186.

Comley, M. (1998) 'Counselling and therapy with older refugees', *Journal of Social Work Practice* 12: 181–187.

Compton, B. R., Galloway, B. and Cournoyer, B. R. (2005) *Social Work Processes* (7th edition), Pacific Grove, CA: Brooks Cole.

Crawford, A. and Newburn, T. (2005) *Youth Offending and Restorative Justice*, Cullompton: Willan Publishing.

Cree, V. and Davis, A. (2007) *Social Work: Voices From the Inside*, Abingdon: Routledge.

Crisis (2003) *Mental Health and Social Exclusion: Crisis's response to a consultation request from the Social Exclusion Unit*, London: Crisis UK.

Crown Prosecution Service (2007) *Achieving best evidence in criminal proceedings: Guidance on interviewing victims and witnesses, and using special measures*, available from: http://www.cps.gov.uk/publications/docs/Achieving_Best_Evidence_FINAL.pdf, accessed 26.2.2016.

Daniel, B. (2000) 'Judgements about parenting: What do social workers think they are doing?', *Child Abuse Review* 9: 91–107.

Daniel, B. (2007) 'Assessment and children' in Lishman, J. (ed) *Handbook for Practice Learning in Social work and Social Care: Knowledge and Theory*, London: Jessica Kingsley.

DANOS (2012) *Developing Standards of Practice in the Drugs and Alcohol Workforce*, available from www.fdap.org.uk, accessed 31.1.2016.

Darragh, E. and Taylor, B. (2009) 'Research and reflective practice' in P. Higham (ed) *Post-Qualifying Social Work Practice*, London: Sage Publications.

Daycare Trust (1995) *Reaching First Base: Meeting the needs of refugee children from the Horn of Africa: Guidelines of good practice*, London: Daycare Trust.

De Jong, P. and Berg, I. K. (2008) *Interviewing for Solutions*, Pacific Grove: Brooks /Cole.

Department for Children, Schools and Families (2009) *The Protection of Children in England: A Progress Report*, Norwich: The Stationery Office, available from: http://publications.everychildmatters.gov.uk/eOrderingDownload/HC-330.pdf, accessed 31.3.2016.

Department for Education and Skills (2003) *Every Child Matters: Change for Children* (DfES/1090/2004), London: HMSO, available from: http://webarchive.nationalarchives.gov.uk/20130401151715/http://www.education.gov.uk/publications/eOrderingDownload/DfES10812004.pdf, accessed 10.6.2016.

Department of Health (1995) *Child Protection: Messages from Research*, London: HMSO.

Department of Health (1996) *Focus on Teenagers Research into Practice*, London: The Stationery Office.

Department of Health (1998) *Modernising Social Services*, London: The Stationery Office.

Department of Health (1999) *The National Services Framework for Mental Health: Modern Standards and Service Models*, London: The Stationery Office.

Department of Health (2000a) *The Framework for Assessing Children in Need and their Families*: London, The Stationery Office.

Department of Health (2000b) *No Secrets: Guidance on Developing and Implementing Multi-agency Policies and Procedures to Protect Vulnerable Adults from Abuse*, London: Department of Health.

Department of Health (2001a) *National Service Framework for Older People*, London: HMSO.

Department of Health (2001b) *Valuing People: A New Strategy for Learning Disability for the 21st Century*, London: The Stationery Office.

Department of Health (2002) *Requirements for Social Work Training*, London: Department of Health.

Department of Health (2004a) *The NHS Improvement Plan: Putting People at the Heart of Public Services*, London: The Stationery Office.

Department of Health (2004b) *Choosing Health: Making Healthier Choices Easier*, London: Department of Health.

Department of Health (2005) *Independence, Well-being and Choice: Our Vision for the Future for the Provision of Social Care for Adults in the Future*, London: Department of Health.

Department of Health (2006a) *Working Together to Safeguard Children: A Guide to Inter-agency Working to Safeguard and Promote the Welfare of Children*, London: The Stationery Office.

Department of Health (2006b) *Our Health, Our Care our Say*, London: Department of Health.

Department of Health (2006c) *Choosing Health: Supporting the physical health needs of people with severe mental illness*, London: Department of Health.

Department of Health (2012) *No Health Without Mental Health: Implementation Framework*, London: HM Government, available from: www.gov.uk.

Department of Health (2015) *The Care Act and Whole Family Approaches*, London: HM Government, available from: http://www.local.gov.uk/documents/10180/5756320/The+Care+Act+and+whole+family+approaches/080c323f-e653-4cea-832a-90947c9dc00c, accessed 10.6.2016.

Devore, W. (2001) 'Ethnic sensitivity: a theoretical framework for social work practice' in L. Dominelli, W. Lorenz and H. Soydan (eds) *Beyond Racist Divides: Ethnicities in Social Work Practice*, Aldershot: Ashgate Publishing Company.

DiClemente, C. C. and Velasquez, M. (2002) 'Motivational Interviewing and the Stages of Change' in W. R. Miller and S. Rollnick (eds) *Motivational Interviewing: Preparing People for Change* (2nd edition), New York: Guilford Publications.

Diggins, M. (2004) *Teaching and Learning Communication Skills in Social Work Education: Resource Guide*, London: SCIE.

Dingwall, R. (1986) 'The Jasmine Beckford affair', *Modern Law Review* 49: 488–518.

Dinham, A. (2006) 'A review of practice of teaching and learning of communication skills in social work education in England', *Social Work Education* 25(8): 838–850.

Dixon, J. (2013) 'Effective Strategies for Communication? Student Views of a Communication Skills Course Eleven Years On', *British Journal of Social Work* 43: 1190–1205.

Dogra, N., Parkin, A., Gale, F. and Frake, C. (2002) *A Multidisciplinary Handbook of Child and Adolescent Mental Health for Front-line Professionals*, London: Jessica Kingsley.

Dominelli, L. (1992) 'An uncaring profession? An examination of racism in social work' in P. Braham, A. Rattansi and R. Skellington (eds) *Racism and Anti-Racism*, London: Sage.

Doyle, C. and Kennedy, S. (2009) 'Children, young people, their families and carers' in P. Highham (ed) *Post-Qualifying Social Work Practice*, London: Sage Publications.

Ebden, P., Bhatt, A., Carey, O. and Harrison, B. (1988) 'The bilingual consultation', *The Lancet* 8581i: 347.

Egan, G. (1990) *The Skilled Helper: A systematic approach to effective helping*, Pacific Grove, CA: Brooks/Cole.

Egan, G. (2007) *The Skilled Helper: A Problem-Management and Opportunity-Development Approach to Helping* (8th edition), Belont: Thomson Brooks/Cole.

Fanning, B. (2004) 'Asylum-seeker and migrant children in Ireland: racism, institutional neglect and social work' in D. Hayes and B. Humphries (eds) *Social Work Immigration and Asylum: Debates, Dilemmas, and Ethical Issues for Social Work and Social Care Practice*, London: Jessica Kingsley.

Featherstone, B., White, S., and Morris, K. (2014) *Re-imagining Child Protection: Towards humane social work with families*, Bristol: Policy Press.

Federation of Drug and Alcohol Professionals (FDAP) (2012) *DANOS 2012: Developing standards of practice in the drugs & alcohol workforce*, available from: www.fdap.org.uk, accessed 31.1.2016.

Fell, P. (2004) 'And now it has started to rain: support and advocacy with adult asylum-seekers in the voluntary sector' in D. Hayes and B. Humphries (eds) *Social Work Immigration and Asylum: Debates, Dilemmas, and Ethical Issues for Social Work and Social Care Practice*, London: Jessica Kingsley.

Ferard, M. L. and Hunnybun, N. K. (1962) *The Caseworker's Use of Relationships*, London: Tavistock Publications.

Field, P., Jasper, C. and Littler, L. (2014) *Practice Education in Social Work: Achieving Professional Standards*, Northwich: Critical Publishing Limited.

Finkelstein, V. (1980) *Attitudes and Disabled People: Issues for Discussion*, New York: World Rehabilitation Fund.

Flores, G., Laws, M. B., Mayo, S. J., Zuckerman, B., Abreu, M. and Medina, L. (2003) 'Errors in medical interpretation and their potential clinical consequences in pediatric encounters', *Pediatrics* 111: 6–14.

Fook, J. (2007) 'Reflective Practice and Critical Reflection' in Lishman, J. (ed) *Handbook for Practice Learning in Social Work and Social Care*, London: Jessica Kingsley.

Forrester, D. and Harwin, J. (2004) 'Social work and parental substance misuse' in R. Phillips (ed) *Children Exposed to Parental Substance Misuse: Implications for Family Placement*, London: British Agencies for Adoption and Fostering.

Forrester, D. and Harwin, J. (2011) *Parents Who Misuse Drugs and Alcohol: Effective Interventions in Social Work and Child Protection*, Chichester, West Sussex: Wiley-Blackwell.

Galvani, S. (2012) *Supporting People with Alcohol and Drug Problems*, Bristol: Policy Press Adults.

Galvani, S. (2015) *Alcohol and Other Drug Use: The Roles and Capabilities of Social Workers*, Manchester: Manchester Metropolitan University, available from: www.mmu.ac.uk/social-care-and-social-work/ accessed 31.1.2016.

Galvani, S. and Forrester, D. (2011) *Social Work Services and Recovery from Substance Misuse: A Review of the Evidence*, Bedfordshire: ADSW/University of Bedfordshire, available from: http://www.gov.scot/resource/doc/346164/0115212.pdf, accessed 10.6.2016.

Garrett, P. M. (2006) 'Protecting children in a globalized world: "race" and "place" in the Laming report on the death of Victoria Climbié', *Journal of Social Work* 6: 315–336.

Gibbs, J. A. (2001) 'Maintaining front-line workers in child protection: a case for refocusing supervision', *Child Abuse Review* 10: 323–335.

Gillingham, P. (2014a) 'Electronic information systems in human service organisations: the what, who, why and how of information', *British Journal of Social Work* 45(5): 1598–1613, available from: https://espace.library.uq.edu.au/view/UQ:366543/UQ366543_OA.pdf, accessed 10.6.2016.

Gillingham, P. (2014b) 'Electronic information systems in human service organizations: Using theory to inform future design', *International Social Work* (doi: 10.1177/0020872814554856): 1–11, available from: https://www.researchgate.net/publication/281164346_Electronic_information_systems_in_human_service_organizations_Using_theory_to_inform_future_design, accessed 10.6.2016.

Gilman, M. (2000) 'Social exclusion and drug using parents' in F. Harbin and M. Murphy (eds) *Substance issue and Child Care: How to Understand, Assist and Intervene When Drugs Affect Parenting*, Lyme Regis: Russell House.

Goodyer, A. and Higgins, M. (2013) 'Applying a mobilities paradigm to a return to social work programme', *Social Work Education* 32(3): 397–410.

Green, J., Free, C., Bhavnani, V. and Newman, T. (2005) 'Translators and mediators: bilingual young people's accounts of their interpreting work in health care', *Social Science and Medicine* 60: 2097–2110.

GSCC (2005) *Specialist Standards and Requirements (Adult Services)*, London: GSCC.

Halliday, S., Burns, N., Hutton, N., McNeill, F. and Tata, C. (2009) 'Street-level bureaucracy, interprofessional relations, and coping mechanisms: a study of criminal justice social workers in the sentencing process', *Law & Policy* 31(4): 405–428.

Harbin, F. and Murphy, M. (2000) *Substance issue and Child Care: How to Understand, Assist and Intervene When Drugs Affect Parenting*, Lyme Regis: Russell House.

Hargie, O. D. W. (ed) (1997) *The Handbook of Communication Skills* (2nd edition), London: Routledge.

Hargie, O. and Dickson, D. (2004) *Skilled Interpersonal Communication: Research, Theory and Practice*, London: Routledge.

Harkness, D. and Hensley, H. (1991) 'Changing the focus of social work supervision: effects on client satisfaction and generalized contentment' *Social Work* 36(6): 506–512.

Health Advisory Service (1995) *Together We Stand: The Commissioning, Role and Management of Child and Adolescent Mental Health Services*, London: HMSO.

Health and Care Professions Council (2012) *Standards for Proficiency for Social Work*, available from: http://www.hpc-uk.org/assets/documents/10003b08 standardsofproficiency-socialworkersinengland.pdf, accessed 10.6.2016.

Health and Care Professions Council (2016) *Standards of Conduct, Performance and Ethics*, available from: http://www.hpc-uk.org/aboutregistration/standards/ standardsofconductperformanceandethics/, accessed 10.6.2016.

Higgins, M. (2015) 'The Struggle for the Soul of Social Work in England', *Social Work Education: The International Journal* 34(1): 4–16, DOI: 10.1080/02615479.2014.946898.

Higgins, M. and Goodyer, A. (2014) 'The contradictions of contemporary social work: an ironic response', *British Journal of Social Work* Advance Access published 16 March 2014.

Higgins, M., Goodyer, A. and Whittaker, A. (2015) 'Can a Munro- inspired approach transform the lives of looked after children in England?', *Social Work Education: The International Journal* 34(3): 328–340, DOI: 10.1080/02615479.2014.999658.

Hildyard, K. and Wolfe, D. (2002) 'Child neglect: Developmental issues and outcomes', *Child Abuse and Neglect* 26: 679–695.

HM Government (2012) *Social Justice: transforming lives*, available from https:// www.gov.uk/government/uploads/system/uploads/attachment_data/ file/49515/social-justice-transforming-lives.pdf, accessed 10.6.2016.

HM Government (2015) *Working Together to Safeguard Children: a guide to interagency working to safeguard and promote the welfare of children*, London: Department for Education (DfE).

HMI Probation (2009) *Joint Inspection of Youth Offending Teams: End of Programme Report 2003–2008*, Manchester: HMI Probation.

Holland, S. (2000) 'The assessment relationship: Interactions between social workers and parents in child protection assessments', *British Journal of Social Work* 30: 149–163.

Hollis, F. (1964) *A Psycho-social Therapy*, New York: Random House.

Holmes, L., Munro, E. R. and Soper, J. (2010) *Calculating the Cost and Capacity Implications for Local Authorities Implementing the Laming (2009) Recommendations*, Loughborough: Centre for Child and Family Research, Loughborough University.

House of Lords (2009) *Judgements - R (on the application of G) (FC) (Appellant) v London Borough of Southwark (Respondents)*, available from: http://www. publications.parliament.uk/pa/ld200809/ldjudgmt/jd090520/appg-1.htm, accessed 10.6.2016.

Houston, S., Magill, T., McCollum, M. and Spratt, T. (2001) 'Developing creative solutions to the problems of children and their families: communicative reason and the use of forum theatre', *Child and Family Social Work* 6: 285–293.

Howe, D. (1998) 'Relationship based thinking and practice in social work', *Journal of Social Work Practice* 12: 45–56.

Howe, D. (2005) *Child Abuse and Neglect: Attachment, Development and Intervention*, Basingstoke: Palgrave Macmillan.

Howe, D., Brandon, M., Hinings, D. and Schofield, G. (1999) *Attachment Theory, Child Maltreatment and Family Support: A Practice and Assessment Model*, Basingstoke: Macmillan.

Howitt, D. (1992) *Child Abuse Errors: When Good Intentions Go Wrong*, Hemel Hempstead: Harvester.

Humphrey, C. (2006) 'Tomorrow's social workers in the UK', *European Journal of Social Work* 9: 357–373.

International Federation of Social Workers (2000) 'Global Definition of Social Work', Retrieved 5 August 2011, available from: http://www.ifsw.org /f38000138.html, accessed 31.1.2016.

Ivey, A. E. and Ivey, M. B. (2008) *Essentials of Intentional Interviewing: Counselling in a Multicultural World*, Belmont, CA: Thomson/Brooks Cole.

Jack, G. (2001) 'Ecological perspectives in assessing children and families' in J. Horwath (ed) *The Child's World: Assessing Children in Need*, London: Jessica Kingsley.

Jack, G. and Donnellan, H. (2010) 'Recognising the person within the developing professional: Tracking the early careers of newly qualified child care social workers in three local authorities in England', *Social Work Education* 29(3): 305–318.

Jack, J. and Gill, O. (2003) *The Missing Side of the Triangle*, Ilford: Barnardo's.

Jacobsen, T., Edelstein, W. and Hofmann, V. (1994) 'A longitudinal study of the relationship between representations of attachment in childhood and cognitive functioning in childhood and adolescence', *Developmental Psychology* 30: 112–124.

Jay, A. (2014) *Independent Inquiry into Child Sexual Exploitation in Rotherham, 1997–2013*, Rotherham Metropolitan Borough Council.

Jewett, C. (1984) *Helping Children Cope with Separation and Loss*, London: British Agencies for Adoption and Fostering.

Jones, P. H. (2003) *Communicating with Vulnerable Children*, London: The Royal College of Psychiatrists.

Kadushin, A. and Kadushin, G. (1997) *The Social Work Interview* (4th edition), New York, NY: Columbia University Press.

Kadushin, A. and Harkness, D. (2002) *Supervision in Social Work* (4th edition), New York: Columbia University Press.

Kaptani, E. and Yuval-Davis, N. (2008) 'Participatory Theatre as a Research Methodology: Identity, Performance and Social Action Among Refugees', *Sociological Research Online* 13: 5, available from: http://www.socresonline.org .uk/13/5/2.html, accessed 31.1.2016.

Killick, J. and Allan, K. (2001) *Communication and the Care of People with Dementia*, Buckingham: Open University Press.

Kitwood, T. (1997) *Dementia Reconsidered: The Person Comes First (Rethinking Ageing)*, Buckingham: Open University Press.

Kohli, R. (2006) *Social Work with Unaccompanied Asylum Seeking Children*, Basingstoke: Palgrave Macmillan.

Koprowska, J. (2005) *Communication and Interpersonal Skills in Social Work*, Exeter: Learning Matters.

Koprowska, J. (2008) *Communication and Interpersonal Skills in Social Work* (2nd edition), Exeter: Learning Matters.

Kroll, B. (1995) 'Working with children' in F. Kaganas, M. King and C. Piper (eds) *Legislating for Harmony: Partnership Under The Children Act 1989*, London: Jessica Kingsley.

Kroll, B. and Taylor, A. (2003) *Parental Substance Misuse and Child Welfare*, London: Jessica Kingsley.

Laird, S. E. (2008) *Anti-Oppressive Social Work: A Guide for Developing Cultural Competence*, London: Sage Publications.

Lambley, S. and Marrable, T. (2012) *Practice Enquiry into Supervision in A Variety of Adult Care Settings Where There Are Health and Social Care Practitioners Working Together* (Report to SCIE), Brighton: University of Sussex.

Laming, Lord (2003) *The Victoria Climbié Inquiry: Report of an Inquiry by Lord Laming*, London: The Stationery Office, available from:https://www.gov.uk/government/uploads/system/uploads/attachment_data/file/273183/5730.pdf, accessed 10.6.2016.

Laming, Lord (2009) *The Protection of Children in England: A Progress Report*, London: The Stationery Office, available from: https://www.gov.uk/government/publications/every-child-matters, accessed 10.6.2016.

Lefevre, M. (2012) *Becoming Effective Communicators with Children in Social Work Practice: who you are, not just what you know and do*, Doctoral thesis (DSW), University of Sussex.

Le Riche, P. and Tanner, K. (1998) *Observation and its Application to Social Work: Rather Like Breathing*, London: Jessica Kingsley.

Lincoln, Y. S. and Guba, E. (1985) *Naturalistic Enquiry*, Beverley Hills, CA: Sage.

Lishman, J. (2009) *Communication in Social Work* (2nd edition), Basingstoke: Palgrave Macmillan.

Luckock, B., Lefevre, M. and Orr, D., Jones, M., Marchant, R. and Tanner, K. (2006) *Knowledge Review: Teaching Learning and Assessing Communication Skills with Children in Social Work Education*, SCIE (Social Care Institute for Excellence), Bristol: The Policy Press, available from: http://www.scie.org.uk/publications/knowledgereviews/kr12.asp, accessed 14.2.2016.

Lyons-Ruth, K., Alpern, L. and Repacholi, B. (1993) 'Disorganized infant attachment classification and maternal psychosocial problems as predictors of hostile – aggressive behaviour in the pre-school classroom', *Child Development* 64: 572–585.

Macer, J., Murphy, J. and Oliver, T. (2009) *Training care home staff to use Talking Mats® with people who have dementia*, York: Joseph Rowntree Foundation, available from: https://www.jrf.org.uk/report/training-care-home-staff-use-talking-mats%C2%AE-people-who-have-dementia, accessed 10.6.2016.

Marchant, R. and Page, M. (2003) 'Child protection practice with disabled children' in National Working Group on Child Protection and Disability (ed) *It Doesn't Happen To Disabled Children*, London: NSPCC.

Marthinsen, E. and Julkunen, I. (2012) *Practice Research in Nordic Social Work: Knowledge production in transition*, London: Whiting and Birch.

Mattinson, J. and Sinclair, I. (1979) *Mate and Stalemate*, Oxford: Basil Blackwell.

McGregor, K. (2013) 'Social workers more likely to turn to food than to managers as way of coping with stress', *Community Care*, 2 December 2013, available from: http://www.communitycare.co.uk/2013/12/02/social-workers-more-likely-to-turn-to-food-than-managers-to-cope-with-stress/ accessed 31.1.2016.

McLeod, J. (1998) *An Introduction to Counselling*, Buckingham: Open University Press.

Mehrabian, A. (1972) *Non-verbal Communication*, Alberta: Aldine.

Mental Health Foundation (1997) *Knowing Our Own Minds*, London: Mental Health Foundation.

Mental Health Foundation (1999) *Bright Futures: Promoting Children and Young People's Mental Health*, London: Mental Health Foundation.

Mental Health Foundation (2000) *Strategies for Living: A Summary Report of User-led Research into People's Strategies for Living with Mental Distress*, London: Mental Health Foundation.

Menzies, I. E. P. (1960) 'A case study in the functioning of social systems as a defence against anxiety: a report on a study of the nursing service in a general hospital', *Human Relations* 13: 95–121.

Miley, K. K., O'Melia, M. and DuBois, B. L. (1998) *Instructors annual and Testbank for Generalist Social Work Practice – An Empowering Approach*, Boston: Allyn and Bacon.

Miller, N. R. and Rollnick, S. (2002) *Motivational Interviewing: Preparing People to Change Addictive Behaviour*, London: Guildford Press.

Mitchell, W. and Glendinning, C. (2007) *A Review of the Research Evidence Surrounding Risk Perceptions, Risk Management Strategies and their Consequences in Adult Social Care for Different Groups of Service Users*, York: University of York Social Policy Research Unit.

Morales, A. and Sheafor, B. W. (2001) *Social Work: A Profession of Many Faces* (6th edition), Needham Heights, MA: Allyn and Bacon.

Morazes, J. L., Benton, A. D., Clark, S. J. and Jacquet, S. E. (2010) 'Views of specially-trained child welfare social workers: a qualitative study of their motivations, perceptions, and retention', *Qualitative Social Work* 9(2): 227–247.

Moriarty, J., Baginsky, M. and Manthorpe, J. (2015) *Literature Review of Roles and Issues Within the Social Work Profession in England*, London: Kings College London, Social Care Workforce Research Unit, available from: http://social welfare.bl.uk/subject-areas/services-activity/social-work-care-services/socialcare workforceresearchunit/174392moriarty-et-al-2015-PSA.pdf, accessed 31.1.2016.

Morris, J. (2002) *A Lot to Say! A Guide for Social Workers, Personal Advisors and Others Working with Disabled Children and Young People with Communication Impairments*, London: Scope.

Morris, J. (2004) *Services for People with Physical Impairments and Mental Health Support Needs*, York: Joseph Rowntree Foundation.

Munro, E. (2005) 'A systems approach to investigating child abuse deaths', *British Journal of Social Work*, 35(4): 531–546.

Munro, E. (2010) *Part One: A Systems Analysis*, London: Department for Education, available from: http://www.education.gov.uk/munroreview/ accessed 31.1.2016.

Munro, E. (2011a) *The Munro Review of Child Protection. Interim report: The child's journey*, London: Department for Education.

Munro, E. (2011b) *The Munro Review of Child Protection. Final report: A child-centred system*, London: Department for Education.

Narey, M. (2014) *Making the Education of Social Workers Consistently Effective*, available from: https://www.gov.uk/government/publications/making-the-education-of-social-workers-consistently-effective, accessed 10.6.2016.

National Assembly for Wales (2000) *In Safe Hands: Protection of Vulnerable Adults in Wales*, Cardiff: National Assembly for Wales.

National Assembly for Wales (2003) *Requirements for a Degree in Social Work*, Cardiff: National Assembly for Wales.

National Institute for Clinical Excellence (2002) *Clinical Guideline 1. Schizophrenia: Core Interventions in the Treatment and Management of Schizophrenia in Primary and Secondary Care*, London: NICE.

National Institute for Mental Health England (2005) *NIMHE Guiding Statement on Recovery*, London: Department of Health.

Nelson-Jones, R. (2005) *An Introduction to Counselling Skills*, London: Sage.

Nicolson, P. (1993) 'Motherhood and women's lives', in D. Richardson and V. Robinson (eds) *Introducing Women's Studies*, Basingstoke: Macmillan.

Oliver, M. (1990) *The Politics of Disablement*, Basingstoke: Macmillan.

Oliver, M. (1996) *Understanding Disability: From Theory to Practice*, Basingstoke: Macmillan.

Oliver, M. and Sapey, B. (1999) *Social Work with Disabled People* (2nd edition), Basingstoke: Macmillan.

Oliver, M. and Sapey, B. (2006) *Social Work with Disabled People* (3rd edition), Basingstoke: Palgrave Macmillan.

Orford, J. (2001) *Excessive Appetites: A Psychological View of Addictions* (2nd edition), Chichester: John Wiley.

Osborn, D. P. J., King, M. B. and Nazareth, I. (2003) 'Participation in screening for cardiovascular risk by people with schizophrenia or similar mental illnesses: cross sectional study in general practice', *British Medical Journal* 326: 1122–1123.

Outhwaite, W. (1994) *Habermas: A Critical Introduction*, Cambridge: Polity Press.

Oxfordshire Safeguarding Children Board (2015) *Serious Case Review into Child Sexual Exploitation in Oxfordshire: from the experiences of Children A, B, C, D, E, and F*, Oxfordshire Safeguarding Children Board, available from: http://www.oscb.org.uk/wp-content/uploads/SCR-into-CSE-in-Oxfordshire-FINAL-FOR-WEBSITE.pdf, accessed 10.6.2016.

Parker, J. (2000) 'Social work with refugees and asylum seekers: a rationale for developing practice', *Practice* 12: 61–76.

Parker, J. (2004) *Effective Practice Learning in Social Work* (Transforming Social Work Practice Series), Exeter: Learning Matters.

Parr, S., Byng, S., Barnes, C. and Mercer, G. (2004) *Social Exclusion of People with Marked Communication Impairment Following Stroke*, York: Joseph Rowntree Foundation, available from: https://www.jrf.org.uk/report/social-exclusion-people-marked-communication-impairment-following-stroke, accessed 10.6.2016.

Parsloe, P. (2000) 'Generic and specialist practice' in M. Davies (ed) *Blackwell Encyclopaedia of Social Work*, Oxford: Oxford University Press.

Parton, N. (1991) *Governing the Family: Child Care, Child Protection and the State*, London: Macmillan.

Parton, N. (2004) 'From Maria Colwell to Victoria Climbie: reflections on a generation of public inquiries into child abuse', *Child Abuse Review*: 13: 80–94.

Parton, N, Thorpe, D. and Wattam, C. (1997) *Child Protection: Risk and the Moral Order*, London: Macmillan.

Pawson, R., Boaz, A., Grayson, L., Long, A. and Barnes, C. (2003) *Types and Quality of Knowledge in Social Care*, London: SCIE.

Paylor, I. (2008) 'Social work and drug use' in K. Wilson, G. Ruch, M. Lymbery and A. Cooper (2008) *Social Work: An Introduction to Contemporary Practice*, Harlow: Pearson Education.

Paylor, I., Measham, F. and Asher, H. (2012). *Social Work and Drug Use*, Maidenhead: Open University Press.

Payne, M. (2007) 'Performing as a "wise person" in social work practice', *Practice* 19(2): 85–96.

Perry, B. (2002) 'Childhood experience and the expression of genetic potential: what childhood neglect tells us about nature and nurture', *Brain and Mind* 3: 79–100.

Petit-Zeman, S., Sandamas, G. and Hogman, G. (2002) *Doesn't it make you sick?*, London: Rethink Publications.

Phelan, M., Stradins, L. and Morrison, S. (2001) 'Physical health of people with severe mental illness', *British Medical Journal* 322: 443–444.

Piaget, J. (1983) 'Piaget's theory' in P. H. Mussen (ed) *Handbook of Child Psychology: 1: Theory and Methods*, New York: Wiley.

Pile, H. (2009) 'Social worker shortage after Baby P puts children at risk', *The Guardian*, 28 August, available from: http://www.guardian.co.uk/society/joepublic/2009/aug/28/social-worker-shortage-baby-p, accessed 14.2.2016.

Potter, C. and Whittaker, C. (2001) *Creating Enabling Communication Environments for Children with Autism and Minimal or No Speech*, York: Joseph Rowntree Foundation.

Preston-Shoot, M. (2004) 'Responding by degrees: Surveying the education and practice landscape', *Social Work Education* 23(6): 667–692.

Prins, H. (1999) *Will They Do It Again?*, London: Routledge.

Prochaska, J. O. and DiClemente, C. C. (1983) 'Stages and processes of self-change of smoking: Toward an integrated model of change', *Journal of Consulting and Clinical Psychology* 51: 390–395.

Prochaska, J., DiClemente, C. and Norcross, J. (1992) 'In search of how people change' *American Psychologist* 47: 1107–1114.

Proctor, G. (2001) 'Listening to older women with dementia: relationships, voices and power', *Disability and Society* 16: 361–376.

Quality Assurance Agency for Higher Education (QAA) (2000) *Social Policy and Administration and Social Work: Subject Benchmark Statements*, Gloucester: QAA.

Reder, P., Duncan, S. and Gray, M. (1993) *Beyond Blame: Child Abuse Tragedies Revisited*, London: Routledge.

Reder, P. and Lucey, C. (1995) *Assessment of Parenting: Psychiatric and Psychological Contributions*, London: Routledge.

Reder, P. and Duncan, S. (2001) 'Abusive relationships, care and control conflicts and insecure attachments', *Child Abuse Review* 10: 411– 427.

Reid, D., Ryan, T. and Enderby, P. (2001) 'What does it mean to listen to people with dementia?' *Disability and Society* 16: 377–392.

Rhodes, P. and Nocon, A. (2003) 'A problem of communication? Diabetes care among Bangladeshi people in Bradford', *Health and Social Care in the Community* 11: 45–54.

Richards, S., Ruch, G. and Trevithick, P. (2005) 'Communication skills training for practice: the ethical dilemma for social work education', *Social Work Education* 24: 409–422.

Richardson, D. (1993) *Women, Motherhood and Childrearing*, Basingstoke: Macmillan.

Royal College of Psychiatrists (1998) *Changing Minds: Every Family in the Land. Recommendations for the Implementation of a five year Strategy*, London: Royal College of Psychiatrists.

Ruch, G. (2005a) 'Relationship-based and reflective practice in contemporary child care social work', *Child and Family Social Work* 4: 111–124.

Ruch, G. (2005b) 'Relationship-based practice and reflective practice: holistic approaches to contemporary child care work', *Child and Family Social Work* 10: 111–123.

Ruch, G. (2007) 'Reflective practice in child care social work: the role of containment,' *British Journal of Social Work* 37: 659–680.

Ruch, G. (2009) 'Identifying the critical in a relationship-based model of reflection', *European Journal of Social Work* 12: 349–362.

Ruch, G. (2012) 'Where have all the feelings gone? Developing reflective and relationship-based management in child-care social work', *British Journal of Social Work* 42(7): 1315–1332.

Ruch, G., Turney, D. and Ward, A. (2010) (eds) *Relationship-Based Social Work: Getting to the Heart of Practice*, London: Jessica Kingsley.

Rustin, M. (2005) 'Conceptual analysis of critical moments in Victoria Climbié's life', *Child and Family Social Work* 10: 11–19.

Rutter, J. (2003) *Working with Refugee Children*, York: Joseph Rowntree Foundation.

Rutter, M. (1985) 'Resilience in the face of adversity. Protective factors and resistance to psychiatric disorder', *British Journal of Psychiatry* 147: 598–611.

Salzberger-Wittenberg, I. (1970) *Psycho-analytical Insight and Relationships: A Kleinian Approach*, London: Routledge and Kegan-Paul.

Sanford, F., Fox, J. and Murray, K. (1981) *Children Out of Court*, Edinburgh: Scottish Academic Press.

Sapey, B. (2009) 'Engaging with the social model of disability' in P. Higham (ed) *Post-Qualifying Social Work Practice*, London: Sage.

Schön, D. (1983) *The Reflective Practitioner: How Professionals Think in Action*, London: Temple Smith.

Schofield, G. (1998) 'Inner and outer worlds: a psychosocial framework for child and family social work', *Child and Family Social Work* 3: 57–67.

Schore, A. N. (2001) 'Effects of a secure attachment relationship on right brain development, affect regulation, and infant mental health', *Infant Mental Health Journal* 22: 7–66.

Sheppard, M. and Ryan, K. (2003) 'Practitioners as rule using analysts: A further development of process knowledge in social work', *British Journal of Social Work* 33: 157–176.

SCODA (Standing Conference on Drug Abuse) (1997) *Drug-related Early Intervention: Developing Services for Young People and Families*, London: SCODA.

SCOPE (2007) *Communication Aid Provision: Review of the Literature*, London: SCOPE.

Scottish Office (1999) *Aiming for Excellence – Modernising Social Work Services in Scotland*, Edinburgh: Scottish Office.

Scottish Executive (2004) *Hidden Harm: Scottish Executive Response to the Report of the Inquiry by the Advisory Council on the issue of Drugs*, Edinburgh: Scottish Executive.

Scottish Executive (2006a) *Social Work: A 21st Century Profession*, Edinburgh: Scottish Executive.

Scottish Executive (2006b) *Changing Lives: Report of the 21st Century Review of Social Work*, Edinburgh: Scottish Executive.

Seden, J. (2005) *Counselling Skills in Social Work Practice,* Maidenhead: Open University Press.

Shaw, D. S., Owens, E. B., Vondra, J. I., Keenan, K. and Winslow, E. B. (1996) 'Early risk factors and pathways in the development of early disruptive behaviour problems', *Development and Psychopathology* 8: 679–699.

Sheppard, M. (1998) 'Practice validity, reflexivity and knowledge for social work', *British Journal of Social Work* 28: 763–781.

Sheppard (now Woodcock), J. (2000) 'Learning from personal experience: Reflexions on social work practice with mothers in child and family care', *Journal of Social Work Practice* 14: 38–50.

Sheppard, M. (2007) 'Assessment: from reflexivity to process knowledge' in Lishman, J. (ed) *Handbook for Practice Learning in Social Work and Social Care*, London: Jessica Kingsley.

Shulman, L. (1998) *The Skills of Helping Individuals, Families and Groups* (4th edition), Illinois: Peacock Publishers.

Shulman, L. (2009) *The Skills of Helping Individuals, Families, Groups and Communities* (6th edition), Belmont, CA: Wadsworth Publishing.

Silverman, D. (2004) *Qualitative Research: Theory, Method and Practice*, London: Sage.

Skills for Care (2002) *National Occupational Standards for Social Work*, Leeds: Topss, available from: https://www3.shu.ac.uk/HWB/placements/SocialWork/documents/SWNatOccupStandards.pdf, accessed 10.6.2016.

Skills for Care (2015) *Care Act Briefing: Care Act Implications for Safeguarding Adults*, London: Skills for Care, available from: http://www.skillsforcare.org.uk/document-library/standards/care-act/learning-and-development/care-act-implications-for-safeguarding-adults-briefing.pdf, accessed 31.1.2016.

Skills for Care and Development (2008) *Health and Social Care National Occupational Standards*, Leeds: Skills for Care and Development.

Smale, G. and Tuson, G. with Biehal, N. and Marsh, P. (1993) *Empowerment, Assessment, Care Management and the Skilled Worker*, London: HMSO.

Smart, C. (1996) 'Deconstructing motherhood', in S. E. Bortolaia (ed) *Good Enough Mothering: Feminist Perspectives on Lone Motherhood*, London and New York: Routledge.

Social Care Institute for Excellence (SCIE) (2004) *Teaching and Learning Communication Skills in Social Work Education*, London: SCIE.

Social Care Institute for Excellence (SCIE) (2009) *Dignity in Care Practice Guide 02*, London: SCIE.

Social Care Institute for Excellence (SCIE) (2013a) *Effective Supervision in a Variety of Settings, Guide 50*, London: SCIE.

Social Care Institute for Excellence (SCIE) (2013b) *Narrative Summary of the Evidence Review on the Supervision of Social Workers and Social Care Workers in a Range of Settings Including Integrated Settings*, London: SCIE, available from: http://www.scie.org.uk/publications/guides/guide50/files/supervisionnarrativesummary.pdf, accessed 31.1.2016.

Social Care Institute for Excellence (SCIE) (2015) *Adult Safeguarding: Types and Indicators of Abuse*, London: SCIE, available from http://www.scie.org.uk/publications/ataglance/69-adults-safeguarding-types-and-indicators-of-abuse.asp, accessed 31.1.2016.

Social Services Directorate (2006) *Safeguarding Vulnerable Adults: Regional Adult Protection Policy and Guidance (Northern Ireland)*, Ballymena: Northern Health and Social Services Board.

Social Services Inspectorate (SSI) (2002) *Improving Older People's Services: Policy into Practice*, London: DoH Publications.

Social Services Inspectorate (2004) *Building a Better Future for Children: Key Messages from Inspections and Performance Assessment*, London: Department of Health, available from: http://www.scie-socialcareonline.org.uk/building-a-better-future-for-children-key-messages-from-inspection-and-performance-assessment/r/a11G00000017wMAIAY, accessed 26.2.2016.

Social Work Reform Board (SWRB) (2010) *Building a Safe and Confident Future: detailed proposals from the Social Work Reform Board*, London: Department for Education, available from: https://www.gov.uk/government/publications/building-a-safe-and-confident-future-detailed-proposals-from-the-social-work-reform-board, accessed 26.2.2016.

Social Work Reform Board (SWRB) (2011) *Building a Safe and Confident Future: Improving the quality and consistency of initial qualifying social work education and training*, London: Department for Education, available from: www.collegeofsocialwork.org/uploadedFiles/TheCollege/Practice/ Improving%20the%20quality%20and%20consistency%20of%20initial%20qualifying%20social%20work%20education%20and%20training.pdf, accessed 26.2.2016.

Social Work Reform Board (SWRB) (2012) *Building a Safe and Confident Future: maintaining momentum*, London: Department for Education, available from: https://www.gov.uk/government/publications/building-a-safe-and-confident-future-maintaining-momentum-progress-report-from-the-social-work-reform-board, accessed 26.2.2016.

Social Work Taskforce (2009) *Facing up to the Task: The interim report of the Social Work Task Force*, London: Department of Health and Department for Children, Schools and Families, available from: http://webarchive. nationalarchives.gov.uk/20130401151715/http://www.education.gov.uk/ publications/eOrderingDownload/DCSF-00753-2009.pdf, accessed 26.2.2016.

Speltz, M. L., Greenberg, M. T. and De Klyen, M. (1990) 'Attachment in preschoolers with disruptive behaviour: A comparison of clinic – referred and nonproblem children', *Development and Psychopathology* 2: 31–46.

Sroufe, L. A. (1983) 'Infant-caregiver attachment and patterns of attachment in pre-school: the roots of maladaptation and competence', in M. Perlmutter (ed) *Minnesota Symposium in Child Psychology* 16: 41–81, Hillsdale, NJ: Erlbaum.

Stack, D. W., Hill, S. R. and Hickson, M. (1991) *An Introduction to Communication Theory*, Fort Worth: Holt, Rinehart and Winston.

Stepney, P. (2006) 'Mission impossible? Critical practice in social work', *British Journal of Social Work* 36: 1289–1307.

Strauss, A. and Corbin, J. (1990) *Basics of Qualitative Research: Grounded Theory Procedures and Techniques*, London: Sage.

Taylor, A. (1999) 'The elephant in the interview room: working with the process of denial with chronic drinkers', *Probation Journal* 46: 19–26.

Taylor, A. and Kroll, B. (2004) 'Working with parental substance misuse. Dilemmas for practice', *British Journal of Social Work* 34: 1115–1132.

Taylor, C. and White, S. (2000) *Practising Reflexivity in Health and Welfare: Making Knowledge*, Buckingham: Open University Press.

Taylor, H. (2008) 'Judgements of Solomon: anxieties and defences of social workers involved in care proceedings', *Child and Family Social Work* 13: 23.

TCSW/BASW (2012) *Assessing Practice Using the PCF Guidance*, London: The College of Social Work (now held by The British Association of Social Workers), available from: https://www.basw.co.uk/pcf, accessed 31.1.2016.

TCSW/BASW (2013) *Practice Educator Professional Standards for Social Work*, London: The College of Social Work (now held by The British Association of Social Workers), available from: https://www.basw.co.uk/resources/tcsw/PEPS, accessed 31.1.2016.

Thomas, C. (1999) *Female Forms: Experiencing and Understanding Disability*, Buckingham: Open University Press.

Thomas, C. (2007) *Sociologies of Disability and Illness: Contested Ideas in Disability Studies and Medical Sociology*, Basingstoke: Palgrave Macmillan.

Thompson, N. (1995) *Age and Dignity: Working with Older People*, Aldershot: Arena.

Tibbs, M. A. (2001) *Social Work and Dementia: Good Practice and Care Management*, London: Jessica Kingsley.

TOPSS (Training Occupational Standards for the Personal Social Services) (2002) *The National Occupational Standards for Social Work*, Leeds: TOPSS.

Trevithick, P. (2005) *Social Work Skills: A Practice Handbook*, Maidenhead: Open University Press.

Trevithick, P. (2012) 'The generalist versus specialist debate in social work education in the UK' in J. Lishman (ed) *Social Work Education and Training*, London: Jessica Kingsley Publishers.

Trevithick, P., Richards, S., Ruch, G. and Moss, B. (2004) *Teaching and Learning Communication Skills in Social Work Education: Knowledge Review 6*, London: SCIE.

Triangle (2002) *How It Is: An Image Vocabulary for Children About Feelings, Rights and Safety, Personal Care and Sexuality*, Leicester: NSPCC, available from: www.howitis.org.uk/ accessed 26.2.2016.

Tsui, M. (2005) *Social Work Supervision, Contexts and Concepts*, London: Sage.

Turney, D. (2000) 'The feminising of neglect', *Child and Family Social Work* 5: 47–56.

Turnell, A. (2012) *The Signs of Safety Comprehensive Briefing Paper*, Resolutions Consultancy Pty Ltd., available from: http://www.aascf.com/pdf/Signs%20 of%20Safety%20Breifing%20paper%20April%202012.pdf, accessed 14.2.2014.

Turnell, A. and Edwards, S. (1999) *Signs of Safety: A safety and solution orientated approach to child protection casework*, New York: W.W. Norton & Company.

Turnell, A., Elliott, S. and Hogg, V. (2007) 'Compassionate, Safe and Rigorous Child Protection Practice with Biological Parents of Adopted Children', *Child Abuse Review* 16(2): 108–119.

Unison (2009) *Still Slipping Through the Net? Front-line Staff Assess Children's Safeguarding Progress*, London: Unison, available from: http://www.scie-socialcareonline.org.uk/still-slipping-through-the-net-front-line-staff-assess-childrens-safeguarding-progress/r/a11G00000017zWbIAI, accessed 31.1.2016.

Urek, M. (2005) 'Making a case in social work: the construction of an unsuitable mother', *Qualitative Social Work* 4(4): 451–467.

University of York (1999) 'Facts, feelings and feedback: a collaborative model for direct observation', Interviewing Skills and Direct Observation Project Team, available at http://www.worldcat.org/title/facts-feelings-and-feedback-a-collaborative-model-for-direct-observation-a-video-for-trainers-practice-teachers-and-social-work-students/oclc/224083224, accessed 10.6.2016.

Velleman, R. (2001) *Counselling for Alcohol Problems* (2nd edition), London: Sage.

Ward, A. (2010) 'Use of Self in Relationship-based Practice' in G. Ruch, D. Turney and A. Ward (eds) *Relationship-Based Social Work: Getting to the Heart of Practice*, London: Jessica Kingsley.

Warren, S. L., Huston, L., Egeland, B. and Sroufe, L. A. (1997) 'Child and adolescent anxiety disorders and early attachment', *Journal of the American Academy of Child and Adolescent Psychiatry* 32: 165–178.

Wastell, D., White, S., Broadhurst, K., Peckover, S. and Pithouse, A. (2010) 'Children's services in the iron cage of performance management: street-level bureaucracy and the spectre of Švejkism', *International Journal of Social Welfare* 19(3): 310–320.

Welsh Assembly Government (2006) *National Service Framework for Older People*, Cardiff: WAG.

Wikström, P.-O. and Sampson, R. (eds) (2009) *The Explanation of Crime: Context, Mechanisms and Development*, Cambridge: Cambridge University Press.

Williams, C. and Soydan, H. (2005) 'When and How Does Ethnicity Matter? A Cross-National Study of Social Work Responses to Ethnicity in Child Protection Cases', *British Journal of Social Work* 35: 901–920.

Williams, S. and Rutter, L. (2013) *The Practice Educator's Handbook* (2nd edition), London: Learning Matters, Sage.

Wilson, J. C. and Powell, M. (2001) *A Guide to Interviewing Children: Essential Skills for Counsellors, Police, Lawyers and Social Workers*, London: Routledge.

Wilson, K. and Ryan, V. (2001) 'Helping children by working with their parents in individual child therapy', *Child and Family Social Work* 6: 209–217.

Wilson, K., Ruch, G., Lymbery, M. and Cooper, A. (2008) *Social Work: An Introduction to Contemporary Practice*, Harlow: Pearson Education.

Wilson, K., Ruch, G., Lymbery, M. and Cooper, A. (2011) *Social Work: An Introduction to Contemporary Practice* (2nd edition), Harlow: Pearson Education.

Woodcock, J. (2003) 'The social work assessment of parenting: An exploration', *British Journal of Social Work* 33: 87–106.

Woodcock, J. and Sheppard, M. (2002) 'Double trouble: maternal depression and alcohol dependence as combined factors in child and family social work', *Children and Society* 16: 232–245.

Woodcock, J. and Tregaskis, C. (2008) 'Social Work Communication Skills with Parents of Disabled Children: A Combined Social Model & Social Work Analysis', *British Journal of Social Work* 38: 55–71.

Woodcock Ross, J. (2011) *Specialist Communication Skills for Social Workers*, Basingstoke: Palgrave Macmillan.

Woodcock Ross, J. (forthcoming) *Specialist Social Work Communication Skills with Parents and Carers who are Christian*, Doctoral thesis, Institute of Education, University College London.

Woodcock Ross, J. and Crow, C. (2010) 'Social Work Practice Strategies and Professional Identity within Private Fostering: A Critical Exploration', *Adoption and Fostering* 34: 41–51.

World Health Organisation (2001) *World Health Day. Mental health: Stop Exclusion: Dare to Care*, Geneva: World Health Organization, Department of Mental Health and Substance Dependence, available from: www.who.int/world-health-day, accessed 31.1.2016.

World Health Organisation (2005) *Mental Health Action Plan for Europe. Facing the Challenges, Building Solutions*, Helsinki, WHO European Ministerial Conference on Mental Health, available from: www.euro.who.int/mentalhealth/publications/20061124_1, accessed 31.1.2016.

Youth Justice Board (2006) *Asset: an assessment framework for young people involved in the youth justice system*, London: Youth Justice Board, available from: https://www.gov.uk/government/publications/asset-documents, accessed 10.6.2016.

Youth Justice Board (2008) *Assessment, Intervention Planning and Supervision (Source Document)*, London: Youth Justice Board.

Zeanah, C. H., Boris, N. W. and Scheeringa, M. S. (1997) 'Psychopathology in infancy', *Journal of Child Psychology and Psychiatry* 38: 81–99.

Index

A

Abuse and maltreatment, 20, 79, 82, 86–87, 96, 104, 134, 149–150, 164, 189, 198, 234, 238

Accuracy, 36, 70, 82, 135
  assessing for truthfulness, 119
  non-leading questions, 97
  Statement Validity Analysis, 119
  appraising evidence and types of evidence, 135

Achieving a shared purpose, 55, 60–68, 76, 88–89, 111, 138, 170–171, 193, 200, 217, 259, 262, 278

Active listening, *see* reflective listening

Actively look for the channels of communication the service user is using, 188, 192, 198, 203, 234, 240, 246

Addressing service user fears of stigmatisation, 160, 173, 278

Adversity, 81–84

Ageism, 231

Agendas, 47, 61–67, 89, 138, 142, 147, 151, 171, 220, 240

Aggression (and hostility), 12, 57, 61, 138, 213, 217, 255, 257

Ambivalence, 12, 25, 61, 71, 88, 91, 95, 110, 138, 162, 176

Assessing communication skills, 28–53
  direct observation, 44–48
  holistic assessment of developmental progression, 28–30, 42, 47, 48, 52
  service user feedback, 48–51
  supervision, 39–43

Assessing for remorse and willingness to reform, 107, 111, 122–123

AssetPlus,106–110, 114

Asylum legal process, 263

Attachment styles, 17, 58, 83–84, 87, 138, 169

Attitudinal obstacles, 21, 32, 37, 39, 45, 79, 137, 223, 276, 279

Attuned, 18, 55, 66, 94, 167, 277

Augmentative communication, 82, 187

Authenticity, 31, 62

Authority (legislative) role, 20, 24, 26, 57, 61–66, 71, 88, 95, 98, 137, 147, 164, 170–171, 262, 274, 276, 279

Avoid exhortations to change, 174

Avoiding the how and why questions, 97

B

Basic communication skills, 11, 54–76, 85, 120, 169, 171, 193, 245, 263

Being open to communication at all levels, 221–222

Beginning communication, 55

Body language, *see* non-verbal communication

C

The Care Act (2014), 3–4, 61, 78, 132, 187–188, 190, 212, 230–231, 275–276

Care Mapping Approach, 233

Challenging, 12, 77, 94, 162, 193

Change processes, 162, 175

Channel of communication, 16, 187–188, 192, 198, 203, 221, 230, 234–235, 240, 245–246, 279

Child in need, 118, 131–132
The Children Act (1989), 2, 77, 118, 131–132, 163, 263
The Children Act (Scotland) (1995), 163
The Children Act (2004), 78, 131,163, 263
The Children and Families Act (2014), 4, 60, 77–78, 132, 263, 275,
Choice (giving choice), 3, 5, 24, 60, 77, 93, 105, 111, 113–114, 132, 174, 187–188, 191, 204, 222, 231, 234, 276
Clear about purpose, 24, 55, 60–68, 72, 88–90, 96, 113, 138, 152, 170–172, 193, 197, 200, 215, 217, 238, 241, 259, 262, 279
Clear on role, 11, 24, 54, 62–65, 71, 88–89, 111, 131, 161, 170, 193, 259
Closed questions, 12, 119, 151, 173, 203–204, 263
Communication enhancing environment, 82–83
Communicating consequences in a non-threatening manner, 105, 114, 279
Communicating empathy for the experience of systemic barriers, 187, 197, 200
Confidentiality, 51, 62, 89, 214
Containing a child's feelings by being a safe place in which feelings can be explored, 77, 85, 94, 278
Containment, 18, 37, 85, 142–144, 221–222, 239, 264, 278
Contracting, 62
Co-production, 3, 61, 78, 276, 278
Counter-transference, 17, 86
Creative arts (*see also* pictures), 233
Crime and Disorder Act (1998), 105
Cultural awareness, 254
Cultural background, 60, 62, 68, 133
Cultural competence, 257
Cultural differences, 20, 69, 80, 160, 232, 257

Cultural expectations (and role), 56, 204, 262–263, 265
Cultural relativism, 20, 80, 133–134, 254, 263
Cultural sensitivity (and culturally relevant), 86, 122, 150, 213, 253–254, 257–258, 266
Cultural stereotyping (and assumptions), 16, 19–20, 36, 37, 41, 56, 58, 59, 68, 70, 79, 133, 136, 149, 151, 160–161, 163, 167–168, 204, 217, 232–233

D

Decision-making capacity (*see also* developmental competence), 90, 188, 198, 231
Defending the rights of the service user, 105, 113
Dementia, stroke and other cognitive impairments, 199, 215, 232–234, 238
Demonstrating cultural acceptance, 253, 257–258
Demonstrating knowledge of the individual child, 130, 148, 151, 280
Developing early rapport, 105, 109, 111–113, 279
phatic communication, 109
Development, 15–16, 20, 21, 58, 65, 71, 78, 79, 81–90, 95, 97, 98, 121–122, 130, 131–136, 141, 144, 147–150, 160, 163, 212
developmental delay, 78, 122, 147–148
reflective function, 87
Developmental competence (including positive framing), 78, 90, 130, 151, 280
learning disabilities and learning difficulties, 107, 122, 147, 198
Dignity, 3, 132, 187, 198, 200, 222, 231, 234
Disability Discrimination Act (2005), 187, 190

Disability Discrimination (Northern Ireland) Order (2006), 187
Distress, 58, 82, 120, 161, 192, 200, 203, 211, 213–214, 216, 223, 253, 255, 264–265, 278

E

Ecological approach (also systemic barriers), 15, 21, 37, 80, 130, 134, 137, 141, 143–144, 151, 173, 187, 191, 193, 197, 200, 204, 279–280
Emotional support, 172, 213
  being (alongside), 95, 222
  emotionally available, 216
Emotional warmth, 35, 57, 66, 68, 90, 96, 143, 200, 221, 254, 264
Empathy (*see also* preparatory empathy), 12, 37, 41, 46, 51, 54, 55, 62, 67–72, 85, 88, 95, 105, 110, 120–122, 138, 141, 144, 152, 169–170, 187, 197, 200, 203, 216, 220, 262–265
  communicating empathy for the experience of systemic barriers, 141, 151, 187, 197, 200
Emphasising or exaggerating non-verbal communication without being patronising, 230, 239, 245
Endings, 73–74, 97
Enter the world of substance using families, 159, 172–173, 279
  genograms and ecomaps, 279
Establish a vocabulary of feelings, 77, 96
Every Child Matters (2003), 78, 130, 131
Experience the child's world, 77, 81, 83, 278
Experiencing service user feelings (asylum seekers and refugees), 253, 265, 278
Experiential Learning, 6, 277, 282
Expressing empathy and understanding without necessarily signifying agreement, 105, 110, 121

F

Fear (and mistrust), 18, 24, 34, 59, 61, 66, 71, 82, 87, 95, 108, 134, 137, 147, 163, 169–171, 173, 200, 213, 215, 217, 220, 223, 234, 244, 253–254, 256, 263, 265, 278
Fear of failure (and repercussions), 34–36, 59, 80, 86
Feelings as medium of communication, 18, 35, 56, 77, 81, 86–90, 98, 121, 277, 279
Forum theatre, 6, 141, 150, 172, 199, 239–240, 264–265, 277, 278, 282–285
The Framework for the Assessment of Children in Need and their Families, 15, 131, 144, 168
Frustration, 57, 80, 88, 136, 85, 89, 136–137, 141–143, 191, 203, 233, 240, 244

G

Gathering facts, 73–74, 120
Genograms and ecomaps, 151, 173, 279
Give time to process thoughts or feelings and respond, 222, 244

H

Harm reduction model, 168
Hidden Harm (2004), 163
High order concepts (use short, simple sentences), 121–122, 215, 263, 77–78, 182, 244
Hostility, *see* aggression

I

Identify coping and strengths, 84, 136, 162
Identify, discuss and empathise with systemic barriers, 143, 280
Identify, validate and use the child's medium of communication, 18, 35, 77, 81, 86, 88–90, 97

Identifying a practical response of seeking to overcome the systemic barriers, 130, 142–144, 149, 280
Identifying social worker's personal attitudes and preconceptions of parenting, 130, 150, 168, 280
Illusion of work, 67, 151
Immediacy, 24, 42, 54, 66–67, 171
Independence, Well-being and Choice (2005), 187
Individual differences, 38, 133, 137
Influence of self when managing uncertainty, 4, 11, 15, 35, 106, 135, 214
Informed consent, 93, 114, 214
communicating consequences in a non-threatening manner, 114, 279
Interpreters, 254–255, 262–263
Isolation, 143, 168, 213, 254, 265

J

Jasmine Beckford, 79
Judgemental attitudes, 12, 137
Non-judgemental, 118, 149, 160, 174–175, 220

K

Knowledge and Skills Statements (KSS), 10, 99–104, 124–129, 152–158, 177–186, 205–210, 225–229, 247–252, 267–272, 274–276

L

Listening for clues, 105, 118
Loss, 58–59, 62, 73, 86, 134, 213

M

Maintain a non-threatening body position, 211, 223
Managing aggressive situations, 94–95, 223
Marginalisation, 161, 164, 168, 176, 216
Maria Colwill, 20

Media, 36, 59, 61, 80, 138
Media packages, 192, 198
Medical model of addiction, 167
Memory, 119, 215,
Mental Capacity Act (2005), 3,188–190, 214, 231
The Mental Health Act (2007), 211
Metaphors and images, 222
Mirroring, 12, 221, 230, 233, 235
Motivating service users to decide to make changes, 174–175
Motivational interviewing, 174, 188

N

Non-verbal communication, 12, 47, 91, 95, 121, 144, 147, 200, 232–235, 238–240, 245, 263, 265, 284
maintain a non-threatening body position, 223
managing aggressive situations, 94, 223

O

Observing, 6, 47, 68, 95, 221, 282
Obstacle, 19, 21, 24, 32, 37, 39, 45, 67, 71, 95, 136–137, 177, 223, 240, 245
authority obstacle, 65, 94, 220, 223, 240, 245, 276, 279, 281
intimacy obstacle, 220
societal taboo obstacle, 79, 182, 279
ONSET, 106
Open question, 70, 73, 119, 141, 151, 173, 175, 203, 220–221, 263, 265

P

Paraphrasing, 12, 70, 91, 172, 175, 220, 221
Parent-child relationship, 17, 83, 143
Parenting, 80–100
normative expectations, 19–21
theoretical frameworks, 131–132

Parenting assessment (including influence of self), 15–16, 59, 108, 131–133, 135–136, 143, 148–149, 151, 163, 167–168, 191
  attitudinal, cultural and societal templates, 59, 133–134, 149, 151, 164, 280
  cultural relativism 133–134
  natural love, 133–134
  rule of optimism, 133
  surface-static, 134
Parents who use substances, 162–164, 167–176, 172–173
Parents with disabled children, 13, 21, 82, 130–152, 199
Partnership working, 55, 170
Personalisation, 3, 23
Person-centred, 3, 4, 8, 14, 61, 78, 87, 130, 132, 187, 212, 213, 216, 230–232, 246, 275–279
Peter Connolly, 39, 79–80, 133, 138
Phatic communication, 109
Physical contact (touch), 232, 233, 235, 239–240, 265
Physical health symptoms, 107, 122, 214–215
Pictures, 49, 89, 97, 190, 192, 203, 215, 233, 259
Positioning, 68–69
Positive communication, 190
Positive framing of development rather than using deficit notions, 151, 280
Power differential, 24, 34, 36, 49, 60, 79, 88, 97, 279
Private knowledge, 21, 141–143, 151, 199, 279
  private voice, 141, 144, 265
Professional anxiety (*see also* emotional challenge), 18, 24, 35–38, 79–80, 121, 134, 149–150, 212, 214, 246
Professional development, 1, 4, 11, 13, 22, 23, 25, 28–52, 273, 276–277
  developing capability, 22, 29, 32, 40, 160
  holistic assessment of developmental progression, 28–30, 42, 47, 48, 52

Promises, 199–200
Promoting understanding of links between experiences and symptoms, 214
Provide affirmation, 174
Psychodynamic approach, 16, 81
Psychological defences, 12, 17, 18, 35, 79, 122, 238–244
Purpose (being clear), 24, 55, 60–68, 72, 88–90, 96, 113, 138, 152, 170–172, 193, 197, 200, 215, 217, 238, 241, 259, 262, 279
Putting feelings into words, 42, 68, 70–71, 73, 96, 110, 141, 144, 174, 197, 203, 220, 239, 245, 262, 265

Q

Questioning, 12, 20, 73
  closed questions, 119, 151, 173, 203, 204, 263
  critical questioning, 41
  focused questioning, 119
  open questions, 119, 151, 173, 175, 203, 220–221, 263

R

Racism, 255–257
Reach for feedback, 62, 88, 170, 193
Reach for feeling, 42, 68, 70, 71, 174, 245
Recovery model, 161, 212–213
Reflecting back (mirroring), 221
Reflective listening, 12, 42, 54, 68–69, 92, 95, 120, 147, 151, 171, 174, 200, 220–221, 263
Reflexive processes, 18–19, 26, 37, 38, 71, 217
Reflexivity, 18–19, 164
Relationship-based practice, 8, 14–16, 56
Religious and spiritual beliefs, 133, 214, 257
Reminiscence, 233
Resistance (including passive resistance), 61, 135, 138
Respect, 3, 14, 20, 49, 51, 66, 90, 93, 120, 144, 162, 190, 199–200, 222, 233, 244, 264, 276, 279

Risk (including assessing risk and managing risk), 3, 4, 11, 15, 16, 23, 35, 39, 49, 78, 84, 106–107, 131–136, 161, 163, 164, 168, 188, 189, 204, 214, 231
   risk of offending, 107–108, 119

S

Safeguarding (children and adults), 3, 15, 24, 78, 80, 106, 131–3, 150, 163, 198, 203, 214, 279
   new approaches to adult safeguarding, 188–189, 212, 231
   proportionate safeguarding solutions, 135, 189
Secrecy and denial, 160–161, 163, 169, 171, 279
Shared agenda, 62, 66–67, 89, 95, 138, 147, 171, 220, 240
Sharing social worker feelings, 72–73
Short, simple sentences (*see also* high order concepts), 121–122, 215, 263, 77–78, 182, 244
Signs of Safety practice approach, 78, 87, 135, 148
Silences, 12, 42, 69, 72, 91, 174, 222, 264
Social constructionist approach, 16, 19, 36
Social exclusion
   physical health, 214–215
   inequalities, 214–215
   isolation, 143, 213, 254, 265
   marginalisation, 161, 164, 168, 176, 216
   stigmatisation, 160, 161, 162, 173–174, 212, 217, 257, 278
Social model of disability, 13, 14, 21, 23, 26, 143, 190–191, 193, 279
Societal barrier, 136, 256, 258–259
Southwark ruling, 118
Stigmatisation, 160, 161, 162, 173–174, 212, 217, 257, 278
Strengths, *see* identify coping and strengths
Stroke, dementia and other cognitive impairments, 199, 215, 232–234, 238

Substance use, 107, 151, 159–186, 214, 278
Summarising, 12, 55, 70, 74, 147, 175
Supervision, 39–43
Systemic barriers, 15, 21, 37, 80, 130, 134, 137, 141, 143–144, 151, 173, 187, 191, 193, 197, 200, 204, 279–280
Systemic perspective, 134

T

Take time, 91, 93, 162
   give time to process thoughts or feelings and respond, 191, 222, 232, 263
Third ear (objective distancing), 45, 67, 171, 222
Three Houses technique, 87, 279
Total communication, 68, 190, 192, 198, 203, 221
Touch (physical contact), 232, 233, 235, 239–240, 265
Tuning in, 55–60, 62, 83, 86, 118, 137, 168, 169, 193, 216, 234, 256, 262, 277
   tuning in to experience the child's world, 83, 278
   tuning in to experience the individual experience of mental distress, 216, 278
   tuning in to fear and uncertainty over citizenship, 256, 266
   tuning in to social worker's personal attitudes and preconceptions of people who use substances, 167, 278
Transference, 17, 18, 36, 71, 86, 141, 149, 216, 239, 244, 265, 278
   Counter-transference, 17, 86

U

Unconditional regard, 120
Use of self, 16, 18, 19, 22, 32, 62, 74, 135
Use of the 'third object', 93
Using a storyline, 88–90

Using humour, 113, 121
Using the whole communication
    spectrum (*see also* total
    communication), 192, 198, 203,
    232, 240, 245, 259, 279

V

Validation, 233, 235, 239, 245, 279
Valuing People (2001), 187, 190
Victoria Climbie, 17, 79, 82, 138

W

Well-being, 3, 4, 12, 15, 42, 48, 61,
    78, 98, 130, 132, 137, 151, 161,
    167–168, 172, 188, 190, 197,
    211–212, 231, 275
Wishes and feelings of children, 77
Working Together to Safeguard
    Children (HM Government,
    2015), 15, 55, 78, 82, 130–132,
    143, 145, 168